RELIGION TODAY: TRADITION, MODERNITY AND CHANGE

BELIEF BEYOND BOUNDARIES: WICCA, CELTIC SPIRITUALITY AND THE NEW AGE

RELIGION TODAY: TRADITION, MODERNITY AND CHANGE

BELIEF BEYOND BOUNDARIES: WICCA, CELTIC SPIRITUALITY AND THE NEW AGE

EDITED BY JOANNE PEARSON

Ashgate

in association with

The Open University

This publication forms part of an Open University course AD317 *Religion Today: Tradition, Modernity and Change*. Details of this and other Open University courses can be obtained from the Call Centre, PO Box 724, The Open University, Milton Keynes MK7 6ZS, United Kingdom: tel. +44(0)1908 653231, e-mail ces-gen@open.ac.uk

Alternatively, you may visit the Open University web site at http://www.open.ac.uk where you can learn more about the wide range of courses and packs offered at all levels by The Open University.

To purchase this publication or other components of Open University courses, contact Open University Worldwide Ltd, The Open University, Walton Hall, Milton Keynes MK7 6AA, United Kingdom: tel. +44 (0)1908 858785; fax +44(0)1908 858787; e-mail ouwenq@open.ac.uk; web site http://www.ouw.co.uk

British Library Cataloguing in Publication Data

Belief beyond boundaries. – (Religion today:
tradition, modernity and change; v.5) / edited by Joanne Pearson.
  1. Cults
  I. Pearson, Joanne. II. Series.
  291.9

Library of Congress Control Number: 2001053654

Co-published by

The Open University	Ashgate Publishing Ltd	Ashgate Publishing Company
Walton Hall	Gower House, Croft Road	Burlington, VT 05401-5600
Milton Keynes MK7 6AA	Aldershot, Hants GU11 3HR	USA

Ashgate web site: http://www.ashgate.com

First published 2002.

Edited, designed and typeset by The Open University.

Printed and bound in the United Kingdom by The Bath Press, Bath.

ISBN 0 7546 0744 5 (hbk)
ISBN 0 7546 0820 4 (pbk)

1.1

25462B/ad317b5prelimsi1.1

Religion Today: Tradition, Modernity and Change – an Open University/Ashgate series

The five textbooks and Reader that make up this series are:

- *From Sacred Text to Internet* edited by Gwilym Beckerlegge
- *Religion and Social Transformations* edited by David Herbert
- *Perspectives on Civil Religion* by Gerald Parsons
- *Global Religious Movements in Regional Context* edited by John Wolffe
- *Belief Beyond Boundaries* edited by Joanne Pearson
- *Religion Today: A Reader* edited by Susan Mumm

Each textbook includes:

- an introduction to the issues and controversies relevant to the topic under discussion
- a series of detailed case studies, which allow readers to see the theories and debates at work today in the experience of religious practitioners from various parts of the world
- extracts from other publications, which address the same issue from different perspectives (except *Perspectives on Civil Religion*)
- extensive references to other published material on the same topics
- supporting colour and black-and-white illustrations

The series offers an in-depth introduction to contemporary themes and challenges in religious studies. The contents highlight the central issues and ideas that are shaping religion today – and will continue to do so tomorrow. The textbooks contain plentiful contemporary case studies spanning many countries and religions, and integrate methods of analysis and theoretical perspectives. They work to ensure that readers will understand the relevance of methodologies to lived experience and gain the ability to transfer analytic skills and explanatory devices to the study of religion in context. The textbooks focus on the following key issues in contemporary religious studies: representation and interpretation; modernity and social change; civil religion; the impact of globalization on religion; and the growth of alternative religion.

The accompanying Reader presents primary and secondary source material structured around these core themes. It will serve as an invaluable resource book, whether used to accompany the textbooks in the series or not.

Contents

Preface   ix

Introduction   1
JOANNE PEARSON

PART ONE

**Chapter 1 The history and development of Wicca   15
and Paganism**
JOANNE PEARSON

Chapter 2 Contemporary Celtic spirituality   55
MARION BOWMAN

**Chapter 3 Aspirational Indians: North American   103
indigenous religions and the New Age**
SUSAN MUMM

Chapter 4 Witches and Wicca   133
JOANNE PEARSON

Chapter 5 Religion, science and the New Age   173
RODERICK MAIN

PART TWO

The roots of modern Paganism   225
RONALD HUTTON

Madame Blavatsky's children: Theosophy and its heirs   239
KEVIN TINGAY

**The faith of the fringe: perspectives and issues in   251
'Celtic Christianity'**
DONALD E. MEEK

**Wanting to be Indian: when spiritual searching turns   277
into cultural theft**
MYKE JOHNSON

From the Devil's gateway to the Goddess within: **295**
the image of the witch in neopaganism
WOUTER J. HANEGRAAFF

The witch in history   **313**
DIANE PURKISS

Acknowledgements   325

Index   327

Preface

Belief Beyond Boundaries is the last of a five-volume series entitled *Religion Today: Tradition, Modernity and Change*, published by Ashgate Publishing Ltd in association with The Open University. Like all the volumes in the series, *Belief Beyond Boundaries* has been compiled primarily with the needs of Open University undergraduate students in mind. However, it is hoped that the contents of the volume will also be of interest and value to other readers who would like to know more about the place of religion in the world today.

The authors have benefited greatly from the careful and constructive comments on the first drafts of their chapters by Professor Kim Knott of the University of Leeds (external assessor), Professor Ken Thompson of the Faculty of Social Sciences at The Open University (reader) and Dr Claire Disbrey (tutor consultant). Any inaccuracies or questionable judgements are the responsibilities of the authors alone. Thanks are also due to the writers and publishers who permitted the texts to be reprinted in Part Two of the volume.

The authors wish to acknowledge the contribution made to the production of this volume by: Adrian Roberts (course manager), Julie Bennett, Kate Clements and Peter Wright (editors), Paul Smith (picture researcher), Richard Hoyle (designer) and Pip Harris (compositor).

The authors of the five chapters in the volume are:

- Joanne Pearson, Department of Religious Studies at The Open University
- Marion Bowman, Department of Religious Studies at The Open University
- Susan Mumm, Department of Religious Studies at The Open University
- Roderick Main, Lecturer in Psychoanalytic Studies at the University of Essex.

Introduction

JOANNE PEARSON

As the title suggests, this book is concerned with traditions and practices around which it is difficult to draw boundaries; where they are drawn, they tend to be permeable and fluid rather than fixed. As such, this book includes religions and spiritual groups that fall outside the traditional remit of mainstream religion, both contemporary and historical, although it does not attempt to cover all such groups. Instead, the chapters here focus on Paganism, Wicca, Celtic spirituality, Native American spirituality, and the New Age, which is discussed in relation to religion and science, specifically through the work of the psychiatrist C.G. Jung in the twentieth century.

Such traditions constitute observable religious practice outside what many would conventionally regard as religion, and in some cases, such as that of Celtic spirituality, represent significant bridges between the 'alternative' and the 'mainstream'. This brings us to our first boundary: at what point does the 'alternative' become 'mainstream' (or vice versa) and are such categories helpful or indeed useful? To what are these spiritualities an alternative? How do we determine what is mainstream? On the one hand, to many people witchcraft certainly falls outside what is considered to be mainstream religion, while on the other, the New Age Movement, which began as part of the 1960s counter-culture, has now permeated vast areas of life. Celtic spirituality is to be found not only among Pagans and New Agers, but also constitutes a strong movement within Christianity, a long-standing 'mainstream' religion. To look at the problem another way, the religious beliefs, practices and traditions of tribes of North America are clearly not 'alternative' to the tribes themselves. Nevertheless, practices such as Native American vision quests might well be regarded as an alternative to a mainstream western way of life, which is regarded as over-civilized and ecologically unsound by the 'aspirational Indians' considered in Chapter 3. We must, then, ask ourselves not only *what* such practices are alternatives to, but to *whom* they are alternative.

The boundaries shift and flow in the arena of mainstream versus alternative. But this shifting is just as evident between religion and science, and within and between the religious and spiritual groups themselves. You will find, for example, that the opening chapter of this volume differentiates between Paganism and the New Age, while Chapter 5 treats Paganism as part of the New Age Movement. This demonstrates that it is notoriously difficult to define what is generally known as New Age, just as it is to make generalizations about alternative or non-aligned spirituality. The field of study thus becomes more confused, for we are not considering here religions whose limits have been strongly defined, but rather those areas where any boundaries may seem arbitrary and artificial. So at one end of the spectrum, Paganism might well overlap with the New Age, Celtic spirituality might be practised by New Agers and Pagans, and both might adopt some Native American techniques and practices or engage on some level with Jungian psychology. We could conceivably present a composite figure of an individual who practises techniques and holds beliefs drawn from all of these areas, yet it is highly unlikely that such a person would self-identify as both Pagan *and* New Ager.[1]

Indeed, even within Paganism, for example, the differences suggest that the term 'Paganism' itself is also a somewhat arbitrary boundary drawn around a variety of traditions and practices. Commonalities include reverence for nature as sacred, drawing inspiration from pagan religions of the past, the creative use of ritual and myth, a seasonal cycle of festivals, and a tendency towards polytheism and pantheism rather than monotheism, at least to the extent of accepting the divine as both male and female and thus including both gods and goddesses in their pantheons. These traditions include initiatory Wicca, Pagan Druidry, Asatru/Heathenism[2] (influenced by Scandinavian and Teutonic myth and practices, honouring deities such as Odin and Freya), Pagan shamanism (sometimes influenced by Native American Indian tribes and practices), and what we might call 'non-aligned' Pagan groups because they do not identify with any of the above but simply call themselves

[1] In academic studies, alternative spiritualities have been variously interpreted as New Age (Heelas, 1996; Hanegraaff, 1998), as New Religious Movements (Barker, 1989), as revived religious traditions (Hutton, 1999; Crowley, 1998) and as nature religions (Crowley, 1998; Harvey, 1997). Such a range of possibilities can be confusing, but as I have pointed out above, it is extremely difficult to provide definitive boundaries, and many of these categorizations can thus prove useful in establishing ways to discuss the forms of spirituality that are addressed here. However, they can also prove to be a 'sticky spider's web of concepts and assumptions' (Beckford, 1984, p.260), which have created argument and debate in fields that are themselves subject to contestation.

[2] Some scholars and most Heathens argue that Heathenism is different from Paganism. (See Harvey, 1997, pp.53ff.)

'Pagans'.[3] In a very real sense, then, the term describes a religiosity that embraces a range of different religions rather than a specific religion. This is in keeping with a generally held Pagan view that no one belief system is correct, and that each person has the freedom to choose his or her own religion.

Such a description of Paganism leads one to draw the conclusion that there are many 'Paganisms' – indeed, that there are as many Paganisms as there are Pagans – and we shall find that this is also true of Celtic spirituality, Native American spirituality and the New Age! However, although there are Pagans who operate in a solitary capacity, Paganism is for the most part a sociable form of spirituality which attracts people who wish to join together in groups. These groups take many forms, and entry into them may be by formal rituals of initiation, dedication to a particular deity or deities, or simply through friendship. Some groups may extol the efficacy of magic, deeming it to be a requisite part of Paganism, while others eschew magic and follow instead a path of different inclination. But there is common ground as well.

Ritual

One of the basic shared characteristics of Pagan groups, and some Celtic, Native American Indian and New Age groups, is their use of ritual. Although rituals may vary between different groups, and even between different individuals in the same group, in Paganism there is a framework that is common to most groups ('The Wheel of the Year', which we shall look at later) and the variety of interpretations is seen as a strength. Individual creativity is highly regarded and encouraged, allowing personal interests to be followed in a ritual setting and preventing repetition of what some scholars call 'the routinization of spontaneity'. Ritual, as one would expect, is usually performed by a group of people rather than by solitary individuals. Although the latter is also common within Paganism, here we shall concentrate on group ritual.

Wicca, for example, is made up of hugely varied networks of autonomous covens into which members are initiated. A coven is thus composed of a group of witches who have been initiated into that coven and meet regularly for religious festivals and for training. Druids meet in groups called 'groves', and some Druid orders, such as the Order of Bards, Ovates and Druids, have governing councils.

---

[3] In this volume we focus predominantly on Wicca, Druidry and non-aligned Paganism.

Heathens meet in groups called 'hearths' and some groups, such as the Odinic Rite, have a ruling council called the Court of Gothar, 'gothar' being the plural of gothi (male) and gythja (female) which mean 'priest'. Shamans usually work alone, only occasionally gathering together with other shamans. Non-aligned Pagans often form groups with others with whom they wish to associate, and such groups are therefore often fluid in terms of membership and longevity. Many Pagans, particularly Wiccans, refer to meetings of their groups as 'circles', a reference to the circular sacred space in which rituals are typically held.

Inspiration for ritual is drawn from ancient pasts (e.g. Celtic, Egyptian and Greek civilization) discovered through archaeology, classics, myth and history, or from indigenous peoples such as the First Nation tribes of North America – the idea of 'medicine' for example, as considered in Chapter 3 – or the Australian aborigines. Practices and beliefs are revived and recreated to fit the context of modern day life. Some practitioners also use ideas and concepts developed by Jung to add another level of meaning to their rituals. Pagan rituals fall into roughly four categories: rites of passage (marking the birth of a new child, menarche, manhood, marriage, menopause, ageing and death); initiation rituals (marking an individual as a first, second or third degree Wiccan, for example, or as Bard, Ovate or Druid in Druidry); seasonal festivals; and rituals that celebrate the phases of the moon.

Perhaps the most well-known and extensively celebrated rituals are the eight seasonal festivals which together constitute the mythic-ritual cycle known as 'The Wheel of the Year' (see Colour Plate 1). The 'wheel' is made up of the four solar festivals which mark the winter and summer solstices and the spring and autumn equinoxes. These are more or less fixed, the winter and summer solstices occurring around 21 December and around 21 June, and the spring and autumn equinoxes around 21 March and around 21 September.[4] In between these dates are the cross-quarter days, also known as the fire festivals or Greater Sabbats. These four festivals celebrate the agricultural year, and take place on or around 31 January/1 February (Candlemas, or Imbolc), 30 April/1 May (May Day, or Beltane),

---

[4] In the southern hemisphere, the dates are reversed so that Imbolc (see footnote 5) falls on 1 August and Lammas on 1 February, the winter solstice on 21 June and the summer solstice on 21 December.

31 July/1 August (Lammas or Lughnasadh) and 31 October/1 November (Hallowe'en/Samhain).[5]

The Wheel of the Year is of great importance to an understanding of Paganism, representing the ritual framework of the year in which the seasonal changes in nature are celebrated and in some groups symbolized in the myth of the Goddess and God. The existence of such an eight-fold calendar is contested, however, for there is no irrefutable evidence for it and, as Chapter 2 points out, it is unlikely that identical seasonal ceremonies would have been kept throughout the whole of the British Isles, given the variant temperatures, agricultural practices and daylight hours that exist between the far north of Scotland and the south-western tip of Cornwall. The calendar is most likely an academic construction dating from the eighteenth and nineteenth centuries, but nevertheless the Wheel of the Year is now of profound importance to Paganism. Through the rituals,

> ... gods and humans are intimately and inextricably linked and energies flow from feminine to masculine and back again. Sexuality and death are emphasized as normal stages of an ever-repeating cycle of nature, in what Eliade calls the myth of the eternal return. By repeating the primeval deeds of the gods, humans become as gods, and through ritual the gods become alive once again as the human body becomes the vehicle for their descent.
>
> (Hume, 1997, p.124)

The sacred is thus present in the mundane, the sun and the earth are perceived in close relationship to each other, the ordinary and the extraordinary are celebrated together in a multi-layered cycle of celebration as Pagans observe and immerse themselves in the life cycle of the earth.

All groups work rituals differently, though maintaining a common and recognizable framework for both the mythic cycle as a whole and for the particular rituals which are the Wheel of the Year's constituent parts. Since the sequence of rituals is cyclical, there is no official beginning. For some, the festival of Samhain or Hallowe'en (31 October) marks the start of the year, as it is believed to be the ancient Celtic New Year. For others, however, Imbolc (1 February) is the new

---

[5] A diverse range of names are used for these festivals. Some follow a 'Celtic calendar', as explained in Chapter 2, using names such as Imbolc, Beltane, Lughnasadh and Samhain; others use Candlemas, May Eve/Day, the Anglo-Saxon Lammas and Hallowe'en. The winter solstice is also known as Yule, Alban Arthuan (the Light of Arthur) and Midwinter, and the summer solstice as Litha (after the name used in J.R.R. Tolkien's *Lord of the Rings*, 1954–5), Alban Hefyn (the Light of high summer) and Midsummer.

year, marking the beginning of new growth in early spring. Thus, each group will celebrate in some way the rebirth of the sun at Yule, on or near 21 December; the precise content of the ritual, however, varies considerably from year to year, from person to person and group to group. The style and content of the rituals thus reflect the diversity of Paganism, and not all celebrate all eight festivals: many Heathens, for example, disregard the Wheel of the Year as too recent in origin, preferring to celebrate the festivals of Anglo-Saxon, Teutonic and other northern European peoples, such as Winternights, Yule and *Sigrblot*. In whatever format they are celebrated, however, the seasonal festivals of the Wheel of the Year tie in to the ever-changing cycle of nature and provide a meaningful perspective for this passing of time, and by attuning themselves through ritual with the cycles of nature, Pagans claim to gain greater understanding of their own life cycles.

The New Age

As already mentioned, the inclusion of Paganism under the New Age rubric is contested in this volume. Wicca is, for example, regarded as 'more overtly religious and precisely defined than the New Age' according to Amy Simes (1995, pp.490–8, cited in Hutton, 1999). However, given the use of terminology borrowed from Jungian psychology in popular books on Wicca such as Vivianne Crowley's *Wicca: The Old Religion in the New Millennium* (1996), with much reference to individuation and the search for the Self, it is easy to see why a connection has been made between Wicca and the characteristic 'Self-spirituality' (Heelas, 1996, p.18) of the New Age (see Chapter 5). But the New Age Movement is a term used chiefly to describe various religious movements that emerged in the 1960s on the west coast of the USA and spread throughout North America and Europe, while contemporary Paganism emerged in the UK in the 1950s and then spread to North America. The New Age Movement is characterized by a sense that a new age of spiritual awareness is dawning, for underlying the concept of the New Age is the theory of precession of the equinoxes. This states that, roughly every 2,000 years, a new age of world history begins under the auspices of a different constellation of the zodiac; at present, we are on the verge of the Age of Aquarius (the water bearer) and leaving the Age of Pisces (the dark and light fishes). It is in this sense that the New Age and Paganism are similar, for many Pagans also see the change from

Pisces to Aquarius as a sign that spiritual awareness is growing and that spirituality must therefore change.

However, in many other ways the two are quite distinct. The New Age is, generally, more utopian, with an emphasis on light and healing, whereas Paganism tends to be more pragmatic, recognizing and appreciating darkness and death as part of life's cycle, as well as healing and light. Such distinctions belie a more transcendental attitude within New Age, whereas Paganism regards the divine as immanent. Paganism considers itself to be less consumer oriented and less mainstream than New Age, although this may change as some forms of Paganism become more acceptable to the mainstream. Both Paganism and the New Age operate across an entire spectrum of attitudes, practices and 'beliefs', and there are thus areas where the two overlap – where there are Pagan New Agers as well as New Age Pagans – just as there are areas where the two are wholly distinct. However, just as New Agers tend to react with horror when they are classified as Pagan, so Pagans regard themselves as practising something wholly distinct from the New Age, which they tend to regard with scorn.

New Religious Movements and revived religion

Contrary to the reaction against being labelled New Age, however, practitioners generally find it more or less acceptable to be classified as new religions while recognizing that the term is not particularly accurate. The term 'New Religious Movement' (NRM) has been used to cover 'a disparate collection of organizations, most of which have emerged in their present form since the 1950s, and most of which offer some kind of answer to questions of a fundamental religious, spiritual or philosophical nature' (Barker, 1989, p.9). Many, however, prefer the term 'revived religion', since practitioners draw on ancient traditions and manipulate them for the twenty-first century. Thus, Wiccans and Pagans draw on ancient Paganism as well as indigenous practices, people drawn to Celtic spirituality see the Celt as the upholder of a spiritually superior past, those who have adopted Native American techniques claim a more relevant and spiritually satisfying tradition which is held up as being more ecologically aware, while the New Age claims the rebirth of ancient esoteric teachings, whether from Atlantis[6], Avalon[7] or extra-terrestrials. Gods and goddesses are adopted from a whole range of pantheons, including Egyptian, Greek, Roman, Celtic, Nordic, Saxon, Teutonic, Native American, aboriginal, and even from science fiction. Research into the mystery cults of the ancient world forms the basis of some spiritual practices, and these can be found in archaeological and historical material, classical mythology, and other writings.

Revived religion is not, however, an appropriate or specific enough term for use in distinguishing religions, since all religions have a tendency to use what has gone before and could therefore be called revived religions. As Irving Hexham points out, 'the thing that is "new" in new religions is the content of their mythological idioms and their conscious use of images, practices and theories from anywhere [and indeed, any time] in the world' (Hexham and Poewe, 1997, p.162). Since many practitioners have in common an attitude towards 'nature-as-sacred', however, scholars and practitioners have also favoured definition as 'nature religion'.

Nature religion

'Nature religion' is a relatively recent academic construct under which to group a variety of religions, including Paganism, eco-spirituality and indigenous religions. Yet at present, 'nature religion' is a contested designation, and is itself an emerging field. The current use of the term stems from Catherine Albanese's usage in her book *Nature Religion in America: From the Algonkian Indians to the New Age* (1990). Albanese defined nature religion as beliefs, behaviours and values that make nature a 'symbolic centre'. While recognizing the value of the construct in bringing to light the diversity of religious practices that take nature as a symbolic referent, Albanese's term has been criticized as too broad to be of practical use. Bron Taylor (1999, pp.22–4) suggests instead that we use phrases such as 'the natural dimension of religion', or 'nature influenced religion', to distinguish those religions that see nature as important but not sacred, and keep 'nature religion' exclusively for reference to religions that regard nature as sacred.

[6] Mythical island of the Atlantic ocean, believed to be a repository of ancient wisdom until it was overwhelmed by the sea.

[7] Legendary land to which King Arthur was transported after his death to await the time for his return. In Welsh mythology, Avalon is the kingdom of the dead. It is sometimes regarded as the Land of Fairy and the home of the last vestiges of indigenous British Paganism.

As we shall see, many practitioners of alternative spirituality do regard nature as sacred, and market their beliefs as 'green religion'. However, their response to nature is often confused, revealing both intimacy and distance as they shape nature with the Wheel of the Year, sacred circles and ritual to suit their own needs for relationship with the earth. The nature/culture duality thus persists in nature religion, reflecting a turn to nature as a source of revitalization, an attempt to re-engage with a nature from which participants feel estranged, to re-enchant the natural world which has been exploited and dominated. Since practitioners are not generally involved with salvation religions, they do not reject the world or the everyday reality of living in the world, but seek to enhance life on earth. Earthly existence is not regarded as fundamentally sinful or binding, with a need for salvation or escape. How much one takes this as a need to defend and protect the earth, however, is open to question.

Often, a past golden age or the spiritual practices of indigenous peoples are held up as being more ecologically sound or closer to nature, and as seeming to offer an alternative to what is perceived as modern western destruction of nature. Science is largely blamed for this destruction of nature, and as we shall see in Chapter 5, non-western and pre-modern religions (or their modern revived versions) are seen to be insulated from scientific developments and thus untainted by it. Sometimes, however, it is the growth of environmental awareness that changes attitudes to nature. As Vivianne Crowley points out in her discussion of 'Wicca as Nature Religion', Wicca has only recently identified itself closely with the natural world – growing popular awareness of environmental concerns brought an influx of changes, and Wiccans realized that 'a nature religion implies a nature to worship ... the ethos of Wicca and Paganism was beginning to evolve from one of nature veneration to nature preservation' (Crowley, 1998, p.175). Direct links had already been made with the natural world in ritual texts such as the 'Great Charge', written by Doreen Valiente in the 1950s, which contains the following lines:

> I, who am the beauty of the green Earth and the white Moon among the stars, and the mystery of the waters, and the desire in the heart of man, call unto thy soul: Arise, and come unto me. For I am the Soul of nature who gives life to the universe.
>
> (Crowley, 1998, p.173)

Yet among 'organized' Pagan traditions such as Wicca and Druidry, few practitioners involve themselves in direct action. Emma Restall Orr, Joint Chosen Chief of the British Druid Order, explains the Druid perspective:

> While the extraordinary courage and dedication of the young folk who are willing to risk their own lives for the sake of the forests and the meadows, the wildlife, the SSSIs (Sites supposed to be protected because of their Special Scientific Interest), never ceases to amaze me, most Druids would not work at the cutting edge of confrontation.
>
> (Restall Orr, 1998, pp.153–4)

Thus, the impact of environmental awareness and activism begs the question as to whether attitudes towards nature are merely a religious rendering of secular concerns. The concept of 'nature' is, however, itself diffuse and fractured, and it may be for this reason that attitudes to nature as sacred, and the refusal to place boundaries around a constructed 'nature', necessarily leave the observer with the impression of a confused and ill thought-out response to the natural world. Yet new designations such as 'revived religion' and 'nature religion' are proving to be more applicable as terms of categorization than the very general labels of 'New Age' or NRM.

Outline of the book

The chapters, along with the texts in Part Two of this volume, discuss the emergence into relative popularity of alternative spirituality over the course of the past one hundred years. Focusing particularly on Wicca and Paganism, the first chapter evaluates the influence of the rise of magical, secret societies during the late Victorian age on the development of alternative spirituality during the second half of the twentieth century. The volume then moves on to three extended case studies, which consider Celtic spirituality, Native American spirituality and Wicca. All three studies question the authenticity of spiritualities based on the reclamation of 'ancient truths and peoples', and ask why these forms of spirituality are so popular in the contemporary UK and USA. The emergence of such forms of spirituality in the closing decades of the twentieth century gives rise to the question: why have they appeared at a time when science and technology have permeated every aspect of human life? The closing chapter thus considers the impact of the rise of science on religion, noting interactions between the two before progressing to a detailed examination of New Age spirituality as a response to scientifically led modernization, secularization and globalization, using the psychology of Jung, and in particular his theory of synchronicity, as an illustrative example.

The texts in Part Two present an overview or illustrate specific examples of the themes of the chapters in greater detail. Ronald

Hutton's 'The roots of modern Paganism' outlines the influences on the development of Paganism, while Kevin Tingay's 'Madame Blavatsky's children' deals specifically with the Theosophical Society. Donald Meek's 'The faith of the fringe' draws attention to the way in which Celticism has been imposed on an idea of early Christianity in Britain, and Myke Johnson's 'Wanting to be Indian' focuses on issues raised by the use of First Nations' practices and beliefs by non-Indians. Wouter Hanegraaff's 'From the Devil's gateway to the Goddess within' examines in detail the shifting emphases in the image of the witch from its development in the fourteenth century to today's neopagans, while Diane Purkiss' 'A Holocaust of one's own' explores the importance of the witch to feminists. 'Against the self-images of the New Age' by John Hedley Brooke and G.N. Cantor deals explicitly with the relationship between science and religion, and looks at how that relationship has been portrayed in the work of one writer influential on the New Age: Fritjof Capra. Throughout, the volume suggests some possible answers to the questions that have been asked. How do we categorize these new forms of spirituality? How might we best study them? And lastly, are we looking at a new understanding of religion – what do the terms 'spirituality' and 'religion' mean to both practitioners and scholars in the twenty-first century?

References

Albanese, C. (1990) *Nature Religion in America: From the Algonkian Indians to the New Age*, Chicago: Chicago University Press.

Barker, E. (1989) *New Religious Movements: A Practical Introduction*, London: HMSO.

Beckford, J. (1984) 'Holistic imagery and ethics in new religious and healing movements', *Social Compass*, 32, pp.259–72.

Crowley, V. (1996) *Wicca: The Old Religion in the New Millennium*, London: Thorsons (first published 1989, Wellingborough: Aquarian).

Crowley, V. (1998) 'Wicca as Nature Religion', in J. Pearson, R.H. Roberts and G. Samuel (eds), *Nature Religion Today: Paganism in the Modern World*, Edinburgh: Edinburgh University Press, pp.170–9.

Hanegraaff, W.J. (1998) *New Age Religion and Western Culture: Esotericism in the Mirror of Secular Thought*, New York: SUNY.

Harvey, G. (1997) *Listening People, Speaking Earth: Contemporary Paganism*, London: Hurst.

Heelas, P. (1996) *The New Age Movement*, Oxford: Blackwell.

Hexham, I. and Poewe, K. (1997) *New Religions as Global Cultures: Making the Human Sacred*, Colorado/Oxford: Westview Press.

Hume, L. (1997) *Witchcraft and Paganism in Australia*, Melbourne: Melbourne University Press.

Hutton, R. (1999) *The Triumph of the Moon: A History of Modern Pagan Witchcraft*, Oxford: Oxford University Press.

Restall Orr, E. (1998) *Spirits of the Sacred Grove: The World of a Druid Priestess*, London: Thorsons.

Simes, A. (1995) 'Contemporary Paganism in the East Midlands', unpublished PhD thesis, University of Nottingham.

Taylor, B. (1999) 'Nature and supernature – harmony and mastery: irony and evolution in contemporary Nature Religion', *The Pomegranate: A New Journal of NeoPagan Thought*, 8 pp.21–7.

PART ONE

CHAPTER I

The history and development of Wicca and Paganism

JOANNE PEARSON

Introduction

> Who else have civilised the world, and built the cities, if not the nobles
> and kings of Paganism? ... They have filled the earth with settled forms
> of government, and with wisdom, which is the highest good. Without
> Paganism the world would be empty and miserable.
>
> (Thabit ibn Qurra, in Scott, 1985, p.105)

> ... the Paganism of today has very little in common with that of the past
> except the name, which is itself of Christian coinage.
>
> (Hutton, 1993, p.337)

> [Wicca is] neither the descendant of a continuous sectarian witch cult,
> nor [was it] born fully fledged from the imagination of one man in the
> 1940s. It is, on the contrary, a particular, and extreme, incarnation of
> some of the broadest and deepest cultural impulses of the nineteenth
> and twentieth century British world.
>
> (Hutton, 1996, p.13)

Paganism has been described as a term that 'implies a polytheistic [1]
nature religion whose deities are meant to be personifications of
nature, often as they were found within the ancient pantheons'
(Luhrmann, 1994, p.83). These ancient pantheons formed part of the
paganism of the ancient world – of the Egyptian civilization, classical
Greece or Rome, or of Celtic or Nordic Europe. It may therefore seem
strange to speak of modern-day Pagans communing with these same
gods and goddesses – Isis and Osiris, the Olympians, Minerva,
Rhiannon or Thor. Yet contemporary Paganism draws inspiration

---

[1] Belief in or worship of more than one god.

from the ancient past discovered through archaeology, classics, myth and history, reinventing the past to give meaning to the present.

This can, of course, cause problems for Religious Studies scholars in that it is easy to confuse ancient paganism and modern-day Pagans. In this chapter, therefore, we shall refer to contemporary Pagans and Paganism with a capital 'P', and use lower case to denote ancient paganism. In North America, 'neo-Paganism' is the preferred term in academic circles, in order to differentiate between the paganism of the ancient world and modern Paganism, and we will come across this in readings and quotations from some scholars, and in other chapters in this volume. However, this prefix is not universally applied, and 'neo-Paganism' is not in common use in the UK. But where does the term 'Paganism' come from, and what does it mean? Having decided how we shall refer to contemporary Paganism and ancient paganism, we need to examine the meanings of the word 'pagan', and to consider how contemporary Pagans interpret these meanings.

Interpretation 1: 'Country dweller'

There are three meanings that have been attributed to the word 'pagan' (Hutton, 1993, p.xiv). In the first meaning, 'pagan' is taken to refer to a 'country dweller', an interpretation that seems to have developed mainly with the Romantic literature of the late eighteenth and early nineteenth centuries, and Victorian urban growth from the mid-nineteenth century. Romantic literature combined in varying degrees admiration for ancient Greece, nostalgia for a vanished past, and desire for organic unity between people, culture and nature (Hutton, 1999, p.21), its main enthusiasts in England being poets such as John Keats and Percy Bysshe Shelley. By the mid-nineteenth century, towns had grown at a rate that led some to celebrate nature as a form of resistance to its perceived disappearance. According to the Census of 1851, for example, the English urban population outnumbered the rural for the first time. Between 1821 and 1841, the population of London rose by 20 per cent, those of Manchester, Leeds and Sheffield increased by 40 per cent, while that of Bradford rose by a spectacular 65 per cent (Williams, 1975, p.188). It has been suggested that this growth of urban areas during the Victorian era caused 'an almost hysterical celebration of rural England' from the 1870s onwards, with the Arcadian goat-god Pan being invoked as the great god of nature,[2] and the idea of the Greek goddess Gaia as Mother Nature and Mother Earth becoming popular (Hutton, 1996, p.9).

The growing interest in the environment, and the urge to leave behind the towns and cities and enter once more into communion with 'nature' as 'the countryside' encouraged popular usage of the term 'pagan' as one who dwells in the rustic areas, and the engagement of poets and authors with nature and the countryside certainly influenced the development of Wicca and Paganism. However, it is the very growth of the city that accounts for what is a primarily urban phenomena – most Wiccans and Pagans live in towns and cities – at the same time as it provides a focus for discontent and an opposition to idealized nature.

The veneration of nature in modern Paganism, the concern for the earth as deity and the **pantheism**[3] of seeing the divine in all of nature has led modern Pagans to maintain an attitude of reverence for the wild, untamed countryside on the one hand, and of sadness or revulsion at human estrangement from this ideal, living in towns and cities away from the land, on the other. For some Pagans, veneration of nature and identification as 'Pagan' manifests as a romantic attachment to the countryside, a dream of living away from the towns and nurturing a closer relationship with nature; but it has been pointed out that 'most [Pagans] are urban, as is usually true of those who love nature (the farmers are too busy fighting it)' (Russell, 1991, p.171). For others, direct action against the destruction of the environment – at road protests, proposed building sites, Manchester Airport's second runway in 1998–9, or simply to protect an old tree – is the favoured means of expressing their concern for nature and their belief that nature is divine, ensouled (i.e. is animated, has a soul) or, at the very least, alive. Others, however, see nature as all-inclusive, regarding all that we do as 'natural', for we, as humans, are also part of nature. While it is a fact that most Pagans live in urban areas, and very few depend directly on the land for their living, for many Pagans, 'respectful and intimate relationships with nature include[s] the awareness that "nature" includes all that we eat and drink' (Harvey, 1997, p.12), which presumably includes food and drink bought from supermarkets!

[2] We might cite as examples Arthur Machen's 1894 novel *The Great God Pan*, and Saki's short story 'The Music on the Hill' (1911), both of which feature Pan as a central figure, while Kenneth Grahame's *The Wind in the Willows* (1907) and J.M. Barrie's *Peter Pan* (1906) made Pan accessible to children.

[3] Note that definitions for words printed in bold are to be found in the Glossary at the end of each chapter.

However, most town dwellers were in fact pagan at the time the term 'pagan' was coined. Thabit ibn Qurra, a Sabian[4] from Harran (835–901), praised ancient paganism to the Caliph of Baghdad with the words that appear in the quotation at the beginning of this chapter, which clearly has nothing to do with a rustic existence; and by the early fifth century, *pagani* was used by Christians simply to refer to those who were not members of their own religion. Since resistance to Christianity in late antiquity was led by the nobility and academics, it is highly unlikely that 'pagan' was used to relate to religions exclusively of the countryfolk.

Interpretation 2: 'Civilian'

This brings us to the second meaning of 'pagan', that of 'civilian' (Fox, 1986, pp.30–1). By the second and third centuries, the *pagani* were those who had not enlisted as part of God's 'army', as *militia Christi* (soldiers of Christ) against the forces of Satan. Among early Christians, *pagani* thus came to be used to distinguish the *militia Christi* from mere 'civilians'. This meaning, however, died out by about the fourth century. By this time, the pagans were simply those who had not yet received baptism, and the term seems to have been used objectively as a term of identification rather than as a pejorative term of contempt. 'Pagan' as 'civilian', as one not enlisted in the 'army of God', expresses the synonymity of 'pagan' with 'heretic' in the popular mind, sometimes as non-Christian and often as anti-Christian. Undoubtedly, many Pagans today see themselves as opposing Christianity, identifying with the persecution of witches in early modern Europe by the Christian Church, and reacting against the patriarchal, monotheistic religion of western culture. This may be particularly true among people who have recently decided to identify themselves as Pagans, and who are perhaps rebelling against their upbringing, education, society and culture. Indeed, one historian has argued that the writings of contemporary British Pagans exhibit:

> ... an intense and consistent hostility to the Christian Church. The follies and deficiencies of this institution are regularly held up to ridicule and abuse. Such bitterness may be therapeutic for those who

---

[4] The name taken by a group of esotericist non-Muslims living in Harran (near the river Euphrates) when forced by the Caliph of Baghdad to reveal who they were in 830. Since Islam offered protection to peoples officially recognized in the Qur'an (see Wolffe, 2002, Book 4 in this series, Chapter 3), they called themselves Sabians, people from Saba (the biblical Sheba), a region of southern Arabia now comprising Yemen. To gain full recognition and protection, they were required to name the book of their sacred scripture, and cited certain texts ascribed to **Hermes Trismegistus**. Hermeticism thus became the official religion of the Sabians.

have recently rejected Christianity, and is natural in view of the conviction of modern pagans that the Church was directly responsible for the Great Witch Hunt with whose victims they identify.

(Hutton, 1993, p.336)

Such an attitude of 'being Pagan' in opposition to 'being Christian' is growing more rare. Rather, Pagans tend to be tolerant and respectful towards other religions and spiritual practices. Much changed in the 1990s, as the influence of historical research permeated Paganism and historical claims were re-evaluated. Any links between Wicca and the Great Witch Hunt[5] of early modern Europe, for example, are now seen in terms of self-identification rather than as historical facts (see Chapter 4 of this volume). Along with this re-evaluation of the past has come a re-evaluation of Christianity. Wiccans and Pagans have been, and are at present, involved in the development of interfaith meetings with members of other religions, and as Paganism has grown in popularity,[6] and public awareness of it has increased, it has adopted a less reactive posture which no longer requires legitimization through false histories or hatred of the Christian Church.

Interpretation 3: 'Locality'

The definitive account of the word 'pagan', however, argues that pagan simply meant 'followers of the religions of the "pagus" or locality; i.e. the old, rooted faiths instead of the new universal one' (Chuvin, 1990, cited in Hutton, 1993, p.xiv), and thus, by the sixth century, *pagani* had indeed come to mean 'non-Christian'. The interpretation of 'pagan' as a follower of the religion of the locality is becoming more noticeable among modern Pagans, who perceive themselves to be creating links with the energy of the land at a local level, celebrating their rituals with reverence for the *genius loci*, the spirit of the place, or with gods and goddesses traditionally associated with a locale. A recent account of Pagan Druidry by Emma Restall Orr, Joint Chief of the British Druid Order, expresses this interpretation of Paganism as local religion:

> [Paganism] is a religion of locality, i.e. it is where the devotees revere the spirits of the landscape around them, the water courses and wells on which they depend, the soil of the fields and forests that surround

[5] A name used to denote the witchcraft persecutions of early-modern Europe, also called the Witch Craze.

[6] The most recent estimated number of Pagans in the UK is 120,000 (see later in this chapter).

them, the sprites and elementals, sometimes to deification. It is a basic attitude in the Pagan mentality that the spirit of the land is the most potent force.

(Restall Orr, 1998, p.140)

The term 'pagan' can thus be interpreted by modern Pagans according to all three definitions provided above, indicating 'country dweller', non-Christian and the religion of the locality. The latter interpretation is, however, by far the most popular among modern Pagans, who are well aware of their own and ancient pagans' urban rather than rustic existence, and who are reluctant to define themselves in terms of reference to Christianity. In the multi-faith, globalized world of the late twentieth century, it is no longer deemed appropriate for any religion to be named according to its relationship with Christianity, and consequently labelled 'non' – or 'anti' – Christian. Paganism today, then, refers to a number of religions that view nature as sacred, ensouled or alive, which tend to be pantheistic, **polytheistic** and/or **duotheistic** rather than **monotheistic**, including both gods and goddesses in their pantheons, who try to live in balance and harmony, accepting darkness and light, life and death, as part of one sacred whole.

So, where did this contemporary Paganism come from? As the quotations cited at the beginning of this chapter indicate, today's Paganism is not the same as that of the ancient world, nor has it continued unbroken for thousands of years. 'The roots of modern Paganism' by Ronald Hutton, which is reprinted in Part Two of this book, provides an outline of modern Paganism's development. It shows that to untangle the roots of contemporary Paganism we must go back just over 100 years to the late-Victorian period known as the *fin de siècle*, and from there to Wicca and the beginnings of twentieth- and twenty-first-century Paganism.

The influence of the *fin de siècle*

The nature of the *fin de siècle* has been subject to varying characterizations, relating to both a specific historical era and the spirit of that particular era. As such, the *fin de siècle* denotes the period of time immediately before and immediately after the end of one century and the beginning of the next, and constitutes an image of transition, of society imbued with anxiety and insecurity. Our concern here is with the transition period between the end of the nineteenth century and the beginning of the twentieth, from the 1880s to the beginning of the First World War in 1914. The thirty to forty years constituting this *fin de siècle* have been characterized as a period in which the process of cultural fragmentation 'threw the norms of the Victorian age into crisis: empires were threatened, feminism was on the march, and the first socialist parties in Britain were formed' (Ledger and McCracken, 1995, p.1). The *fin de siècle* was a period of spiritual and psychological exploration, which saw the beginnings of a trend that has continued throughout the twentieth century. The whole period has been characterized as 'the flight from reason', in which 'the resulting crisis of human consciousness produced a revulsion from the methods of thought and action that were responsible for the insecurity of Western man' (Webb, 1976, p.8). The rejection of reason resulted in the revival of the 'underground of rejected knowledge, [which] has as its core the varied collection of doctrines that can be combined in a bewildering variety of ways and that is known as the occult' [literally 'hidden' or 'concealed', referring to an immense body of magical, mystical and religious knowledge gathered over thousands of years] (Webb, 1976, p.9).

The publication of Charles Darwin's *On the Origin of the Species by Means of Natural Selection* in 1859 had 'deprived man of his divine image and replaced it with that of an ape' (Webb, 1976, p.8). It thus became a focus in the conflict between science and religion, a thread that will be picked up in Chapter 5. Humankind was no longer God's special creation, and into this spiritual crisis new waves of scholarship brought further erosion of the Christian establishment. Biblical criticism, for example, was closely examining the documents on which Christianity was built, and such developments undermined the security of establishment religion.

Spiritualism in particular became increasingly attractive, particularly among women as it openly advocated the feminism which had begun to emerge in the mid-nineteenth century. By the 1890s, some women were no longer satisfied with the same role models that had inspired their mothers, and some began to forge new roles for themselves, particularly in the realm of religion. Among these women were many important figures of the occult revival, including Helena Petrovna Blavatsky (1831–91) and Annie Besant (1847–1933) of the **Theosophical Society**, and Anna Kingsford (1846–88), who established the Hermetic Society[7] as an offshoot of the Theosophical Society. From the **Hermetic Order of the Golden Dawn**, women such as Annie Horniman (1860–1937) 'rebelled against the restrictions that her parents sought to impose on her, and ... rebelled even more heartily against those imposed on her sex by society' (Howe,

---

[7] The Hermetic Society is different from the Hermetic Society of the Golden Dawn.

1972, p.66), and Florence Farr (1860–1917) was, according to the playwright George Bernard Shaw, 'in violent reaction against Victorian morals, especially sexual and domestic morals' (ibid., p.68). Moina Mathers (1865–1928), wife of S.L. MacGregor Mathers, head of the Golden Dawn, played a major role in the development of the Order, writing many of its rituals, and headed the Alpha et Omega temple in London after her husband's death in 1918.

Societies such as the Theosophical Society and, in particular, the Hermetic Order of the Golden Dawn, were influenced by the close-knit secrecy of **freemasonry** and its claims to be the guardian of a powerful secret of ancient provenance. They set about popularizing their own claims to ancient wisdom, reviving the **hermetic** and **kabbalistic** teachings gathered together by Renaissance scholars such as Marsilio Ficino (1433–99) and Giovanni Pico della Mirandola (1463–94). Most of the leading occultists of the late nineteenth/early twentieth century were already members either of Masonic or quasi-Masonic fraternities, but in keeping with the early feminism of the *fin de siècle,* the new societies were open to both men and women on an equal basis.

Figure 1.1 Madame Blavatsky, co-founder of the Theosophical Society. Mary Evans Picture Library.

Figure 1.2 Annie Horniman, patron of the arts, occultist and member of the Golden Dawn. Abbey Theatre Collection. Photo: Rex Roberts.

Figure 1.3 Florence Farr, actress and head of the London temple of the Golden Dawn from 1893–1900. Mander and Mitchenson Theatre Collection.

Figure 1.4 Moina Mathers, wife of MacGregor Mathers. After his death she headed the Alpha et Omega breakaway group of the Golden Dawn. Aquarian Press/HarperCollins Publishers.

The Western Esoteric Tradition

Such societies for seekers after eastern wisdom and western magic drew enormously on what is now known as the **Western Esoteric Tradition**, a vast field comprising a body of material gathered together in the West since the end of the fifteenth century by men such as Ficino and Mirandola mentioned above. This material includes the kabbalah, hermeticism, **Gnosticism** and the occult sciences of **astrology**, **alchemy** and magic, and has its origins in a body of magical and philosophical texts attributed to Hermes Trismegistus, collectively known as the *Corpus Hermeticum* and said to originate on an emerald tablet inscribed by the Egyptian god Thoth (Hermes Trismegistus in the Graeco-Roman tradition).

In the late fifteenth century, these manuscripts, containing elements of Platonism, **NeoPlatonism**, **Stoicism**, **Neo-Pythagoreanism**, and Jewish and Persian influences, were brought to Cosimo de Medici, ruler of Florence. Marsilio Ficino, a physician and scholar, was immediately instructed to begin their translation. At the same time, refugees from the expulsion of the Jews from Spain in 1492 brought the Jewish kabbalah to Florence. The Jewish kabbalah was blended with hermeticism by Giovanni Pico della Mirandola who, along with Ficino, was one of the founders of Italian Renaissance hermetism, or 'the hermetic-cabbalist tradition' (Yates, 1991, pp.86, 257). This fertile marriage of Egyptian, Greek and Jewish thought produced 'a practical, spiritual "way" – an attempt to understand the self, the world and the divine' (Fowden, 1986, p.xvi). With a strong emphasis on astrological and alchemical lore, the teachings of the corpus claimed that, through the power of mystical regeneration, it is possible for humankind to regain the supremacy over nature that was lost at the time of the biblical Fall.

When they first appeared in the fifteenth century, the manuscripts were thought to date from vast antiquity, long before Plato and even longer before Christ – indeed, Hermes Trismegistus was believed by some to be a contemporary of Moses, and by others to have lived at the same time as Noah. The corpus was, however, misdated and it is now known that the writings were by various authors and of varying dates: Isaac Casaubon, in 1614, is generally regarded to have been the first person to disprove the pre-Christian provenance of the hermetic manuscripts. They are now regarded as 'the records of individual souls seeking revelation, intuition into the divine, personal salvation, gnosis, without the aid of a personal God or Saviour, but through a religious approach to the universe' (Yates, 1991, p.22). After the Renaissance, esotericism survived the Enlightenment under the aegis of Romanticism and occultism, not unchanged but reinterpreted, and to a certain extent secularized, as esoteric cosmology came to be increasingly understood in terms of new evolutionism and scientific cosmologies (Hanegraaff, 1998, p.406).

The popularization of the terms 'esotericism' and 'occultism' by the influential French occultist Eliphas Lévi from 1856 'provided useful generic labels for a large and complicated group of historical phenomena that had long been perceived as sharing an *air de famille*' (Hanegraaff, 1998, p.385). During the nineteenth century, Lévi came to be regarded 'as a kind of saint of the new occult movement' (Wilson, 1987, p.23), responsible 'for the surfacing, in an admittedly romanticised form, of the whole underground magical tradition' (King, 1989, p.22), and influencing the Hermetic Order of the Golden Dawn and Aleister Crowley (who claimed to be a reincarnation of Lévi) in particular. Thus, the Western Esoteric Tradition emerged into the twentieth century, and is still with us today. Its influences can be recognized to greater and lesser degrees within Wicca, Paganism, magical orders and some New Age practices, into which it has filtered through many organizations including the Theosophical Society and the Golden Dawn.

The Theosophical Society

The Theosophical Society was established in 1875 in New York to explore the alternatives provided by eastern literature, religion and science. As Kevin Tingay reveals in 'Madame Blavatsky's Children' in Part Two of this volume, the society spread to England and from there to the English-speaking world where it has flourished to this day. The foundation of the Theosophical Society by Helena Petrovna Blavatsky and Colonel Henry Steel Olcott established an organization, open to both men and women, for research and study. Its published aims were:

1 to form a nucleus of the Universal Brotherhood of Humanity, without distinction of race, creed, sex, caste or colour;
2 to encourage the study of comparative religion, philosophy and science;
3 to investigate unexplained laws of nature and the powers latent in man.

(Ransom, 1938, p.545)

When theosophy was introduced to England in January 1883, it was immediately attractive to those who were spiritually unsettled by religious doubts arising from the Darwinian controversy.

The work of the Theosophical Society was a mission to correct the misapprehensions of spiritualism, to expand the horizons of science, and to oppose dogmatic Christianity (Godwin, 1994, p.307). The means to do this were drawn from Egyptian occultism, both ancient and modern, and from the Western Esoteric Tradition. However, it was eastern wisdom, particularly from India, which was to become the overriding influence. Blavatsky believed that all eastern philosophies and religions surpassed those of the West, and embraced Hinduism and Buddhism. She had reached the extreme conclusion that western society and western religion contained nothing good, and her ultimate mission was to supplant western ignorance with eastern wisdom (Godwin, 1994, p.305).[8]

This contrasts with similar organizations, such as Anna Kingsford's and Edward Maitland's Hermetic Society and the Hermetic

---

[8] In its early days, the Theosophical Society was treated as a bit of a joke, and eventually Blavatsky was disgraced as the movement became more closely linked to broader Indian interests under Annie Besant (1847–1933), who was president of the society from 1907 until her death in 1933.

Figure 1.5 Madame Blavatsky and Colonel Olcott, co-founders of the Theosophical Society. Mary Evans Picture Library.

Brotherhood of Luxor, both founded in 1884. Like the Golden Dawn, both of these were loyal to the Western Esoteric Tradition – making use of eastern knowledge and wisdom but not subservient to it. Kingsford had been president of the London lodge of the Theosophical Society from 1883 to 1884, but resigned precisely because she disliked the emphasis on eastern ideas. In founding the Hermetic Society, she aimed to promote western esoteric philosophy. By the mid-1880s, freemasonry, spiritualism and theosophy had firmly woven themselves into the fabric of British occultism and into the subculture of secret societies. But it was at the close of the 1880s that the most influential occult society came into being.

The Golden Dawn

The Hermetic Order of the Golden Dawn opened its Isis Urania Temple in London in 1888 under the leadership of Dr William Wynn Westcott, S.L. MacGregor Mathers and Dr W.R. Woodman. Westcott, a London coroner and **Rosicrucian**, obtained part of a manuscript from a freemason, Revd A.F.A. Woodford, in 1887. On deciphering

Figure 1.6 Samuel Liddell MacGregor Mathers, Chief of the Golden Dawn, and regarded as one of the main contenders, with Aleister Crowley, for the role of chief magician in Europe. Aquarian Press/ HarperCollins Publishers.

the manuscript, Westcott claimed to have discovered that it contained fragments of rituals from the Golden Dawn, a previously unheard of German occult order that admitted women as well as men. MacGregor Mathers developed the fragments into full-scale rituals, which he based largely on freemasonry, and papers were forged to give the Golden Dawn a history and authenticity. The original manuscript was later shown to be a forgery also, and it was on such dubious grounds that the Hermetic Order of the Golden Dawn was established in London.

The Golden Dawn organized itself as an association of individuals, with its headquarters in London and lodges in Weston-super-Mare, Bradford, Edinburgh and Paris, and a leader (Mathers) who based himself, for the most part, in Paris. The secret society quickly caught on, with 315 initiations taking place during its heyday (1888–96) before, in 1897, members unearthed Westcott's questionable role in 'discovering' the Golden Dawn, and irreparable schisms began to form. In addition, although the Golden Dawn recognized the importance of the feminine aspect of the divine (goddesses), admitted women to equal membership alongside men, and aimed to provide a coherent structure for learning and magical advancement, hierarchy was inherent within the extensive degree system,[9] competition between individuals was rife, and splinter groups proliferated. The eventual disintegration of the Golden Dawn in the early twentieth century has predominantly been interpreted as a natural consequence of the clash of egos between various people involved in the Order.

From 1888 to 1896, however, the Golden Dawn members gathered together western magical knowledge, including studies on the **Kabbalistic Tree of Life**, the **Key of Solomon**, **Abramelin Magic, Enochian Magic**, as well as material gleaned from the **Egyptian Book of the Dead**, William **Blake's Prophetic Books** and the **Chaldean Oracles**. The legacy of the Golden Dawn for contemporary alternative spirituality is immense, and this is largely due to the very individualism of the members who undertook research into diverse areas of history, myth, archaeology, magic and languages. As a result, the Order has been described as 'the sole depository of magical knowledge, the only occult order of any real worth that the West in our time has known' (Regardie, 1989, p.16). It was 'the order that would virtually redefine the British occult world for the Twentieth Century' (Godwin, 1994, p.223).

The Golden Dawn formulae were, in essence, pagan and hermetic, using pre- or non-Christian names of power (i.e. the names of God, which in Jewish thought are so powerful that they cannot be spoken) which were to be found in Hebrew, Greek, Coptic, Egyptian and Chaldean sources, but it took no official stance against establishment Christianity. Like the Theosophical Society, the spiritualist movement and freemasonry, the Golden Dawn attracted many people who were at least uncomfortable with, if not in direct revolt against Christianity; on the other hand, some members (such as the author A.E. Waite) made use of the pre-Christian and magical methods to facilitate their Christian spiritual development. For many members, there existed no abyss between Christianity and the occult, and they found no difficulty in neatly dovetailing their Christian faith with their occult interests and magical leanings. From a Christian, particularly a Catholic standpoint, the Golden Dawn would be condemned simply because it demanded a vow of secrecy from its members. But

---

[9] An elaborate hierarchy was created consisting of ten grades or degrees, which were divided into three orders – the Outer (Neophyte, Zelator, Theoricus, Practicus, Philosophus, Adeptus Minor), the Second (Adeptus Major, Adeptus Exemptus) and the Third Order (Magister Temple, Magus, Ipsissimus) made up of the astral chiefs with whom only Mathers could communicate.

Christian or not, members only had to acknowledge their belief in the existence of a 'supreme being', and the old pagan gods were just as welcome as, and in fact more popular than, those of conventional religion.

In general, there was a largely amicable split between western magic and eastern philosophy in the occult community of the *fin de siècle*: those interested in researching and studying the wisdom of the East joined the Theosophical Society; those who wished to study the Western Esoteric Tradition and perform ritual within an initiatory system joined the Golden Dawn. A few occultists, including W.B. Yeats, were members of both organizations, bringing together the traditions in a more global fashion, a trend that became more popular after the First World War.

By the start of the First World War, the stage was set for the emergence of Wicca and Paganism out of the occult revival: magic and ritual were being practised systematically, large amounts of knowledge and information had been gathered and translated, women held important positions within secret societies and steered the development of magical religion, and nature was celebrated as at once mystical, powerful and divine, and as under threat, in need of protection.

In the inter-war years, this form of occultism was kept alive and promoted by such figures as Dion Fortune (1890–1947) and Aleister Crowley (1875–1947). Dion Fortune (born Violet Mary Firth) was a member of both the Theosophical Society and of a Golden Dawn offshoot, the Stella Matutina, before forming her own Fraternity of the Inner Light in 1924. Gradually, the Inner Light moved away from its Golden Dawn heritage and, although the Fraternity still exists today, it 'can no longer be considered a magical fraternity, it rather more resembles a heterodox semi-Christian cult' (King, 1989, p.158). Fortune does not appear to have considered herself 'Pagan', although she has been described as a 'proto-Pagan' (Crowley, 1998, p.170), and her writings, particularly her novels *The Sea Priestess* (1938) and *Moon Magic* (1956), can be found on the bookshelves of many Pagans and are standard reading for most Wiccans. Fortune was always as much involved in esoteric Christianity as she was in specifically Pagan ritual and magic; her flirtation with Christian Science, which came to Britain in 1898, 'was the first manifestation of the dichotomy which ran right through her life: between the Gods and the one God; between the Mystery at Bethlehem and those of Karnak[10], Atlantis, and Avalon' (Richardson, 1991, p.42).

---

[10] An Egyptian village near Luxor which is a site of ancient monuments, including temples of Egyptian gods.

Figure 1.7 Dion Fortune, prominent occultist and founder of the Fraternity of the Inner Light. Reproduced with permission from *The Story of Dion Fortune as told to Charles Fielding and Carr Collins*, Loughborough, Thoth Publications, 1985.

Figure 1.8 Aleister Crowley, the Great Beast. Hulton Getty.

Aleister Crowley, on the other hand, was vehemently anti-Christian. He was initiated into the London temple of the Golden Dawn in November 1898 at the age of 23, and initially used the Order as a launching pad for his invectives against Christianity, a kind of 'therapeutic blasphemy' (Hutton, 1996, p.5; cf. Godwin, 1994, p.286) for a hatred that stemmed from his **Plymouth Brethren** upbringing. Although at first close to Mathers, he became intensely competitive with the Chief and was subsequently expelled from the Order. Confident of his own abilities, however, Crowley awarded himself the highest grade of Ipsissimus, and went on to found the Argenteum Astrum (AA), or Order of the Silver Star, through whose journal, *The Equinox,* he published many of the Golden Dawn's secret rituals between 1909 and 1913. In 1912, Crowley became involved in the **Ordo Templi Orientis** (OTO), a German system of occultism, becoming the head of the Order in 1922. In 1920, he founded his Abbey of **Thelema** in Sicily, which he envisioned as a magical colony from which to launch the new aeon, the Age of Horus, of which Crowley considered himself to be the chosen prophet. However, the new aeon seemed not to be destined to begin in Sicily after all, as Crowley was expelled by Mussolini in 1923.

Crowley's thought was propagated through the Argenteum Astrum and his prolific writings, the most important of which is his *Book of the Law,* dictated, so Crowley claimed, by the manifested presence of his guardian angel, Aiwass, on three consecutive afternoons between noon and 1pm in April 1904. The most important and most remembered of these laws is the Law of Thelema – 'Do what thou wilt shall be the whole of the law' (Crowley, 1989, pp.31 and 400) – set as a positive universal rule in contrast to the Christian Ten Commandments, of which nine are 'thou shalt nots'. The similarity of this law to the Wiccan Rede (literally, 'advice' or 'counsel'), 'An it harm none, do what thou wilt', indicates the influence of Crowley on the development of Wicca and Paganism (see later in this chapter). Just prior to the outbreak of the Second World War, Gerald Gardner (1884–1964), a civil servant who had spent most of his life managing tea and rubber plantations in Ceylon, North Borneo and Malaya, returned to England from the Far East and proceeded to develop Wicca. He met Crowley before the latter's death in 1947, and was made an honorary member of Crowley's OTO.

A brief history of Wicca

Wicca was developed in the UK in the 1950s as a highly ritualistic, nature venerating, polytheistic, magical and religious system, operating within a predominantly western framework like that which emerged during the occult revival from the 1880s onwards. It arose from the cultural impulses of the *fin de siècle*, but it is largely undisputed that the modern religion of Wicca was formulated by Gerald Gardner, who gradually wove together various threads in the 1940s. It slowly became more widespread and public after the repeal of the **Witchcraft Act** in 1951. Gardner was born in the early years of the *fin de siècle* in 1884, in Crosby, Liverpool, and was a freemason, Rosicrucian, and member of the Ordo Templi Orientis and other secret societies. In 1936, he returned to England from the Far East and two years later retired to the New Forest with his wife, Dorothea, usually known as Donna.[11] Here he became involved with the Fellowship of Crotona, an occult group of Co-Masons[12] established by Mrs Besant-Scott, a daughter of the theosophist Annie Besant. The Fellowship of Crotona allegedly contained a hidden inner group of hereditary witches,[13] who initiated Gardner in 1939, though quite what this group was remains unclear.

With the permission of the **coven**, and under the pseudonym Scire, Gardner included the rituals of witchcraft in a novel called *High Magic's Aid* (1949). However, Gardner was not able to publish more open accounts of witchcraft under his real name until 1951, when the 1736 Witchcraft Act was repealed and replaced with the Fraudulent Mediums Act, which gave freedom for individuals to practise witchcraft so long as no harm was done to person or property. No longer threatened by a law that enabled persecution of a person alleged to have magical powers,[14] Gardner wrote *Witchcraft Today* which was published in 1954, followed by *The Meaning of Witchcraft* in 1959. He broke away from the New Forest coven and established his own coven, moving to the Isle of Man where he became 'resident witch' at Cecil Williamson's Museum of Witchcraft and Magic in Castletown (now in Boscastle, Cornwall).

[11] Gardner married Donna, a nurse, after a whirlwind romance at the age of 43. She did not share Gerald's interest in spirituality and had no involvement in Wicca, but their marriage lasted until her death in 1960.

[12] Co-Masons admitted women as well as men, unlike freemasonry.

[13] Witches who claim to belong to a family of witches, in which witch lore is passed down through the ages.

[14] Despite, at the same time, asserting that such magical powers did not exist!

Figure 1.9 Gerald Brousseau Gardner, founder of modern Wicca. Fortean Picture Library.

Figure 1.10 Alex Sanders, charlatan and magician. Wandel/Corbis.

Witchcraft Today vaulted Gardner into the public spotlight, and he made numerous media appearances. The media attention and popular appeal was something totally unexpected, and Gardner revelled in it. Believing witchcraft to be a dying religion, he propelled it into the public domain, initiated many new witches, and encouraged covens to spring up, operating according to the outlines provided in his books. By the mid-1950s, Gardner's love of publicity had drawn the religion to the attention of the public, and in the early 1960s it was exported to North America. Gardner died in 1964, but his tradition of **Gardnerian Wicca** was firmly established, much to the annoyance of those who practised Traditional and Hereditary witchcraft, which they believed to be a witchcraft religion older than Gardner's Wicca.[15] Into this stream was injected another current in the 1960s, as Alex Sanders brought a stronger application of high ritual magic to his branch of Wicca.   Alex Sanders, a resident of Manchester who claimed a witch ancestress from Snowdonia, established his own version of Wicca along with his wife Maxine, which became known as **Alexandrian Wicca**. He, like Gardner, was a prolific initiator, but did not confine himself to the UK: many covens in Germany and elsewhere in Europe sprang from his visits to the continent. Sanders sought publicity from the very beginning, and many Gardnerian witches reacted against this in the 1960s and 1970s. The 'wars' between the Alexandrian and Gardnerian traditions superseded those between the early Gardnerians and the Traditionals/Hereditaries. Sanders was regarded as a maverick, seeking sensational publicity in newspapers and on the television (as Gardner had done). He was seen to be bringing Wicca into disrepute, and as a result many of the Gardnerians went underground. The schism was made worse when, in the 1970s, two of his initiates, Stewart and Janet Farrar, published many of the Wiccan rituals which were supposed to be kept for initiates only. Over time, however, it was recognized that the Alexandrian stream of Wicca was as valid as the Gardnerian, and the rifts started to heal. Thus, in 1989, nine months after the death of Sanders, the editors of the Pagan Federation journal *The Wiccan* announced an end to hostilities:

> ... our members include not only 'Elders' ... from Gerald Gardner's original covens of the 1950s, their continuations and daughter covens, but Witches from other traditions, both newer and older; even, amazing as it may seem to original readers, many Alexandrians. Whoever is of good will, who loves Nature, and who worships both the Goddess and the God, is welcome in our Federation, and the current started in the 1960s by that old ritual magician A. Sanders has stood the test of time.
>
> (*The Wiccan*, issue 91, February 1989, p.2)

[15] We have already noted that no evidence has yet been produced which can prove the existence of pre-Gardnerian Wicca, but the claims were often vehement. Doreen Valiente notes, 'the real traditional witches, I have been told, were furious at the behaviour of Gerald Gardner in "popularizing" the Old Religion and regarded such enterprises as the opening of his museum on the Isle of Man as a disaster' (Valiente, 1989, p.85). She further states that she thinks it was Robert Cochrane, who claimed to be a Hereditary witch, who 'invented the word "Gardnerian" – originally as a term of abuse' (p.122), and that Cochrane 'frequently expressed hatred of "Gardnerians" ... [and] relished the prospect of having what he called "a Night of the Long Knives with the Gardnerians"' (p.129). In her book, Valiente produces references to newspaper articles which back up her recollections of division and denigration between traditional and Gardnerian witches in the 1960s.

Sanders is now considered to have made Wicca more accessible and to have brought about greater public awareness of it.

Today's Gardnerian and Alexandrian Wiccans are those with a provable line of descent by initiation from Gerald Gardner or Alex and Maxine Sanders, or both. Gardnerian Wiccans trace their initiatory lines back to Gardner and practise a form of Wicca subtly different from that of Alexandrian Wicca. Alexandrians trace their initiatory lineage back to Alex and Maxine Sanders. Gardnerian and Alexandrian Wicca are based on autonomous covens (groups of witches, traditionally thirteen in number) run by a High Priestess and/ or a High Priest, and centre on the worship of the Goddess and her consort, the Horned God. Polarity in all things is stressed – female/ male, dark/light, negative/positive – and the cycle of birth, death and rebirth is celebrated, along with fertility, through the eight seasonal festivals. Nature is honoured and all things, including oneself, are regarded as part of nature.

Alexandrian Wicca is quite clearly based along Gardnerian lines, though with greater emphasis on ritual ceremonial magic, angels and spirits, and magical healing. Both are initiatory traditions, in which a woman is initiated into a coven by a man, and a man by a woman. [16] There are three degrees of initiation: first, second and third degree. First degree witches are initiated as 'priestess and witch' or 'priest and witch', while second and third degree witches are titled High Priestess or High Priest. The degrees are not regarded as hierarchical but as a mark of proficiency and experience in Wicca, in which all members are regarded as equal. Due to increased dialogue between Gardnerian and Alexandrian Wicca, many practices are in fact a synthesis of the two traditions, and an increasing number of Wiccans are initiated jointly or separately into both traditions, thus tracing their lineage back to both Gardner and Sanders. The differences between the two traditions have been played down, and the similarities and synthesis emphasized to such an extent that some Wiccans claim that there is no difference between them. And while others retain a 'pure' Gardnerian or Alexandrian practice, a great deal of ritualizing and socializing occurs between practitioners of both traditions. Both traditions have influenced each other, and many regard them as so similar that we can now talk of 'Alexandrian and Gardnerian Wicca' in one breath, or conflate the two and refer to them as 'Alexandrian/ Gardnerian', especially given the number of Wiccans who are initiates of the two traditions combined.

---

[16] Although there are exceptions to this practice, and instances of initiation by someone of the same gender are becoming more frequent.

However, Gardnerian and Alexandrian Wicca are not the only types of witchcraft. The growing popularity of witchcraft over the last three decades has seen the development of a variety of forms of witchcraft and Paganism which have fanned out from the original forms of Wicca. In 1996, the estimated number of Pagans in the UK was between 110,000 and 120,000, of whom approximately 20,000 were initiated or formally inducted members of organized and distinctive Pagan traditions. Of this 20,000, 10,000 were initiated Wiccans and 6,000 were Pagan Druids, with smaller traditions making up the remaining 4,000 (Hutton, 1999, p.401).

Wicca and witchcraft: the UK and the USA

It was in the context of late 1970s and 1980s North America that the development and movement of Paganism beyond its traditional boundaries took place, at a time when the New Age Movement was becoming conscious of itself as a movement and when feminist spirituality was emerging (Hanegraaff, 1998, pp.85–7). This should draw our attention to obvious parallels between the three move-ments. An example of the development of new forms of witchcraft will suffice to illustrate the point. Wicca as it was traditionally practised in the UK, was exported to the USA by Raymond Buckland in the 1960s, where it was transformed into a 'very different kind of religion' (Orion, 1995, p.143). Differences include a less formal and hierarchical ritual style which is more inventive and celebratory, Native American influences such as shamanism and drumming, the superimposition of psychotherapy on to Wicca, and the application of Wicca to political activism. In particular, Wicca was adapted by the women's spirituality movement, resulting in the development of Pagan Goddess spirituality and feminist witchcraft traditions such as Dianic and **Reclaiming** witchcraft.[17] This 'mutant "Feminist Witch-craft"' (Salomonsen, 1996, p.32) developed as female witches gradually took part in the Women's Movement and 'in some cases met, in other cases helped create, the Goddess Movement' (ibid., p.32; Bonewits, 1989, p.110). The Goddess Movement, however, has not adopted witchcraft but has used its ritual expression for inspiration – it does not associate itself with the occult, magical tradition or with Paganism; 'although Neopagan men (and women) may worship the Goddess, women in the Goddess Movement do not

---

[17] See later in this chapter for further discussion of these types of witchcraft.

regard them as feminists' (Salomonsen, 1996, p.33). Wicca and feminist/Goddess spirituality thus blend into each other, and it is predominantly this blurring of distinctions between the original British Wicca and North American feminist witchcraft into a normative, generally applied (mis)understanding of Wicca/witchcraft that has created problems for scholars attempting to categorize these forms of spirituality.

The distinctly feminist branch of witchcraft shares little in common with Alexandrian and Gardnerian Wicca in the UK beyond an initial framework consisting of the ritual **Wheel of the Year** (see the introduction to this volume). Feminist witchcraft, for example, explicitly emphasizes the Goddess as representative of divinity, attempts to maintain an explicitly non-hierarchical organization inherited from the feminist consciousness movement (in which women rotate leadership and make collective decisions) and engages in political activism. Alexandrian and Gardnerian Wicca, however, emphasize both Gods and Goddesses as representative of divinity, allow a 'hierarchy of experience' (implicit in their organization in covens led by a High Priestess and/or High Priest and the structure of three degrees of initiation), and tend to maintain a distance between spirituality and politics. Thus, whereas Alexandrian and Gardnerian Wicca can be considered one entity, feminist witchcraft is an altogether different entity, consciously distinct from its non-feminist kin.

In order to distinguish between these two currents, we might refer to Alexandrian and Gardnerian 'Wicca' and to feminist 'witchcraft'. This distinction in part reflects the terminology used by practitioners. On the one hand, Wiccans use the term 'Wicca' to denote a **mystery religion** involving a process of initiation and rigorous training within a cosmos polarized between male and female forces, all of which is an inheritance from the magical secret societies from which Wicca is descended. The term is also used in order to differentiate between the anthropological study of primitive and tribal witchcraft and the Wiccan religion of western, literate, post-industrial society developed into its contemporary forms since the 1950s. On the other hand, feminist witches prefer the term 'witchcraft', using it to describe a religious practice based on the human (female) witch becoming empowered through interaction with the Goddess as divine counterpart of the witch, an empowerment which is sought in order to provide personal liberation for the individual woman and thus sustain women in their struggle against patriarchy. Feminist witchcraft is thus located within the wider feminist spirituality and Goddess movements, making use of a constructed image based on a feminist reading of the witchcraft persecutions of the sixteenth and seventeenth centuries and a myth of matriarchy,[18] both of which are preferred alternatives to a legacy from secret societies (which are regarded as a predominantly male preserve) and Gerald Gardner as founding *father*.

The two best-known forms of feminist witchcraft are **Dianic witchcraft** and Starhawk's Reclaiming community, and an exploration of these may illustrate the merging streams and influences on various branches of witchcraft. The Dianic tradition of witchcraft emerged in the USA from the feminist consciousness movement, and characteristically stresses the worship of the Goddess, sometimes exclusively. Dianic covens are largely feminist and/or matriarchal in orientation, with an emphasis on rediscovering and reclaiming female power and divinity, and consciousness raising.[19] Often, they are radical and lesbian in orientation. By the 1980s, the increasing number of feminists joining Dianic covens made feminist witchcraft the fastest growing segment of witchcraft in the USA. Its popularity among feminists was assured by the writings of the radical feminist Zsuzsanna Budapest, and later by Starhawk.

As well as her engagement with Dianic, feminist witchcraft, Starhawk is also an initiate of **Faery Wicca**. Faery Wicca was developed by Americans Victor and Cora Anderson and Gwyddion Pendderwen in the 1970s, and is based on the myth of the Tuatha De Danaan, the Tribe of Dana, a race of people skilled in magic, healing and crafts, who arrived in Ireland bringing with them a Great Mother Goddess called Dana. This mythical race eventually retreated into the Otherworld, the World of Faery. Faery Wicca was originally a very small and secretive tradition, but many of the fundamentals of the tradition have become widespread through the writings of Starhawk. Faery Wicca is polytheistic and does not emphasize male/female polarities as much as other traditions. Nature is honoured and deities (whose names are secret) personify the forces of nature, life, fertility, death and rebirth. Emphasis is placed on pragmatic magic, self development and **theurgy**. It is an initiatory tradition, and thus some material is kept secret, though much is now taught openly and has been published.

It was from her basis in Faery Wicca, feminism, and environmental and political activism that Starhawk and others established Reclaiming witchcraft. As the name suggests, feminist witchcraft as

[18] The belief among feminist witches that civilization was once ruled and led by women, based on a matriarchal system, and enjoyed peace and harmony before being overthrown by patriarchal invaders.

[19] A feminist practice, which allows for the exploration of women's preconscious wishes and desires outside psychoanalysis.

practised and taught by Starhawk is based largely on reclaiming the image of the witch and empowering women (and men) with the Goddess in order to effect political, environmental and social change. The Reclaiming 'Principles of Unity' (September 1998) explicitly set out these aims: 'we work for all forms of justice: environmental, social, political, racial, gender and economic. Our feminism includes a radical analysis of power, seeing all systems of oppression as interrelated, rooted in structures of domination and control'. In Chapter 4 we shall return to feminist witchcraft in a consideration of the attraction of witchcraft to feminists and attempts to reclaim the image of the witch.

Wiccan/Pagan relations, 1970–99

Historically, Wicca has been regarded as a core group around which Paganism has emerged. In September 1970, the Pagan Front was established, and its inaugural meeting was held in London at **Beltane** on 1 May 1971. It was not until 1989 that the organization changed its name to the Pagan Federation, which even then saw itself as 'speaking for the mainstream of revived Wicca in this country', offering a referral service between covens and 'genuine enquirers' and providing a 'forum for dialogue between Wicca, which spearheaded the re-emergence of Nature religion in our time' (*The Wiccan,* issue 91, p.2). Wiccans thus worked hard to establish the Federation, and every Pagan Federation president until 1997 was Wiccan. Added to this, Wicca also provided much of the available Pagan literature until the 1990s.

This formative period for Paganism is now over. As Paganism has grown considerably in popularity, it has come to consider itself autonomous and distinct from Wicca. In 1994, the title of the journal of the Pagan Federation changed from *The Wiccan* to *Pagan Dawn,* and the election of the first non-Wiccan Pagan Federation President in 1997 has given added weight to this process of differentiation. During 1999, the Pagan Federation conducted written discussions about the three principles it adheres to, the second of which was deemed problematic. The first principle is 'Love for and kinship with nature: reverence for the life force and its ever-renewing cycles of life and death'; the third is 'Honouring the totality of Divine Reality, which transcends gender, without suppressing either the female or male aspect of Deity' (*Pagan Dawn,* issue 126, Imbolc 1998, p.14). The second of the three principles has caused some controversy among Pagans. Called the Pagan Ethic, it is, in fact, the Wiccan Rede

Figure 1.11 Zsuzsanna Budapest, a key figure in the development of feminist witchcraft. Cinetel Productions Pty Ltd.

Figure 1.12 Starhawk, founding member of Reclaiming, and self-proclaimed Jewitch. Courtesy of Starhawk.

(developed from Aleister Crowley's Law of Thelema): 'An it harm none, do what thou wilt'. This principle, according to an article in *Pagan Dawn*,

> ... was instituted and named back in the early 1970s, when Wicca and Paganism were synonymous in the minds of the PF leadership. Today, this is simply no longer appropriate ... Since the PF is no longer a Wiccan organization, it does us little good to identify ourselves as such in the minds of many by continuing to use this 'Wiccan Commandment'.
>
> (*Pagan Dawn*, issue 126, Imbolc 1998, p.15)

Such thinking reflects the growth in popularity of Paganism as distinct from initiatory Wicca, which constitutes only a small number of overall Pagans.

There are various reasons why initiatory Wicca remains small despite the growth of Paganism. Although some Pagans perhaps desire initiation into a Wiccan coven, many regard Wicca as hierarchical in structure, and élitist in that it requires initiation of 'the chosen few', retaining 'secrets' which it does not share with the rest of the Pagan community, leading to claims that Wicca constitutes an élite Pagan 'priesthood'. Pagans tend to be non-hierarchical, and so the majority remain outside the initiatory Wiccan traditions, being committed to Paganism in general rather than to a specific spiritual tradition.[20] Wiccan priests and priestesses do not consider themselves to be 'clergy' to a Pagan 'laity'. Rather, they regard themselves as priests and priestesses within their own particular religion, with no laity, although they do perform ceremonies such as handfastings (weddings) and rituals open to the public as and when required, as do many Druid priests and priestesses and those who feel inspired to act as celebrants whether or not they have been formally initiated or inducted into any specific group. Since Wiccan initiates are heavily outnumbered by people who identify themselves as Pagans yet do not belong to any formal Pagan group or tradition, the aura of élitism is perpetuated, and Wicca (as we shall see in Chapter 4) does use initiation, secrecy, and intimate community to maintain strong, concrete boundaries which demarcate who is an 'insider' and who is an 'outsider'. This keeps its structure and practice distinct from the general mêlée of Paganism in which 'inside' and 'outside' status is not an issue.

As Paganism has increased in popularity and alternative traditions to Wicca have become established, the distinctiveness of Wicca in

---

[20] Although increasingly Paganism is regarded as a specific spiritual tradition in its own right, rather than as an umbrella term for a host of traditions.

relation to the wider, non-aligned Pagan community has become, somewhat paradoxically, both more and less pronounced. Within Wicca, practitioners increasingly feel that the growing popularity of Pagan spiritualities has eroded the traditional secrecy of Wicca, and that the distinctiveness of Wicca needs to be re-established. Outside Wicca, however, the distinctiveness of Wicca is less pronounced as the popularity of the religion has led to new and 'unorthodox' derivations of Wicca and conflation between the various forms, resulting in the erosion of boundaries.

Increasingly, at the level at which Wicca interacts with popular culture, there appears to be a certain amount of 'trendiness' attached to identifying oneself as Pagan and, especially, Wiccan. For example, the film *The Craft* (1996)[21] proved especially influential with teenagers, and teenage girls in particular wrote to the Pagan Federation for advice about joining a coven. Certainly, in the 1990s the 'teen witch' image was increasing in popularity, with Silver Ravenwolf's book *Teen Witch: Wicca For A New Generation* (1998)[22] proving to be a bestseller in the USA. The February 1999 issue of *The Cauldron: Pagan Journal of the Old Religion*, contained the following list of witch-types: 'white witches, grey witches, black witches, green witches, teen witches, feminist witches, media witches, hedge witches, kitchen witches, New Age witches, and even weekend witches' (issue 91, p.30).

This list reflects a growing awareness that 'witchcraft' and 'Wicca' can be used to describe very different paradigms. On the one hand, 'Wicca' is used to refer to 'covens' of friends who have no initiation or training but gather together to celebrate the seasons or full moons. The growing popularity of books written by practitioners of Wicca has led to the formation of many self-styled groups who refer to themselves as covens, thus creating a 'popular' Wicca made up of people who have read a book on Wicca and joined together with friends in groups, but who are not initiated into an established Wiccan tradition. On the other hand, 'Wicca' is an esoteric religion and a mystery tradition operating in small, closed groups, to which entry is solely by initiation ceremonies which include oaths of secrecy and which are designed to trigger personal transformation.

As Wicca becomes increasingly popular and the figure of the witch maintains its hold on the human imagination, appropriation of the word 'Wicca' becomes an increasing source of annoyance to those who see themselves as practitioners of a serious religion which

---

[21] A film telling the story of four teenage witches.

[22] A book aimed at teenage girls in particular.

demands a great deal of commitment and dedication. Whereas even ten years ago one could assume that those who identified themselves as 'Wiccan' were initiates of the Alexandrian and/or Gardnerian traditions of Wicca, there is no longer any guarantee that someone who describes themselves as 'Wiccan' is an initiated witch. The feminist author Mary Daly (1981, p.221) wrote in *Gyn/Ecology* that 'to limit the term [witch] only to those who have esoteric knowledge of and participation in "the Craft" is the real reductionism'. While it is not appropriate for 'witch' and 'witchcraft' to be limited to those initiated into Wicca, since anyone can call themselves a witch quite legitimately, it should be noted that Wicca does require initiation into, and the practice of, an esoteric mystery religion, and the two terms thus refer to different entities.

The terminology of identification has thus become confused. Many initiated Gardnerian/Alexandrian Wiccans claim that Wicca is being simplified through 'how to' books in order to make it more acceptable, and regard it as important to preserve Wicca as distinct from Paganism. One way of preserving such distinctions is to portray Gardnerian/Alexandrian Wicca as an 'esoteric' mystery religion which is distinguishable from 'exoteric' witchcraft and Paganism.

The development of more open, easily accessible Paganism, including witchcraft, 'whose principal function is not to practise magic or to initiate into the mysteries as such' (Crowley, 1994, p.19), allows some original forms of Wicca to remain secretive and initiatory:

> ... within modern Paganism we have seen initially a revival of the inner esoteric aspects of Pagan tradition. These are small, closed groups to which entry is solely by initiation ceremonies ... More recently we have seen the growth of exoteric Paganism, whereby modern Pagans have devised rites and ceremonies, held more and more often in public, to celebrate marriage, the birth of children and death, and whereby Pagans have sought to develop religious teaching for their children and to extend ministry to those of the community who are in need, whether in hospital, hospice or prison.
>
> (Crowley, 1996, pp.81–2)

Esoteric Wicca and exoteric witchcraft and Paganism differ predominantly in their aims and practices rather than in their religious outlook. Nevertheless, a shared terminology and under-standing of what is and is not 'Wicca' helps maintain important boundaries, aiding the differentiation between Wiccan priests and priestesses who are initiates of the self-styled esoteric mystery religion of Wicca on the one hand, and other forms of witchcraft and Paganism on the other. There are, in fact, a variety of forms of witchcraft rather than a monolithic or normative Wicca or witchcraft. Of these some, such as feminist witchcraft, may be exoteric, while others, such as Gardnerian/Alexandrian Wicca, might well be esoteric in nature.

Conclusion

In this chapter we have discussed the various interpretations of the words 'Pagan' and 'Wiccan', and traced their development from the magical and philosophical societies of the *fin de siècle*. In addition, we have indicated the forerunners of the occult revival in the Western Esoteric Tradition. The history of Wicca and Paganism thus has a long trajectory back in time, for

> ... if Wicca and its successors are viewed as a form of ritual magic,[23] then they have a distinguished and very long pedigree, stretching back through the Ordo Templi Orientis and the Golden Dawn to Lévi, the New Templars, the Rosicrucians and the freemasons, and so beyond these to the early modern and medieval texts which derived by many stages from those of Hellenistic Egypt.
>
> (Hutton, 1993, p.337)

We have also traced the growing differentiation between Wicca and Paganism. That there is considerable overlap between Wicca, witchcraft and the wider Pagan movement is not in doubt – witchcraft and Paganism have drawn from a heritage popularized by Wicca which includes, for example, the Pagan seasonal cycle of eight festivals which make up the Wheel of the Year and the practice of a Goddess/God nature-based spirituality. That there are distinctions, however, is often overlooked. In the UK, very few Pagans are Wiccan initiates, and the two terms are considered to be distinctive.

Wicca can be characterized as a pagan religion and, historically, was central to the variety of Pagan revivals in the UK and the USA which now constitute modern Paganism. However, although Paganism and feminist witchcraft may have developed out of Wicca, Wicca itself is not wholly situated within Paganism. Rather, Wicca 'is a neo-pagan development of traditional occultist ritual magic, but ... the latter movement is not itself pagan. In other words ... [Wicca] gradually and almost imperceptibly shades into a non-pagan domain' (Hanegraaff, 1998, p.86). Thus, although Wicca has been intricately

---

[23] Although the use of magic does not in itself have anything to do with religion, it is a constitutive element of Wicca which encompasses both magic and religion, blurring their distinctions. The magical heritage of Wicca is therefore important to the development of the religion and the identity of its practitioners.

bound up with the development of exoteric Paganism, there is increasing evidence of growing differentiation between the two. Wicca therefore occupies an ambiguous position *vis-à-vis* other forms of witchcraft and Paganism: it is at once central to and on the margins of both.

Glossary

Abramelin Magic *The Sacred Book of Abramelin the Mage* was discovered by S.L. MacGregor Mathers in a manuscript in the Bibliothèque de l'Arsenal in Paris, and was claimed to have been written by one Abraham the Jew in 1458, who travelled to Egypt in search of teachers of secret traditions and became a pupil of Abramelin in Arachi. He collected his knowledge in this book, which was translated into French around 1700. This was the version read by Eliphas Lévi and found and translated by Mathers. It instructs the magician on the magical operations necessary for contacting his or her Holy Guardian Angel, and lists angels and demons who can be invoked for specific purposes. Aleister Crowley was fascinated by this book and spent a long time preparing to perform the Abramelin magic, for which purpose he bought Boleskine Lodge near Loch Ness.

alchemy a combination of chemistry and spirituality, the purpose of which in ancient times was to find the philosopher's stone or elixir of life which would grant immortality. The word is derived from the old name of Egypt, Khem, and the practice grew largely from Gnostic texts on metallurgy dating from the second century, and later from texts that came to light via the Arab world whence the *Corpus Hermeticum* arrived in Europe in the late fifteenth century. It was immensely popular in Christian Europe between 1400 and 1700, with eminent scientists such as Robert Boyle (1627–91) and Sir Isaac Newton (1642–1727) committed to its quest. The psychiatrist, C.G. Jung did much to revive interest in alchemy in the twentieth century, and in Paganism it tends to be regarded as an analogy of the search for the true self, for the grail, symbolized in previous eras by the search to transmute base metal into gold.

Alexandrian Wicca form of Wicca founded by Alex Sanders in the 1960s.

astrology the interpretation of the movements and positions of the planets through the celestial sphere as an influence on human affairs. One of the most ancient surviving occult sciences, astrology constitutes one of the three streams of the **Western Esoteric Tradition**.

Beltane one of the eight seasonal festivals which make up the **Wheel of the Year**. Beltane is celebrated on May Eve and May Day, and reflects the burgeoning fertility of the land.

Blake's Prophetic Books works by William Blake (1757–1827) which include *Songs of Innocence and Experience* and *The Marriage* *of Heaven and Hell*. It was not until 1887 that all the Prophetic Books were published, in a limited and expensive edition edited by Edwin J. Ellis and W.B. Yeats (who was initiated into the Golden Dawn in 1890).

Chaldean Oracles chronicles written by and about the inhabitants of the ancient country of Chaldea which formed part of Babylonia, in what is now southern Iraq.

coven a coven is made up of a group of witches who have been initiated into that coven and meet regularly for religious festivals and for training. Jeffrey Russell (1991, p.157) suggests that the word 'coven', which first appears as a Scottish invention in the sixteenth century, derives from the French *couvent* and the Latin *conventus*, meaning 'gathering' or 'meeting'.

Dianic Witchcraft a branch of radical feminist, often lesbian, witchcraft which began in the USA. Named after Diana, the goddess of the witches, it is usually purely goddess oriented.

duotheistic belief in two deities

Egyptian Book of the Dead more accurately known as 'The Book of Coming Forth by Day', the Book of the Dead is a collection of religious and magical texts from ancient Egypt aimed at helping the soul survive the journey through hell (Amenti).

Enochian Magic a form of angelic magic discovered and practised by Dr John Dee and Edward Kelly in sixteenth-century Elizabethan England.

Faery Wicca an American tradition of witchcraft developed in the 1970s. Its most famous initiate is Starhawk.

freemasonry a secret, fraternal association open only to men, claiming ancient provenance but beginning in its present form with the founding of the Grand Lodge in London in 1717.

Gardnerian Wicca the branch of Wicca founded by Gerald Gardner.

Gardnerian/Alexandrian Wicca popular form of Wicca in the UK which combines the Gardnerian and Alexandrian traditions.

Gnosticism knowledge of spiritual and esoteric mysteries. The Gnostics were originally a heretical Christian movement dating from the second century, though partly based on pre-Christian ideas and infused with Greek philosophy and other pagan sources. The power of gnosis to redeem the spiritual in humans was emphasized. The Gnostics believed in the dualism of a supreme and remote divine being and a demiurge who controlled the world and was antagonistic to all that was spiritual. Christ was seen as an emissary from the supreme divine being, bringing gnosis. Their teachings were known only through the anti-heretical texts of such writers as the Greek theologian Iraneus (*c*.130–*c*.200) and Tertullian (a Roman Christian, born in Carthage *c*.160–*c*.240) until a collection of Gnostic texts was found near Nag Hammadi, Egypt, in 1945–6 and 1948. These latter are known as the Dead Sea Scrolls and have provided a new basis for the interpretation of Gnostic beliefs and influences.

Hermes Trismegistus Greek derivation of the Egyptian god Thoth, tutelary deity of writing, learning, magic, philosophy and mysticism. In hermetic literature, he is described as a sage. 'Trismegistus' means 'thrice great', and was an epithet of Thoth in Upper Egypt.

hermetic the intellectual study of magic which began in Renaissance Italy with Marsilio Ficino after he had translated the Greek manuscript of the *Corpus Hermeticum*, the body of lore attributed to **Hermes Trismegistus**. Hermeticism eventually spread throughout western Europe, including England, and even though its pre-Christian provenance was disproved by Isaac Casaubon in 1614, it remains popular to this day.

Hermetic Order of the Golden Dawn a secret, magical society formed in London in 1888.

kabbalistic 'kabbalah' means to receive or to accept, and is often translated as 'tradition': the kabbalah is the Jewish mystical tradition, and in particular relates to a system of esoteric mystical thought and practice that developed during the twelfth and thirteenth centuries, although it dates back to the first century. The kabbalah has been very influential on western magic. Other spellings include cabbala, qabala, kabbala, from the Hebrew root 'kbl'.

Kabbalistic Tree of Life a glyph, or symbol, showing the ten emanations of the divine. The tree of life is symbolic of the entire universe and its patterns of interaction.

Key of Solomon a famous magical grimoire or book of spells, attributed to the biblical King Solomon.

monotheistic belief that there is only one God.

mystery religion the secret religious rites honouring various deities which flourished during the Hellenistic period were known as mystery religions. They involved rites of initiation and spiritual transformation, which Wicca and some forms of contemporary Paganism attempt to emulate.

NeoPlatonism a philosophical and religious system originating in the third century with Plotinus but based on Platonic ideas as well as elements from the philosophies of Pythagoras (*c*.560–*c*.480 BCE), Aristotle (384–322 BCE) and the Stoics (founded *c*.300 BCE). It postulated a hierarchy of being, with the transcendent One at the apex, immaterial and indescribable. The human being aspires to knowledge of this One by rising above the imperfection and multiplicity of the material world through ascetic virtue and sustained contemplation. NeoPlatonism included overtones of eastern mysticism and was the dominant philosophy of the pagan world from the mid-third century to 529, when the Roman emperor Justinian closed the pagan schools, and was a strong influence on medieval and Renaissance thought.

NeoPythagoreanism a secret religious, political and scientific sect, originally founded by the Greek philosopher Pythagoras (*c*.560–480 BCE), which believed that the soul is condemned to a cycle of reincarnation from which it can only escape by attaining a state of purity.

Ordo Templi Orientis a German occult order founded in 1904 by the occultist and freemason Karl Kellner, headed by Aleister Crowley in the 1920s. Derived from mystical freemasonry, it was influenced by the writings of French occultist Eliphas Lévi, Indian traditions of tantra and yoga, and myths of the Knights Templar. It is still in existence today, and emphasizes sexual magic, natural lore and hermetic magic.

pantheism the widespread belief among Pagans that the divine is immanent in the forces and substances of nature, and is thus identifiable with nature. It also refers to the admissibility or toleration of all deities, another deeply held Pagan value.

Plymouth Brethren a fundamentalist Christian Protestant denomination, established in 1830 by John Nelson Darby in Plymouth. It has no formal creed, but emphasizes an expected millennium and combines elements of Calvinism and Pietism. It has a very austere outlook, renouncing many occupations except those compatible with New Testament standards. A split in 1849 resulted in the formation of the Exclusive Brethren and the Open Brethren.

polytheistic belief in or worship of more than one god.

Reclaiming witchcraft community founded by Starhawk and others in San Francisco, California, in 1980 (now worldwide).

Rosicrucian the Rosicrucians, or Order of the Rose and Cross, are members of a worldwide esoteric society, apparently founded in medieval Europe by Christian Rosenkreutz (an allegorical figure), which has as its aim the spiritualization of individuals. Members strive for perfection and the attainment of true knowledge or cosmic consciousness over many lifetimes.

spiritualism the belief that spirits of the dead can communicate with the living, particularly through a medium. The spiritualist movement began in 1848 in New York when the Fox sisters claimed to have communicated with spirits through a system of rappings, and this led to the formation of spiritualist churches and societies, where seances were held and mediums attempted to communicate with dead loved ones.

Stoicism an ancient Greek school of philosophy founded *c.*300 BCE by Zeno of Citium and named after the Stoa Poikile (painted colonnade) in Athens in which its founder used to lecture. The Stoics taught that the highest good, virtue, is based on knowledge, and that only the wise are truly virtuous, living in harmony with the divine Reason that governs nature and thus indifferent to the vicissitudes of fortune as well as to pleasure and pain.

Thelema Greek for 'will'. The name of a religious and occult order founded by Aleister Crowley and based on Nietzschean philosophy of the will. Crowley believed, like Friedrich Nietzsche, that human progress was facilitated by discovering one's own true will and making it manifest.

Theosophical Society theosophy is literally 'divine wisdom'. The society was set up in 1875 by Blavatsky and Olcott to seek and spread this wisdom, which eventually was regarded as coming from the East.

theurgy early NeoPlatonic system of white magic; the art of securing divine or supernatural help in human affairs.

Western Esoteric Tradition a vast field comprising a body of material gathered together in the West since the end of the fifteenth century, including the kabbalah, hermeticism, gnosticism and the occult sciences of astrology, alchemy and magic. It pertains to the connections between man and the universe (microcosm and macrocosm).

Wheel of the Year the name for the cycle of eight seasonal festivals celebrated with rituals by Wiccans and Pagans. The festivals are Yule (*c.*21 December), Imbolc (1 February), spring equinox (*c.*21 March), Beltane (1 May), midsummer (*c.*21 June), Lammas (1 August), autumn equinox (*c.*21 September), and Samhain (31 October).

Witchcraft Act this replaced witchcraft acts in England and Scotland when they were repealed in 1736. It both allowed a person to be prosecuted if he or she was alleged to have magical powers *and* denied the possibility of such powers' existence. It was replaced in 1951 by the Fraudulent Mediums Act, which gave freedom for individuals to practise witchcraft so long as no harm was done to person or property.

References

Albanese, C. (1990) *Nature Religion in America: From the Algonkian Indians to the New Age*, Chicago: Chicago University Press.

Barker, E. (1989) *New Religious Movements: A Practical Introduction*, London: HMSO.

Barrie, J.M. (1906) 'Peter Pan in Kensington Garden', in *The Little White Bird*, London: Hodder & Stoughton.

Beckford, J. (1984), 'Holistic imagery and ethics in new religious and healing movements', *Social Compass*, 32, pp.259–72.

Bonewits, I. (1989) *Real Magic*, York Beach, Maine: Samuel Weiser (first published 1971).

Chuvin, P. (1990) *A Chronicle of the Last Pagans*, Cambridge MA: Harvard University Press.

Crowley, A. (1989) *The Confessions of Aleister Crowley: An Autobiography*, edited by J. Symonds and K. Grant, Harmondsworth: Arkana (Penguin) (first published 1979).

Crowley, V. (1994) *Phoenix From the Flame: Pagan Spirituality in the Western World*, London: Thorsons.

Crowley, V. (1996) 'Wicca as modern-day mystery religion' in G. Harvey and C. Hardman (eds) *Paganism Today: Wiccans, Druids, the Goddess and Ancient Earth Traditions for the Twenty-first Century*, London: Thorsons, pp.81–93.

Crowley, V. (1998) 'Wicca as Nature Religion', in J. Pearson, R.H. Roberts and G. Samuel (eds) *Nature Religion Today: Paganism in the Modern World*, Edinburgh: Edinburgh University Press, pp.170–9.

Daly, M. (1981) *Gyn/Ecology: the Metaethics of Radical Feminism*, London: The Women's Press (first published 1978).

Faivre, A. (1994) *Access to Western Esotericism*, New York: SUNY.

Fortune, D. (1989) *The Sea Priestess*, Wellingborough: Aquarian Press (first published in 1938).

Fowden, G. (1986) *The Egyptian Hermes: A Historical Approach to the Late Pagan Mind*, Cambridge and New York: Cambridge University Press.

Fox, R.L. (1986) *Pagans and Christians in the Mediterranean World from the Second Century AD to the Conversion of Constantine*, Harmondsworth: Penguin.

Gardner, G.B. (1959) *The Meaning of Witchcraft*, London: Aquarian Press.

Gardner, G.B. (1954) *Witchcraft Today*, London: Rider.

Gardner, G.B. (1993) *High Magic's Aid*, London: Pentacle Enterprises (first published 1949).

Godwin, J. (1994) *The Theosophical Enlightenment*, New York: SUNY.

Grahame, K. (1908) *The Wind in the Willows*, London: Methuen.

Hanegraaff, W.J. (1995) 'Empirical method and the study of esotericism', in *Method and Theory in the Study of Religion*, vol.7, no.2, pp.99–129.

Hanegraaff, W.J. (1998) *New Age Religion and Western Culture: Esotericism in the Mirror of Secular Thought*, New York: SUNY.

Harvey, G. (1997) *Listening People, Speaking Earth: Contemporary Paganism*, London: Hurst.

Heelas, P. (1996) *The New Age Movement*, Oxford: Blackwell.

Hexham, I. and Poewe, K. (1997) *New Religions as Global Cultures: Making the Human Sacred*, Colorado/Oxford: Westview Press.

Howe, E. (1972) *The Magicians of the Golden Dawn*, London: Routledge & Kegan Paul.

Hutton, R. (1993) *The Pagan Religions of the Ancient British Isles: Their Nature and Legacy*, Oxford: Blackwell (first published in 1991).

Hutton, R. (1996) 'The roots of modern Paganism', in G. Harvey and C. Hardman (eds) *Paganism Today: Wiccans, Druids, the Goddess and Ancient Earth Traditions for the Twenty-First Century*, London: Thorsons, pp.3–15.

Hutton, R. (1999) *The Triumph of the Moon: A History of Modern Pagan Witchcraft*, Oxford: Blackwell.

King, F. (1989) *Modern Ritual Magic: The Rise of Western Occultism*, Dorset: Prism Press.

Ledger, S. and McCracken, S. (eds) (1995) *Cultural Politics at the Fin de Siècle*, Cambridge: Cambridge University Press.

Luhrmann, T.M. (1994) *Persuasions of the Witches' Craft: Ritual Magic in Contemporary England*, Basingstoke: Picador (first published in 1989).

Machen, A. (1993) *The Great God Pan*, London: Creation Books (first published 1894).

Meštrovic, S.G. (1991) *The Coming Fin de Siècle: An Application of Durkheim's Sociology to Modernity and Postmodernity*, London: Routledge.

Needleman, J. and Baker, G. (eds) (1978) *Understanding the New Religions*, New York: Seabury Press.

Orion, L.L. (1995) *Never Again the Burning Times: Paganism Revived*, Prospect Heights, Illinois: Waveland Press.

Pearson, J.E. (1998) 'Assumed affinities: Wicca and the New Age', in J. Pearson, R.H. Roberts and G. Samuel (eds) *Nature Religion Today: Paganism in the Modern World*, Edinburgh: Edinburgh University Press.

Puttick, E. (1997) *Women in New Religions: In Search of Community, Sexuality and Spiritual Power*, London: Macmillan.

Ransom, J. (1938) *A Short History of the Theosophical Society*, Adyar: Theosophical Publishing House.

Ravenwolf, S. (1999) *Teen Witch: Wicca for a New Generation*, St Paul, Minnesota: Llewellyn Publications.

Regardie, I. (1989) *The Golden Dawn: The Original Account of the Teachings, Rites and Ceremonies of the Hermetic Order of the Golden Dawn*, St Paul, Minnesota: Llewellyn (first published 1941).

Restall Orr, E. (1998) *Spirits of the Sacred Grove: The World of a Druid Priestess*, London: Thorsons.

Richardson, A. (1991) *The Magical Life of Dion Fortune: Priestess of the Twentieth Century*, London: Aquarian Press.

Russell, J.B. (1991) *A History of Witchcraft: Sorcerers, Heretics and Pagans*, London: Thames & Hudson (first published 1980).

Saki (Hector Hugh Munro) (1982) 'The Music on the Hill', from *The Chronicles of Clovis* (1911), in *The Complete Saki*, Harmondsworth, Penguin, pp.161–6.

Salomonsen, J. (1996) '"I Am a Witch – A Healer and a Bender": An Expression of Women's Religiosity in the Contemporary USA', unpublished PhD thesis, University of Oslo.

Scott, W. (ed.) (1985) *Hermetica: the Ancient Greek and Latin Writings which contain Religious or Philosophical Teachings ascribed to Hermes Trimegistus*, Boston: Shambala.

Simes, A. (1995) 'Contemporary Paganism in the East Midlands', unpublished PhD thesis, University of Nottingham.

Taylor, B. (1999) 'Nature and Supernature – harmony and mastery: irony and evolution in contemporary Nature Religion', *The Pomegranate*, vol.8, May, pp.21–7.

Tiryakian, E. (1974) 'Toward the sociology of esoteric culture', in E. Tiryakian (ed.) *On the Margin of the Visible: Sociology, the Esoteric and the Occult*, New York: Wiley, pp.257–80.

Truzzi, M. (1974) 'Definition and dimensions of the occult: towards a sociological perspective' in E. Tiryakian (ed.) *On the Margin of the Visible: Sociology, the Esoteric and the Occult*, New York: Wiley, pp.243–55.

Valiente, D. (1989) *The Rebirth of Witchcraft*, Washington: Phoenix Publishing.

Webb, J. (1971) *The Flight From Reason: Volume 1 of the Age of the Irrational*, London: MacDonald.

Webb, J. (1976) *The Occult Establishment*, La Salle, Illinois: Open Court.

Williams, R. (1963) *Culture and Society*, Harmondsworth: Penguin.

Williams, R. (1975) *The Country and the City*, St Albans: Paladin.

Wilson, C. (1987) *Aleister Crowley: The Nature of the Beast*, Wellingborough: Aquarian Press.

Wolffe, J. (ed.) (2002) *Global Religious Movements in Regional Context*, Aldershot: Ashgate/Milton Keynes: The Open University.

Yates, F.A. (1991) *Giordano Bruno and the Hermetic Tradition*, Chicago and London: University of Chicago Press.

York, M. (1995) *The Emerging Network: A Sociology of the New Age and Neo-Pagan Movements*, Maryland: Rowman & Littlefield.

CHAPTER 2

Contemporary Celtic spirituality

MARION BOWMAN

Introduction

> The world has need of its Celtic connections and Celtic recollections to enable modern man in his urban wilderness to find again the verdant place within himself, and to give back to him a true sense of belonging to his kind, with nature, with past-present-future, and most of all that healing of self which comes when he is again free to live beyond reductionist boundaries.
>
> (Constantine, 1993, p.10)

> Celtic matters are in fashion these days. At various levels of awareness, both physical and spiritual, a sense of Celticness or Celtic identity, real or imagined, is awakening.
>
> (Meek, 1991, p.13)

> The terms 'Celt' and 'Celtic' have become a battleground.
>
> (Sims-Williams, 1998, p.1)

The purpose of this chapter is to explore the phenomenon of contemporary Celtic spirituality, to examine why people are turning to the Celts and the Celtic past for spiritual inspiration, and to demonstrate how varied and complex this phenomenon is. In order to contextualize the different images of 'Celticity' which are evolving in the contemporary spiritual milieu, we shall look at ways in which understandings of the terms 'Celt' and 'Celtic' have changed over time, from appellations based on archaeological, linguistic, geographical or ethnic criteria to the rise of the idea of 'Celticity' as a quality to be acquired and aspired to in a variety of ways for spiritual ends. By examining different perceptions of Celtic spirituality and its attractiveness to a variety of spiritual seekers, we shall seek to understand why, in the context of contemporary religion, Celtic is 'cool'.

More specifically, however, this chapter is about contemporary *perceptions* of Celtic spirituality. Think 'Celtic spirituality' and who or what do you envisage? Druids performing sunrise rituals at Stonehenge? The Book of Kells?[1] Harp music? Scenes of remote sea-lashed islands or wild moors, preferably with standing stones? The General Assembly of the Church of Scotland? The eisteddfod? Iona or Glastonbury? There is no right or wrong answer to this question, but the fact that there are so many possible responses is indicative of the breadth and complexity of contemporary images of who the Celts were/are, and what might be meant by Celtic spirituality.

The term 'Celtic *spirituality*' is being used here in its broadest sense, covering those who are within or on the peripheries of an identifiable religion (such as Christianity) and those who, though formally 'non-aligned', perceive themselves to be 'spiritual' or involved in spiritual activity. Modern Celtic spirituality thus takes a great variety of forms, including Celtic Christianity, Celtic Paganism, Druidry and Celtic-influenced New Age. While some Celtic spirituality is conducted within specific groups (for example, Druid Orders, the Celtic Orthodox Church), for many spiritual seekers Celtic spirituality simply adds a particular 'flavour' to their chosen form of religiosity, which is sometimes highly individualistic. (This makes it extremely hard to quantify how many people are involved in some form of Celtic spirituality.) There is a further reason for referring in this context to Celtic spirituality, and that is the widespread perception of a 'Celtic spirit', expressed in many forms – musical, artistic, religious – simultaneously intangible but somehow identifiably Celtic.

The extent to which people consider themselves (or are considered by others) to be engaged in 'authentic' Celtic spirituality is a difficult issue, as we shall see. However, in Religious Studies generally, authenticity is a tricky area; for example, given the huge internal variety, what counts as 'authentic' Christianity or 'authentic' Buddhism? Because of the very different ways in which contemporary Celtic spirituality is envisaged and practised, very different ideas have emerged about what Celtic spirituality is or was, and the extent

---

[1] The Book of Kells is 'a richly ornamented and illustrated gospel book dating from *c*.900' (Maier, 1997, p.40). It is not known where the Book of Kells originated; many believe that it was made in Iona, off the west coast of Scotland, and taken to Kells (forty miles north-west of Dublin) when the Iona monks abandoned their monastery after a Viking attack in 806. It is now on display in Trinity College, Dublin.

to which it can be reconstructed or revived with any accuracy. Thus we shall examine a variety of views, beliefs and practices concerning the Celts and Celtic spirituality, and then return to the authenticity issue later in the chapter. This is undoubtedly a context where the Religious Studies usage of 'myth' as a neutral term to describe a 'significant story', making no value judgement as to truth or falsehood, is particularly useful.

Celtic revival

The Celtic mists are swirling again and we are once more in the throes of a Celtic revival. There have been periods of fascination with the Celts in the past, for example, among seventeenth- and eighteenth-century antiquarians or eighteenth- and nineteenth-century Romantics. Perhaps we should say that there has been a history of continuous interest in the Celts in recent centuries, marked by peaks

Figure 2.1 'Celtic Dawn' – an example of contemporary Celtic revivalist writing and artefact, sold in Glastonbury. Copyright: Bahli Mans-Morris.

Figure 2.2 An example of contemporary Celtic artwork on the cover of *Celtic Connections: The Journal of Celtic and Related Subjects.* Copyright David James.

and troughs; the *fin de siècle*, whether eighteenth, nineteenth or twentieth century, seems particularly susceptible to the call of the Celts. It might be argued that what is happening now is essentially similar to previous revivals, but whereas Celts have in the past captured the imagination of antiquarians, Romantics, folklorists, artists, poets and minority interest groups, the present phenomenon is significantly more varied and broadly based. At the popular (and commercial) level, there are huge quantities of books relating to Celtic art, archaeology and mythology; there is a plethora of Celtic music; jewellery, pottery and clothing decorated with Celtic motifs abound; 'Irish' pubs seem to be a global phenomenon.

Moreover, and most significantly for our purposes, the *spiritual* aspects of this revival are also considerably more developed and diverse than ever before (see Bowman, 1993; 1994; 1996; 2000). Increasingly, for a variety of reasons and in varying ways, the Celts are being seen as providers of a particularly attractive 'brand' of spirituality. Many people in Britain, Ireland, western Europe, North America, New Zealand, Australia and elsewhere are now putting considerable effort into being restorers, reclaimers, rediscoverers, re-establishers, reinventors of Celtic spirituality, or 'innovators' within it. The Celts are being looked to for inspiration by a variety of spiritual seekers, Christian, New Age and Pagan, while even some Buddhist and Hindu-derived groups are articulating Celtic connections.[2] The obvious question is 'why?'.

In order to appreciate the attraction of Celtic spirituality and how it is perceived and practised, we shall have to examine some of the intellectual infrastructure around which images of the spiritual Celt are constructed and examine some trends in the history of ideas. We shall also look briefly at the sources from which information and ideas about Celts are constructed. An image commonly used in some branches of Celtic spirituality is shape shifting (the ability to take on different forms) and this seems an apt metaphor for the Celt, whose form appears to differ at various points in history, and whose shape has been shifted by a variety of interest groups – ideological, political, nationalist, academic and religious.

[2] This connection has a long history; see Catherine Robinson's article 'Druids and Brahmins: a case of mistaken identity?' in the electronic journal *DISKUS* 6, 2000.

Periphery, progress and primitivism

Have you ever considered the implications of the term 'the Celtic fringe'? That designation only makes sense if you feel you are in some way at a centre from which areas considered Celtic are perceived to be on the periphery. It is said (possibly apocryphally) that a Church of Scotland minister on Great Cumbrae (a very small island off the west coast of Scotland) used to conclude his services with the words, 'Lord pour out thy blessings on the Great Cumbrae and the Wee Cumbrae and the neighbouring islands of Great Britain and Ireland'. It would be a real marker of changed perceptions, for example, if post-devolution Scots were to start referring to southern England as the 'Anglo-Saxon fringe'. The archaeologist Simon James literally gives a new perspective on 'the Celtic fringe' by producing a map of Europe 'as seen from the Atlantic archipelago' (1999, pp.14–15).

The idea of the Celts as people on the edge, seen from a distance in terms of either time or space, is expressed in the following passages. The historian Ian Bradley wrote in *The Celtic Way* (1993, p.30):

> The great upsurge of interest in Celtic Christianity in recent years can be compared to the re-evaluation of the religious beliefs of other peoples who have lived on the margins like the Australian Aborigines and the Native Indians of North America. It reflects a realisation that what is primitive and simple can also be profound and highly original.

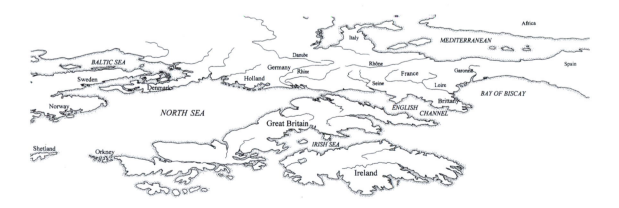

Figure 2.3 A different perspective on 'the Celtic fringe'; Europe as seen from the Atlantic archipelago. Copyright Simon James. Reproduced with permission.

In similar vein, Pamela Constantine, of the New Age 'New Romantic Movement', has written:

> I think the reason there is such a Celtic Revival is because the human spirit has been restricted so long by a society in which science and materialism and profit motive predominate. It has been dammed up and is now urgent for expression. It seems to me the Celts have a natural ability to reopen the 'magic casements' and to help people reconnect with the lost dimensions of themselves.
>
> (personal communication to author)

Those who write in this way – and there are many – are honouring the people and traditions of which they speak; there is an extent to which the Celts are being looked to as spiritual midwives and role models. But as the Celtic Studies scholar Donald Meek has pointed out (1996), would Celtic Christians (including the producers of the magnificent Book of Kells and Lindisfarne Gospels) really have seen themselves as marginal, primitive and simple? Have Celts really not been exposed (and succumbed) to science, materialism and profit motive? For some, it seems that Celts and the Celtic past have come to epitomize that which is lost but longed for in contemporary society. The remedy for dissatisfaction with the present is being sought in a particular (some would say distorted) reflection of the past; the antidote to dissatisfaction with the mainstream is being sought in the margins. What has made the Celts and the Celtic past so desirable?

The concept of progress, characterized as 'the idea that mankind constantly improves itself to its greatest advantage in the quest for perfectibility in the future' (Grobman, 1982, p.1), has a long pedigree, appearing in various forms in the classical period, and in Renaissance and Enlightenment thought. However, it was during the nineteenth century that concepts of evolution, particularly influenced by Charles Darwin's *The Origin of Species* (1859), brought the subject to the forefront. As the historian of religious studies Eric Sharpe puts it, before the end of the nineteenth century 'evolution, from being a theory, had become an atmosphere' (Sharpe, 1986, p.89).

Herbert Spencer, in his *First Principles* (1862), claimed that 'the law of organic evolution is the law of all evolution', and that 'this same advance from the simple to the complex, through successive differentiations, holds uniformly' (quoted in Sharpe, 1986, pp.33–4). In 1870, in *The Origin of Civilization and the Primitive Condition of Man*, Sir John Lubbock applied the theory of unilinear evolution to religion: 'Races in a similar state of mental development, however distinct their origins may be, and however distinct the regions they inhabit, have very similar religious concepts' (quoted in Sharpe, 1986, p.52).

What was being presented at this time was a definite view of progress. This affected not only biology and technology, but also ideas, and specifically religious ideas. It was assumed that there would be a universal and predictable progression in culture, regardless of time or space, from irrationality to rationality, from 'primitive' religion to ethical monotheism or, some thought, ultimately to scientifically informed atheism. It was presumed at this time that in the 'civilized' world later was better, the present was technologically, intellectually and religiously superior to the past. From exotic, 'less advanced' foreigners in small-scale societies it was possible to learn about the behaviour of ancestors in some remote, less enlightened past. However, the assumption was that no matter how quaint or interesting, they were among the losers in the evolutionary race.

Meanwhile, seemingly at odds with the ideas of 'progress' displayed in cultural evolution, the concepts of Noble Savage, the Golden Age and Primitivism developed. The cultural historian Stuart Piggott wrote, in relation to the history of ideas, of

> ... a recurrent series of speculations which seem to arise in civilized communities as the result of a subconscious guilty recognition of the inadequacy of the contemporary social order, and involve the concept of simpler and more satisfactory systems, remote either in time (Golden Ages in the past), or in place (Noble Savages at or beyond the edges of contemporary geographical knowledge).

(Piggott, 1993, p.20)

Cultural primitivism has been defined as 'the belief of men living in a relatively highly evolved and complex cultural condition that a life far simpler and less sophisticated in some or all respects is a more desirable life' (Lovejoy and Boas, 1965, p.7). The corollary of this is that 'The model of human excellence and happiness is sought in the present, in the mode of life of existing primitive, or so-called "savage" peoples' (ibid., p.8).

Primitivism is generally characterized as hard primitivism or soft primitivism. Hard primitivism has usually been the result of first-hand contact between people who consider themselves culturally superior to a group they consider primitive; there is a tendency to believe the worst of the newly discovered group, with descriptions that are basically empirical if unsympathetic. Soft primitivism tends to come about 'when distance in time or space lends enchantment to the view, and desirable qualities are not only sought for, but discovered and idealized' (Piggott, 1993, p.92). A Noble Savage becomes more noble and less, as it were, savage with distance, be that distance geographic, temporal or imaginary. What frequently paves the way for an upsurge in noble savagery is Romanticism, which in the British context has tended to be 'the spiritual and intellectual *alter ego* of urban industrialism – a glorification of things rural, non-industrial and pre-industrial' (Chapman, 1992, p.129).

Further fuel was added to this particular fire by the development in Britain of the field of folklore – described by Sharpe as 'the home missions department of anthropology' (1986, p.50) – and the notion of 'survivals' posited by Edward Tylor in his book, *Primitive Culture: Researches into the Development of Mythology, Philosophy, Religion, Language, Art and Custom* (1871). Survivals, he contended:

> ... are processes, customs, opinions, and so forth, which have been carried on by force of habit into a new state of society different from that in which they had their original home, and thus they remain as proofs and examples of an old condition of culture out of which the newer has been evolved.
>
> (Quoted in Sharpe, 1986, p.54)

Alice and Lawrence Gomme, writing on British folklore, remarked:

> In every society there are people who do not progress either in religion or in polity with the foremost of the nation. They are left stranded amidst the progress. They live in out-of-the-way villages, or in places where general culture does not penetrate easily; they keep to old ways, practices, and ideas, following with religious awe all their parents had held to be necessary to their lives. These people are living depositories of ancient history – a history that has not been written down, but which has come down by tradition. Knowing the conditions of survivals in culture, the folklorist uses them in the ancient meaning, not in their modern setting, tries to find out their significance and importance in relation to their origin, and thus lays the foundation for the science of folklore.
>
> (Gomme and Gomme, 1916, p.10)

While Irish, Scottish Gaelic and Welsh texts had been the object of study (and occasional forgery) in previous centuries, and the curious ways of the folk had been commented on by antiquarians, the conscious search for 'survivals' and an active desire to 'reconstruct' led to a new bout of confident assertions (as opposed to tentative suggestions) about the beliefs and lifestyle of the Celts, and for some reinforced the desirability of a Celtic revival. Folklore collectors went out looking for 'survivals' on the margins of industrialized Britain, which further 'associated rurality with age; and conflated age and rurality with spirituality' (Bennett, 1993, p.87), and we shall see how this has had an impact on images of the Celts in the twentieth and twenty-first centuries.

Having looked at some of the ideas that have influenced how we regard progress, the past and people on the 'periphery', we shall now examine a variety of sources for images of the Celts. These influential images of Celts, developed at different periods, now have an impact on the perceptions of Celts that appear in contemporary Celtic spirituality.

Where does the spiritual Celt come from?

It is important to grasp that there is no one authoritative, universally accepted version of 'the truth' about the Celts, past and present; there are shifting ideas and images, scholarly and popular, all of which have contributed to the immensely varied and vibrant phenomenon of contemporary Celtic spirituality, examples of which we shall encounter later in this chapter. Without getting submerged in the detail of different branches of Celtic scholarship, I want to establish not just that scholarly methodology develops and academic fashions change, but also that what people look for affects what they see and how they present their findings. While there might be 'solid' academic evidence about the Celts, approaches to it can be partial and partisan, affected by the socio-political milieu of the scholar. That is to say, academic study of the Celts is not necessarily neutral, and is certainly contested; moreover, it is in abandoned scholarly theory that popular perceptions of Celts frequently have their genesis.[3] Context and perspective have played and continue to play a large part in how Celts are perceived and studied in archaeological, historical, geographical, literary and linguistic terms, and by extension in how Celts are envisaged and Celticism is experienced in spiritual or religious terms.

So who are the Celts in contemporary Celtic spirituality? Within the British Isles, 'Celtic' has popularly become increasingly broadly interpreted to embrace all Scots, Irish, Welsh, Manx, Northumbrians, and people from the West Country. Some look to geography, some to language, some to ancestry, to establish Celtic credentials, but increasingly there are what I have referred to elsewhere as 'Cardiac Celts' – people who feel in their hearts that they are Celtic (Bowman, 1996). Tim Sebastion, Chosen Chief of the Secular Order of Druids,

---

[3] While modern academic folklore is no longer obsessed with the hunt for 'survivals', some contemporary Pagans regard certain calendar customs (whose origins can sometimes only be traced back to the eighteenth century) as unquestionably prehistoric survivals, and are confidently 'reclaiming' them as pre-Christian traditions.

(SOD)[4] is of the opinion that ultimately *everyone* in Britain is of Celtic descent; but anyway, he claims, as 'Celtic' describes culture not ethnicity, anyone can 'tap into' Celticity. Who or what constitutes 'Celtic' at present is fluid, one might even say 'up for grabs'.

Simon James uses the term 'Atlantic Celts' for the people who are considered or consider themselves to be modern Celts geographically, living on the 'Atlantic façade' of Europe. The term 'Atlantic Celts' is also apposite because, in the English-speaking world, the majority of people of 'Celtic' ancestry now live on the other side of the Atlantic in the Americas (such as Irish and Scots in North America, and Welsh in Patagonia). Although this chapter is largely concerned with the British situation, then, there are millions of people in the Celtic diaspora (including Australia and New Zealand), which makes Celticity a global rather than a purely British or European issue.

The physical remains of the material cultures of the many Iron Age peoples of Europe have conventionally been used to give a picture of Celtic life and culture. Indeed, Celtic remains, artefacts and artwork are possibly among the best known and most attractive aspects of Celtic culture. However, the archaeologist Timothy Champion makes the point that 'Archaeological remains do not speak for themselves, they have to be interpreted' (1996, p.62). In an article entitled 'The Celt in archaeology', Champion shows how European archaeologists of different nationalities at various times have focused on specific aspects of Celtic material culture in order to emphasize what best suited their purposes – Celts as warriors, Celts as artists, Celts as king makers, Celts as resistance fighters. Thus, archaeology

> ... served to provide Celts suitable to the needs of nineteenth-century Europe, whether that was for an artistic society in need of control, or for heroes and heroines to authenticate the aspirations of European nation states ... The society of the Iron Age Celts was reconstructed as the wished-for prototype of nineteenth-century patriarchy and militarism.
>
> (Champion, 1996, p.75)

Champion notes that the Celts are again being 'rewritten' in the current context of political moves towards a unified Europe. This was seen in both an exhibition of the early Iron Age Hallstatt culture held in Austria in 1980, with the subtitle 'An early form of European unity', and the spectacular 1991 Venice exhibition entitled 'The Celts: the origins of Europe'. For the latter:

---

[4] The Secular Order of Druids, based in the West Country, seeks to revive the relevance of Druidry by, among other things, reviving folk traditions.

Circumstances demanded that the artistic rather than the military side of the Celts was stressed, and it was without doubt the biggest and most stunning exhibition of Iron Age artistic and technical achievement ever gathered together ... Nevertheless, it required considerable distortion of the archaeological evidence to accommodate the vision of a pan-European Celtic culture zone as a precursor of the longed-for federal Europe, but this was simply the most recent example of the dynamic interaction between the interpretation of the archaeological evidence and the wider intellectual and political context of archaeological practice that has shaped our vision of the Celts for the last three hundred years.

(Champion, 1996, p.76)

The point is that physical remains do not come handily labelled with the exact context, intentions and meanings of those who made them; as the archaeologist Angela Piccini admits, 'because we come into contact with these things in the present, we make meanings for them in the here and now' (1999, p.20). That is as true for practitioners of Celtic spirituality as it is for archaeologists. Thus, some would argue that monuments such as West Kennett Long Barrow in Wiltshire, explained by conventional archaeology simply as burial mounds, were originally constructed for ritual purposes to represent the womb of the Goddess, and such rituals are now being 'revived'.

Furthermore, the contested nature of interpretation is such that Simon James has gone so far as to suggest that developments in archaeological technology, the discrediting of earlier theories of mass migration and waves of invasions, and a fresh appraisal of the diversity of archaeological evidence from Iron Age communities in the British Isles lead to the conclusion that 'our established belief that these islands, like much of continental Europe, were occupied by Celts in later prehistory, is simply wrong: the insular Ancient Celts never existed' (James, 1999, p.16). Some have accused James of 'genocide', while others (such as the anthropologist Malcolm Chapman in *The Celts: The Construction of a Myth*, 1992) join him in seeing Celts as essentially a fairly modern invention. Thus, at a time when in popular culture we are surrounded by 'proofs' of the Celts' ancient and continued existence – Celtic languages, Celtic music, Celtic artefacts, Celtic exhibitions, Celtic art, Celtic writings, Celtic ceremonies, a huge Celtic industry and myriad forms of Celtic spirituality – some scholars are actually questioning the whole concept of a Celtic tradition.

When thinking or reading about, or, as some are trying to do, capturing the spirit of the Celtic past, we need to be aware of the contested and contingent nature of history. As James contends, we do not discover history as 'unambiguous truth', we *create* history:

> In the broadest sense – covering both document-based historical studies and material-based archaeology – history is the construction by modern minds of imagined (although not wholly imaginary!) pasts, from the fragmentary surviving debris of past societies. History is what *we* think, say and write about the evidence of the past.
>
> (James, 1999, p.33)

This is not to say that anything goes, for 'the evidence forms the all-important framework for, and places constraints on, the models of the past that we construct' (James, 1999, p.33). Judgements based on fact can be made on some of the more dubious claims about Celtic spirituality, for example, Edain McCoy's assertion in *Witta: An Irish Pagan Tradition* (1993) that the ancient Irish revered the potato – 'Because they grew underground, potatoes were sacred to the Goddess and used in female fertility rites' (p.82) – when we know that potatoes were introduced to Ireland from the Americas in the sixteenth century. We just need to bear in mind that history is not a neutral discipline, that at different times the same events and evidence may be viewed quite differently, that our knowledge-base develops and changes, and that 'all invented traditions, so far as possible, use history as a legitimator of action and cement of group cohesion' (Hobsbawm, 1984, p.12).

Classical sources

One of the most influential sources for details about the Celts has traditionally been Greek and Roman accounts of them, and many scholarly summaries and reappraisals of these classical sources have appeared in recent years (e.g. Chapman, 1992; Collis, 1996; Piccini, 1996; James, 1999). Many stereotypes taken from this classical literature have contributed to the present view of the Celts, including their passionate nature, their love of ornamentation, their bravery and bravado, their high-spiritedness, and so on. However, it needs to be remembered that 'The Celts were only one of many groups described as being quick to anger, illogical and intemperate – the direct opposite of how the Greek and Roman societies liked to view themselves' (Piccini, 1999, p.19).[5] Malcolm Chapman has likewise suggested that when the term 'Keltoi' was used, this was frequently not careful ethnography of particular people, but a conflation of 'foreigners'. Ancient Greek and Roman authors writing about the strange people with whom they came in contact frequently tell us as

[5] Comparisons might be made with British imperialist rhetoric concerning India and Africa.

much about themselves and their attitudes to 'others' as they do about those being described.[6]

It is probably the Druids, described in classical literature as the priestly caste of the Celts, and associated with mistletoe, oak, golden sickles, sacred groves, esoteric learning and (rather more controversial, and variously interpreted) human sacrifice,[7] who are most eagerly seized upon from these writings for clues about Celtic spirituality. However, Piggott describes the classical sources on Druids as, once again, 'scanty and scrappy, frequently in second-hand quotation' (1993, p.18). Thus, while there is much information in the classical sources and some treat them as accurate, eye-witness accounts, they are not without controversy, being open to a number of interpretations and the charge that they are written by 'outsiders' who have their own agendas.

Celtic language and literature

One of the most tangible sources of information about the Celts is that of Celtic language and literature. The continental Celtic group of languages includes Gaulish, Celtiberian, Lepontic and Galatian, all of which had died out by the early Middle Ages, while the insular Celtic group comprises Breton, Cornish, Cumbrian, Irish, Manx, Scottish Gaelic and Welsh (Maier, 1997, p.165). The academic discipline of Celtic Studies has thus come to be based on the study of 'all linguistic utterances of the Celtic peoples from ancient times to the present day' (Maier, 1997, p.66).

However, the term 'Celtic languages' has hidden agendas. In 1707, the Welsh scholar and patriot Edward Lhuyd, Keeper of the Ashmolean Museum in Oxford, published *Archaeologia Brittanica*, 'a significant landmark in the history of the study of language' (James, 1999, p.45). After years of research into the ancient and modern languages of Ireland, Scotland, Wales, Cornwall and Brittany, Lhuyd identified a family of languages related to the extinct language of the Ancient Gauls of France, which he called 'Celtic'. We should bear in mind the political climate of the time, for 1707 was also the year that

---

[6] In *Inventing Ireland*, the Irish academic Declan Kiberd makes the similar point that 'Through many centuries, Ireland was pressed into service as a foil to set off English virtues' (1995, p.1).

[7] Some Druids simply deny that there was ever any human sacrifice, claiming stories of it were 'smear tactics' by classical authors to discredit enemies. Others claim that the sacrifice would have been of a willing victim, for whom it was a great honour.

the Treaty of Union between England and Scotland officially created 'a new *political* identity called "British"' (James, 1999, p.47). Thus, 'the name of Briton – the best, and time-honoured, potential collective label for those peoples of the island who saw themselves as other than English – was appropriated for all subjects of the new, inevitably English-dominated superstate' (James, 1999, p.48). Lhuyd's work was not only of scholarly interest, then, but it provided 'the basis for a wholly new conception of the identities and histories of the non-English peoples of the isles, which at that moment were under strong political and cultural threat' (James, 1999, p.47).

Just as philology, the study of languages, was extremely influential in the early academic study of religion and the creation of 'Orientalism',[8] philology in the eighteenth and nineteenth centuries played a considerable part in the creation of 'Celticism'. As the Celtic scholar Joep Leerssen points out, Celticism means:

> ... not the study of the Celts and their history, but rather the study of their reputation and of the meanings and connotations ascribed to the term 'Celtic'. To the extent that 'Celtic' is an idea with a wide and variable application, Celticism becomes a complex and significant issue in the European history of ideas: the history of what people wanted that term to mean.
>
> (Leerssen, 1996, p.3)

The conclusion that the Celtic languages formed an independent branch of the Indo-European linguistic family (which also includes Sanskrit), and the idea that there was one language group (albeit, 'a group of *mutually unintelligible* languages' (James, 1999, p.138)) gave the popular impression of a common language, which was interpreted by some as a common culture, cultural identity and 'spirit'. In this perception of commonality lay the roots of pan-Celticism, which has come to mean in some circles that all Celtic cultures/peoples were/are the same, thought/think the same, and in the realm of religion had/ have a shared spirituality, whether pagan or Christian, past or present.

Another linguistic issue relevant to contemporary Celtic spirituality is the fact that most people encounter Celtic myth, poetry, prayers and so on in the *same* language, namely English. From Celtic literature appearing in English for an English-speaking audience has emerged a sort of hybrid 'Celtlish', which reflects the style of English

[8] Edward Said describes Orientalism as 'the corporate institution for dealing with the Orient – dealing with it by making statements about it, authorizing views of it, describing it, by teaching it, settling it, ruling over it: in short, Orientalism as a Western style for dominating, restructuring, and having authority over the Orient' (1995, p.3).

to emerge in translations of Celtic literature, involving formulaic – frequently threefold – repetition, metrical forms, short lines and archaic turns of phrase (e.g. 'Power of storm be thine, Power of moon be thine, Power of the sun ...'). Thus, to the linguistically uninitiated, Celtic literature comes in a homogenized package, with Irish, Welsh, Cornish and Gaelic writings (which we rarely see in their varied original versions) seeming all the same. Similarly, there is a collapsing of chronology, as translations of early medieval, nineteenth- and twentieth-century texts frequently appear together without differentiation, often with the implication that these are all 'ancient' writings. (The antiquity and influence of oral tradition is undoubtedly an important factor, but the fact remains that the texts themselves are often of far more recent date than is implied.) As Mary Low cautions:

> At times, the search for pre-Christian and Indo-European ideas has been carried on so enthusiastically that the thoroughly Christian context of the texts has been overlooked ... It is important to understand that there are no pre-Christian Irish documents dealing with religion, or indeed with any other subject.
>
> (Low, 1996, p.15)

It is no wonder, then, that Celtic writings seem 'timeless', for they are often presented in a completely atemporal manner; and because of the pervading 'Celtlish' style, Celtic prayers, blessings and ritual/ liturgical speech being written now, whether Christian, Druid, New Age or Pagan, frequently sound similar – and that in turn all feeds back into the impression of the 'sameness' and solidity of Celtic spirituality.

While there is a rich variety of literature in Celtic languages – myth, poetry, legal and theological texts, history, song, hagiography – one item of Celtic literature, Alexander Carmichael's 'collection of a remarkable range of orally transmitted Gaelic lore' (Meek, 2000, p.60), known as *Carmina Gadelica*, has become above all 'the "bible" of Celtophiles' (p.72). Collected in Gaelic in the Scottish Hebrides in the late nineteenth century, the *Carmina Gadelica* includes a huge variety of prayers and invocations, blessings for everyday tasks (for example, milking, weaving, grinding), addresses to saints, charms (for example, for toothache, the evil eye, indigestion), journey prayers and songs. *Carmina Gadelica* was first published in six volumes from 1900; Carmichael produced translations for the first two volumes, and over a period of years translations for the remaining volumes were completed. Whereas earlier editions had Gaelic texts alongside English translations by Carmichael and others, in the most recent edition (published by

Floris Books in 1992 with subsequent reprintings) *Carmina Gadelica* appears only in English.

Carmichael had a number of motivations in collecting the *Carmina:* it was a time when folklore collecting was being actively pursued for fear that it would be lost – and also when a certain amount of polishing, reworking or restoring of collected texts was common. There was a political aspect, for Carmichael hoped 'that by making the book up in as good a form as I could in matter and material, it might perhaps be the means of conciliating some future politician in favour of our dear Highland people' (quoted in Meek, 2000, p.61).

Finally, very much a product of his time, Carmichael believed in the special spirituality of the Highland Celt and the antiquity of the material he collected:

> It is the product of faraway thinking, come down on the long stream of time ... Some of the hymns may have been composed within the cloistered cells of Derry and Iona, and some of the incantations among the cromlechs of Stonehenge and the standing-stones of Callarnis.
>
> (Introduction to *Carmina Gadelica*, vol.1, quoted in Meek, 2000, pp.63–4)

In contemporary Celtic spirituality this assumption of antiquity for the *Carmina* is accepted, indeed asserted. As Angela Piccini comments, 'Past and present in the western and northern reaches of Britain eventually came to be transformed into a Celtic always' (Piccini, 1999, p.20).

Celts and natives

A most important contribution to the popular image of the Celt emerged in relation to native peoples. Between the sixteenth and the eighteenth centuries, stories of encounters with 'primitive' peoples by explorers returning from voyages of discovery seemed to have some resonance with classical accounts of Celts. By the sixteenth and seventeenth centuries, views of ancient Britons and Celts were being gained not so much from looking at contemporary Celts, but from accounts and illustrations of Native Americans and other encounters with indigenous peoples, and pictures of newly encountered native peoples influenced artists' impressions of ancient Britons (see Piggott, 1989, pp.13–33). John Aubrey, writing in the seventeenth century, described the ancient Britons of Wiltshire as 'two or three degrees I suppose less savage than the Americans' (Piggott, 1989, p.130).

Eighteenth-century Celts and Druids

By the eighteenth century, however, Druids were becoming in some eyes less savage and more noble, and it was a time of burgeoning interest in Celts. Here I will just draw attention to some of the figures from that period who were to be particularly influential, both at the time and in relation to contemporary Celtic spirituality. William Stukeley, a Lincolnshire doctor with antiquarian interests, became fascinated by Wiltshire ancient monuments and in 1740 published *Stonehenge: A Temple Restor'd to the British Druids.* Although Aubrey had made the connection in the previous century, Stukeley is considered to have been one of the most influential figures in forging the popular link between Druids and Stonehenge and Avebury, and using 'Celts' as an alternative to 'Britons'. He also distorted his archaeological fieldwork findings to support his religious arguments after he became a clergyman. Stukeley envisaged the Druids coming to England with the Phoenicians, 'during the life of Abraham, or very soon after', with a religion 'so extremely like Christianity, that in effect it differ'd from it only in this; they believed in a Messiah who was to come, as we believe in him that is come' (Piggott, 1989, p.145).

The architect John Wood the Elder, responsible for some of the most striking architecture of eighteenth-century Bath, had very definite ideas about the Druids: King Bladud was their founder, and they had a Metropolitan Seat at Bath. Wood saw himself as the

Figure 2.4 Aerial view of Bath, showing John Wood the Elder's design of the Royal Crescent (left) and the Circus, which can be interpreted as representing the moon and the sun. Simmons Aerofilms.

'restorer' of Bath, which he believed had been a great city built by the Britons, three times the size of Roman Bath. The design for the Circus was influenced by Stonehenge and the stone circles of Stanton Drew (which he considered a Druid college), and the Circus and Royal Crescent together were representative of temples to the sun and the moon which Wood claimed to have found in the hills above Bath (Wood, 1765, reprinted 1969; Mowl and Earnshaw, 1988). The work of William Blake (artist, poet and visionary) in the late eighteenth and early nineteenth centuries increasingly contained images of and references to Druids, Stonehenge and Avebury, as he became convinced that Druids had originated in England and spread throughout the earth; in the poem *Jerusalem* he declared, 'All things Begin and End in Albion's Ancient Druid Rocky Shore' (Keynes, 1979, p.649).

Meanwhile, in the 1780s and 1790s, the Welsh patriot, freemason and Unitarian Edward Williams – better known as Iolo Morganwg – presented and promoted what he claimed was an authentic, ancient Druidic tradition of the British Isles which had survived in Wales through the bardic system, the distinctive Welsh language poetic tradition. The first Welsh Gorsedd (assembly of bards or poets) was

Figure 2.5 *The Serpent Temple*. Engraving by William Blake, inspired by William Stukeley's 'reconstruction' of the prehistoric remains at Avebury, Wiltshire. Blake has added a Stonehenge-style ring of trilithons (two upright stones with a third across the top) to the Avebury circle of standing stones. Jerusalem Plate 100, Fitzwilliam Museum, Cambridge.

held in 1791 on Primrose Hill in London. In 1819, the Gorsedd became affiliated to the Welsh Eisteddfod (itself an eighteenth-century revival of a medieval literary and musical competition), which promotes Welsh language and culture, and is still held annually in Wales. Morganwg claimed that ceremonies were to be held outside, 'in the eye of the sun', and were to start by honouring the four directions; he also taught the Gorsedd Prayer, which he attributed to the primeval bard Talhaiarn:

> Grant, O God! thy refuge,
> And in refuge, strength,
> And in strength, understanding,
> In understanding, knowledge,
> In knowledge, knowledge of right,
> In knowledge of right, to love it;
> In loving it, the love of all essences,
> In love of all essences, love of God,
> God and all Goodness

(Quoted in Morgan, 1975, p.51)

Morganwg's claims and writings were accepted as genuine at the time, and it was not until the late nineteenth century that they were revealed as forgeries. By that time, however, their influence had been established and it continues to this day.

It is interesting that from the eighteenth century onwards we see a parallel development of esotericism (see Chapter 1, pp.23–5) and Celtic identity, with literatures and claims (of varying degrees of authenticity) to support them. As the Celtic scholar Terence Brown comments, 'Both occultism and cultural nationalism involve belief in hidden realities which must be made manifest' (1996, p.222).

Theosophical Celts

An important but frequently overlooked contribution to the contemporary image of Celts and Druids has been made by theosophy (see Chapter 1 and the extract 'Madame Blavatsky's children' by Kevin Tingay in Part Two). Among the ideas put forward by H.P. Blavatsky and her followers were the existence of an ancient wisdom tradition, esoteric in character but manifest through exoteric religious traditions; the existence of adepts or masters of the wisdom; channelling of this wisdom to those attuned to receive it; a particular understanding of reincarnation and Karma; spiritual as well as physical evolution; a vision of universal brotherhood. However, some thought it more appropriate to seek a native British form of mysticism than to pursue those of India or Tibet. As the British mystic Lewis Spence wrote:

> We Britons are much too prone to look for excellence outside of the boundaries of our own island ... That we should so weakly rely on alien systems of thought while it is possible for us to re-establish our own is surely miserable. In no individual born in these islands does there not flow the blood of Druid priests and seers, and I confidently rely on British mystics, whatever their particular predilections, to unite in this greatest of all possible quests, the restoration of our native Secret Tradition.
>
> (Spence, 1993, p.256)

Many of the figures involved in the Celtic revival of the late nineteenth/early twentieth centuries had theosphical connections, including the poet W.B. Yeats (who edited a collection of *Fairy and Folk Tales of Ireland*, and wrote *The Celtic Twilight*), George Russell (who wrote on mysticism under the pseudonym 'Æ'), the artist John Duncan (see Figure 2.6), and William Sharp (who wrote mystical

Figure 2.6 John Duncan, *St Bride*, 1913, tempera on canvas, 122 x 145 cm. Copyright Trustees of the National Galleries of Scotland. The painting illustrates the legend that St Bride was carried by angels to the Holy Land to be midwife to Mary and Christ's foster-mother.

prose and verse under the pseudonym Fiona Macleod). What Michael McGrath, modern Archdruid of Tara and Ireland, wrote of the Druids is indicative of this theosophical influence in combination with Celtic Romanticism:

> Some were sent on across fifteen centuries on a sacred mission to this time and place for the benefit of humanity, bearing the Holy Grail of Druidry just hidden, never quite lost, to a whole new generation. The Door of Druidry is now open to all across the planet. You have only to step through to find out. It is significant that after fifteen centuries the Spirit of Druidry is revived universally. Once again the sacred flame is lit and sitting around it we can hear those Masters of the Universe whisper in our ear.
>
> (*The Druids' Voice*, summer 1997, p.35)

Having looked at the many threads from which contemporary Celtic spirituality has been woven, we shall now look at various ways in which the Celtic spiritual vision is being realized today.

Celtic spirituality as native religion

For many Pagans, pre-Christian Europe is regarded as a Golden Age, and they seek to recover, reactivate or capture the spirit of their ancestral, 'native' traditions. While some Pagans seek to reconnect with Norse or Saxon traditions, or revere ancient Greek or Egyptian deities, for many Pagans it is Celtic deities, Celtic sacred places, and the Celtic calendar that provide the means to tap into that bygone age and, some hope, to bring about the re-enchantment of the contemporary world. Not only is contemporary Paganism diverse, as we saw in Chapter 1, but Celtic Paganism itself is very varied. It includes assorted forms of Druidry, groups and individuals with a specifically Irish, Welsh, Scottish, Cornish or Breton focus, some aspects developed from groups such as the Hermetic Order of the Golden Dawn, some eco-protest groups, and assorted 'free-range Celts', individuals who mix their own 'Celtic cocktail'.

Many of these diverse Celtic spirituality practitioners feel that they reconnect both with the Celtic past and with nature through keeping what is known in these circles as the 'eightfold' or Celtic calendar (see Colour Plate 1, discussed in the introduction and Chapter 1). This 'Wheel of the Year', as it is frequently called, is widely believed to reflect how the Celts measured and perceived the year, which is popularly held to have started on 1 November. Many feel that observing this calendar, both as an individual and in group rituals, fosters an awareness of the seasons and the cycle of life, death and rebirth. Samhain is a time for remembering the ancestors and the dead and contemplating the darker aspects of life, while Imbolc, which some associate especially with the goddess Brighde (widely believed to have been Christianized as St Bride) marks the emergence from winter. Beltane celebrates fertility and the coming of summer, while Lughnasadh (also referred to as Lammas) is a time for thanking the Earth for her bounty. Customs and rituals have been and are being 'revived', rediscovered or invented in observing this calendar, frequently drawing in 'survivalist' manner on folk traditions whose original pagan meanings are being 'restored'. In Glastonbury, for example, some women celebrate Imbolc, 'the festival of Brighde, the Triple Fire Goddess', by making 'Bride Crosses' and 'Bride Dolls' following an Irish folk Catholic tradition. Celtic camps, courses and events are often held at these significant times. Keeping the eightfold calendar is one of the few consistent and unifying aspects of Celtic Paganism, as a sort of temporal community is created by people celebrating together at these times.

In line with the general Pagan resacralizing of the land, there is an 'honouring' of and pilgrimage to what are considered to be ancient Celtic sacred sites (such as stone circles, standing stones and barrows) (see Figure 2.7), in addition to natural features such as springs and wells. Offerings of flowers are frequently left beside what are perceived as sacred springs, for example, and tree dressing is becoming popular. Rag wells, springs beside trees to which strips of cloth are tied (also known in some areas as cloutie wells), survived in popular tradition in some areas, frequently associated with healing and often named after a saint.[9] Such rag-well activity has increased markedly, both at existing and new sites, and is seen as a revival or continuance of an ancient Celtic tradition of votive offerings around water. Some Pagans revere specific local Celtic gods and goddesses (such as Sul in Bath); others see the ancient Celtic deities simply as aspects or local forms of the universal sacred female.

An important element in the current practice of Celtic Pagan spirituality is the assumption by some practitioners that Britain's native religion was and is akin to the beliefs and practices of Native Americans and Australians, and indeed any other indigenous or tribal group. As an English informant 'with Celtic blood' who attended a Native American weekend workshop commented, it is 'very close to the Celtic thing'; 'When it comes to spirituality, it's all the same in the end'. Whereas in the past this connection between native peoples

---

[9] Amy Hale recounts incidents of contestation around holy wells in Cornwall, when Christian and Pagan Celtic practitioners have clashed over use of and entitlement to such sites (Hale, 2001).

Figure 2.7 Men-an-tol (the holed stone) at Anguidal Down, Madron, Cornwall. Reproduced from J.T. Blight, *Ancient Crosses and Other Antiquities in the East of Cornwall*, 1858.

and ancient Britons was made largely to help reconstruct the past for antiquarian or archaeological purposes, the present connections are being made to expand and enrich the practice of what is perceived as Celtic native religion. Thus, while some look to Celtic myth and literature to reconstruct ancestral belief and practice, very much in the spirit of cultural evolutionism, there is an assumption in some circles that whatever is present among contemporary native peoples must have been part of Celtic spirituality, and therefore some consider it logical to copy and Celticize it, or at least to merge it with what is known of Celtic tradition.

Shamanism is one example of this trend. The term 'shaman' is derived from the Tungus people of Siberia, but it has come to be used generally for the role of 'mediator between the human world and the world of the spirits' (Jakobsen, 1999, p.1), one who 'journeys' to the unseen realms and communicates with the spirits encountered there. Shamanism enjoys great popularity among a variety of spiritual practitioners and has spawned numerous related books, workshops and training sessions, some of which incorporate practices and paraphernalia from a variety of native traditions. While some feel that to 'revive' shamanism it is necessary to look to contemporary indigenous religion, others, such as Caitlin and John Matthews, feel that Celtic literature and cultural tradition support and preserve Celtic forms of shamanic practice which can be made relevant for the present day. John Matthews' book *The Celtic Shaman: A Handbook* (1991) has been influential in this respect, and Caitlin and John Matthews have been running a 'Foundation Course in Celtic Shamanism' for many years. The publicity for this course, entitled 'Walkers between the Worlds', describes it thus:

> The two-part [two weekends] Foundation Course aims to impart the principles of Walking between the Worlds or shamanic journeying between our worlds and the otherworlds within a safe and friendly context. Drawing on the lore, practice and background of Celtic and ancestral methods of shamanism, participants will directly receive the bright knowledge of the many beings who maintain the thresholds between the worlds, gaining their own allies, learning to quest, heal and arbitrate along the ancient paths of wisdom.

However, not all Pagans share the current enthusiasm for Celtic shamanism, and some feel there are issues of spiritual and cultural exploitation in this trend, as a Welsh Pagan, John Davies, demonstrates in this trenchant criticism:

> I doubt if it is possible to become a 'celtic shaman', and it is a mistake to try. Because if you do; if you come to Wales (as I fear you may), wearing beads, and funny hats adorned with feathers and pieces of stick; if you come laden with rattles and spirit callers and suchlike paraphernalia; if you come following an expensive workshop leader who can't even pronounce, let alone speak, any Welsh; whose only qualifications are a set of distinctly cranky ideas, assembled from fragments torn loose from our heritage and a hotpotch of others; plus, of course, a fast line in chat to convince you that this system offers instant enlightenment at a price (the fast-food version of spirituality); then you will be obvious for the fool you are.
>
> (Davies, 1993, p.1)

Contemporary Druids

For many, Celtic spirituality *par excellence* is to be found in Druidry. Stuart Piggott writes of 'Druids-as-known' who can be inferred from archaeological and literary sources, and 'Druids-as-wished-for', the result of 'unconscious or conscious creation of Druid idealizations or myths' (Piggott, 1993, p.11). Piggott concludes that contemporary Druids are very much Druids-as-wished-for, and traces their development from the sixteenth to the twentieth centuries in the light of Romanticism, scholarly fashion, changing views of British and European history and popular fancy. Nevertheless, Druidry is a varied and vibrant movement within contemporary Celtic spirituality, and one that can have a huge impact on people's lives.

Without becoming overwhelmed by the detail of differences and disputes, we should note the division between what might be called 'cultural' Druidry and esoteric or 'believing' Druidry.[10] Whatever religious vision he may have had, Iolo Morganwg's major concern, culminating in the Welsh Gorsedd, had been the preservation and promotion of the Welsh linguistic, literary and cultural tradition. Similarly, when a Cornish Gorseth (assembly of bards or poets) was established in 1928, its purpose was to assert Cornwall's Celtic credentials and promote the revival and preservation of the Cornish language and cultural tradition. Thus, although the ceremonial of the Welsh 'Gorsedd of Bards of the Isle of Britain' and the Cornish Gorseth look most impressively and romantically 'Druidic' with Welsh white-robed and Cornish blue-robed bards uniformly attired, the symbol /|\ for Awen (bardic inspiration) displayed, and Iolo's Druidic prayer recited, these are primarily cultural rather than religious expressions.

As one modern Welsh bard has written:

> I do not believe in the Druidic ancestry of the Gorsedd, but I do believe in what that imaginative myth symbolises – the rich and splendid tradition of Welsh bardism, which can be traced as far back as the Sixth Century. [*sic*]

> (Cynan, 1989, p.65)

The former Cornish Grand Bard George Ansell is quoted as saying:

> The gorseth provides a focus for Cornish nationality and allegiance. We also meet throughout the year and pronounce on important matters to do with Cornwall and Cornishness, such as the closure of hospitals and threats to our main-line railway. If you don't have a community, you don't have a culture.

> (*The Times* 'Weekend', 24 July 1999)

A flyer distributed by the Cornish Gorseth before the 1999 ceremony stated categorically 'The Gorseth is non-political, non-religious and non-profit making and contrary to some belief, *has no connection with Druidism nor any pagan practices*' (Hale, 2000).[11] In terms of

---

[10] For an excellent summary of the issues and sensitivities involved here, see Amy Hale's article 'In the eye of the sun: the relationship between the Cornish Gorseth and esoteric Druidry', 2000.

[11] Of course, few things connected with Celtic spirituality are straightforward, and although the overwhelming majority of people connected with the Welsh Gorsedd and the Cornish Gorseth were and are Christian (or nowadays 'spiritually non-aligned'), I know of 'cultural Druids' who also have personal Druidic or Pagan beliefs but who cannot express this in the bardic forum.

Figure 2.8 Bards at the Cornish Gorseth, July 1999. Apex Photo Library.

contemporary Celtic spirituality, then, these colourful but cultural
bards are not our main concern.

In popular perception, Druidry and Stonehenge are inextricably
linked – a connection made, as we saw, by the antiquarian Aubrey in
the seventeenth century and popularized in the eighteenth century
by William Stukeley. Archaeologists now tend to date the building of
Stonehenge to several phases, between *c.*3000 and 1500 BCE,
considerably earlier than the people conventionally recognized as
the Celts are reckoned to have arrived in Britain.[12] While many
contemporary Druids concede that Stonehenge may not have been
built by Druids originally, they argue that as a sacred site of obvious
significance to different peoples at different times, it would undoubtedly have been a place where Druids would have held ceremonies. I
have been assured by one Druid that in the 1980s a hoard of golden
sickles was uncovered at Stonehenge, 'proving' the connection
between Druidry and Stonehenge; this was 'hushed up' by the
authorities opposing the rights of Druids to have free access to the

[12] Just as archaeological views of Stonehenge have changed over time, so have
explanations as to how it was built. While in the thirteenth century Geoffrey of
Monmouth suggested that it had been erected by Merlin, who had magically
transported the stones from Ireland, I have been assured that the ancients simply
put the stones on ley lines, along which they travelled to Stonehenge. See Burl
(2001) for continuing speculation concerning the building of Stonehenge.

site at festival times for ceremonial purposes. However, Druid ceremonies are held at numerous sites, including Avebury in Wiltshire and other stone circles, or simply in places without any (pre)historical connections which are considered appropriate. Some feel, for example, that rather than travelling to distant sites, people should be honouring and sacralizing their local landscape.

Druids tend to observe the eightfold calendar, although nowadays ceremonies (particularly relating to Imbolc, Beltane, Lugnasagh/ Lammas and Samhain) are often held on the nearest Saturday or Sunday to allow more people to attend. Rituals are held 'in the eye of the sun' (i.e. usually in the middle of the day), the spirits of the four directions are honoured, and Morganwg's prayer is said (sometimes adapted to include God *and* Goddess, or God*s*). Ceremonies tend to reflect on the time of year, the passing of the seasons, and connectedness with both the land and the ancestors. 'Celtlish' language is frequently used,[13] and one may well encounter the *Carmina Gadelica*. Reviewing the 1992 Floris Books paperback edition of the *Carmina*, Philip Shallcrass of the British Druid Order (BDO) enthused:

> The Druidic interest in this collection of folk lore lies in its obvious antiquity, as well as its lyrical beauty. As raw material for ritual it is invaluable ... Many of these are heavily Christianised, but many more are not, and sing out clearly of our pagan past.
>
> (Shallcrass, 1993, p.37)

Some groups take costuming more seriously than others, but it is generally fair to say that no strict dress code is adhered to; a participant is as likely to wear a T-shirt bearing a Celtic design as a 'traditional' long white robe.

A number of Gorseths (or Gorseddau) have been established (or some would say 're-established') by contemporary Druid groups, such as the BDO. These are frequently connected with what are perceived as sacred sites (such as Avebury and Stonehenge in Wiltshire, and the Rollright Stones and the Uffington White Horse in Oxfordshire), although in 1998 the BDO inaugurated the Gorsedd of the Bards of Caer Troia in Milton Keynes! Generally speaking (and in sharp contrast with the Welsh Gorsedd and Cornish Gorseth), people become bards at such Gorseths by self-selection (i.e. without audition or demonstration of their poetic or musical talent) and with no reference to Celtic language, by taking part in a ceremony during which the Awen (inspiration) is called down or conferred upon them.

---

[13] One English Druid described the Welsh Gorsedd as 'racist' because of its insistence on the use of the Welsh language.

That is not to say, however, that becoming a bard is not regarded by participants as a serious undertaking. Awen can be understood not simply as poetic or creative inspiration, but 'the divine inspiration that flows, spirit to spirit, between the people, the land and the ancestors'.[14]

There is considerable variety within contemporary Druidry (Pagan Druids and Christian Druids, even self-styled Zen Druids and Hassidic Druids) and differing levels of commitment, formality and seriousness. The Cotswold Order of Druids, for example, declares that 'Druidry is not a hobby; it is a vocation' (Shallcrass and Restall Orr, 2001, p.59), while the Berengaria Order of Druids is 'dedicated to the aims, ideals and whatever else of Star Trek ... and Babylon 5 ... plus any other sci-fi that takes our fancy' (ibid.). While some view Druidry as something that existed in the past and about which we have limited information, for many practising Druids it is a living tradition. As the BDO declares:

> We draw inspiration from the sacred land and from our ancestry; the mud and blood of Britain, whose myths and mysteries are the well-spring of our tradition ... Although we work with the long spiritual and cultural heritage of Britain, we are not bound by any one aspect of it. We are not seeking to recreate a Druidry that may have existed 5000, 2000, 200 or 50 years ago. We see Druidry as a process of constant change and renewal whereby the tradition is continually recreated to address the needs of each generation.
>
> (*The Druids' Voice*, vol.8, summer 1997, p.31)

Some see Druidry as specifically rooted in Celtic tradition. The French Druids of Ecole Druidique des Gaules 'believe that, on the deep roots of Druidry, Europe could be rebuilt, and that the spirituality of the Celts is the only one which represents the collective Indo-European heritage common to all Europe' (Shallcrass and Restall Orr, 2001, p.80). One of the aims of the Insular Order of Druids[15] is 'to spread and encourage interest in Celticism, and the general knowledge of our heritage and lore, poems and myths and anything Celtically cultural' (ibid., p.65). However, as Druidry is seen as a living phenomenon, another aim is 'to recreate to the best of their knowledge authentic Celtic ritual, minus the bloodshed, within the framework of twentieth-century law and ethics, in a working form

---

[14] This description of Awen is taken from the publicity for the BDO's midsummer camp 2001, 'Awen: the spirit of inspiration'.

[15] The founder of this group was described in a Druid publication as someone who 'used to practise the shamanic arts of body piercing and tattooing at Labyrinth, a New Age gift shop and centre for Celtic spirituality in Portsmouth' (Shallcrass and Restall Orr, 2001, p.65).

relevant for today' (ibid., p.66). Similarly, the Charnwood Grove of Druids:

> ... see Druidry as a modern adaptation of our native British spirituality which addresses contemporary problems and dilemmas in a manner that is uniquely suited to our needs ... We believe that people working together are capable of raising power which can balance and heal the Earth. We focus our energy at local sacred sites and we honour the Celtic god and goddess forms as personifications of the land and the seasons. We seek inspiration from our ancestors and we work with traditional Celtic symbols, myths and the tree *ogham* to reveal the power of our inner guides and totems.
>
> (Shallcrass and Restall Orr, 2001, pp.56–7)

For some of those regarding Druidry as native spirituality, it seems natural to incorporate elements from other native traditions; thus, the groom at a Druidic handfasting (wedding) at Avebury wore a long white robe with a digeridoo slung on one shoulder throughout the ceremony, and there are now Druidic sweat lodges (sweat lodges are discussed in Chapter 3). Again, opinions vary as to whether this is justified 'revival', creative borrowing and respectful enhancement of one native tradition by reference to another, or rather dubious cultural theft.

In 1964, the Order of Bards, Ovates and Druids (OBOD) was formed. According to its publicity leaflet:

> The Order is not a cult or religion – it simply represents a particular way of working with, and understanding the Self and the natural world.

OBOD's stated aims are 'to help each person to develop their spiritual, intellectual, emotional, physical and artistic potential' and 'to work with the natural world, to cherish and protect it, and to co-operate with it in every way – both esoterically and exoterically' (Shallcrass and Restall Orr, 2001, p.70). Since 1988, OBOD has run a correspondence course in Druidry, and through readings, tapes and workbooks one can progress through the different grades, from Bard to Druid. At the Bard level, the student studies basic subjects such as the four elements, the circle of nature, the Sun, the Earth, the calendar, poetry and the development of the artistic self. After initiation into the Ovate grade, the student works on healing and divinatory skills, a study of sacred trees, animals and plants, sacred sites and ley lines,[16] and Arthurian legend. At the Druid Grade, study

---

[16] Ley lines are considered to be lines or tracks conveying some sort of earth energy, and are a common feature of alternative spirituality; for a useful summary, see Marcus, 1987, pp.1–10.

of the Grail and Arthurian myths continues, and the Druid is also shown how to open and lead a grove. (Various other Druidic qualifications exist, offered by an assortment of groups and individuals, including the Degree in Druidry certified by the Druid College of Avalon in Glastonbury.[17])

The Druid Order (also known as The British Circle of the Universal Bond) claims to be a continuation of the Mount Haemus Grove which it asserts was founded in Oxford in 1245, 'reconstituted' in 1717 from Druid groups which had continued to exist in various parts of the British Isles and Brittany; it claims Stukeley and Blake among its former chieftains. Deriving from 'a previous phase of human development long since vanished from the earth's surface', the Order claims that Druidry recognizes each person as 'a miniature cosmos, internally sourced with light, energy and wisdom' (introductory leaflet).

There are those who see in the current Celtic and Druidic revival the fulfilment of ideas which started to be 'revealed' in the eighteenth century. Some have been attracted to the city of Bath, for example, because of its supposed Druidic connections. In August 1995, Tim Sebastion, Chosen Chief of the Secular Order of Druids, held a ceremony on Solsbury Hill (which he claimed was 'one of the old bardic sites of the chief Druids') to establish a 'Bardic Chair' in Bath. On 28 November 1997 (William Blake's birthday), at noon, a Gorsedd of Caer Badon (Bath's 'Celtic' name) was held in Bath at the Circus designed by John Wood (Figure 2.9). Overseen by Arthur Uther Pendragon[18] as Champion and Protector of the Gorsedd, the ceremony was attended not only by members of SOD, but by Druids from the Cotswolds Order of Druids and OBOD, some guests, and some curious members of the public who were invited to join in. Sebastion declared that Wood was a Druid, explained the Druidic nature of Wood's design for the Circus, and claimed that Wood had designed the Circus as a forum for Druidic ceremony (Bowman, 1998). Thus, some feel that Wood's Druidic vision of Bath is at last being realized, and, as Sebastion commented that day, 'We are seeing the return of everything Blake talked of'.

---

[17] Some believe that Glastonbury was once the site of a huge Druidic University, to which students came from all over Europe.

[18] Arthur Uther Pendragon believes that he is a reincarnation of King Arthur, who in legend was thought to lie sleeping until some great time of national emergency; Arthur Uther Pendragon claims this is a time of *spiritual* emergency for Britain, and he is involved in various Druid gatherings.

Figure 2.9 Arthur Uther Pendragon (left) and Tim Sebastion of the Secular Order of Druids in a Druidic ceremony at the Circus, Bath, 1997. Copyright Marion Bowman.

Christians and Druids

Although at times in the past Druids were portrayed as cruel tormentors of Christian missionaries (see Figure 2.10) and some lives of Celtic saints present Druids and Christians as arch enemies, it is increasingly common in some circles to view the transition from the old religion to Christianity as essentially smooth and harmonious. Very much in the spirit of eighteenth-century writers such as Stukeley, who saw Druids as proto-Christians, the Druids are said to have foreseen the coming of Christianity, even to have welcomed it. Sebastion has commented: 'the Druidic colleges were merely replaced by Christian cells ... There was, it would appear, absolutely

Figure 2.10 William Holman Hunt, *A Converted British Family Sheltering a Christian Priest from the Druids*, 1850, oil on canvas on panel, 111 x 141 cm. Ashmolean Museum, Oxford.

no conflict between the early Celtic Christian tradition and the pagan, or Druidic tradition' (Shallcrass and Restall Orr, 2001, p.73).

So strong is this belief that it is sometimes assumed that wherever there was Celtic Christianity, it would have been preceded by Druidry. In some branches of contemporary Celtic spirituality, then, it is believed that the 'unique nature' of Celtic Christianity owed much to the fact that it preserved a body of esoteric wisdom, known to Druids but unknown to other branches of Christianity.

Celtic Christianity

To put the contemporary interest in Celtic Christianity into context, it is useful to note Ian Bradley's claim that what we are experiencing now is the sixth and latest form of 'Celtic Christian revivalism' (1999, p.viii). The first revival he places in the eighth and ninth centuries, 'when hagiographers first created idealised portraits of the Celtic saints and Bede compared the purity of the golden age of Aidan and Cuthbert with the corruption of his own day', while the second arose in the twelfth and thirteenth centuries, 'stimulated partly by the new

Anglo-Norman rulers of the British Isles and partly by the outburst of romantic imagination that produced the Arthurian legends and the Quest for the Holy Grail' (p.viii). The Reformation sparked 'interest in and appropriation of the Celtic Church as a prototype of sturdy independent British Protestantism',[19] while in the eighteenth and nineteenth centuries 'antiquarianism, growing national conscious-ness, denominational rivalries and the influence of the romantic movement' (p.viii) gave shape and appeal to Celtic Christianity. The fifth revival grew out of the late nineteenth/early twentieth-century Celtic revival mentioned earlier, and focused on Iona as 'a place of exceptional spiritual power, ecumenical potential and renewal of the church' (p.viii), and we are now still experiencing the sixth revival, which started in the late twentieth century. Bradley points out that in all the revivals, 'the leading protagonists have generally, although not exclusively, been non-Celts' (p.viii), and that 'A persistent vein of nostalgia has allowed those Christians who lived in the sixth and seventh centuries, about whose faith and work we know next to nothing first hand, to become paragons of a pure and primitive faith' (p.ix).

For many Christians, as I have already indicated, Celtic Christianity tends to be seen as more spiritual, more intuitive, more egalitarian, more in tune with nature than other brands of Christianity – all qualities that are felt by many to be missing from the institutionalized Church. However, what exactly is meant by Celtic Christianity, how that Celtic Christianity can best be recaptured, exactly what it was, and who can rightfully claim to be the heirs of Celtic Christianity, are all matters for debate. ('The quest for Celtic Christianity' by Donald E. Meek, a native Gaelic speaker from Tiree and Professor of Celtic at Aberdeen University, is reproduced in Part Two of this volume. It explores a number of issues concerning what is said about the Celtic Church and what there seems to be evidence for, and the reasons that there is sometimes a mismatch in perception between these two.)

Is Celtic Christianity the same as the Celtic Church? If so, does it start in the fourth century, or the first? Does the Celtic Church end with 664, the Synod of Whitby, portrayed by some as the clash between the Gaelic and the Anglo-Saxon strands of Christianity, the point when the Roman Church imposed its will on the Celtic Church over the dating of Easter?[20] There is undoubtedly an element of

[19] I have been told by a lapsed Anglican, now a Druid, that Henry VIII's 'real plan' was to restore the Celtic Church, but it all got horribly subverted.

[20] Meek points out that by 633 some churches in southern Ireland had already adopted the Roman (or Dionysian) dating, and that the Welsh churches did not adopt the Dionysian method of calculating Easter until 768 (Meek, 2000, pp.137–8).

religious Euroscepticism – if not denominational antagonism – in some of this. A number of people have spoken to me of the Celtic Church as 'our roots' or 'our native Christianity' before Roman Christianity 'was imposed on us'. A staunch Presbyterian commented, 'You and I both know that if the Church of Rome hadn't taken over the Celtic Church, there probably would have been no need for the Reformation.'

Was there in fact one institution, the Celtic Church, covering early Scotland, Ireland, Wales, Cornwall, Brittany and, through missionary activity from Iona, the north of England? Or, as Meek suggests, was there:

> ... a 'Gaelic Church' which functioned in the Gaelic-speaking regions of Ireland and Scotland, a 'Welsh Church' in Wales, and the corresponding entities in Cornwall, Brittany and Northumbria, each with a different complexion depending upon the prevailing local culture?

(Meek, 2000, p.105)

Does Celtic Christianity simply comprise Christianity in what are perceived as Celtic areas? If so, that would embrace such varied bedfellows as Scottish Highland Catholicism, Welsh Methodism and Ulster Protestantism, none of which entirely coincide with the popular, 'soft' image of Celtic Christianity.

While there are things we know with some certainty about the early Gaelic church of Ireland and Scotland – the dating of Easter; the distinctive tonsure,[21] mixed houses of both monks and nuns (indeed, married religieux, because celibacy was not a condition of holy orders); a large penitential literature detailing the private penances to be enacted for various sins (such as standing up to the waist in freezing sea water); passionate and persistent missionary activity; a tendency to withdraw to remote and hostile environments, either singly or in small groups – these tend not to be the hallmarks of contemporary Celtic Christianity. Rather, contemporary Celtic Christianity tends to be perceived and experienced in terms of closeness to nature, tolerance, holism and 'freedom of spirit'. It is expressed visually in Celtic crosses and artwork, verbally in 'Celtlish' prayers, blessings and literature, and physically in pilgrimage.

Celtic Christianity tends to be characterized as gentle, 'green', meditative, holistic Christianity. Shirley Toulson, for example, claims that 'if we want to understand the depths of Celtic spirituality we shall

---

[21] Among monks, the front part of the hair was shaved sideways (i.e. from the forehead to a line ear to ear over the top of the head), rather than the more familiar tonsure involving the crown of the head being shaved.

find the nearest parallels in the Buddhist teaching of today as well as in the creation spirituality of such Christian teachers as Matthew Fox' (Toulson, 1996, p.15).[22] The growth of interest in what are perceived as important Celtic Christian places and people connected with them (such as Iona and St Columba, Lindisfarne and St Aidan, Kildare and St Bride), and the revival of traditions associated with Celtic holy wells and springs, reinforces the idea of closeness to nature. Iona, for example, has become important for a great variety of Christians, a place of spiritual refreshment, remote and beautiful, very much 'on the edge' for most people travelling there, thus conforming to and confirming a particular image of 'otherworldly' Celtic Christianity. For many, the Iona Community (founded in the 1930s and very much rooted in Presbyterian social concern) seems to have become an icon of Celtic spirituality, its ecumenism taken to be a reflection of Celtic Christianity, which is perceived as relaxed and gentle, not bogged down in internal division. Iona Community songs (sometimes set to Scottish folk tunes) and prayers are felt by a variety of denominations to add a Celtic flavour to worship.

Celtic Christianity has become a means whereby Protestant denominations can act atypically and experimentally, for example, by going on pilgrimage. As Meek points out:

> Members of relatively old denominations and religious bodies such as Baptists, historically hostile to monasticism, wary of liturgies, and suspicious of symbols such as crosses, are prepared to accommodate these elements into their 'Celtic' experiments.
>
> (Meek, 1996, p.153)

In worship and writings on Celtic Christianity, much use is made of Carmichael's collection of Gaelic texts from the Hebrides, *Carmina Gadelica*, and a whole genre of 'writing in the Celtic tradition' has emerged (Meek, 2000, pp.12–13). The latter includes the work of David Adam, Vicar of Holy Isle (Lindisfarne), whose modern 'Celtlish' prayers and blessings, written since 1980, often appear alongside older translated material in Celtic anthologies, underlining the seemingly timeless and homogenous nature of Celtic Christianity. Examples of this literature also tend to appear on prayer cards edged with knotwork, the visual clue that this is Celtic (see Colour Plate 3).

---

[22] Connections between Buddhism and Celtic spirituality are often made, both directly and indirectly. The Tibetan Buddhists of Samye Ling monastery in southern Scotland have purchased as a place of retreat Holy Isle (off the Scottish island of Arran), said to have been inhabited by a Celtic saint.

In Christian denominations that have robes or ecclesiastical embroidery, Celtic motifs (particularly Celtic crosses) are appearing more frequently.[23] Celtic paraphernalia (Celtic crosses, Celtic prayers and merchandise decorated with Celtic motifs and Celtic lettering) have become increasingly popular in British cathedral and church shops, and residential courses and workshops on various aspects of Celtic Christianity proliferate. So, through a variety of means – verbal, visual and active – people can feel close to, or participate in, what seems a purer, more 'spiritual' form of Christianity.

Among the 'proofs' of Celtic Christianity's holism are the many blessings and prayers to be found in the *Carmina Gadelica* that deal with the most mundane aspects of life. Meek suggests, however, that:

> It could be argued that the prayers and charms in the *Carmina* tell us nothing whatsoever about the way in which Highlanders viewed spirit and matter as such; rather, the *Carmina* focus on the activities and the day-to-day lives of the people, and invoke the blessing of God and the saints on all relevant human endeavour. Such invocation surely implies that the material world is a hostile environment which inspires fear and requires to be kept under control by superior and more benign forces.
>
> (Meek, 2000, p.70)

Alternatively, in the popular perception of Celtic Christianity's holism, and with it the realization that the sacralizing of everyday life might be both possible and desirable, it could be argued that at the turn of the third millennium Christians are rediscovering pre-modern perspectives and what has been and remains self-evident to religious adherents around the world – that religion *is* a way of life.

Issue of authenticity

> … any picture of Early Celtic Europe is necessarily based upon a rather comprehensive ignorance. I make this point, since one could be forgiven for thinking, after reading one of the many illustrated books on the Celts, that the authors had been round pre-Roman barbarian Europe with camera and tape-recorder.
>
> (Chapman, 1992, p.6)

---

[23] *The Grapevine* (official newspaper of the Anglican diocese of Bath and Wells) for January 1998, for example, reported 'A Celtic theme for new vestments for St Andrew's, Cheddar, was chosen by their designer Janet Knox to "compliment the Church and its very long history"'. They include a set 'embroidered with versions of the four evangelists described in the Revelation of St John and in the style of Celtic manuscripts' (vol.8, no.1, p.10).

> There's something there, a wonderful ambience, and we can localize it
> as no one is sure who the Celts really were. It doesn't matter about
> strict historicity – it sets up a wonderful warm glow of hope, helps you
> feel more integrated. What we need in the West is a Celtic renaissance.
>
> (comment of a self-styled New Ager in Glastonbury)

There is no doubt that a great number of people consider their spiritual lives enriched and enhanced by Celtic spirituality, and I have briefly given some flavour of its diversity and vitality. One of the most striking contrasts between some Celtic scholars and contemporary Celtic spirituality practitioners is the degree of certainty with which the latter present their vision of the past. Scholars are aware of gaps in archaeological evidence and the unreliability of some historical sources, and they acknowledge limits as to what can safely be inferred from the available evidence. They point out that the people now described as Celts would not actually have identified themselves thus, and that the Celts in the British Isles were not one homogenous group, nor are they now. Some practitioners of Celtic spirituality, however, perceive a self-aware pan-Celtic culture and worldview, details of which are confidently enumerated. They believe they have achieved – or are well on their way to constructing – a complete picture of the Celts and their world, through inspiration, interpretation of cultural tradition and esoterically transmitted knowledge. Is it either possible or desirable to bridge that gap between scholarly tentativeness and spiritual certainty?

To some extent, it is a matter of perspective. In contemporary Celtic spirituality, for example, Celtic language material is often regarded in the same way as other previously 'hidden knowledge' which is now surfacing. Meek uses the example of the cover notes of Robert Van de Weyer's *Celtic Fire* (1990) – 'Composed in languages long extinct, Celtic literature has been inaccessible for many centuries' – to make the point that:

> Both these claims – about the extinction of the Celtic languages and
> the inaccessibility of the literature – are manifestly incorrect. What
> they do tell us is that Celtic literature is falling into the hands of some
> people who know nothing about its background, and assume that
> nobody else does either.
>
> (Meek, 1992, p.14)

While some involved in Celtic spirituality are learning Celtic languages to enable them to read material in the original, to express solidarity with the Celtic people, or to enhance their ritual practice, for the most part it is the message not the medium that is considered important. It is the experience and efficacy of Celtic spirituality which confirm people in their belief and practice, not linguistic expertise.

Another area where academic and practitioner viewpoints might diverge concerns the Celtic calendar. Although keeping the eightfold calendar is one of the few consistent and unifying aspects of Celtic Paganism, the existence of such a calendar is contested. The historian Ronald Hutton contends that there is 'absolutely no firm evidence in the written record that the year opened on 1 November in either early Ireland or early Wales, and a great deal in the Welsh material to refute the idea' (Hutton, 1996, p.410).

While some use varied material from Celtic myth and literature to support and explain the calendar (e.g. Matthews, 1989, pp.83–93), others express scepticism that identical seasonal ceremonies and the same calendar would have been kept throughout the British Isles (let alone Europe), with their variations in temperature, agriculture and daylight hours. Hutton suggests instead that:

> The notion of a distinctive 'Celtic' ritual year, with four festivals at the quarter-days and an opening at Samhain, is a scholastic construction of the eighteenth and nineteenth centuries which should now be considerably revised or even abandoned altogether.
>
> (Hutton, 1996, p.411)

Nevertheless, whether or not there *was* an eightfold Celtic calendar, it is *now* firmly part of the spiritual life of those who regard themselves as practitioners of contemporary Celtic spirituality.

Caitlin Matthews has been described as an 'initiator within the Celtic tradition', which captures the apparent need for Celtic roots coupled with the element of personal choice and inspiration which is a hallmark of contemporary religiosity. She writes of practitioners of Celtic spiritual traditions that:

> Celtic ethnicity is not necessarily a prerequisite, as might be imagined. We have entered a phase of maturity wherein *spiritual lineage* transcends blood lineage ... The impulse for joining such groups often springs from exposure to the lands of Britain and Ireland, or from reading stories and myths deriving from Celtic tradition. A sense of belonging is also often felt from perceived memory of previous incarnation.
>
> (Matthews, 1993, p.7)

Thus, being or feeling Celtic is something that can be acquired, from contact with the land, or from encountering some aspect of Celtic cultural tradition – a sort of contagious Celticity. People visiting what are perceived to be 'Celtic' destinations, whether Ireland, Scotland, Wales and Cornwall in general, or more specific locations like Iona, Glastonbury, Lindisfarne, New Grange and Avebury, often comment on the 'feel' or 'energy' of such places. There is thus the authenticating nature of the experience of place.

Matthews' comment on the perceived memory of previous incarnation is also extremely significant. Ideas of reincarnation are being used by some to explain or express their current feelings of Celticity. For example, one American told me that as soon as he went to Scotland, he realized he had been a Scot in a past life. If reincarnation is connected with going back to the past for an explanation of the present, we should remember that much of what is being said about the Celtic past is the result of 'channelling',[24] which is largely about the past coming to the present, a way of being authoritative about the past in the present, and experiencing the past in the present. The Insular Order of Druids believes that 'As Druidry is a growing movement ... the channelling of new Druidic information is of paramount importance'. Thus, at its meetings, you will not only 'hear genuine Celtic stories told in the bardic way. You will hear new channelled material' (Shallcrass and Restall Orr, 2001, p.73).

The difference between the emic and etic (outsider/insider, academic/practitioner) approaches to Celtic myth might be compared to the difference between Biblical Studies scholars, sifting through texts while engaged in scholarly criticism, and those for whom the Bible is the word of God which speaks to them in a personal and meaningful way, and to which they can turn for inspiration and answers. Thus, while for the scholar of Celtic literature the overriding concerns are those of dating, provenance, authorship, authenticity and so on, for the practitioner Celtic myths and poetry or material derived from them are read for clues to the beliefs, lifestyles and worldviews of the Celts. They can also have a far more active role. Matthews writes of the use of such material as spiritual exercises:

> ... traditional stories and myths are memorised and retold, not in any pretentious folkloric way, but as living pathways of spiritual wisdom. The spiritual beings encountered in these scenarios give actual teaching and often provide otherworldly and ancestral guidance to those bereft of ordinary reality tutors. By meditative interface with these stories, the Celtic tradition is passed on.
>
> (Matthews, 1993, p.7)

This internalized, interactive transmission is obviously not something which lends itself to 'objective' or external checking.

---

[24] Channelling occurs when a person acts as a channel for, or transmitter of, messages and information from the spirit world or other dimensions, frequently from individuals (such as spiritual teachers) who have lived in the past but are able to communicate in the present.

One of the major problems some scholars (and practitioners) have with contemporary Celtic spirituality in its myriad forms is that they see it as inaccurate and 'inauthentic'. However, from the foregoing it should be becoming obvious that ideas of authenticity are tricky, for the criteria of authenticity and modes of authenticating which are operating in the various forms of contemporary Celtic spirituality are not necessarily located in the Celtic past, nor are they available for empirical scrutiny. They are more often situated in the traits of religiosity at the turn of the third millennium which were discussed earlier. One of the points you frequently have to make as a Religious Studies scholar is that you are not *doing* religion, you are *studying* it. Conversely, Celtic spirituality is not an exercise in Celtic Studies; people are *doing* Celtic spirituality. A frequently quoted maxim in Religious Studies is that 'God is real for Christians whether or not he exists' (Smart, 1973, p.54). Similarly, we might now say that the 'spiritual Celt' is real for a great variety of believers, whether she or he existed or exists.

From Celtic fringe to cyberspace

> Everywhere, cultural identities are emerging which are not fixed, but poised, in *transition*, between different positions; which draw on different cultural traditions at the same time; and which are the product of those complicated cross-overs and cultural mixes which are increasingly common in a globalized world.
>
> (Hall *et al.*, 1992, p.310)

The term 'Celtic revival' is ambiguous. It is unclear whether it means those who are traditionally thought of as Celts are 'reviving', or that non-Celts are turning to and 'reviving' Celtic culture and traditions. In the present context, there is an element of both. To put it another way, it is not just a case of who are the Celts but *whose* are the Celts in contemporary Celtic spirituality.

Although 'Celtic' is being used in some contexts as code for 'long ago and far away' and Celts are to some extent being honoured as Noble Savages, Celtic lands and those being designated Celts are not distant in time and space. Indeed, many people are flocking to 'Celtic' destinations. At the intersection of 'Cardiac Celts' – people who feel in their hearts that they are Celtic (Bowman, 1996) – and conventional Celts, there is the possibility of friction; a conventional Celt may see a Cardiac Celt as a cultural imperialist or cultural transvestite rather than as a kindred spirit. John Davies has forcefully expressed some of his reservations and exasperation in this respect:

> I do not wish to see Ireland marketed for its sad air of the uncanny, when that is because it is full of ghosts; the ghosts of the million who starved to death in the famine of 1846/7 ...
>
> I do not wish to see the empty landscape of the Hebrides extolled for its beauty, when it is empty because of brutal clearances.
>
> I do not wish to see you create a homogenised pabulum of Celtic culture ...
>
> I do not wish to encounter hordes of eager-eyed acolytes who don't know the first thing about the reality of Wales. I do not wish to meet their teacher; some self-appointed Saxon expert on Celtia, whose tongue stumbles over the simplest Welsh place-names.
>
> I do not wish to see the less acceptable aspects of my ancestors glossed over, in order to create yet another sanitized 'noble savage' for your consumption.
>
> (Davies, 1993, p.5)

For, whatever it was in the past, 'Celtic' nowadays is not simply a designation or label applied by outsiders. Even writers such as Chapman and James, who have attracted (often virulent) criticism for their denial of the existence of self-designated, self-aware Celts in the past, agree that Celts do exist now:

> Not only are there large groups of people thought to be Celts by others (as has happened before), but there are also large groups of people that think they are Celts themselves. This is a very modern phenomenon, but is nevertheless real: if people think they are Celts, who is to gainsay them?
>
> (Chapman, 1992, p.251)

With the developing nationalisms of the eighteenth and nineteenth centuries, many embraced Celtic identity as a way of distinguishing themselves from the English cultural 'other', a process that continues in the current post-devolution consideration of British national identity. 'Celtic' has become an 'ethonym', an appellation adopted by people themselves, not simply applied to them by outsiders.

Moreover, it should be remembered that ambiguous identities existed, and indeed continue to exist, *within* those lands now designated Celtic by both insiders and outsiders. In Scotland, for example, there was traditionally an element of internal 'fringery' on the part of Lowland, Protestant, Scots-speaking Scots in relation to the Catholic, Gaelic-speaking Highlanders. After the defeat of Highland forces supporting 'Bonnie Prince Charlie' at Culloden in 1746, however, the Highlanders, no longer regarded as dangerous, became 'a wild and romantic Other' (James, 1999, p.128). This image was fostered in the eighteenth century by the Ossian forgeries in which

Highlanders were depicted as noble savages,[25] bolstered in the nineteenth century by the Lowlander Sir Walter Scott's romantic novels, and is perpetuated now in films such as 'Braveheart' and 'Rob Roy' – the soft primitivism of the tartan shortbread tin in which Scots have consistently colluded.

So we might say that there are now two ways of describing Celts: Celts as 'other' – the designation of the fringe by the mainstream; and Celts as 'not English', the ethonym adopted by 'geographical' Celts such as Welsh, Irish, Scots, Cornish – the self-designation of the fringe in relation to the mainstream.

However, might it be possible to argue for a third description – the Cardiac Celts, Celts as the result of elective affinity, or indeed elective ethnicity – the designation from the heart? As we have seen, the spiritual Celt is to an extent the product of modern Celticism and the contemporary religious milieu. For being Celtic not only allows one to be 'not English'; it allows one to be 'not British' (with all the attendant imperial baggage), 'not like the mainstream', 'not exploiter' of either other peoples or the environment; in short, 'not guilty'.[26] For the Cardiac Celt, to feel Celtic is to become Celtic; to become Celtic is to become part of an ancient yet still developing, universal yet highly individual, pure spiritual tradition. And what is more, nowadays that can even be done from the comfort of one's own home.

Ironically, as Celticity becomes regarded as a quality that can be commodified and acquired, it provides 'roots' while itself becoming increasingly uprooted or physically rootless. This is perhaps epitomized by the CyberCelts. There is a considerable and varied Celtic presence in cyberspace. The Celtic Thistle Awards for 'excellence in Celtic-oriented websites', for example, includes among past winners not just 'Scottish Crafts Direct', but 'Raven's Moon Pagan Page' (2000), 'The Techno Pagans Unlimited' (1999) and 'Celtica – The Virtual Nation of the Celts' (1999). (Something about the latter can be found on http://celt.net.)[27]

In the realm of cyber community, as with other 'communities of assent', familial relations are replaced with 'metaphorical brothers, mothers, sisters and fathers' (Morris, 1996, p.239). Thus, there are various Cyber Clans. Clann an Fhaoil-Choin (Clan of the Wolfhound),

[25] In the 1760s, James Macpherson published two 'translations' of epic poems by the bard Ossian, which he claimed to have discovered in the Highlands.

[26] One American Pagan described to me how liberating it had been for her to discover her Celtic (Irish) roots, for instead of being 'Anglo', 'the oppressor', she was thereafter able to identify and more easily interact with Native Americans and other oppressed minorities.

[27] All web sites listed in this chapter were most recently accessed in January 2002.

for example, describes itself as 'a Celtic family, come together from many backgrounds to honour our ancestors and keep alive the Celtic ways' (http://www.flash.net/~bellbook/faolcu/). In self-consciously romantic and anachronistic manner, the Clan records 'hits' (i.e. the number of times the site has been logged on to) with the words 'Our cyber-hearth has been visited xxxx times'. Summerlands (http://summerlands.com) is 'an online Celtic Pagan Community ... who meet online daily to discuss Celtic and Druidic ways' (Shallcrass and Restall Orr, 2001, p.102).

The CyberCelts provide the example *par excellence* of ahistorical and ageographical Celticism. In 1998, for example, Clan Keltoi announced 'the formation of a new clan':

> This is a call to those who cherish the pre-christian Celtic ways! It is a call to those who are proud to be Celts but don't 'fit in' to the 'established' revisionist description of Celtic society! Please note that the question IS NOT ... 'are you of Scottish, Irish or Welsh heritage?'. Celtic heritage does not begin nor end in these places, but rather extends to nearly every corner of the globe. It's not where your family came from ... it is a passion in your heart that makes you a Celt!
>
> (http://celt.net/Keltoi.home.html)

Conclusion

Contemporary Celtic spirituality floats on a raft of ideas of comparatively recent construction. Thus, the focus of this chapter has not been what happened in the Celtic past (whenever and however that might be dated) to Celts (however they might be defined), but what today's spiritual searchers *believe* happened to people *perceived* as Celts, and how that impacts on their religious belief and practice in the present. Or, to put it another way, this has been an exercise in Celticism: 'not the study of the Celts and their history, but rather the study of their reputation and of the meanings and connotations ascribed to the term "Celtic"' (Leerssen, 1996, p.3).

The varied and vibrant phenomena of contemporary Celtic spirituality challenge and renegotiate a number of boundaries: temporal, spatial, linguistic, denominational, disciplinary, methodological, national, cultural and personal. They also reinforce and revisit a number of themes and issues we encounter elsewhere in this volume, particularly representation, appropriation and identity.

The folklorist Henry Glassie claims that 'tradition is the creation of the future out of the past', and that history 'is an artful assembly of materials from the past, designed for usefulness in the future' (1995, p.395). What we have seen in this brief exploration of contemporary Celtic spirituality is an 'artful assembly of materials' not so much from the Celtic past but from previous periods of interest in and speculation about Celts, and how these interact with contemporary religious trends. We have also seen examples of the creation of tradition from a variety of sources.

Perhaps the two most apposite images with which to end are the Celt as walker between the worlds and the Celt as shape shifter. The worlds the spiritual Celt walks between are not just this world and the other world of spirits, but also between the post-industrial landscapes of Wales, Scotland and Cornwall and the spiritually imbued never-never land of the highlands and islands, the Welsh hills, the Cornish moors, perceived as untarnished by materialism and modernity. As we have seen, the shape of the Celt has been shifted over the centuries by diverse interest groups, ideological, political, nationalist, academic and religious. However, the agility of this image, and the ability of the Celt to meet a variety of emic and etic needs, seems to indicate that the Celt will continue to provide a powerful 'anam chara', or soul friend, for assorted spiritual seekers for many years to come.

References

Bennett, G. (1993) 'Folklore studies and the English rural myth', *Rural History*, vol.4, no.1, pp.77–91.

Bowman, M. (1993) 'Reinventing the Celts', *Religion*, vol.23, no.1, pp.47–56.

Bowman, M. (1994) 'The commodification of the Celt: New Age/Neo-Pagan consumerism', *Folklore in Use*, vol.2, no.1, pp.43–52.

Bowman, M. (1995) 'The noble savage and the global village: cultural evolution in New Age and Neo-Pagan thought', *Journal of Contemporary Religion*, vol.10, no.2, pp.139–49.

Bowman, M. (1996) 'Cardiac Celts: images of the Celts in contemporary British Paganism', in G. Harvey and C. Hardman (eds) pp.242–51.

Bowman, M. (1998) 'Belief, legend and perceptions of the sacred in contemporary Bath', *Folklore*, vol.109, pp.25–31.

Bowman, M. (2000) 'Contemporary Celtic spirituality', in A. Hale and P. Payton (eds) *New Directions in Celtic Studies*, Exeter: Exeter University Press, pp.69–91.

Bowman, M. and Harvey, G. (eds) (2000) *Pagan Identities*, http://www.uni-marburg.de/religionswissenschaft/journal/diskus/ 6 (electronic journal).

Bradley, I. (1993) *The Celtic Way*, London: Darton, Longman & Todd.

Bradley, I. (1999) *Celtic Christianity: Making Myths and Chasing Dreams*, Edinburgh: Edinburgh University Press.

Brown, T. (1996) 'Cultural nationalism, Celticism and the occult', in T. Brown (ed.) pp.221–30.

Brown, T. (ed.) (1996) *Celticism*, Amsterdam: Studia Imagologica (Amsterdam Studies on Cultural Identity, 8).

Burl, A. (2001) 'Stonehenge: how did the stones get there?', *History Today*, vol.51, no.3, pp.19–25.

Champion, T. (1996) 'The Celt in archaeology' in T. Brown (ed.) pp.61–78.

Chapman, M. (1992) *The Celts: The Construction of a Myth*, New York: St Martin's Press.

Collis, J. (1996) 'The origin and spread of the Celts', *Studia Celtica*, vol.xxx, pp.17–34.

Constantine, P. (1993) 'Borderlands: the Celtic world of imagination, and the arts', *Celtic Connections*, vol.5, December, pp.9–10.

Cynan (1989) 'I believe in the Gorsedd of Bards', Programme for the Proclamation Ceremony of the Royal National Eisteddfod of Wales, Rhymney Valley, 1990, in The Gorsedd Circle, Bargoed Park, Bargoed.

Davies, J. (1993) *Three Things There Are, That Are Seldom Heard: A Comment on Modern Shamanism*, London: House of the Goddess.

Glassie, H. (1995) 'Tradition', *Journal of American Folklore*, vol.108, no.430, pp.395–412.

Gomme, A. and Gomme, L. (1916) *British Folk-Lore, Folk Songs, and Singing Games*, London: National Home-Reading Union.

Grobman, N.R. (1982) 'Primitivism versus progress: the Scottish Enlightenment's reaction to epic and mythology', *Lore and Language*, vol.3, no.6, pp.1–17.

Hale, A. (2000) 'In the eye of the sun': the relationship between the Cornish Gorseth and esoteric Druidry', in P. Payton (ed.) *Cornish Studies Eight*, Exeter: Exeter University Press, pp.182–96.

Hale, A. (2001) 'Whose Celtic Cornwall? The ethnic Cornish meet Celtic spirituality', in D.C. Harvey, R. Jones, N. McInroy and C. Milligan (eds) *Celtic Geographies: Old Cultures, New Times*, London and New York: Routledge.

Hall, S. (1992) 'The question of cultural identiy', in S. Hall, D. Held and T. McGrew (eds) *Modernity and its Futures*, Cambridge: Polity Press in association with the Open University.

Harvey, G. and Hardman, C. (eds) (1996) *Paganism Today*, London: Thorsons.

Hobsbawm, E. (1984) 'Introduction: inventing traditions', in E. Hobsbawm and T. Ranger (eds) *The Invention of Tradition*, Cambridge: Cambridge University Press, pp.1–14.

Hutton, R. (1996) *The Stations of the Sun: A History of the Ritual Year in Britain*, Oxford: Oxford University Press.

Jakobsen, M.D. (1999) *Shamanism: Traditional and Modern Approaches to the Mastery of Spirits and Healing*, New York and Oxford: Berghahn Books.

James, S. (1999) *The Atlantic Celts: Ancient People or Modern Invention?*, London: British Museum Press.

Keynes, G. (ed.) (1979 edn) *Blake: Complete Writings*, Oxford: Oxford University Press.

Kiberd, D. (1995) *Inventing Ireland*, London: Jonathan Cape.

Leerssen, J. (1996) 'Celticism', in T. Brown (ed.) pp.1–16.

Letcher, A. (2000) '"Virtual Paganism" or direct action? The implications of road protesting for modern Pagans', in M. Bowman and G. Harvey (eds) (electronic journal).

Lovejoy, A.O. and Boas, G. (1965) *Primitivism and Related Ideas in Antiquity*, New York: Octagon Books.

Low, M. (1996) *Celtic Christianity and Nature: Early Irish and Hebridean Traditions*, Edinburgh: Edinburgh University Press.

McCoy, E. (1993) *Witta: An Irish Pagan Tradition*, St Paul, Minn.: Llewellyn.

Maier, B. (1997) *Dictionary of Celtic Religion and Culture*, Woodbridge: Boydell & Brewer.

Marcus, C.C. (1987) 'Alternative landscapes: ley-lines, feng shui and the gaia hypothesis', *Landscape*, vol.29, no.3, pp.1–10.

Matthews, C. (1989) *The Elements of the Celtic Tradition*, Shaftesbury: Element Books.

Matthews, C. (1993) 'A Celtic quest', in *World Religions in Education* 1993/1994, London: The Shap Working Party, pp.6–9.

Matthews, J. (1991) *The Celtic Shaman: A Handbook*, Shaftesbury: Element Books.

Meek, D.E. (1991) 'Celtic Christianity: what is it, and when was it?', *The Scottish Bulletin of Evangelical Theology*, vol.9, no.1, pp.13–21.

Meek, D.E. (1992) 'Modern Celtic Christianity: the contemporary revival and its roots', *The Scottish Bulletin of Evangelical Theology*, vol.10, no.1, pp.6–31.

Meek, D.E. (1996) 'Modern Celtic Christianity', in T. Brown (ed.) pp.143–57.

Meek, D.E. (2000) *The Quest for Celtic Christianity*, Edinburgh: Handsel Press.

Morgan, P. (1975) *Iolo Morganwg*, Cardiff: University of Wales Press.

Morris, P. (1996) 'Community beyond tradition', in P. Heelas, S. Lash and P. Morris (eds) *Detraditionalization: Critical Reflections on Authority and Identity*, Oxford and Cambridge, Mass.: Blackwell, pp.223–49.

Mowl, T. and Earnshaw, B. (1988) *John Wood: Architect of Obsession*, Bath: Millstream Books.

Piccini, A. (1996) 'Filming through the mists of time: Celtic constructions and the documentary', *Current Anthropology*, vol.37 (Supplement), pp.87–111.

Piccini, A. (1999) 'Of memory and things past', *Heritage in Wales*, Issue 12 (Spring), pp.18–20.

Piggott, S. (1989) *Ancient Britons and the Antiquarian Imagination*, London: Thames & Hudson.

Piggott, S. (1993) *The Druids*, London: Thames & Hudson (first published 1968).

Robinson, C. (2000) 'Druids and Brahmins: a case of mistaken identity?', in M. Bowman and G. Harvey (eds) (electronic journal).

Said, E.W. (1995) *Orientalism*, Harmondsworth: Penguin Books.

Shallcrass, P. (1993) book review of *Carmina Gadelica* in *The Druids' Voice*, vol.3, autumn, p.37.

Shallcrass, P. (ed.) (1995) *A Druid Directory 1995: A Guide to Modern Druidry and Druid Orders*, British Druid Order.

Shallcrass, P. and Restall Orr, E. (2001) *A Druid Directory: A Guide to Druidry and Druid Orders*, St Leonards-on-Sea: The British Druid Order.

Sharpe, E.J. (1986) *Comparative Religion: A History*, London: Duckworth.

Sims-Williams, P. (1998) 'Celtomania and Celtoscepticism', *Cambrian Medieval Celtic Studies*, vol.36 (Winter), pp.1–35.

Smart, N. (1973) *The Science of Religion and the Sociology of Knowledge*, Princeton: Princeton University Press.

Spence, L. (1993) *The Mysteries of Britain: Secret Rites and Traditions of Ancient Britain*, London: Bracken Books.

Sutcliffe, S. and Bowman, M. (eds) (2000) *Beyond New Age: Exploring Alternative Spirituality*, Edinburgh: Edinburgh University Press.

Tingay, K. (2000) 'Madame Blavatsky's children: theosophy and its heirs', in S. Sutcliffe and M. Bowman (eds) pp.37–50.

Toulson, S. (1996) *The Celtic Year*, Shaftesbury: Element Books.

Van de Weyer, R. (1990) *Celtic Fire: An Anthology of Celtic Christian Literature*, London: Darton Longman & Todd.

Wood, J. (1969) *A Description of Bath*, Bath: Kingsmead Reprints (first published 1765).

CHAPTER 3

Aspirational Indians: North American indigenous religions and the New Age

SUSAN MUMM

Each part of our religion has its power and its purpose. Each people have their own ways. You cannot mix these ways together, because each people's ways are balanced. Destroying balance is a disrespect and very dangerous. That is why it is forbidden. Many things are forbidden in our religion. The forbidden things are acts of disrespect, things which unbalance power. These things must be learned, and the learning is very difficult. That is why there are very few real 'medicine men' among us; only a few are chosen.

(Matthew King, a Lakota elder, cited in Churchill, 1991, p.14)

I have a right to practise any religion that has meaning for me. In my heart I am Lakota. No one has a right to fuck with my religion.

(New Age environmental activist)

These people [those who charge for participation in 'Indian religious rituals'] have insisted upon making themselves pariahs within their own communities, and they will have to bear the consequences of that. As to white people who think it's cute, or neat or groovy or keen to hook up with plastic medicine men, to subsidise and promote them, and claim you and they have some fundamental 'right' to desecrate our spiritual traditions, I've got a piece of news for you. You have *no* such right. Our religions are *ours*. Period. We have very strong reasons for keeping certain things private, whether you understand them or not. And we have every human right to deny them to you, whether you like it or not. You can either respect our basic rights or not respect them. If you do, you're an ally and we're ready and willing to join hands with you on other issues. If you do not, you are a thief of the sort who is willing to risk undermining our sense of the integrity of our cultures for your own perceived self-interest.

(Russell Means, cited in Churchill, 1991, p.15)

Interest in North American indigenous religions has soared since the 1960s, when a poet's interpretation of the Hopi religion, published in a popular form,[1] first attracted numbers of countercultural youth to reservations in the south-west USA. But missionaries and anthropologists had been compiling and publishing accounts of Indian religious practices and beliefs for 400 years by that time, with the biases inherent to their backgrounds and occupations. At the same time, traditional teachings were being eroded and changed by contact with other tribes, Europeans and European religions.

From the time of the first European contact, there was an insistence on lumping together more than 500 nations in places ranging from the Arctic to Central America as 'Indians' – because Columbus had mistakenly believed he had reached the Indies. With the linguistic generalization came an assumption that all the peoples of North America were a collective entity, with identical characteristics, culture, beliefs and practices.

> Native Americans were usually described not for what they were in their own eyes but from the viewpoint of the invaders into their lands. Images of the Indian, accordingly, were and are usually what they were not or had not in White terms and ideals, rather than in terms of individual tribal cultures and social systems ... Europeans and Americans [used] anti-images of themselves to describe Indians and the anti-images of Indians to describe themselves.
>
> (Berkhofer, 1988, pp.526–7)

Early descriptions were sometimes positive, although saturated with the paternalism of the European arrivals. The Dominican Bartolomé de Las Casas wrote in the sixteenth century:

> God created these simple people without evil and without guile. They are most obedient and faithful to their natural lords and to the Christians whom they serve. They are most submissive, patient, peaceful and virtuous. Nor are they quarrelsome, rancorous, querulous, or vengeful. Moreover they are more delicate than princes and die easily from work or illness. They neither possess or desire to possess worldly wealth. Surely these people would be the most blessed in the world if only they worshipped the true God.
>
> (Berkhofer, 1988, p.523)

This view of native North Americans was reinforced by ideas derived from the Romantic movement, and its belief in a pastoral Golden Age, complete with the Noble Savage, free from 'history's burdens and

---

[1] Frank Waters' *Book of the Hopi* (1963), while a bestseller, has been attacked for seriously misrepresenting Hopi beliefs and customs.

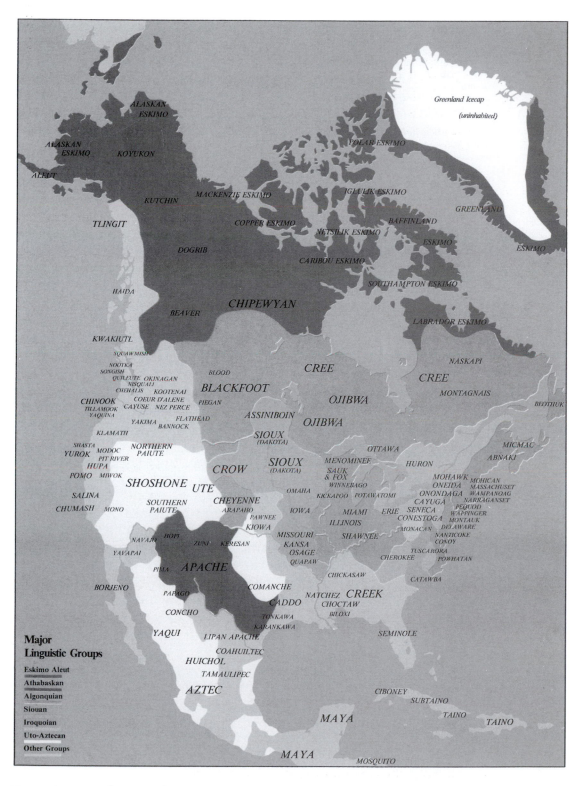

Figure 3.1 Distribution of Native American tribes. © Bill Yenne. From Bill Yenne (1986) *The Encyclopedia of North American Indian Tribes*, London: Bison Books. Attempts to trace the copyright owner have failed, but all rights acknowledged.

modern society's complexities' (Berkhofer, 1988, p.529). This was, of course, an oblique criticism of European culture, a theme resurrected today by aspirational Indians. Others, especially in the more racist climate of the nineteenth century, associated Indians with everything negative: from cowardice through cruelty to drunkenness. What all united in agreeing in these various 'descriptions from deficiency' was that indigenous religions should be suppressed, if not eradicated, and replaced by Christianity. Even a century ago, missionaries on Indian reservations were describing indigenous religions as primitive superstitions, and explaining away their apparent efficacy through ascribing their power to the work of the devil. They were routinely described as 'pagan'.[2] Indians were also the subject of study by anthropologists, who shared the wider EuroAmerican view of First Nations as historyless and without change until they had contact with Europeans (Berkhofer, 1988, p.528).[3]

Today, large numbers of people are turning to 'Native Indian religion' as a more globally relevant and spiritually satisfying alternative to the traditions they were born into. Amanda Porterfield defines 'American Indian Spirituality' as a countercultural movement which seeks to employ insights from indigenous traditions to restore the earth to its former sanctity and intactness (Porterfield, 1990, p.152). This is an important perceptual change: from being perceived as demonic to being believed to be our only hope for global survival suggests a paradigm shift of considerable importance.[4]

Majority culture assumed that the solution to the 'Indian problem' was assimilation to AmerEuropean culture and a complete abandonment of indigenous custom, religion and language. At the same time, however, there had always been a small proportion of AmerEuropeans who admired elements of indigenous culture and wished to imitate it. In the early years of the twentieth century, both the Boy Scouts and the Woodcraft Society borrowed many practices, such as ritual dances, from Indian sources. Ernest Seton, the Canadian naturalist who was involved with the founding of both groups, wrote that Indians were 'the most heroic race the world has ever seen, the most physically perfect race the world has ever seen, the most

[2] See Chapter 1 in this volume for a discussion of how the meaning of paganism gradually shifts to a pejorative sense as it is used here.

[3] While the term 'Indian' is sometimes used in this chapter, largely because of its ubiquity, 'First Nations' or 'indigenous' are more accurate and more satisfactory terms, and also can be used to encompass Inuit groups.

[4] Some, of course, continue to perceive Indian beliefs as being opposed to what they consider to be true religion.

spiritual Civilisation the world has ever seen' (Seton, 1970, p.108). For much of the twentieth century a group of enthusiasts known as 'hobbyists' attempted to replicate indigenous patterns of dress, art, dancing and singing. Some went so far as to seek adoption by First Nations' families living on reservations (Powers, 1988, pp.557–61). In the 1960s, the anthropologists and hobbyists visiting tribes were joined by large numbers of countercultural adherents, church-based youth missionaries and service volunteers 'bent on doing good and seeking their own identity or salvation but often simply getting underfoot' (Lurie, 1988, p.555). The counterculture, in particular, as a pervasive Romantic movement, saw First Nations' people as ideal: 'ecologically aware, spiritual, tribal, anarchistic, drug-using, exotic, native, and wronged, the long genuine holdouts against American conformity and success' (Brand, 1988, p.570). Sales of anything 'Indian' rocketed, from headbands to books of spiritual practices, and voluntary primitivists sought to align themselves with native causes. So what exactly was coming to the attention of young AmerEuropeans in the 1960s, and igniting an interest that has become widespread among New Age adherents and 'deep environmentalists'?[5]

This is not an easy question to answer. First, there is no valid category that can be labelled 'North American Indian religion'. Before the arrival of Europeans, North America was populated by a large number of Indian societies, thinly scattered across a vast continent now divided into Canada, the USA and Mexico. A recent estimate has suggested that there were about 500 of these 'First Nations'.[6] Each of these societies, or tribes, had its own religion, its own language and its own social practices. They lived in relatively isolated settlements with varying degrees of inter-tribal contact. Instead of a single, unitary Indian religion, there were and are a vast range of religions, varying widely in belief, practices and influence, and undergoing subtle changes as the tribes came into contact with one another. Most of these religions have a written history that dates only from the eighteenth or nineteenth century, after considerable contact with Europeans and European religion had occurred. The verbal/oral histories of the religions vary enormously in scope, depending largely on how well the tribes have been able to maintain at least some of their traditional practices.

[5] Deep environmentalists combine environmental activism with the conviction that the earth itself is a deity, rather than having been created by a deity.

[6] Berkhofer claims there were 'at least two thousand cultures and more societies' (1978, p.3).

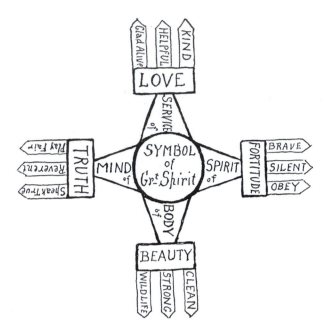

The Woodcraft Way

Figure 3.2 Ernest Seton's depiction of First Nations'
values for adoption by the Woodcraft Society.
Frontispiece of Ernest Seton, *The Birch Bark Roll
of Woodcraft*, 1925, New York: Brieger Press.

The huge diversity of First Nations' tribes means that a comprehensive discussion of their belief systems is beyond the scope of
anything less than an encyclopedia. What is certain is that the
religions known today as indigenous comprise sectarian offshoots of
other native religions, incorporations from Aztec and Maya influences, with a significant infusion of Christianity and, more recently,
New Age ideas. In addition, there is a considerable difference in the
strength of the religions of the various Indian nations: some,
especially the smaller ones whose languages have been virtually
eradicated, have lost much of their original belief system as well;
others, especially the larger tribes, have religious teachings so
vigorous that they have been accused of 'colonizing' the religions of
other tribes.

While it is dangerous to generalize, it would be foolish to launch
into a discussion of this topic without any attempt to sketch a very
broad picture of indigenous beliefs. First Nations' religions do share
some common tendencies. One commonality is the refusal to

Figure 3.3 An example of countercultural appropriation: poster for 'Pow Wow: A Gathering of the Tribes', 14 January 1967. © Stanley Mouse Studios/ Courtesy of the Bancroft Library, University of California, Berkeley.

recognize any split between sacred and secular (similar to the position of Hinduism on this point), which creates an essentially religious worldview, supporting all of tribal life, existence and self-identity. Like Hinduism, many traditional practitioners describe indigenous religions as ways of life and not sets of principles or credal formulations. Again like Hinduism, some insist that these religions cannot be adopted by outsiders, but must be born into: few, even among those who reject this position, would actively seek converts. The local terrain is considered to be saturated with sacredness, and natural objects possess consciousness and power. Ceremonial rituals are carried out, individually and in groups, to ensure communal and individual prosperity. Usually ceremonies and rituals are highly elaborate and rigorously performed, while the theology underlying them remains fuzzy and undefined. They are not primarily religions of theology, but of ritual practice (like Shinto, the indigenous religion of Japan). Indian religions also often share a set of ideas about the nature of the divine. As Vine Deloria Jr, a prominent spokesman for native rights and traditional religions, points out, in general indigenous religions do not perceive God anthromorphically (Deloria, 1995, p.31). But again, it is important to remember that indigenous religions can often vary from each other as dramatically as Buddhism from Judaism, or Christianity from Shinto.

Because there are so many varieties of Indian religion, I would be reluctant to generalize much beyond the few concepts mentioned above. To illustrate the point, consider the following definitions of the essential nature of indigenous religions.

1 Traditional religions are fundamentally a 'not easily accessible inner reality which is first experienced on the level of tribe, clan, and extended family'. There is no practice of native religions for personal empowerment. They are communal and communitarian (Weaver, 1997, p.viii).

2 J.S. Slotkin concluded that the Indian, epistemologically speaking, 'is an individualist and empiricist: he believes only what he himself has experienced' (Weaver, 1997, p.xx).

3 'To speak in terms of "religion" as normally conceptualized in western thought, and Native community and traditions is, in fact, to be engaged in a kind of incommensurate discourse. Native religion does not concern itself – does not try to know or explain – "what happens in the other world". Native languages do not even have words for "religion" or "theology" or "philosophy". Instead, for example, "Hopi" designates both tribe and religious practice. The Navajo call themselves "Diyin dine'e" (Children of the Holy

Figure 3.4 Vine Deloria Jr. Courtesy of the Publications Department of the University of Colorado at Boulder/Photo: Casey Cass.

People) ... And the word in Cherokee usually translated as "religion", "eloh", also means, at one and the same time, land, history, law, and culture. Forbes[7] has speculated sarcastically that there may be no need for a word for religion until a people no longer have religion' (Weaver, 1997, pp.vii, viii).

So are indigenous religions communitarian or individualist? Inner oriented or focused on ritual practice? Is it simply impossible to generalize, given their diversity? I would argue that this last position, despite its superficial appeal, is not helpful to the student of religions seeking to gain a basic understanding of indigenous religions. For if diversity is so great as to make generalization impossible or unprofitable, what of the perceived commonalities that have made 'Indian religion' so important to AmerEuropeans within New Age and environmentalist movements? While it is possible to argue that the

---

[7] Jack D. Forbes, Professor of Native American Studies, University of California at Davis.

religion that these groups find so attractive is an artificial and inauthentic invention (and some do take this position), those who identify with such groups would refute this position with energy.

One useful way out of this definitional impasse may be that suggested by Guy Cooper in an article on Navajo religion. He points out that within the enormous variety of religious beliefs and practices found in indigenous religions, there are two 'broad types' of religions: hunters and horticulturists. He follows the eminent Stockholm-based scholar Abe Hultkrantz in seeing the hunting groups as primarily 'oriented toward animal ceremonialism, personal quests for power, shamanism and annual ceremonies of cosmic rejuvenation'. On the other hand, horticulturally based tribes emphasize 'rain and fertility ceremonies, priestly ritual, medicine societies and calendrical rites. In general, hunting societies are strongly oriented toward individualism and horticultural ones toward collectivism' (Cooper, 1990, p.67). Cooper goes on to point out that religion in the hunter-based societies 'can at times attain the level of an almost individual religion'. After identifying these two focal orientations, it is important to remember that many groups blend them in varying degrees.

Like the counterculture in the 1960s, the New Age has taken to North American indigenous religions with enthusiasm. There has been a gigantic outpouring of publications, courses, web sites, guidebooks, seminars, articles, self-help manuals and courses introducing EuroAmericans to 'Indian religion'. Aspiring Indians can pay $150 to attend a sweat lodge[8] ceremony and $1000 to Sundance,[9] buy books that offer to initiate into Indian religion, and join 'clans' designed especially for them. Others undertake serious courses of reading in an attempt to find out more about indigenous religious beliefs and practices, or in a search for rituals that they can incorporate into their own personal philosophies.[10] These develop-

---

[8] A sweat lodge is a small shelter used for purification, often before participating in a particularly sacred activity, such as the Sundance.

[9] The Sundance is practised by about 40 tribal groupings; it is a major feature of the religious practice of many Plains Indians groups. It is a calendric rite of world and life renewal that takes place in spring or at midsummer. Among other things it involves the construction of a sacred lodge, drumming, singing, prolonged fasting and the infliction of severe physical suffering on the participants. It is sometimes performed in fulfilment of a vow. Typically the Sundance lasts three to four days.

[10] There is an excellent web site that assists enquirers in assessing the authenticity of Internet sites that make claims to be native. See 'Evaluation guidelines for web sites about American Indian peoples', http://www.u.arizona.edu/~ecubbins/webcrit/html. (All web sites listed in this chapter were most recently accessed in January 2002.)

Figure 3.5 A sweat lodge. Photo courtesy of South Dakota State Historical Society, State Archives.

ments have been viewed with dismay by traditionalists. The 'Resolution' of the fifth annual meeting of the Traditional Elders' Circle of the Northern Cheyenne Nation declared that New Age leaders were invalid because of their lack of training. 'The medicine men are chosen by the medicine and long instruction and discipline is necessary before ceremonies and healing can be done. These procedures are in the Native tongue; there are no exceptions and profit is not the motivation' ('Resolution', 1992, p.15).

A prominent example of a contentious 'medicine man' is Sun Bear, who markets ceremonies. His books, in which he promises his audiences and customers access to Native American spiritual wisdom, have reached an international audience. However, he claims that the ceremonies he sells in workshops, and describes in his how-to manuals, are not Indian, but are based on Indian models. Sun Bear, like many others who popularize indigenous traditions among a EuroAmerican audience, contends that his activities are legitimate precisely because they are synchronistic: they are derived from a variety of tribes and some elements, such as crystal healing, are not derived from First Nations' practices. His 'Sun Bear Tribe' is exclusively EuroAmerican, and he appears to have dissociated himself entirely from the Chippewa reservation on which he was raised. A similar fee-paying group in Florida has been established by an individual calling himself (risibly) 'Chief Piercing Eyes', who has recently written that the core of spirituality is cheerfulness (Churchill, 1991, p.14; 'Religion Made Simple', *Earthkeeper Magazine* web site, earthkeeper.freeservers.com).

Chief Piercing Eyes Penn is typical of non-Indian spokespersons influential in the New Age. Completely independent of tribal controls, he espouses a 'red road' comprising ideas derived from different First Nations' religions, and argues that his client group is made up of people with Indian blood, although without tribal backgrounds. Presumably many of them are 'aspirational Indians', those without firm evidence of Indian ancestry. Porterfield identifies the audience for such spokespersons as the disaffected: those who feel let down by 'American government, capitalism, and technology' (Porterfield, 1990, p.155). In the Pan-American Indian movement, charges are made for the group's services and products. Chief Piercing Eyes describes the Pan-American Indians (previously known as the Thunder Chicken Tribe) as a non-profit group founded in 1984 with about 3,500 members.[11] Groups such as the Pan-American Indian organization highlight the issues of authenticity implicit in the three quotations that opened this chapter.[12] Such groups disregard traditional emphasis on the difference between tribal customs and claim that tribal affiliation is unnecessary. Porterfield sees the difference as a reflection on the 'culture wars' currently being fought.

> Distinctions between authentic spokespersons and pretenders is a persistent theme in discussions about American Indian spirituality. Although the nature of these distinctions often seems to be racial, with critics of Storm[13] and Highwater,[14] for example, implying that these men are spiritually inauthentic because their parents were not full-blooded Indians, the real distinction behind this preoccupation with authenticity is a cultural one. Representatives of American Indian spirituality who actually participate in tribal culture speak with the authority of tribal rootedness. Their involvement in tribal culture sanctions their interpretation of American Indian spirituality.
>
> (Porterfield, 1990, p.153)

Cultural Studies has done much in recent years to expand our conception of culture: culture can now be understood as an

---

[11] www.nonprofits.org/gallery/alpha/paia.

[12] For another view of the issue of authenticity, see Chapter 2 in this volume.

[13] Hyemoyohsts Storm, controversial New Age reinterpreter of Cheyenne culture to non-Indians.

[14] Jamake Highwater, a controversial figure of Greek descent.

expression of lived experience, which expresses the consciousness of an entire group. It is 'popular' as well as 'high'; it encompasses language and body, myths and belief structures, ideology and religion, forms of communication, as well as how the society is organized and how relationships within it are built and maintained. This understanding of culture is one shared both by First Nations' groups (think, for example, of the meaning of the Cherokee word 'eloh') and by aspirational Indians.

Aspirational Indians see themselves as setting up a new culture, taking the best from both worlds, while traditionalists focus on protecting what is left of their old culture. By traditionalists I mean First Nations' people who see their religions as something so embedded in culture that 'elective affinity' is an impossibility. 'Traditionalist', however, should not be equated with 'conservative' as the term is usually understood. Such traditionalists, while highly conservative on the question of religion, are often deeply engaged in advocacy, and may be on the left in terms of political and social activism. Traditionalists see their religion and their culture as one, a view not shared by 'wannabes': if their religion becomes open to all, and thus is changed by the values and preoccupations of aspirational Indians with an AmerEuropean cultural background, their culture will also be changed.

While writing this chapter, I performed a quick search for web sites selling 'medicine bags'. These are traditionally viewed as sacred, highly personal, ritual objects by the indigenous groups that employ them. The design of the bag and its contents are rigidly prescribed by tradition. I found dozens of sites purporting to sell these bags to all comers, varying in price from $10 to $900. Some sold them purely as works of art; others advertised them as fashion statements ('If you like the idea of wearing "medicine", you might enjoy carrying a fetish or something else personally meaningful in a leather bag around your neck or waist'),[15] still others suggested that the purchaser would benefit from the spiritual powers of the bag. This seems to confirm that traditionalist fears of cultural erosion may have some basis, as a sacred object becomes a commercial commodity and fashion statement. For Christians, the equivalent might be like finding hundreds of web sites purporting to sell consecrated sacramental wafers fashioned into earrings or as good-luck charms.

Totem poles, while primarily visual statements about the family identity and ceremonial status of those who erected them, are often regarded as having profound religious meaning. Their construction

---

[15] For example, see www.keshi.com/medicinebags.html.

was limited to six tribes in western Canada and south-eastern Alaska. Their spiritual significance is underlined in a number of recent 'repatriations' of totem poles from museums in North America and Europe. Contemporary indigenous artists erect new poles with specific symbolic meanings, such as the installation of 40 poles during the 2001 First Peoples' Festival in the Jardin botanique de Montréal.

The 'Ghost Shirt' is another example of the increasing flood of repatriation of sacred objects. Ghost Dancing, which arose in 1889, was a complex ceremonial which developed in response to a medicine man's prophecy that victory for the indigenous forces and the restoration of the land to its natural state was possible if they underwent spiritual revival. The Ghost Shirt consecrated by this ritual was believed to render its wearer impervious to bullets. In 1892, a member of Buffalo Bill's Wild West Show sold a Lakota Ghost Shirt, which was believed to have been worn at the massacre of Wounded Knee in 1890, to Glasgow Museums (see Colour Plate 5). In 1992, the Lakota tribe became aware that the shirt was on display in Glasgow, and negotiations for its return began. After some resistance from Glasgow City Council and museum conservators, the shirt was returned to South Dakota, with elaborate and extended ceremonial, in 1999.

Religious Studies has always been fascinated by syncretism (the blending of practices or ideas from two traditions) and bricolage (the amalgamation of many elements from a number of diverse traditions), and these concepts can be of considerable help when considering what is underlying both the growth of interest in First Nations' religions and the resistance to EuroAmerican involvement in them.

What exactly is syncretism? The term originates with the first-century Greek historian Plutarch, who used it to refer to the overcoming of differences to face a common enemy. In the seventeenth century, it acquired the meaning of an incorrect and inappropriate combining of elements. This negative interpretation has become the dominant popular understanding of the term. In academic Religious Studies, syncretism can be an objective, neutral term, or a subjective concept that views religious mixing as negative, or, more rarely, positive. However, regardless of perspective, syncretism brings debate. 'Syncretism is in the first place *contested* religious interpenetration' (Droogers, 1989, p.20).

Meanings can change while forms remain constant; this concept is basic to modern understandings of syncretism, where it is called *Verschiebung*, or transposition (Droogers, 1989, p.9). An example of this is the way in which worship of the Virgin Mary is often transposed on to the cult of an older female goddess.[16] This is what makes syncretism so threatening to those who oppose religious intermingling; public ritual can remain virtually unchanged while the popular understanding of the ritual has changed radically.

Syncretism can be both the cause and effect of religious change, and as such it is inevitably paired with conflict. It would also be simplistic to assume that the outside influence can only be that of a competing religion. As André Droogers reminds us, 'syncretism may occur between currents of one religion, between a religion and an ideology, between religion and science, and between religion and culture' (1989, p.13). It is a complicated concept where cause and effect are usually unclear.

> One must also choose between syncretism as the *process* of religious interpenetration, or as the *result* of such a process, or a combination of both. When one speaks of a 'syncretistic religion', this may mean a religion which is the result of a period of religious encounter. But the term may also refer to an extremely tolerant and permanently absorbent religion, ready to adopt and adapt whatever may present itself. One may therefore ask whether syncretism is a temporary or a permanent phenomenon.
>
> (Droogers, 1989, p.13)

Both contemporary First Nations and their fellow travellers see themselves as countering EuroAmerican Christianity with a religion of their own. Both also agree that indigenous religions are of great value. However, a crucial difference is that native traditionalists see the New Agers as perpetuating yet another form of cultural theft. It is evident that syncretism is viewed negatively by native traditionalists such as Ward Churchill and Vine Deloria Jr. They fear that the two-way process implicit in syncretism will inevitably dilute what has survived of native culture, and believe that eroded cultural foundations can lead to cultural disintegration. Some observers of contemporary adaptations of First Nations' beliefs feel that the process is itself changing from syncretism to briocolage (see the discussion of Bron Taylor's case study below).

A central question for traditionalists and aspirational Indians is whether a community-based, ritual faith with a considerable ancestral element can be adopted by outsiders in an authentic way. Traditionally, the puberty rituals of isolation/vision quests in which adolescents find their 'true name' are not only sacred but potentially

---

[16] There are parallels to this in the relationship between Japanese New Religious Movements (NRMs) and Catholicism; see Chapter 2 in *Global Religious Movements in Regional Context* (Wolffe, 2002), Book 4 in this series.

dangerous, both to the body and the psyche: Lame Deer (John Fire) warns that 'Out in the plains we got our visions the hard way, by fasting and by staying in the vision pit for four days and nights, crying for a dream'[17] (Fire and Erdoes, 1973, p.61). The adoption of modified versions by non-Indians has led some traditionalists to conclude that their religion is so acculturated and so tied to ancestral land-memory that any use of it by outsiders is a provocative act. In 1993, several Lakota leaders issued the 'Declaration of War Against Exploiters of Lakota Spirituality', which is reproduced as an appendix to this chapter.

This debate over the ownership of First Nations' religions highlights the issue of ownership, control and power within contemporary religious practice. While the New Agers might decry all three of these concepts, traditionalists routinely conclude their defence of exclusivity with a warning that unwarranted meddling by outsiders in a religion that is not meant for them could be dangerous to their spiritual wellbeing. To the Indians, their religious traditions are part of their core identity, and cannot be transferred beyond the group where they developed without damage to both appropriator and religion. Religion gives power to those to whom it rightfully belongs, and New Agers who appropriate it do so at their peril, at worst, and at best are deluded in their belief that it can meet their spiritual needs.

On the other hand, some have argued that American Indian spirituality mediates between tribal and middle-class western values. Both indigenous peoples and New Agers tend to agree on the damage done to the world by the western exploitation of nature, and on the sacramental nature of the intact environment and natural ecosystem. Both share a conviction that 'American Indian attitudes are opposite to those of American culture and morally superior on every count, and an underlying belief that American Indian attitudes toward nature are a means of revitalising American culture' (Porterfield, 1990, p.154). Some natives do welcome AmerEuropeans as participants in even the most sacred of ceremonies, such as the Sundance. Advocates argue that it may be a way for disconnected non-natives to ground themselves in something real. Woody Kipp (Blackfeet Nation) argues:

> In the heat and dust and suffering of the Sundance, with the blood of humankind being sacrificed in an act of mass love, the non-native

---

[17] A vision quest involves a period of extended physical deprivation in the wilderness or sensory deprivation in a vision pit, where the initiate fasts and seeks to find his name or spirit totem.

> Sundancers maybe find a connection that is hard to find in an air-conditioned church with the toss of a few alms into the church coffers the only sacrifice ... Sam Spotted Eagle, a noted Blackfoot healer and metaphysician, told his disciples that when one fasts, when one Sundances, when one suffers in a spiritual fashion, everything in the universe receives help from that kind of sacrifice.
>
> (Kipp, 1999, p.7)

Even Kipp insists, however, that non-natives should go through a seven-year apprenticeship before being considered fully qualified to Sundance. In the mid-1990s, a Sundance was shut down mid-ritual because of concern that whites were participating in order to learn the ritual details that would permit them to sell the ceremony in urban workshops (Kipp, 1996, p.6). Many aspirational Indians are genuinely confused and hurt by traditionalist reluctance to acknowledge their sincerity and their desire to add to their knowledge of the tradition they covet. Coming largely out of a Christian culture that sees conversion as not only possible but desirable, they find the concept of a religion that does not receive converts gladly impossible to accept, particularly since they want so desperately to align themselves with it. Deloria, probably the most highly respected scholar working in the field of First Nations' culture today, sees the problem as stemming from a combination of white cultural starvation and romanticism of the primitive:

> Indians can always become whites because the requirements are not very rigorous, but can whites really become Indians? A good many people seriously want to know. They are discontented with their society, their government, their religion and everything around them and nothing is more appealing than to cast aside all inhibitions and stride back into the wilderness, or at least a wilderness theme park, seeking the nobility of the wily savage who once physically fought civilization and now, symbolically at least, is prepared to do it again.
>
> (Deloria, 1995, pp.14–15)

It is not a simple matter of some indigenous leaders rejecting all non-native interest in their belief systems. Even Deloria, who is highly critical of non-indigenous involvement in traditional religions, is willing to praise serious studies of key rituals such as the vision quest.[18] Deloria and Churchill suggest that New Agers turn to what they see as authentic Indian spirituality because they are profoundly alienated from their own lives and cultures. They are accused of looking for a 'quick fix' religion that can be purchased in a bookshop

---

[18] See, for example, Deloria's introduction to Lee Irwin's study of the vision quest, *The Dream Seekers* (1994).

or attained through attending a weekend workshop (Churchill, 1991, p.13).[19] Another point often made by traditionalists, in addition to their concern that the 'wannabes' are not there when Indians are defending land claims or demanding a political voice, is that New Age Indians seldom practise the whole of a traditional religion: for example, burial rituals are almost universally ignored by appropriators. Again, aspirational Indians find it difficult or impossible to accept that their religious affiliations cannot be tailored to meet their own individual needs, combining influences from a number of sources, and omitting those parts that do not speak to them personally. The question remains whether this is evidence of a new and eclectic approach to spirituality (as well as being an example of bricolage), or a reflection of a dominant consumerist culture that teaches that the customer is always right. Deloria places himself on the side of the traditionalists with his argument that religion cannot be acquired in a bookstore or through taking a workshop:

> Bookshelves today are filled with pap – written many times by Indians who have kicked over the traces and no longer feel they are responsible to any living or historic community, but more often by wholly sincere and wholly ignorant non-Indians who fancy themselves masters of the vision quest and sweat lodge. Lying beneath this mass of sentimental slop is the unchallenged assumption that personal sincerity is the equivalent of insight and that cosmic secrets can be not only shared by non-Indians but given out in weekend workshops as easily as diet plans.
>
> (Deloria, introduction to Irwin, 1994, p.ii)

Some of the growth of interest of the New Age in indigenous religions has been ascribed to cultural primitivism, 'the discontent of the civilized with civilization'. This has been defined by Arthur Lovejoy and George Boas as the belief of people 'living in a relatively highly evolved and complex cultural condition that a life far simpler and less sophisticated in some or in all respects is a more desirable life' (Lovejoy and Boas, 1935, p.7). New Agers may not realize it, but their revulsion at the state of mainstream society was shared by a major figure in the history of Religious Studies, Mircea Eliade, who in the 1950s wrote influentially about shamanism, which is often central to New Age ideas of indigenous spirituality. Eliade was fascinated by the idea of a return to primitive, religiously oriented ways of life. In *The Sacred and the Profane*, he wrote that people in archaic societies

---

[19] Note how similar this concern is to that of Gardnerian/Alexandrian Wiccans in respect of the simplification and conflation of their beliefs through the widespread dissemination of 'how-to' books (Chapter 1, p.42).

wanted to live in close relation to the sacred. 'The tendency is perfectly understandable, because for primitives ... the *sacred* is equivalent to *power*, and in the last analysis, to *reality* ... Thus it is easy to understand that religious man deeply desires *to be*, to participate in *reality*, to be saturated with power' (Eliade, 1989, p.13). Central to Eliade's ideas is the importance of the shaman, or shamanism. Shamanism has been defined as 'a visionary tradition, an ancient practice of utilizing altered states of consciousness to contact the gods and spirits of the natural world' (Drury, 1989, p.1). The problem of its appropriateness for modern AmerEuropeans is a genuine one. Shamanism, which develops in preliterate subsistence cultures, is not an obvious candidate for twenty-first-century urban religiosity. Drury claims that it would

> ... be partaking of a fantasy to endeavour to transpose the world of the Shaman to our own contemporary setting ... This point notwithstanding, it is always possible to find some Westerners on retreats, or engaged in personal growth workshops, who enjoy the theatre of dressing up – who believe that by donning Red Indian feather headdresses or by puffing a ceremonial pipe or burning sage, that they can take on a shamanic persona.

> (Drury, 1989, pp.100–1)

The romanticization of indigenous culture, the cult of primitivism, can be considered a religious form of racism. If this claim appears shocking, compare it to the scientific racism of the nineteenth century, or the nineteenth-century claim that women were 'too fine' to debase themselves by political involvement. Consider also the 'cult of the exotic', or orientalism. Lip-service to 'superiority' can be oppressive, because it can box individuals or groups into romanticized roles that limit their human choices. While declaring a group 'inferior' is obviously oppressive, casting others as 'superior' (for example, for money making, careerism or environmental development, or any other quality that the defining group depreciates) can, especially if the categorized group acquiesces in this stereotyping, be as disabling and limiting as assumptions of inferiority.

The power of cultural primitivism would be wiped out if the sacred ways were not authentic, so an important problem for both traditionalists and adopters is the authenticity of the tradition. The following long passage makes clear the tortuous relationship between practice, oral transmission to an outsider, and

FEELING left behind by hi-tech society? Tired of endless New Age seminars and overpriced therapists? Fed up with monotheism? If you're looking for that something extra-special to spice up your life, here's your one and only chance to get in on Do-It-Yourself healing and primitive spirituality...

Become an
Urban Shaman!™

YES. This is the antidote to alienation you've been waiting for: your Direct Line to the Nature-Spirits! Exorcise that emptiness inside you by enrolling now in our **Crash Course in Core Shamanism.** We'll teach you all you need to know to heal your self, your loved ones, even your neighbors, of all the psycho-somatic ills induced by daily life in industrialized civilization.

YOU'LL re-establish contact with the primal authenticity of Nature and your Inner Being at your own leisure. As a certified **Urban Shaman,**™ you'll stand in a proud lineage stretching back into prehistory: artist, doctor, priest, politician, the tribal shamans of the past fulfilled all these roles in one. As a 20th century shaman, you will be able to transcend the demeaning fragmentation imposed by modern society's division of labor, if only in your spare time.

ONLY the choicest shamanic ingredients, culled by a board of professional anthropologists from the most savage, uncivilized cultures left on the face of the earth, make up our crash curriculum designed for the health and happiness of today's dissatisfied urban denizens. In our week-long intensive program, we will teach you our tried and true **E-Z Out** drumming and chanting techniques, guide you on your first **Trance-Journeys** into the spirit-world of the shamans, and instruct you on how to find and train your very own **Spirit-Ally,** who will assist you in all your future endeavors, from astral projection to getting that next job

promotion. You will be guided by actual disciples of original **Aboriginal Shamans,** and supplied with all the customized chants, rituals and magical accessories you'll need to start off on your new adventure as an **Urban Shaman.**™ We even instruct you on how to contruct a sweat-lodge in the comfort of your own apartment or backyard.

NO need to fuss and fret about social critique, no more messy, impractical desires to change the world! Why bother attacking the roots of the dis-ease when you can alleviate its symptoms? As an **Urban Shaman,**™ you can transform your world just by changing your personal life. We're positive you'll find our **Crash Course** to be the perfect placebo for the spiritual and social bleakness endemic to modern life, consumable at your leisure and in the privacy of your own home.

OUR unique crash program has already proven to be just the thing for bringing family and friends closer together by sharing in the exotic thrills of primitive spiritualism. As a member of our **Healers' Network,** you may even meet your future significant other in the intimacy of sacred dances to the money-spirits. Be the first on your block to say, "I'm an **Urban Shaman!**"™ You'll cash in like never before on the cosmic energies of consumer culture when your **Shamanic DreamQuest**™ takes you on visionary tours of the radioactive shopping malls and freeways of the future.

Reproduction of ancient Australian petroglyph said to foretell the coming of Urban Shamans.

REMEMBER, time is running out: the real shamans may be disappearing fast, but if you act now, *you* can be in the vanguard of those helping this time-honored tradition survive into the 21st century and beyond, and only at the low, low cost of $999.99 per person. Just call this toll-free number and we'll sign you up today: 1-800-SHAMANS (VISA and Mastercard accepted). **We guarantee:**

Your life will be transformed
OR YOUR MANA BACK!!!

SHAMANIC PRODUCTIONS, UNLIMITED/"Putting the Primitive to Work for You"

Figure 3.6 A satirical attack on New Age shamanism. Inside front cover of *Do or Die, Voices from Earth First!*, No.5.

AmerEuropean discovery, using the example of Black Elk,[20] who described Lakota belief systems in the first half of the twentieth century. In the passage, William K. Powers suggests that the 'Lakota' traditions transmitted in this way are a literary construct rather than a religious and cultural reality:

> Since the turn of the century, much of what passes today for Indian culture and religion has been fabricated by the white man, or Indians who have been trained in the white man's schools ... Then new medicine men happened upon the scene, all having in common the same as-told-to 'autobiographies', and all written by white men sent for the purpose of recording Lakota religion ... Today, when Black Elk speaks, everybody listens, and everybody hears precisely what he or she feels inclined to hear with little regard for the meanings of the Lakota words.

> Essentially, in *Black Elk Speaks* and other books written by white men for a white audience, the ideas, plots, persons, and situations of these books have been constructed to conform to the expectations of a white audience that generally knows little about what it means to be brought up as a Lakota over the past one hundred years. Of particular significance, I think, is that the only language into which *Black Elk Speaks* and other books have not been translated is Lakota, the native language of the people who presumably are the originators and benefactors of these religious ideas ...

> There are, however, some Lakota today who do look to spiritual guidance from books. The new generation of Indians has moved to the cities away from their direct source of inspiration on the reservations. In many ways their needs are greater, for they must live in constant contact with the people who have attempted to destroy their culture and their religion. For these young Indians, *Black Elk Speaks* and other fabrications of the white man become not only increasingly acceptable but even desirable in the form of literature, given the Judaeo-Christian substructures introduced by contemporary white writers. To survive in the world today, a white man need only be a white man, but for an Indian to survive he must be both Indian and white. In many ways *Black Elk Speaks* is a form [of] literary imperialism as are so many other books on Indians. But it also represents literary compromise in that Indians are allowed to be Indians because the white man has dictated through clever prose and poetry the very

---

[20] Black Elk described the Lakota beliefs and customs of his boyhood to a white author. Black Elk was an Anglican catechist at the time of the book's publication; he later converted to Catholicism, and spent the last thirty years of his life as a catechist and leader of the Catholic community on his reservation. Like many other indigenous Christians, he embraced Christianity without turning his back on native beliefs.

parameters of being Indian. And through this process, the young
Indian accepts a religion, one he calls Lakota religion, manifested in an
acceptable form of literature and written by a white man who knows
little or nothing of the real religion practised by older and younger
Lakotas today on the reservation. And this younger generation of
Lakota doesn't even know the difference.

(Powers, 1990, pp.147–9)

The radical environmental movement, with 'deep ecology' and
ecofeminism in the vanguard has, from its inception, borrowed from
Native American religious symbols and concepts. This appropriation,
sometimes linked with New Age spiritual tendencies within the
environmental movement, has become deeply troubling to Indian
traditionalists, who often want to cement alliances with the environmental movement in other areas in order to protect what is left of the
wilderness. The religious controversy threatens these fragile
alliances. Bron Taylor presents a very useful case study dealing
with these issues, documenting the relationship of the 'radical
vanguard' of environmentalism, Earth First!, and the American Indian
Movement (AIM). He identifies three main perspectives on the issue:

- however well intended, such borrowing represents a form of
cultural genocide, either destroying such traditions by syncretistically
transforming them as they selectively borrow from them, and/or
directly threatening Indian survival by assuming that native spiritualities are dead and in need of resuscitation by whites.

- the appropriation of Native American religion is impossible, since
the resulting phenomenon is no longer Native American religion.

- since the borrowing of myth, symbol, and rite from one group by
another is a central characteristic of cultural and religious evolution, it
is inappropriate for religious studies scholars to categorically condemn such developments. Such condemnations would inevitably
privilege one form of religion over another.

(Taylor, 1997, p.184)

Earth First! carries out campaigns of protest and civil disobedience
against commercial exploitation of the environment. Its members
believe that the earth has intrinsic value and deserves protection from
human abuse. Bron Taylor describes such groups as practising a form
of 'primal spirituality', a blend of pantheism and individual, interior
spiritual experiences linked to nature. Like Gary Snyder, a poet and
leader of the Deep Ecology Movement, they believe that everyone
has the capacity to become psychologically and spiritually Native
American, an idea derived ultimately from Eliade's ideas about
shamanism (Taylor, 1997, p.185). Because they view indigenous

cultures as more spiritually and ecologically balanced, their desire to learn from them 'produces an impulse to borrow ritual practices. In North America, this has been facilitated by the increasing openness of some Native Americans to such cultural sharing and by the proliferation of New Age practitioners and institutes claiming to be authentic bearers of such practices' (Taylor, 1997, p.185).

In addition, the ecology movement blends ideas and practices from other religions with its borrowings from First Nations' teachings. This borrowing is combined with eclectic contributions from Buddhism, neo-Paganism and Wicca, and the self-help movements:

> Among the practices borrowed (explicitly or implicitly) from Native American cultures, are the sweat lodge, the burning of purifying sage, the passing of a talking stick in community meetings, ritual processes such as the Council of All Beings which involve a solitary seeking of nature spirits in a way that resembles vision quests, the taking (or discovery) of 'earth names', group and solitary wilderness experiences undertaken under the influence of peyote or hallucinogenic mushrooms, 'tribal unity' and war dances characterized by ecstatic dancing and prolonged drumming (which bear no resemblance, as far as I can discern, to Native American dancing); neo-pagan ritualizing that sometimes borrows elements from Native American religion such as prayers to the Great Spirit in the four directions; a variety of rhetoric such as 'ho' to express agreement during 'tribal' meetings, and 'hoka-hey', an exclamation sometimes spoken to register approval of expressions of militant defiance against the oppressors of nature. A small number of these activists live in tepees and do not cut their hair sharing the belief held by some Native Americans that their strength would be dissipated were they to cut it.[21]
>
> (Taylor, 1997, p.186)

However, at recent Earth First! gatherings, there has been increased concern and considerable controversy about the appropriateness of sweat lodges run by and for EuroAmericans. Some environmental activists respond much as Sun Bear does to his critics, saying that the practices are inspired by indigenous traditions but are not actually 'Indian'. While there are well-documented cases of EuroAmericans pretending to be Indian, or falsely claiming to have studied with American Indian 'teachers', especially within the New Age movement, the deep ecologists seem more intent on developing their own rituals. These certainly borrow from indigenous (especially Lakota/

---

[21] Of course, some groups in the Judeo-Christian tradition (such as the Nazarenes) have used the example of Samson to the same end.

Dakota/Nakota) practices, but are a part of piecemeal borrowing from a number of traditions:

> The activists engaged in such borrowing do not presume that they are actually practising Native American religion. Rather, they tend to believe that they are developing their own tradition, that their 'tribe' is different from but has spiritual affinity with what they take to be the spiritual perceptions of traditional Native Americans; namely, a sense that the land and all its inhabitants are sacred, related as kin, capable of communicating, and worthy of defense.
>
> (Taylor, 1997, p.198)

Taylor's own view is that Earth First! and other activists are 'developing their own form of tribal nature religion' (Taylor, 1997, p.191). It is becoming common for 'neo-pagan sweats' to be offered as a more appropriate spiritual path for EuroAmericans, and Taylor claims that Native Americans are increasingly urging deep ecology activists to try to rediscover their own pagan and pre-Christian traditions, rather than appropriating Indian beliefs. But the current situation is one of still considerable tension between New Age desires to find a spiritual path, a desire to express connection with the earth, and the fear that appropriating First Nations' religions is just another example of colonial exploitation. As Janet McCloud, a fishing rights activist and elder of the Nisqually Nation sees it:

> First they came to take our land and water, then our fish and game. Then they wanted our mineral resources and, to get them, they tried to take our governments. Now they want our religion as well. All of a sudden, we have a lot of unscrupulous idiots running around saying they're medicine people, and they'll sell you a sweat lodge ceremony for fifty bucks. It's not only wrong, it's obscene. Indians don't sell their spirituality to anybody, for any price. This is just another in a very long series of thefts from the Indian people and, in some ways, this is the worst one yet.
>
> (Cited in Churchill, 1991, p.13)

Myke Johnson, in her influential article 'Wanting to be Indian' (reproduced in Part Two), points up many of the conflicts inherent in the aspirational Indian position, as well as suggesting some practical ways forward for people seeking elective affinity with First Nations' religiosity.

Ultimately, the concern for many traditionalists is that even if no money changes hands, the New Agers will inevitably bring their other religious and cultural influences into Indian ceremonies in which they participate, and these other cultural influences will inevitably influence the host religion. Given the history of direct and indirect destruction of North American Indian society, culture, traditions, language and way of life, it is possible to understand why traditionalists fear contamination of what is left of indigenous religion, which to many seems to be 'the last thing [Indian] people have that's theirs' (Dennis Martinez, cited in Taylor, 1997, p.193). On the other hand, it may be reasonable to argue that religious change is inevitable, and that attempting to preserve a tradition for its 'own' may instead fossilize it.

This whole area of religion, culture and ownership is a complex and contested one. Ecofeminism and green identity movements see in First Nations' religions values that they do not find elsewhere, and initially at least, have had little hesitation in appropriating them. The indigenous spirituality movement became central to their identity construction, and recent traditionalist protests against elective affinity have created a maelstrom of debate and questioning. This centres on the drives for tradition preservation and authenticity and the New Age emphasis on spontaneity and aversion to rules. When thinking about the issues raised by this, it is impossible to avoid contemplating some very basic questions. When does a religion become a lifestyle choice? What has religion become?

References

Berkhofer, R.F. (1978) *The White Man's Indian: Images of the American Indian from Columbus to the Present*, New York: Alfred A. Knopf.

Berkhofer, R.F. (1988) 'White conceptions of Indians', in W.C. Sturtevant and W.E. Washburn (eds) pp.522–47.

Brand, S. (1988) 'Indians and the counterculture, 1960s–1970s', in W.C. Sturtevant and W.E. Washburn (eds) pp.570–2.

Churchill, W. (1991) 'Spiritual hucksterism: the rise of the plastic medicine men', *Twin Light Trail*, vol.3, pp.13–15.

Cooper, G.H. (1990) 'Individualism and integration in Navajo religion', in C. Vecsey (ed.) pp.67–82.

Deloria Jr, V. (1995) *Red Earth, White Lies: Native Americans and the Myth of Scientific Fact*, New York: Scribner.

Droogers, A. (1989) 'Syncretism: the problem of definition', in J. Gort (ed.) pp.1–25.

Drury, N. (1989) *The Elements of Shamanism*, Longmead: Element Books.

Durkheim, E. (1968) *The Elementary Forms of the Religious Life*, London: George Allen & Unwin (first published 1915).

Eliade, M. (1989) *The Sacred and the Profane: The Nature of Religion*, New York: Harcourt, Brace & World (English translation of 1957 German edition).

Fire, J. and Erdoes, R. (1973) *Lame Deer, Sioux Medicine Man*, London: Davis-Poynter.

Gort, J. (ed.) (1989) *Dialogue and Syncretism: An Interdisciplinary Approach*, Grand Rapids: Eerdmans.

Irwin, L. (1994) *The Dream Seekers: Native American Visionary Traditions of the Great Plains*, Norman: University of Oklahoma Press.

Kipp, W. (1996) 'Sun Dance shut down', *American Indian Review*, no.12, p.6.

Kipp, W. (1999) 'Okan, a dreaming place – exclusively Native?', *American Indian Review*, no.23, p.7.

Lovejoy, A.O. and Boas, G. (1935) *Primitivism and Related Ideas in Antiquity*, Baltimore: Johns Hopkins.

Lurie, N.O. (1988) 'Relations between Indians and anthropologists', in W.C. Sturtevant and W.E. Washburn (eds) pp.548–56.

Porterfield, A. (1990) 'American Indian spirituality as a countercultural movement', in C. Vecsey (ed.) pp.152–66.

Powers, W.K. (1988) 'The Indian hobbyist movement in North America', in W.C. Sturtevant and W.E. Washburn (eds) pp.557–61.

Powers, W.K. (1990) 'When Black Elk speaks, everybody listens', in C. Vecsey (ed.) pp.136–51.

'Resolution of the Fifth Annual Meeting of the Tradition Elders Circle, Northern Cheyenne Nation' (1992), *Twin Light Trail*, vol.3, pp.15–16.

Seton, E.T. (1970) *The Gospel of the Redman: An Indian Bible*, London: Psychic Press (first published 1937).

Sturtevant, W.C. and Washburn, W.E. (eds) (1988) *Handbook of North American Indians. Volume 4 History of Indian–White Relations*, Washington DC: Smithsonian Institution.

Taylor, B. (1997) 'Earthen spirituality or cultural genocide? Radical environmentalism's appropriation of Native American spirituality', *Religion*, vol.27, pp.183–215.

Vecsey, C. (ed.) (1990) *Religion in Native North America*, Moscow: University of Idaho Press.

Waters, F. (1963) *Book of the Hopi*, New York: Ballantine Books.

Weaver, J. (1997) *That the People Might Live: Native American Literatures and Native American Community*, New York: Oxford University Press.

Wolffe, J. (ed.) (2002) *Global Religious Movements in Regional Context*, Aldershot: Ashgate/Milton Keynes: The Open University.

Appendix: Declaration of War Against Exploiters of Lakota Spirituality

(Ratified by the Dakota, Lakota and Nakota Nations, June 1993)

WHEREAS we are the convenors of an ongoing series of comprehensive forums on the abuse and exploitation of Lakota spirituality; and

WHEREAS we represent the recognized traditional spiritual leaders, traditional elders, and grassroots advocates of the Lakota people; and

WHEREAS for too long we have suffered the unspeakable indignity of having our most precious Lakota ceremonies and spiritual practices desecrated, mocked, and abused by non-Indian 'wannabes', hucksters, cultists, commercial profiteers, and self-styled 'New Age Shamans' and their followers; and

WHEREAS our precious Sacred Pipe is being desecrated through the sale of pipestone pipes at flea markets, powwows, and 'New Age' retail stores; and

WHEREAS pseudo-religious corporations have been formed to charge people money for admission to phony 'sweat lodges' and 'vision quest' programs; and

WHEREAS sacrilegious 'sun dances' for non-Indians are being conducted by charlatans and cult leaders who promote abominable and obscene imitations of our sacred Lakota Sun Dance rites; and

WHEREAS non-Indians have organized themselves into 'tribes', assigning themselves make-believe 'Indian names' to facilitate their wholesale expropriation and commercialization of our Lakota traditions; and

WHEREAS academic disciplines have sprung up at colleges and universities institutionalizing the sacrilegious imitation of our spiritual practices by students and instructors under the guise of educational programs in 'shamanism'; and

WHEREAS non-Indian charlatans and 'wannabes' are selling books that promote the systematic colonization of our Lakota spirituality; and

WHEREAS the television and film industry continues to saturate the entertainment media with vulgar, sensationalist and grossly distorted representations of Lakota spirituality and culture which reinforce the public's negative stereotyping of Indian people and which gravely impair the self-esteem of our children; and

WHEREAS individuals and groups involved in the 'New Age Movement', in the 'Men's Movement', in [other] 'neo-pagan' cults, and in 'shamanism' workshops all have exploited the spiritual traditions of our Lakota people by imitating our ceremonial ways and by mixing such imitation rituals with non-Indian occult practices in an offensive and harmful pseudo-religious hodgepodge; and

WHEREAS the absurd public posturing of this scandalous assortment of psuedo-Indian charlatans, 'wannabes', commercial profiteers, cultists, and 'New Age Shamans' comprises a momentous obstacle in the struggle of traditional Lakota people for an adequate public appraisal of the legitimate political, legal, and spiritual needs of real Lakota people; and

WHEREAS this exponential exploitation of our Lakota spiritual traditions requires that we take immediate action to defend our most precious Lakota spirituality from further contamination, desecration and abuse;

Therefore we resolve as follows:

1   We hereby and henceforth declare war against all persons who persist in exploiting, abusing, and misrepresenting the sacred traditions and spiritual practices of our Lakota, Dakota, and Nakota people.

2   We call upon all our Lakota, Dakota, and Nakota brothers and sisters from reservations, reserves, and traditional communities in the United States and Canada to actively and vocally oppose this alarming take-over and systematic destruction of our sacred traditions.

3   We urge our people to coordinate with their tribal members living in urban areas to identify instances in which our sacred traditions are being abused, and then to resist this abuse, utilizing whatever specific tactics are necessary and sufficient – for example, demonstrations, boycotts, press conferences, and acts of direct intervention.

4   We especially urge all our Lakota, Dakota, and Nakota people to take action to prevent our people from contributing to and enabling abuse of our sacred ceremonies and spiritual practices by outsiders; for, as we all know, there are certain ones among our own people who are prostituting our spiritual ways for their own selfish gain, with no regard for the spiritual well-being of the people as a whole.

5   We assert a posture of zero-tolerance for any 'white man's shaman' who rises from within our own communities to 'authorize' the expropriation of our ceremonial ways by non-Indians; all such 'plastic medicine men' are enemies of the Lakota, Dakota, and Nakota people.

6   We urge traditional people, tribal leaders, and governing councils of all other Indian nations, as well as the national Indian organizations, to join us in calling for an immediate end to the rampant exploitation of our respective American Indian sacred traditions by issuing statements denouncing such abuse; for it is not the Lakota, Dakota, and Nakota people alone whose spiritual practices are being systematically violated by non-Indians.

7   We urge all our Indian brothers and sisters to act decisively and boldly in our present campaign to end the destruction of our sacred traditions, keeping in mind our highest duty as Indian people: to preserve the purity of our precious traditions for our future generations, so that our children and our children's children will survive and prosper in the sacred manner intended for each of our respective peoples by our Creator.

(source: Ward Churchill, *Indians Are Us? Culture and Genocide in Native North America*, 1994, Monroe, Maine: Common Courage Press, pp.273–7)

CHAPTER 4

Witches and Wicca

JOANNE PEARSON

Introduction

> There is something connected with the word witch that is atemporal, primordial, prehistoric (in *feeling*, whether or not in *fact*), something perhaps 'older than the human race itself'.
>
> (Adler, 1986, pp.44–5)

> When have I last looked on
> The round green eyes and the long wavering bodies
> Of the dark leopards of the moon?
> All the wild witches, those most noble ladies,
> For all their broom-sticks and their tears,
> Their angry tears, are gone.
>
> (from W.B. Yeats, 1915, 'Lines Written in Dejection')

> 'You mean – a witch?'
> 'That's just a vulgar word for it that can mean all kinds of things.'
>
> (Furlong, 1987, p.85)

Just as modern witchcraft has diverse manifestations, as we saw in Chapter 1, so the image of the witch is complex and diffuse. Contemporary interpretations of the image abound in the popular trend for identification as a witch, which reflects similar issues to those underlying the urge to identify as a Celt, discussed by Marion Bowman in Chapter 2. In particular, a perception of the witch as being close to nature, untrammelled by modernity, indigenous to Britain and Europe, and representing a kind of 'authentic spirituality' as opposed to 'institutionalized religion' make the image of the witch a source of inspiration.[1] Nevertheless, significant differences exist between self-identification as a Celt and as a witch.[2] First, whereas

---

[1] For many North American witches, this takes the form of getting back in touch with European family roots.

[2] These differences do not in any way prevent *some* witches from also identifying themselves as Celts, either because they are, for example, Scottish, Irish or Welsh, or because of elective ethnicity, or because Celtic practices are regarded as authentic and indigenous.

there have been previous revivals of Celticism, there have been no equivalent periods of popularization for the witch, despite a few individual identifications early in the twentieth century. Secondly, when people recognize themselves as witches, there is no reference to an existing ethnic group or groups; thus, while identification of oneself as a Celt, or as a Native American Indian, at least in terms of spiritual allegiance, cannot avoid making links to contemporary Welsh, Irish or Scottish people, or to various tribal peoples in North America, identification as a witch does not have to negotiate with an already existing group of people. This lack of connection with such a readily identifiable group makes the witch a less controversial target to a certain extent, since there can be no retribution from other people accusing the witches of stealing their culture and appropriating their spirituality.[3] Thirdly, identification as a Celt is now perceived as overtly and unambiguously positive. Although 'Celt' has been used as a derogatory term in the past, 'witch' continues to be used to describe a woman (usually) one dislikes or perceives as evil, nasty or wicked.

When the word 'witch' is mentioned, a whole variety of images spring to mind, some of the most common being the wicked witch of fairy tales, the evil witch of horror movies, an automatic association with evil or with the devil, and the so-called witches persecuted in the Great Witch Hunt of early modern times.[4] Other examples might be the teenage witches from films such as *The Craft* (1996), or witches and wizards from children's books. Rarely, it seems, does the word 'witch' conjure up an image of an average person doing a normal job who just happens to be engaged in the religion of Wicca. This is because extremely influential representations of the witch have developed throughout history and across cultures, many of which have had an impact on both the popular imagination and on Wicca today. A selection of these representations will be discussed in this chapter. However, first we need to ask some questions about the people who today call themselves witches. How do they come to be involved in Wicca, for example? What are their backgrounds, in terms of education, occupation and religion of upbringing? How do they

---

[3] Although people claiming to be traditional and hereditary witches would argue, of course, for biological continuity, and indeed did accuse Gardnerian Wicca of appropriating their spiritual practices. No evidence has yet been produced which can prove the existence of pre-Gardnerian Wicca, but the claims were often vehement. In the search for authentic identity, Gardnerian Wicca also accused Alexandrian Wicca of appropriating its rituals and bringing them into disrepute. We might even argue that initiation and lineage take the place of biological continuity in Wicca.

[4] From the beginning of the fifteenth to the end of the seventeenth century.

recognize themselves as witches? This will be our concern in the first section of this chapter. We shall then focus on representations of the witch, looking at their relevance to Wicca, and lastly we will examine the identificational links between witches and Wicca in an attempt to determine some of the reasons why people might wish to identify themselves as witches today.

Who are the witches and where do they come from?

The reasons people give for participating in religious activities and joining religious communities are many and varied: reasons for membership are no longer based on remaining within the religion of one's upbringing. As geographic mobility and access to the information superhighway increase, so the religious choices available to people likewise increase: global consciousness affects individual, local choice.

Wicca and Paganism, for example, are now accessible through various sites on the Internet: Elizabeth Puttick (1997, p.206) noted the existence of 40 British Pagan groups on the Internet, including the Association of Hedgewitches, Dragon Environmental Group, the Fellowship of Isis, and the Order of Bards, Ovates and Druids, and a brief scan of the Internet in January 2002 revealed 898 sites (www.witchcraft.org/index.htm)[5] linked to the web page of the Wiccan group, The Children of Artemis. Pagan and Wiccan sites have continued to multiply with access to the Internet, and Wiccan/Pagan mailing lists allow newcomers to talk to other Pagans all over the world. The spread of Paganism internationally is 'greatly facilitated by the World Wide Web and an increasing number of computer Bulletin Board Systems (BBS) which specifically serve the Pagan community' (Hume, 1997, p.96).

Yet, as we saw in Chapter 1, Wicca in the UK styles itself as a modern-day, esoteric, mystery religion[6], adopting the structure of secret, magical societies inherited from the occult revival of the *fin de siècle*. Wicca thus creates and maintains extremely resilient boundaries, operating through unstructured, changeable networks containing small, closed autonomous groups, called covens, with no overarching organizational structure. How, then, do people come to join a religious group as unusual as Wicca?

---

[5] All web sites referred to in this chapter were last accessed in January 2002.

[6] For glossary entry on mystery religions, see p.48 of this volume.

Finding Wicca, finding a coven

Wicca is non-proselytizing, and individual covens only take on a small number of people over a long period of time. Mass recruitment is neither desired nor feasible since numbers are limited by practical considerations: covens perform private rituals held in someone's house (if they are not working outdoors), and coven members often live some distance from each other so that it can be difficult to arrange meeting dates for a large number of people. A further consideration is the issue of intimacy: secrecy, intense ritualization and ritual nudity assume a high level of trust which is unlikely to be realizable in larger groups. Thus, while the maximum number of members in a coven, according to tradition, is thirteen, between five and ten initiates per coven is a more usual figure.

Contrary to the assertion of sociologists Rodney Stark and William Sims Bainbridge that 'new religions [in which they include Wicca] must grow rapidly or fail' (1985, p.365), slow organic growth is the preferred norm in Wicca, and indeed is the most realistic means of increase. Their statement that new religions 'rarely amount to much because modern societies are so large [and] must grow at astonishing rates in order to reach significant size in a generation or two' (p.365) assumes that *all* 'new religions' have a desire to bring large numbers of people under their control and significantly affect society as a whole. Yet Wicca neither grows rapidly nor fails, and its structure in autonomous covens may be in part the reason for its organic growth which, although making it less likely that Wicca will become a mainstream religion, also ensures that it does not fail. Although some covens are short lived, and may even be said, in common parlance, to 'fail', there are many that endure for years, incorporating a whole variety of changes in their membership and structure as fully-trained members '**hive off** to start their own group and new members arrive.

Where do these new members originate? Wider ranging and more open networks and groupings, such as the Pagan Federation and its localized groups, could be seen as the social network that feeds Wicca. As we noted in Chapter 1, Wiccan symbols, rituals and 'laws' have moved through the Pagan network which overlaps the Wiccan network, and a relatively similar worldview is often shared, at least to some extent. Rather than 'recruitment' or 'mobilization', then, Pagans who join Wicca may be said to be 'carried over' from one to the other (Neitz, 1994, p.135). In terms of the market economy, some notion of 'supply and demand' has entered Wicca. Thus, on the one hand, a **neophyting** course might be offered on an 'as and when required basis'. On the other hand, in the south of England, the Wicca Study Group and the Craft of the Wise run a series of workshops each year which are pre-advertised and held in public, rented rooms. To cover the cost of renting a room a charge is made for the workshops, and training for a (relatively) large number of people is facilitated.

The lack of central organization and the inherent secrecy of Wicca mean that statistics regarding numbers of attendees at workshops and other Wiccan events are not readily available. However, the Wicca Study Group figures from 1991 to 1996 record 140 people attending two or more workshops in London. Of these, 58 (41 per cent) are known to have been initiated into Wicca, and a further three were known to be preparing for initiation. Further attendees may have been initiated without the knowledge of the people involved in the running of the workshops. It is also impossible to say whether all 58 people were initiated into London covens, or how far they were spread over a wide geographical area. Of greater importance, however, is the fact that, averaged over the five-year period, only eleven or twelve people per year were initiated into Wicca from this series of workshops; thus, even when Wicca is made relatively accessible, the rate of growth remains small.

American Pagans gave six reasons for becoming involved in Paganism: for development of the imagination, intellectual satisfaction, personal growth, links with feminism and the emphasis on goddess worship, environmentalism, and freedom in religious belief and practice (Adler, 1986, pp.22–3). There are thus a variety of reasons why people identify as Pagans, witches or Wiccans, and a number of means by which they come into contact with covens – from related networks, study groups and workshops, to private letters and chance meetings. 'In most cases, word of mouth, a discussion with friends, a lecture, a book, or an article provides the entry point' (Adler, 1986, p.14), and people come to Paganism through 'extensive reading on a wide variety of subjects or by meeting someone who was already a Pagan, or a combination of both' (Hume, 1997, p.80). But having found Wicca, *why* do people become initiated as witches?

Conversion motifs

In an attempt to reflect the diversity of religious experience in both new religions and in the resurgence of traditional religions at the close of the twentieth century, John Lofland and Norman Skonovd (1983) have argued for an examination of 'conversion motifs' and proposed six such motifs. The first of these is the *intellectual*, cited as relatively uncommon but increasingly becoming important as a mode of entry into a religious community as a result of the widespread accessibility of information technology. The second motif is the *mystical*, referring to an experience, or experiences, believed by the individual to be generated from outside him or herself; emotional arousal is high, sometimes involving ecstasis. Thirdly, the *experimental* conversion motif occurs commonly with New Age groups, involving a low degree of social pressure over a long-term process of conversion. The *affectional*, fourth motif stresses the importance of bonds of affection during the conversion process. Fifthly, the *revivalist* motif refers to conversion caused by profound experience occurring within an emotionally aroused crowd. Lastly, the *coercive* motif concerns prolonged and intense external social pressure to embrace a religion, including brainwashing.[7] In a study applying these conversion motifs to Wicca, Melissa Harrington found it necessary to add a seventh motif, '*recognition*', because 'for many Wiccans the "conversion" happens long before the religion becomes apparent' – they 'recognize' themselves as Wiccan. Thus, the recognition motif 'may only be relevant to minority religions such as Wicca which are not immediately available to the religious querent' (Harrington, 2000, pp.2–3, 6).

Harrington's study of conversion to Wicca was based on pilot interviews of six subjects, followed by a field study of 102 initiated Alexandrian and/or Gardnerian witches conducted by a questionnaire. Of these, 56 were female and 46 male, the mean age was 35.5, 40 were Gardnerian witches, 3 were Alexandrian, and 59 were both Alexandrian and Gardnerian. In Harrington's study, the coercive motif showed very low presence, affectional and revivalist motifs were moderate, and the intellectual and mystical motifs showed a high presence. Older witches showed considerably less experimentation than younger witches.

Given that studies of Wicca are a recent development, and given that witches have to investigate religious alternatives in order to discover Wicca, the high presence of the intellectual motif among Wiccans is unsurprising, despite Lofland and Skonovd's findings that the motif is generally uncommon. In many cases, covens do not advertise their existence (a characteristic shared by Wicca in Australia according to Lynne Hume, who notes that advertising is an uncommon mode of entry and that groups are difficult to find (1997, p.94)). In cases where covens do advertise, it is often in a fairly closed way, in magazines obtainable only by membership in a wider Pagan organization such as the Pagan Federation. Very often, prospective initiates will find covens by word of mouth, or from

---

[7] 'Brainwashing' is a rather dubious concept, not often used by scholars of religion now (cf. Wilson and Cresswell, 1999, p.8).

writing to a public address (such as that of the Wicca Study Group, which may send letters on if it knows of a coven in the vicinity of the person writing). As we have already mentioned, other options may be through a course, such as those organized by the Wicca Study Group or Craft of the Wise, which offer workshops through which attendees might find a group of people with which to work on a casual basis, or through meeting a High Priestess or High Priest of an existing coven which has room for new members. Thus, it requires a high degree of searching to gain access to Wicca, and this time plus the pre-initiation waiting period contribute to reading and thinking prior to membership in a coven. Since Wicca is a self-styled mystery religion, the similarly high presence of the mystical motif is consistent with the nature of the religion, and again contributes to the significant presence of the intellectual conversion motif.

In Wicca, experimentation can only happen after initiation, although interaction at a less intense level than that which occurs within a coven is becoming more feasible through the workshops and open rituals organized by such bodies as the Pagan Federation. This explains the higher presence of the experimental motif among younger witches. Even this low degree of interaction would not have been possible prior to initiation before the late 1980s. In general, people seeking Wiccan initiation are only able to experiment 'blind' with techniques and philosophies derived from other related subjects (such as magic)[8] or books providing outlines of Wicca and ritual. The proliferation of such books has increased the level of experimentation, but this overlaps with the intellectual conversion motif. 'Modern Paganism depends to a great extent upon the literate world. The availability of books, newsletters, computer networks, television and various forms of media, are imperative to the knowledge and spread of Paganism' (Hume, 1997, p.80), and the same is true of Wicca.

Harrington found the relevance of the revivalist motif to be moderate, a finding which

> ... would be unlikely to have occurred ... before the snowballing revival of Pagan Spirituality eroded the closely guarded secrecy of [Wicca]. The fact that people are reporting revivalist conversion experiences within a Wiccan paradigm indicates the extent to which open festivals and Wiccan type workings have taken off in recent years.
>
> (Chapman, 1995, p.11)

---

[8] Thus, someone coming into Wicca having worked previously in a magical group may have experimented already with ritual techniques used in Wicca, such as invocation, and philosophical systems, such as the kabbalah, which they might also find within Wicca.

The negative correlation Harrington found between age and level of experimentation is also consistent with this revival of Pagan spirituality, but apart from more females reporting a higher degree of pressure to join Wicca, Harrington found few differences by tradition, degree of initiation, age or gender.

However, it was Harrington's additional motif of 'recognition' that showed the highest presence in her results. Participants in her pilot study responded negatively to the idea of conversion, regarding themselves as Wiccan before confirming this identity with initiation. She reports four out of the six pilot study subjects using the same words, 'coming home', to describe initiation – treating initiation as confirmation of an identity they already had, as consolidation rather than conversion – for 'people do not convert to Paganism and thus do not "become" Pagan' (Harvey, 1997, p.192). As one Pagan author says, relating her own experience, 'Like most neo-Pagans, I never converted in the accepted sense – I never adopted any new beliefs. I simply accepted, reaffirmed, and extended a very old experience. I allowed certain kinds of feelings and ways of being back into my life' (Adler, 1986, p.20). A sense of 'coming home' appears to be applicable across the board in both Paganism and Wicca. In Australia, 'many say that they felt they were "coming home" or it felt "like home", as if all that they had done before was leading up to this homecoming, coupled with the sense of Paganism as being "right", not in an intellectual sense, but rather in an emotional sense' (Hume, 1997, p.91).

Recognition as motivation for initiation into Wicca has direct implications for the way in which Wiccan covens are organized, and on the structure of Wicca as a whole. Recognition of oneself as Wiccan comes *prior* to actual initiation, but such recognition does not, however, give a potential Wiccan initiate access to Wicca – the organizational structure of Wicca necessitates recognition from, and acceptance by, a coven in order for initiation to proceed. In this way, Wicca maintains its boundaries and preserves its integrity as a mystery religion operating through small, closed groups, intimate community constructed with initiatory rites of entry, passwords, rules of secrecy and ritual communitas. Thus, one can recognize oneself as a witch, or as a Wiccan, but initiates of Wicca only recognize as fellow Wiccans those who have been admitted into the core community of a coven through a Wiccan rite of initiation.

Descent, assent and recognition: children

The recognition factor in seeking initiation into Wicca raises substantial questions as to the nature of the Wiccan religion and community. There are very few people who grew up as Wiccans, but a new generation of children is being brought up by Wiccan parents. No figures are available as yet for the UK, but in the USA, it has been estimated that there are 82,600 children currently being raised in neo-Pagan families (Berger, 1999, p.83). It is important to note that these children are not regarded as 'Pagan' or 'Wiccan' children, but as children of 'Wiccan/Pagan parents'. Pagan parents claim that they are careful not to indoctrinate their children, deeming it important that their children are left to make their own choices when they are old enough. However, they still find it necessary to have accessible material available, for children cannot be expected to keep silent about their parents' religion and resources are thus invariably useful for giving to schools and to the parents of schoolfriends. In addition, the children themselves often want to know what their parents take part in with their friends at Hallowe'en or full moon. As a result, books are being produced to help Wiccan and Pagan parents in the upbringing of their children. The Pagan Federation, for example, has published *A Pagan Child's ABC* by Jeremy and Arihanto (n.d.), and a children's booklet on the eight Pagan festivals written by Sandy B; New Wiccan Publications published D. Weardale's *The Pagan Child* (1994), which is described as 'a handbook for teachers, carers, childminders and all those involved in looking after the children of Pagan parents'. A workshop on parenting was held at the 1994 Pagan Federation conference, and by 1996 a Pagan Family Newsletter was being produced. In 1995, the journal *Pagan Dawn* carried an article on Pagan parenting and the first in a series of advice columns to 'deal with the problems surrounding Pagan Families' (Issue 114, Imbolc, p.19). Such 'problems' appear to take the form of children sharing secrets at school, indulging 'curious friends with tales about [their parents'] practices and beliefs' (p.18), with the resulting fear of victimization, bullying or the involvement of social services.

The children of Wiccan parents tend to be encouraged to learn about many different religious traditions, beliefs and practices, and the mythology found in comparative religions and civilizations. Wiccan parents teach their children to respect nature, and will often perform celebratory rituals with their children at the festivals, often because the children have asked to be included but are not allowed to join in the adult rituals. The children have a great deal of fun and feel that they are doing something special rather than being left out of their parents' special time of year. Christian festivals such as Christmas and Easter are also celebrated with children in mind, though often with an emphasis on myth and narrative; thus, Easter eggs can be explained as a symbol of fertility and new life, and the Easter bunny as the hare, a symbol of the Saxon goddess Eostre. The relationship between Pagan festivals and Christian celebrations is thus outlined, perhaps giving the children of Wiccan parents access to a greater range of traditional religious practices. Thus, while children are clearly influenced by their parents' beliefs and practices, they are not usually under any pressure to 'convert'.

These children will not, therefore, become Wiccans by descent – they are not deemed to be Wiccan because they were born to Wiccan parents, and they will have to recognize themselves as Wiccan and seek initiation when they are old enough to decide their spiritual path for themselves. For most Wiccan covens, initiation is not possible before the age of 18 and, in fact, people tend to be significantly older at the time of their initiation.

Sociological data

As indicated above, the age of Wiccans ranges from 18 upwards, with most falling between the ages of 25 and 45 (see Figure 4.1),[9] the average age being around 35. In the USA, most witches are in their teens, twenties and thirties (Russell, 1991, p.171), and in a Canadian survey more than half the respondents fell within the 20 to 40 age range. Australian covens have 'a fairly wide age spread, though the largest number appear to be aged between 25 and 55, tending towards the younger end of the spectrum' (Hume, 1997, p.103). Given the fact that Wicca is only 50 years old, it is unsurprising that there are only a relatively small number of Wiccans in the older age range of 50 or over. As Wicca continues and grows older itself, we can expect to see age distribution diffusing to cover the range from 50 to 100. The Wiccan practice of not initiating people under the age of 18 means it is unlikely that the age distribution of Wicca will lower to include the under-twenties. Indeed, the Pagan Federation decided in November 1998 not to allow membership below the age of 18, although a network for teenagers interested in Paganism, called Minor Arcana, was established the same year.

[9] Figures 4.1 and 4.2 are both derived from a survey conducted by the author in the UK in 1996.

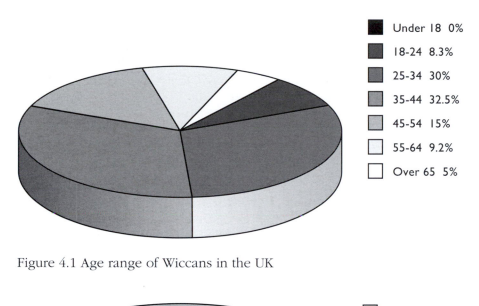

Under 18 0%
18-24 8.3%
25-34 30%
35-44 32.5%
45-54 15%
55-64 9.2%
Over 65 5%

Figure 4.1 Age range of Wiccans in the UK

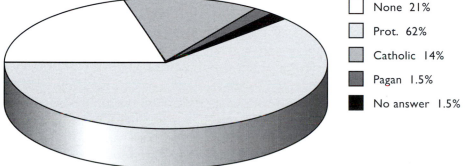

None 21%
Prot. 62%
Catholic 14%
Pagan 1.5%
No answer 1.5%

Figure 4.2 Religious background of Wiccans in the UK

While children are now being brought up by Wiccan and Pagan parents, this is a recent development. Since Wicca has only been established for half a century, the overwhelming majority of those involved in Wicca grew up with a different religious faith. We can see from Figure 4.2 that Wiccans in the UK are overwhelmingly of Protestant religious background. This can be compared with Jone Salomonsen's portrait of the religious background of Reclaiming witches in the USA, where Catholic and Protestant were roughly equal in representation (35 and 32 per cent respectively), and 21 per cent were of Jewish background (Salomonsen, 1996). A 1990 study found 24.5 per cent Catholic, 58.8 per cent Protestant and 9.1 per cent Jewish (Orion, 1995), while a 1986 survey found 23.5 per cent Catholic, 39.2 per cent Protestant and 5.4 per cent Jewish (Adler, 1986). This significant and increasing proportion of Jewish witches in the USA has led to them coining the term 'Jewitch' to describe themselves, Starhawk being the most well known. In contrast, from a survey conducted by the author in the UK in 1996, only one respondent indicated that she had a Jewish *cultural* background, but added that she was brought up with no religion.

That Protestantism is the religious background of the majority of initiated Wiccans in the UK is consistent with the religious background of the general populace at large. Figures from the *UK Christian Handbook* indicate that there are some 32 million Protestants in England and Wales, compared with only 5,500,000 Roman Catholics and 300,000 Jews. We could assume then that Wiccans in the Republic of Ireland, for example, may be of Irish Catholic background, reflecting the religious affinities of the Irish population in general, but this is highly unlikely. It has been argued that Wicca is more popular in Northern European, Protestant countries, where people lack any focus for the divine feminine (i.e. the Goddess), rites of passage and a sense of ritual, factors that remain popular in the Catholicism of southern Europe and the Mediterranean (Crowley, 1998, p.171). Certainly, the very small number of respondents of Catholic background in the UK survey conducted by the author, on which Figures 4.1 and 4.2 are based, together with the fact that responses from Europe outside the UK were from Scandinavia, Germany and Austria rather than Spain, Portugal and Italy, suggest that this assertion may contain some truth. In this study, 76 per cent of Wiccans claimed a Christian background, possibly nominal, but certainly at times practising. Almost a quarter (21 per cent) had no religious background. However, no research has been published to suggest that Wiccans move straight from Christianity to Wicca, and fieldwork suggests that there is usually a gap of some years between people feeling that Christianity is no longer relevant to their lives and finding Wicca. A straightforward disaffection or disillusionment with Christianity is therefore unlikely to be the main cause of Wiccan membership. Instead, as we have seen, rather than asserting any disaffection with Christianity, conversion motifs among Wiccans are predominantly mystical and concerned with recognition of oneself as a witch.

There is almost an equal proportion of men and women in British Wicca, compared with a gender imbalance in the USA, Canada and Australia (Pearson, 2000). In a historical survey of witchcraft which concluded with a study of contemporary North American witchcraft, it was suggested that 'women outnumber men by about two to one, and this imbalance may be growing because of the increase in feminist witchcraft' (Russell, 1991, p.171). However, the study by Kirkpatrick *et al.* (1986) found men and women to be represented equally, whereas a 1990 study showed a split of 38 per cent male and

57.8 per cent female (with 4.2 per cent claiming to be androgynous) (Orion, 1995). Early survey results from Canada in 1995/6 presented by researcher Siân Reid to the Nature Religion Scholars List in June 1999 indicated that three-quarters of her 187 respondents were female, and only one-quarter male. The Australian national census in 1996 resulted in a figure of 1,849 witches, of whom 1,242 were women and 607 were men – that is, two-thirds of Australian witches were female (report made available to the Nature Religion Scholars List, June 1999). The Australian census also revealed 4,353 Pagans and 556 Druids. Figures suggest that Wicca in the UK is not predominantly a religion for women and that its emphasis on the Goddess is attractive to men as well as women. It would thus be inaccurate to assume that Wicca in the UK is merely part of the feminist spirituality movement.

With regard to education, in the UK survey conducted by the author (Pearson, 2000), half of the Wiccans were university educated, seven had a masters degree, nine had doctorates, and one was studying for a doctorate. At least a further 25 per cent of the Wiccans in this study had acquired professional qualifications in nursing, teaching or counselling/therapies. Favoured occupations appear to be healing professions (medicine, counselling, psychotherapy), education (students, academics, teachers), computing, administration and entrepreneurial roles (fifteen had their own businesses). Only one person was seeking employment. In Australia, witches are represented across a wide socio-economic range, including 'university professors, students, school teachers, engineers, musicians, a prison officer, artists, entertainers, sales people, computer specialists, cleaners, chefs, clerks, cashiers and the unemployed' (Hume, 1997, p.102). Occupational profiles of initiated witches reveal 'a higher than usual amount of independence and self-organization ... a greater than usual love of reading and commitment to constant self-education' (Hutton, 1999, p.402), for 'most witches are relatively well educated' (Russell, 1991, p.171).

British witches thus come from a variety of backgrounds and occupations. And yet, despite this wide range, there remains a certain homogeneity about the background of witches. Far from being old women in pointed hats living on the margins of society, the sociological profiles we have just looked at suggest that witches are: (1) men as well as women; (2) well educated; (3) in professional employment; (4) fully integrated with society; (5) aged anywhere from 18 upwards (i.e. neither old *nor* young); and (6) of a religious background comparable to the majority of people in the UK. In addition, we have seen that they actively seek out Wicca, actively seek to be witches; since witches have a predominantly Protestant or

Catholic religious background, there comes a point where they *choose* to identify themselves as witches.

In the next section we look at images of the witch, examining how this figure has been represented in a variety of mediums (including literature, film and art) through a selection of examples.[10] First we consider where the word 'witch' originated and what calling oneself a witch might mean. Why might people of the sociological profile outlined above wish to identify themselves as witches? And what, if anything, is the connection between contemporary Wicca and early modern witchcraft?

The image of the witch

The word 'witch' is notoriously ambiguous and complex – it can mean all kinds of things. Even the etymology of words such as 'witch/craft' and 'Wicca' is debatable. 'Wicca', some Wiccans argue, derives from the same root as the Anglo-Saxon word for knowledge, *wit*, *wittich*, which stems from *weet* meaning 'to know', and such a definition lends itself to modern witches' understanding of themselves as 'wise' men and women who practise the 'Craft of the Wise'. Similarly, some suggest that 'Wicca' derives from the Anglo-Saxon word *wik*, meaning to 'bend or shape', which links nicely with modern witches' definition of magic, which is to bend or shape energy through will in order to make manifest something on the physical plane. However, 'Wicca', it seems, does not stem from the same root as that for knowledge. Rather, 'it was simply the Anglo-Saxon word for a *male* witch (female, "*wicce*")' (Hutton, 1993, p.xiv), the plural form of which may have been 'Wiccan'. The words 'witch' and 'wicca' are therefore linked etymologically, but they are used to emphasize different things today. The word 'witch', for example, is used by many Wiccans in an attempt to reclaim it and place it in a modern context. Others use the term 'Wicca' in an effort to define witchcraft as a religion. This is largely because the word 'witch' may be taken to refer to the practice of 'witchcraft', often perceived to be the use of spellcraft and natural magic on behalf of clients. Such assumptions may regard witchcraft as a craft used to make a living rather than as a religion. As the Wiccan author Vivianne Crowley explains:

> Wicca is the name given by its practitioners to the religion of witchcraft. The word 'Wicca' derives from the Anglo-Saxon word for

[10] However, these examples are not intended to trace the development of representations of the witch through 2,000 years of history.

witch and has been used in its present sense since the 1950s. Within the Wiccan community, the term 'witchcraft' is used in a special sense to mean a Pagan mystery religion and nature religion which worships Goddess and God and is open to both men and women. The words 'witchcraft' and 'witch' are often capitalised by practitioners to distinguish their form of 'witchcraft' from anthropological and other uses of the word.

(Crowley, 1998, pp.170–1)

If the etymology and usage of the words 'Wiccan', 'witch' and 'witchcraft' are contentious, the images produced are even more so. The word 'witch' in particular holds many connotations in the public mind, most of which are negative. It draws the popular imagination to story-book notions of the 'wicked witch', to the historical per-secutions of witches for being 'in league with the devil', and to modern reports of satanic abuse in the sensationalist tabloid press. Somewhat paradoxically, it also tends to hold within it opposing images. Thus, the *Oxford English Dictionary* claims that the witch is both an ugly old woman or hag, and a fascinating girl or woman, a definition not so far removed from that of Ambrose Bierce in his 1911 *The Enlarged Devil's Dictionary*: '(1) An ugly and repulsive old woman, in a wicked league with the devil. (2) A beautiful and attractive young woman, in wickedness a league beyond the devil' (Bierce, 1987, p.318).

It seems that witches polarize opinion in the popular imagination. Young *and* old, beautiful *and* ugly, the witch is perhaps never quite as she seems; she appears to everyone in a different guise, and we read her according to our own context and expectations. Writing at a time when books on Wicca and on witchcraft are commonplace, for example, Terry Pratchett is able to blend the new and the old in the witch books of his Discworld series, which star Granny Weatherwax ('a witch with a whim of steel'), Nanny Ogg (a 'shameless old reprobate') and Magrat Garlick ('the young, desperately earnest New Age witch').[11] *Wyrd Sisters* (Pratchett, 1988) parodies Shakespeare's *Macbeth*, *Witches Abroad* (Pratchett, 1991) opposes rival fairy godmothers in a parody of Cinderella, while in *Equal Rites* (Pratchett, 1987), Granny Weatherwax converses with a tree (which was once a wizard!) on the nature of witchcraft:

> *Women have never been wizards. It's against nature. You might as well say that witches can be men.*
>
> If you define a witch as one who worships the pancreative urge, that is, venerates the basic – the tree began, and continued for several

---

[11] Descriptions of all three witches are from Clute and Grant (1997).

minutes. Granny Weatherwax listened in impatient annoyance to phrases like Mother Goddesses and primitive moon worship and told herself that she was well aware of what being a witch was all about, it was about herbs and curses and flying around of nights and generally keeping on the right side of tradition, and it certainly didn't involve mixing with goddesses, mothers or otherwise, who apparently got up to some very questionable tricks.

(Pratchett, 1987, p.35)

That witches cannot be men seems to be a rule set in stone as far as literature, art and films are concerned. But is the witch good, or is she wicked, and whose definitions of such terms do we accept? For a Wiccan, for example, Arthurian witches such as Vivianne[12] and Morgan le Fay[13] might be considered 'good'. They are regarded as powerful, intelligent women whose dynamism encourages imaginative identification. For a Christian, however, especially one reading Arthuriana in the time of the Great Witch Hunt, they might be regarded as a destructive force, challenging the new Christianity of the British Isles. And while the witch may well have been 'simplified to the point of caricature ... easy to depict ... with a few strokes of the pen or a crude silhouette' (Briggs, 1996, p.20), she might still be evil and frightening to a child enthralled by stories and fairy tales.

Stories from our earliest childhood undoubtedly inform our image of the witch, for good or ill. John Masefield's *The Midnight Folk* (1927) presents witches as evil and as dangerous women who gather in groups but are subordinate to male wizards. Witches are never nice, especially when they come in the form of one's governess! *The Lion, the Witch and the Wardrobe* by C.S. Lewis, published in 1950 and frequently dramatized for stage and television, offers a summation of wicked witch motifs: the nameless archetype may *seem* nice with her offers of warmth and sweets, but she is really an ice queen (a 'white witch'), cold, hard and intractable, descended from **Lilith** rather than Eve, and quite prepared to kidnap children to further her aims.

Children's literature from the 1960s onwards, however, saw a change in the portrayal of the witch that occurred alongside, though independently of, the publicizing of witchcraft and Wicca by Gerald Gardner, Alex Sanders and others (see Chapter 1, pp.32–6). Imogen Chichester's *The Witch-child* (1965) and Helen Cresswell's *Lizzie*

[12] Vivianne, sometimes called Nimüe, is the Lady of the Lake in Arthurian legend, who reputedly stole the wizard Merlin's magical powers before trapping him either in a cave or in the trunk of a tree.

[13] Morgan le Fey is the legendary enchantress and half sister of Arthur. She is also presented as the mistress of Avalon, where she heals Arthur of his mortal wounds.

Dripping (1973), for example, drew on ideas of flying on broomsticks, spells, long robes and pointed hats in their descriptions of witches, but nevertheless challenged the image of the witch as evil: to Lizzie, the witch is a friend, while the witch child, Necromancy Grumblethrush, merely has to come to terms with following in her parents' footsteps and being a witch. For Madeleine Edmonson, in *Anna Witch* (1983), witches are beautiful although 'their hair does not hang down like ours but floats upward from their heads. That is why they wear such tall hats. Witches have chicken feet and pointed ears, and their skin is very light green' (p.7). But still, they are not evil. And Louise Lawrence taps into the link between witches and nature in her description of the Earth Witch, written in the more environmentally conscious 1980s:

> Someone was standing by the corner of the barn, a woman under moonlight. He could see the pale oval of her face and the black drifts of her hair. Her white gown fluttered. Very still she was standing, as if she was sprung from the earth and rooted there. With her gaze she was owning the moors and the meadows, the hills and the trees and the stones ... In the wind was her breathing, and deep she was seeing into the heart of things, touching the seeds with a dream of leaves and flowers.
>
> (Lawrence, 1989, pp.42–3)

Collections and anthologies added to the image of the witch in the 1970s and 1980s. Such works included Jacynth Hope-Simpson's *Covens and Cauldrons* (1977, which included an extract from Gardner's *Witchcraft Today*), Barbara Sleigh's *Broomsticks and Beasticles* (1981) and Dorothy Edward's *Mists and Magic* (1983). The late 1990s saw a revival of the genre on television, including Jill Murphy's *The Worst Witch* (1974), which in 2000 enjoyed its third series on Children's ITV, telling the adventures of Mildred Hubble (the 'worst witch') and her friends at Cackle's Academy for Witches (see Figure 4.3). ITV also broadcast *Sabrina the Teenage Witch*, an American sitcom about a witch family living in modern-day America, very reminiscent of the 1960s series *Bewitched* (itself broadcast by Channel 4 in the late 1990s). Not to be outdone, the BBC televised Kate Saunders' stories of *The Belfry Witches* who, interestingly, are a different species (though they look like humans) who come from Witch Island. The two stars of the show, Skirty and Noshie, are both over 100 years old but look in their mid-teens, have a good relationship with the vicars of the village, and are allowed to live in the church belfry. Perhaps this is significant for the future of Wiccan/ Christian relations!

Figure 4.3 Mildred Hubble is easily recognizable as a witch from her silhouette on the cover of Jill Murphy's book, *The Worst Witch* (Puffin, Harmondsworth, 1983). Illustration copyright © Jill Murphy, 1998.

There is no indication in *The Worst Witch, Sabrina* or *The Belfry Witches* that witchcraft is, or can be, a religion; rather, the stories deal with magic and its use in daily life, and in that sense continue the tradition of feeding children's imaginations with impossible scenes and longings for special powers. In another sense, however, such impossibilities reflect some of the same motifs cited in the Great Witch Hunt, such as the belief that witches could fly through the air on their broomsticks, or that witches are essentially 'different' from 'ordinary people', despite their superficial similarities. But religion does inform the American show *Charmed*, first shown in the UK on Channel 5 in 2000, which specifically refers to 'Wicca' (the first episode was called 'Something Wiccan This Way Comes'), refers to a **Book of Shadows**, and portrays witches as good guys, fighting against the forces of evil. Using the idea of hereditary witchcraft, three adult sisters find out that they are descended from generations of witches through the female line ('it's a chick thing', we are told!), and many of their adventures involve fighting the evil (male) warlocks and similarly threatening patriarchs.

Colour Plate 1 The Wheel of the Year. Designed by Jane Brideson. © Jane Brideson.

Colour Plate 2 Callanish Standing Stones, Isle of Lewis, Outer Hebrides, Scotland. Ancient Art and Architecture Collection. Photo: © 1991 Cheryl Hogue.

**A Blessing
On Leaving Home**

*As you leave your home
God in peace
go with you.
As you leave this shelter
God in power
protect you.
As you leave this love
God in love
enfold you.
God bless and keep you
until in joy
we meet again.*

David Adam

Colour Plate 3 A 'Celtic-style' prayer card. Copyright 1996 David Adam; © Border design by Jean Freer. Reproduced by permission of Tim Tiley Ltd.

Colour Plate 4 Susan J. Davis, Glastonbury, *1990, 46 × 61 cms, oil on canvas. A romantic representation of a druid at Glastonbury. Copyright Susan J. Davis.*

Colour Plate 5 A ghost shirt. Photo: Glasgow Museums; Art Gallery and Museum, Kelvingrove.

Colour Plate 6 'Can you resist the power of the Black Wych?' The Wychwood Brewery uses the image to great effect in advertising its Black Wych stout. Courtesy of The Wychwood Brewery.

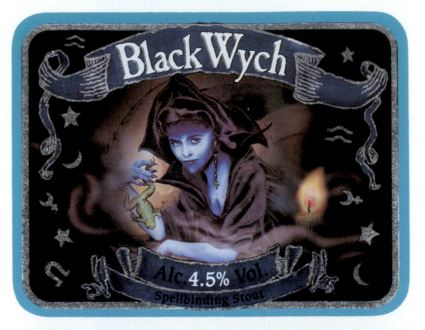

Colour Plate 7 'Welcome to the Witching Hour': good and evil prepare for battle once more. Ronald Grant Archive.

Colour Plate 8 John William Waterhouse, Circe Offering the Cup to
Ulysses, *1891, oil on canvas, 146 × 90 cm. Oldham Art Gallery,
Lancashire/The Bridgeman Art Library.*

Colour Plate 9 *The witch Nimuë weaves her spells around Merlin, in Sir Edward Burne-Jones,* The Beguiling of Merlin, *1874, oil on canvas, 186 × 111 cms. Board of Trustees of the National Museums and Galleries on Merseyside (Lady Lever Art Gallery, Port Sunlight).*

Colour Plate 10 Anonymous, Trial of Galileo, circa 1633, oil on canvas, dimensions not known. Private Collection/The Bridgeman Art Library.

Colour Plate 11 What happened before the Big Bang? Some have pointed to an act of divine creation at this point. Science Photo Library.

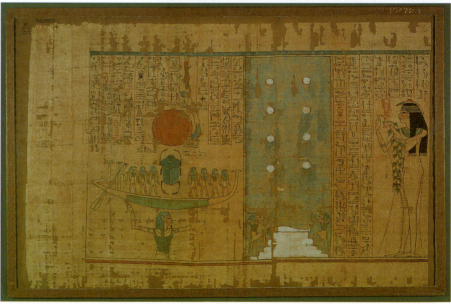

Colour Plate 12 Papyrus of Anhai, Department of Egyptian Antiquities, British Museum. The scarab beetle was an ancient Egyptian symbol of rebirth. © The British Museum.

So it seems that children's and young adults' literature and
television programmes more than meet the demand for witches. But
these are only a few of the representations of the witch. Films such as
The Wizard of Oz (1939, based on Frank L. Baum's 1900 novel, *The
Wonderful Wizard of Oz*) portrayed both the wicked witch (two, in
fact, although the Wicked Witch of the East is killed when Dorothy's
house lands on her at the beginning of the film) and the good witch
(Glinda, the Witch of the North) (see Figure 4.4). Diane Purkiss
begins the introduction to her book *The Witch in History* by
recounting her fascination with *The Wizard of Oz* as a small child:

> To me, the Wicked Witch of the West did not seem to 'belong' to the
> bright and pretty world of Oz; she overwhelmed its illusory harmony;
> her presence was too strong to be contained within its fictional and
> discursive borders ... My identification with her was a secret even from
> me; I wanted to be her partly so that I would not have to be afraid of
> her.

(Purkiss, 1996, p.1)

Interestingly, it is the wicked witch (played by Margaret Hamilton)
Purkiss remembers, not the good witch. The good witch is all frothy
dresses and sparkle, a real fairy godmother, and not at all the

Figure 4.4 Margaret Hamilton as the
stereotypical Wicked Witch of the West
in *The Wizard of Oz* (1939). Ronald
Grant Archive.

Figure 4.5 Cartoon of a witch from *Punch*, 1911.

THE WELSH NATIONAL STEEPLECHASE.

"'OLD WOMAN, OLD WOMAN, WHITHER SO HIGH?'
'TO SWEEP THE STEEPLES OFF THE SKY.'"

Figure 4.6 '*All Hail Macbeth*': Shakespeare's witches as three 'black and midnight hags'. From *Illustrated Stratford Shakespeare*, reproduced by permission of the Birmingham Libraries.

Figure 4.7 '*An Evening with Friends*' – greeting card witches. Courtesy of Julian Williams/ Two Bad Mice.

traditional image of the witch. The stereotypical imagery of witchcraft is saved for the wicked witch, who wears black robes and a pointed hat, has a hooked nose and long finger nails, rides on a broomstick, has strange familiars, and steals children away. This stereotype can be found in cartoons and in literature, from Shakespeare's three 'secret, black and midnight hags' in *Macbeth*, to children's stories, in fairy tales and in film. It even appears on greetings cards and in advertising (see Colour Plate 6).

The juxtaposition of good and evil, light and dark, continues to be embodied in the witch: in 1996, this was made evident in the film *The Craft*, in which, of the four teenage experimenters in witchcraft, Nancy (Fairuza Balk) is portrayed as 'bad', Sarah (Robin Tunney) as 'good', and Bonnie and Rochelle (Neve Capbell and Rachel True) as in thrall to the 'baddie' (see Colour Plate 7). But, of course, it is rarely that easy to separate good from bad, and we should not allow ourselves to become too insistent on the diametrical opposition of wicked witches and good witches, or black witches and white witches. The witch is more complex than that.

We might take as an example Medea, a witch from ancient mythology. Medea combines the 'wild witch' and the 'noble lady', being at once a princess and a priestess, with responsibility for ritual correctness and obligations to the gods and the people, and a wild witch with bare feet and streaming hair howling in the woods at night. She has power over animals, travels widely through the night air to gather the ingredients for her cauldron, has both esoteric and worldly knowledge, and is fearless, going out alone into the woods at night. All these are motifs associated with witchcraft.[14] Yet at the same time Medea is besotted with the Greek hero Jason, and used badly by him. Her ambiguity as a witch and as a woman reveals her to be at once a victim and a criminal, as much sinned against as sinning. In one version of her story, *Metamorphoses 7*, written by the Roman poet and philosopher Ovid (43 BCE – CE 17), it is suggested that society both denies a woman power and rejects her when she acquires it, showing how fragile social conventions are and how ineffective they are to either protect or restrain women (Newlands, 1997, p.208). Such ambiguity appears throughout history in descriptions of witches and people's reaction to and treatment of them, and this may be one of the reasons for the perpetual appeal of Medea. Her story has been reinterpreted over and over again, from its first appearances in Greek and Roman literature to Brendan Kennelly's reworking of Euripides'

---

[14] Pratchett tells us 'Granny Weatherwax ... had walked nightly without fear in the bandit-haunted forests of the mountains all her life in the certain knowledge that the darkness held nothing more terrible than she was' (1991, p.23).

version in 1988 and Christa Wolf's 1998 novel, *Medea: A Modern Retelling*. Our fascination with this witch-woman seems endless, and she appeals to men and women alike.

Before the recent interpretations mentioned above, however, images of witches from the ancient world were resurrected and reinterpreted in the art of the late-Victorian period, contemporaneous with the occult revival in Britain. Artists such as Dante Gabriel Rossetti, Edward Burne-Jones, George Frederick Watts and Frederick Sandys sought to present women as the visible embodiment of the spiritual realm explored partly through representations of powerful female figures from ancient mythology. Here we have men painting witches who continue to be female as opposed to male. While it may be argued that male artists paint women apparently celebrating them while actually trapping them in a specific interpretation, it is nevertheless worth remembering that, whatever the intention of the artists, their paintings can be read by observers in many different ways. Typically dark-haired (an exception being Waterhouse's 1911 painting *The Sorceress*), the Victorian witch is extremely stylish and beautifully dressed, yet remains surrounded by cauldrons, concoctions, and animal familiars such as toads, snakes and ravens. The night still belongs to her, and the fascination of the unknown attracts us at the same time as we fear it. Perhaps, like Purkiss, some women want to be these witches, to own their power partly so that they don't have to be frightened of it. By using the images of the witch in a particular way (see below), Wiccans aim to reclaim the witch rather than allowing her image to be dictated by men, or used to fulfil a male fantasy.

It is in this context that Circe and Medea reappear. Both are divine, or at least semi-divine. And yet, at the same time, they are sorceresses, witches, for to be a priestess of **Hecate**, goddess of the witches, is to be a witch. Medea is depicted as a figure of powerful, though vengeful, womanhood, the most well-known depiction being that painted by Frederick Sandys in 1866–8 where the witch is shown treating with fire the threads with which a magic garment is to be woven. Circe's power as well as her beauty are emphasized in two paintings by John William Waterhouse. In *Circe Invidiosa* (1892), the enchantress, enraged by petty jealousy, is poisoning the sea. However, leaving aside any moral judgement we or the artist might have, it is clear that power flows from her, a power gleaned from the elements suggesting she is at one with them (she is the daughter of Helios the sun god and the ocean nymph Perse). This is a natural force, which she controls because she is part of it – she stands in the centre of a whirlpool, the swirls reflected in her wind-blown hair. In *Circe Offering the Cup to Ulysses* (1891) (see Colour Plate 8), strength and sexuality are again made clear. Circe appears not merely as a femme fatale luring men to their doom, but as a strong and powerful woman (i.e. a witch) seeking her equal – a New Woman, perhaps, who speaks with an undeniably powerful voice which will not be silenced by the Victorian proscription on sorceresses and 'fallen women'.

Waterhouse continued to draw on classical imagery for *The Magic Circle* (1886), where the witch is depicted as a striking young woman in a Mediterranean setting. Her black hair and dark features suggest someone dangerous and powerful, reinforced by the snake coiled around her neck. Her dress of pale grey-blue depicts around the lower half of the skirt scenes from Greek legends, while the amber and jet bead necklace echoes that worn by contemporary witches. She has a purple sash tied around her waist, into which is knotted a bunch of daisies, and her feet are bare as she moves about the circle. In her hands she carries a sickle and a sword with which she draws a magic circle. Other motifs of witchcraft appear in the painting, including seven ravens, a toad, a human skull on which one of the ravens is perched, and umbelliferous plants, such as hemlock and opium poppies with their seed cases – perhaps some of the contents of the brew in the cauldron. In the smoke and steam released from the cauldron appears a demon or spirit, presumably conjured up by the witch. And in the background stands a robed and cloaked woman watching the proceedings, while others wait at the entrance to the cave. This is a powerful depiction of witchcraft: the witch is presented as a dynamic figure, not as the ugly old crone of the popular imagination, and as such the painting has become very popular among contemporary Wiccans.

But it was not just classical mythology that provided images of witches: there were plenty to choose from in Arthurian legend and the canon of British and Irish folklore, where beautiful women in long robes use their power for good or ill with the aid of ravens, owls, cats and potions. Medievalism and the legends of King Arthur became very popular in the second half of the nineteenth century, particularly after the publication of Tennyson's *Idylls of the King* in 1859, and they remain popular to this day, influencing the identities of some Wiccans just as they influence some Celtic identities.[15] The Arthurian style is obvious in Sandys's *Morgan le Fay* (1864). The other famous witch of Arthurian legend, Vivianne/Nimuë, the Lady of the Lake, is depicted by Edward Burne-Jones holding a spell book from which she issues the spell that lulls Merlin to sleep in a hawthorn tree

---

[15] The most obvious example being the Arch Druid King Arthur Uther Pendragon, mentioned in Chapter 2.

in the forest of Broceliande in *The Beguiling of Merlin* (1874), a painting derived from a story in the French medieval *Romance of Merlin* (see Colour Plate 9). The sinuous figure of Nimuë has snakes entwined on top of her head, echoed in the twisting branches of the surrounding hawthorn tree. Arthur Rackham chose an alternative version, of Vivianne entrapping Merlin in a cave, for his illustration of *The Romance of King Arthur and his Knights of the Round Table*, the 1917 abridgement of Sir Thomas Malory's *Morte d'Arthur* (1485).

Figure 4.8 Arthur Rackham's illustration of Vivianne entrapping Merlin, 1917. Mary Evans/Arthur Rackham Collection.

However, earlier depictions, including medieval paintings and engravings of witches, were quite different (see Figure 4.9). Portrayals of witches as female and nude were conventional then and have influenced the modern Wiccan practice of ritual nudity, which Wiccans have sought to legitimate and explain with a variety of provenances and explanations, such as that they are following the traditions of the Celts or the mystery religions of the ancient world (Crowley, 1996, p.98). Other Wiccans cite sources such as ancient Greek and Roman practices of working nude or 'in loose flowing garments', nudity during a ritual of initiation at the Villa of the Mysteries in Pompeii (Valiente, 1989, pp.59, 102; 1993, p.73), and Tantric worship which 'gives further meaning to the custom of ritual nudity, which is found in the east as well as the west' (Valiente, 1989, p.141).

To many Wiccans, being naked, or 'skyclad', allows power to flow from the body unimpeded, and when robes are worn, natural fabrics such as cotton, silk or wool are preferred, as natural fibres are thought to allow magical energy to pass through them.

> The traditional ritual nudity has for its purpose the free flow of power from the naked bodies of the participants ... when a circle of naked or loosely robed dancers gyrates in a witchcraft ceremony, the power flowing from their bodies rises upwards towards the centre of the circle, forming a cone-shape which is called the Cone of Power.
>
> (Valiente, 1993, p.73)

Other witches have reported that nudity 'increases their contact with the powers of nature ... erases class distinctions ... [allows them] to appear before the gods as they were born, with nothing to hide ... [and] gives them a salutary sense of freedom' (Russell, 1991, p.169). Modern witches sometimes point to the painting *Love's Enchantment* (*Der Liebeszauber*, Flemish School 1670–80) as a piece of historical evidence for working in the nude as well as to Hans Baldung Grien's *Two Witches* (1480) (reproduced as Figure 4.9) and Albrecht Dürer's engraving *The Four Witches* (1497). Contemporary witches consider that nudity confers unity by stripping away signs of social differentiation. Yet there are also numerous representations of the witch in art which, while often depicting the witch as female, also paint her fully clothed – Francisco de Goya's *The Spell* (1797–8) and *Witches' Sabbath* (1794–5), for example. Perhaps these later paintings are regarded by Wiccans as less authentic representations of witches than those of the fifteenth century.

Some of these paintings are better known than others, but interest in them is certainly increasing with the staging of major exhibitions, their high cultural visibility in card and print shops, and their active

Figure 4.9 Hans Baldung Grien, *Two Witches* (*Zwei Hexen*), 1523, oil on pine panels, 65 × 45 cms. Städelsches Kunstinstitut Frankfurt/Foto © Ursula Edelmann, Frankfurt am Main.

promotion by British art galleries from London to Liverpool, Oldham to Cardiff. Goya's paintings are frequently used to illustrate books on witchcraft, magic and the occult. These images take their place alongside those of the worship of Hecate in secret groves, **sabbats** on heaths or in caves, and magic beneath the full moon. Shakespeare's *Macbeth* has been particularly influential in this respect, with its famous scene of 'black and midnight hags' gathered around the cauldron:

> *SECOND WITCH:* Fillet of a fenny snake,
> In the cauldron boil and bake;
> Eye of newt, and toe of frog,
> Wool of bat, and tongue of dog
> Adder's fork and blind-worm's sting,
> Lizard's leg, and howlet's wing,
> For a charm of powerful trouble,
> Like a hell-broth boil and bubble.
>
> *ALL:* Double, double, toil and trouble;
> Fire burn; and, cauldron, bubble.
>
> (Act IV, Scene I, lines 12–21)

In a combination of classical and Teutonic mythology, Shakespeare's witches look like hags but invoke Hecate, and the list of cauldron ingredients might well have been drawn from Ovid, who lists hoar frosts, the flesh and wings of a screech owl, the entrails of a werewolf, the scaly skin of a scraggy Cinyphian water-snake, a stag's liver, and the head and beak of a crow more than nine generations old (*Metamorphoses*, 1995, p.162) among the contents of Medea's cauldron. Probably more than any other piece of literature, Shakespeare's portrayal of the witches in *Macbeth* has become the stereotype. How many times do you hear women say to their friends, 'when shall we three meet again?', usually in a voice that is meant to be scary and perhaps with a cackle at the end? The witch in Shakespeare persists to the present in children's literature, historical fiction, education, films, Hallowe'en parties, and so on.

It is likely that the variety and number of representations of the witch will continue to proliferate in the years to come, and an examination of the representations in film reveals a diversity linked to cultural expectations and 'knowledge' in which the witch is manipulated to fit each age. Cinematic witches often draw on the historical stereotype of the witch which was linked to fears about female sexuality, particularly in early documentary films such as the Danish *Häxan* (1922); one of the most commonly cited crimes during the Great Witch Hunt of the early modern period was intercourse with the devil, and one of the most common 'spells' was to cause male impotence. The witch, who is nearly always a woman, certainly represents female power and is predominantly portrayed as a being of sexuality and magnetism – one of the reasons, we might suppose, for the prevalence of pornographic-horror films from the mid-1970s onwards which exploit these ideas. Thus, witches in film are often used to signal the power of female sexuality, its terror, but also the desire which draws women to proclaim themselves witches and which attracts men to them. Sexuality and beauty therefore became dominant symbols of witchcraft in films, from the gothic notions of *la belle dame sans merci* in *The Curse of the Crimson Altar* (1968) (Figure 4.11) to the flowering of teenage girls into young woman-hood depicted in *Blood on Satan's Claw* (1970). It is notable that the period 1960–2000 has seen witches portrayed on screen by actresses such as Barbara Steele, Cher, Nicole Kidman and Elizabeth Montgomery, all of whom have no shortage of admirers!

However, the various representations of the witch in the 1960s were not always concerned with beauty, for they included the hag (*She Beast* in 1965, *The Witches* in 1966), the evil/unnatural (step)mother (*The Witches*), the avenger from beyond the grave (*Black Sunday*, 1960, *The Long Hair of Death*, 1964), as well as the femme fatale. In addition, television spin-offs such as *Bewitched*

Figure 4.10 'Journey to the Sabbat', a still from the 1922 pseudo-documentary on witchcraft, *Häxan*. © 1921 AB Svensk Filmindustri.

Figure 4.11 Barbara Steele as the witch Lavinia in the film, *The Curse of the Crimson Altar*. Courtesy of BFI Films: Stills, Posters, and Designs. Copyright owner unknown/all rights acknowledged.

(1964–71) and its sequel *Tabitha* (1977) represented the witch as tamed and domesticated, with her power to work magic limited to the domestic sphere where it might help make housework easier, keep her husband happy, and allow her to indulge in social one-upmanship. Any suggestion of feminist content was certainly accommodatory rather than revolutionary, despite the presence of witch imagery in the earliest manifestations of proto-feminist witchcraft in North America in the late 1960s, where the witch figure was incorporated into feminist rhetoric as an image of female power. At this point you might find it useful to read the extract 'A Holocaust of one's own' from *The Witch in History* by Diane Purkiss, reprinted in Part Two.

The development of Wicca and Paganism and its emergence into relative popularity has had an effect on the more modern witch movies of the 1980s and 1990s. For instance, the Witchcraft Anti-defamation League complained about the portrayal of witches as bored housewives in the 1987 film *The Witches of Eastwick*, despite the fact that the three witches in the film have the power to send the devil back to where he came from and keep him there. The age-old connection between witchcraft and satanism is apparently broken, with the witches being portrayed as forces for good fighting against the power of the devil whom they unwittingly called up. The film includes the themes of witch-women's independence (Alexandra, played by Cher), sexual licence (Jane, played by Susan Sarandon) and fecundity (Sukie, played by Michelle Pfieffer), but despite at first being taken in by the powerful personality of the devil in the shape of Daryl Van Horn (played by Jack Nicholson) they, in the final analysis, are more powerful than the devil. The film may, therefore, be interpreted as a positive image of witchcraft, yet the reaction of North American witches was to be appalled:

> The Witches' League ... sent out 'awareness packets' to the three actresses pointing out the disservice their portrayals would cause to thousands of women around the world ... We also offered to advise on the script or story line. We received no reply from the actresses, their agents, or Warner Brothers.
>
> (Cabot, 1990, p.80)

More positively, in the 1990s witches have acted as consultants on movies such as *The Craft* (1996) and *Practical Magic* (1998). From being 'outside' the film industry in terms of production and subject matter, witchcraft and Paganism are now in a very different position: after all, according to the advertising slogan for *Practical Magic*, 'there's a little witch in every woman'!

Manipulation of the witch figure has thus created a plethora of witch images throughout the ages and in a multitude of mediums. They can be confusing. As we have seen, some images of the witch are inherently ambiguous. Is Medea a lovesick girl wronged by her husband, a royal princess and priestess of an ancient religion, or a dangerous and powerful witch? Is Morgan le Fey a force for the continuance of Pagan evils, attempting to destroy early Christianity in Britain, or is she to be admired for her strength in upholding the 'indigenous religion' of the British (for which read 'Celtic') people, and guarding the power of women against the patriarchy and sexism which the Christian Church brings with it, as Marion Zimmer Bradley (1983) would have us believe? More importantly, who might wish to focus on this ambiguity, and for what purpose? In view of this complex and at times contradictory heritage, why reclaim the witch? Why should people wish to be identified as witches now?

You might find it informative at this point to turn to Part Two and read Wouter Hanegraaff's chapter 'From the Devil's gateway to the Goddess within', which traces the changing image of the witch and explores its importance to Pagans.

Twenty-first century witches

As we have seen, the image of the witch is often negative. But despite this negativity, one explanation for why some people identify with the witch is because she is imagined as powerful – she can make people sleep for one hundred years, she can see the future, she can curse and kill as well as heal, she can alter the course of history by putting a new king on the throne, she can defy gravity and fly, and, of course, she can turn people into frogs! These rather frivolous vignettes would seem more applicable to answering the question 'why do children dress up and play at being witches?', but nevertheless, it has been suggested that witches are involved in 'recreating a childhood world, enchanting adulthood' (Luhrmann, 1994, p.19). It seems more likely, however, that there are deeper and more serious reasons why contemporary people call themselves witches, reasons that go beyond the enactment of a childhood (or even childish) fantasy and concentrate instead on the image of the witch of the early modern period during the Great Witch Hunt.

The time of the Great Witch Hunt of early modern Europe, still commonly known as 'the Burning Times' despite the fact that witches were hanged rather than burned in England, is perhaps the most important epoch with which contemporary Wiccans, witches and Pagans have identified. An exaggerated nine million women were said to have been put to death during the persecution, and this 'myth of nine million' until recently constituted a substantial mythic thread. It was computed in the late eighteenth century through the false extrapolation of local records by an antiquarian at Quedlinburg, Germany, and was then repeated by various German historians. The feminist writer Matilda Jocelyn Gage made use of the number in *Women, Church and State* in 1893 in order to emphasize the crimes of the Church against women. It is from Gage that the number entered Wiccan mythology. The Museum of Witchcraft and Magic on the Isle of Man, owned by Cecil Williamson with Gerald Gardner as 'resident witch', sported a plaque commemorating the nine million witches who died in the Great Witch Hunt, and Mary Daly's use of the figure in her 1978 book *Gyn/Ecology* (1981, p.183n.) transmitted the myth to feminist witches. Although historical research from the 1970s has revealed a figure closer to 40,000 executed for witchcraft in Europe during this time, feminist witches in particular have continued to make use of the myth of the Burning Times. Through relating the enormous number of witches persecuted to the six million Jews murdered in the Holocaust, witches (and women) are assimilated to persecuted minorities. This general distortion of history suits the political aims of a feminist interpretation of witchcraft (Briggs, 1996, p.8).

Identification as a witch can thus provide a link to those persecuted and executed in the Great Witch Hunt, which can then be remembered as a holocaust against women, a repackaging of history that implies conscious victimization and the appropriation of 'holocaust' as a badge of honour (Meštrović, 1997, p.11) – 'gendercide rather than genocide' (Briggs, 1996, p.8). An elective identification with the image of the witch during the time of the persecutions is commonly regarded as part of the reclamation of female power, a myth that is used by modern feminist witches as an aid in their struggle for freedom from patriarchal oppression. Memories of the past are thus focused on as a central source of meaning, with the Burning Times used as a rallying symbol, and the witch regarded both as a martyr and as a representation of repressed female power. For some feminist witches, this myth is so important that they go so far as to identify themselves as direct inheritors of a corpus of occult knowledge passed on from the witches of the Burning Times. An example is the Hungarian-born feminist witch Zsuzsanna Budapest who, in an interview with *Whole Earth Review* (Spring, 1992, p.42), exclaimed passionately:

> My European ancestors and yours risked the Inquisition's stakes and racks to keep alive a body of knowledge about power and healing. My generation of witches is making this wisdom accessible to those who seek a spiritual foundation for political work.

The representation of the early modern witch has thus been an important part of the development of both Wicca and feminist witchcraft, and remains relevant to the heritage of Wiccans, witches and Pagans in the twenty-first century. It is a representation open to manipulation by witches and non-witches alike, and as such it evolves with the human imagination according to the specifics of cultural influences. Thus, in 1604 a witch was

> ... a woman, or man, who had abandoned Christianity and renounced her baptism, who worshipped Satan as her God and had made a definite act of surrendering herself to him, body and soul, offering herself as an instrument for the evil work he could only perform through a human agent. In exchange she had been promised anything she desired to have.
>
> (Peel and Southern, 1969, p.54)

According to James VI's *Demonology* of 1597, people sought to become witches for two reasons: the lure of food and wealth for the poverty stricken, and the promise of power and revenge on their enemies for the wealthy (Peel and Southern, 1969, p.35).

There would seem to be little reason for people today to identify with such representations of witches or with the reasons cited for becoming one. But in addition to being understood as the victim of propaganda, persecution and patriarchy, the early modern witch is also portrayed as a symbol of strength and power. A feminist reclaiming of the witch as an image of woman victimized, persecuted and derided as evil because of her sexuality and control over the processes of life and death, enables some women to reclaim their own power through identification with her. The image of the witch, even when linked to persecution, thus remains attractive because she lives her own life, defies patriarchal authority, and is strong and independent:

> The advantage of the label 'witch' is that it has all the exciting connotations of a figure who flouts the conventions of normal society and is possessed of powers unavailable to it, at once feared and persecuted. It is a marvellous rallying point for a counter-culture, and also one of the few images of independent female power in early modern European civilization.
>
> (Hutton, 1993, p.335)

The witch thus becomes a trump card in the 'war of the sexes', and is identified with not only as another persecuted minority but also as a source of power. Some witches, such as Leo Martello, see the image of the historical witch as important precisely because 'in Medieval times "the only liberated woman was the witch"' (cited in Adler, 1986, p.213),[16] and indeed this image of the witch as a free woman has maintained its hold. Such sentiments are clearly evident in Sylvia Townsend Warner's *Lolly Willowes, or The Loving Huntsman*, first published in 1926. The narrator of the story, Lolly, has become a witch or, rather, discovered that she is one. She relates her feelings on the subject to Satan (the 'Loving Huntsman') who has taken the form of a gardener:

> 'I can't take warlocks so seriously, not as a class. It is we witches who count. We have more need of you. Women have such vivid imaginations and lead such dull lives. Their pleasure in life is so soon over; they are so dependent on others, and their dependence so soon becomes a nuisance ...

---

[16] It is a common misconception that the Great Witch Hunt dates from the Medieval era (generally considered to be between the fifth and fifteenth centuries, i.e. pre-Renaissance) rather than the early modern period.

When I think of witches, I seem to see all over England, all over Europe, women living and growing old, as common as blackberries and unregarded ...

Some may get religion, then they're alright, I expect. But for the others, for so many, what can there be but witchcraft? That strikes them real ... Even if they never do anything with their witchcraft, they know it's there – ready ... [And] you say: "Come here my bird! I will give you the dangerous black night to stretch your wings in, and poisonous berries to feed on, and a nest made of bones and thorns, perched high up in danger where no one can climb to it". That's why we become witches: to show our scorn of pretending life's a safe business, to satisfy our passion for adventure ... One doesn't become a witch to run round being harmful, or to run round being helpful either, a district visitor on a broomstick. It's to escape all that – to have a life of one's own, not an existence doled out to you by others.'

(Warner, 2000, pp.234, 237–9)

Warner had read Margaret Murray's *The Witch Cult in Western Europe* (1921), and in fact visited Murray to take tea just after the publication of *Lolly Willowes*. She wrote of the meeting, 'I wish I were in her coven, perhaps I shall be', and when the author Virginia Woolf enquired how she knew so much about witches, Warner apparently replied, 'because I am one' (cited in Harman, 1989, p.59). Another influence on Warner was Robert Pitcairn's *Criminal Trials in Scotland* (1833), in which the account of the witch trials was of particular import. Pitcairn stressed that 'the actual speech of the accused impressed upon me that these witches were witches for love; that witchcraft was more than Miss Murray's Dianic cult; it was the romance of their hard lives, their release from dull futures' (cited in Harman, 1989, p.59). This is clearly a central theme of Warner's novel, where the symbolism of the witch conveys, as it does in the story of Medea, the image of an independent, anti-establishment being whose source of power is nature itself, rather than the devil.

Thus, while to a certain extent historical images inform the caricature of the witch that has continued into the present century, 'she' is now an altogether different character. In the second half of the twentieth century, in Wicca and feminist witchcraft, the witch has been reclaimed from her early modern association with 'evil'. No longer allied with Satan except by those religious groups that see the work of the devil everywhere, she instead gains her power from the forces of nature. She has become that mythic figure of our urban age imagined as close to nature, dealing in magic and spellcraft and worshipping the old pagan deities. She is the reclaimer of the lost power of woman, and of the image of the Goddess. And 'she' can also be 'he'. The witch has been incorporated into the priesthood of Wicca as the religion of witchcraft, or has become an activist, or remains the isolated individual whose connection to religion is neither here nor there. The thread thus continues, reminding us 'how easily the pliable figure of the witch can be manipulated to fit the spirit of each age' (Briggs, 1996, p.5).

Conclusion

The witch is undoubtedly a familiar but elusive figure, and this is perpetuated by the secrecy and initiatory structure of Wicca. People often identify as witches before finding Wicca, and thus are informed by representations of the witch from a variety of diverse sources. Initiation into Wicca, it could be argued, provides a framework in which the image of oneself as a witch can be explored and brought into a modern context, where the witch of, say, the Great Witch Hunt coexists with Wiccan sites on the Internet as well as on film, in literature, and so on. The motif of recognition developed by Harrington reveals the importance of the underlying recognition of oneself as a witch, but it does not provide us with information on how the image of the witch is itself recognized. For she has been represented as a dangerous remnant from the middle ages, as a monster from horror movies, as a harmless figure of fun in children's literature, as a representative of women persecuted in the early modern period, as the wicked witch and the good witch of fairy tales, as a hag gathering with others of her kind on the blasted heath, and as a Hallowe'en witch with warts, hooked nose, green skin and a black cat.

Such popular stereotypes confine the witch largely to fantasy or the distant past, and yet, as we have seen, the witch is still very much with us in the twenty-first century. The witch is thus a mythic creature *and* a person in the real world, both during the early modern period of the Great Witch Hunt and as an initiate of the religion of Wicca, a practitioner of feminist witchcraft and a rural wise woman in the present. By identifying themselves as witches, Wiccans identify with a being who has been represented as the possessor of supernatural powers and as the consort of the devil, but also as the victim of horrific persecution at the hands of the Christian Church. Wicca has reclaimed the witch as the guardian of the secret powers of nature and of woman, as the priestess of the Goddess, as the herbalist, and as the practitioner of magic, thus offering a critical synthesis of the polarities and ambiguities of the witch figure to produce a 'witch' who is both modern and timeless.

But if 'historical European witchcraft is quite simply a fiction' (Briggs, 1996, p.6), then modern witches are free to construct their own fiction, to use their imagination to affirm a positive image of the witch. The 'slippery' status of witchcraft 'as a logical and linguistic construct whose boundaries are both arbitrary and insecure' (Briggs, 1996, p.7) can be seen to aid this ongoing process of reinvention, as can the multitude of images stretching back through history, some of which we have examined in this chapter. Thus, the witch appears as an active and powerful figure, culturally constructed throughout history and easily manipulated to fit each age: that people today are happy to call themselves witches is just one more example of this process.

Glossary

Book of Shadows a book in which a witch writes invocations, rituals and other information and lore. The book is copied from the coven into which the witch is initiated, and often added to over the years so that no two books are exactly alike. The Book of Shadows is traditionally kept secret, and only ever shown to a fellow initiate; as its name suggests, it is regarded as a shadowy reflection of the realities of the other world.

Hecate one of the Greek moon goddesses, along with Artemis and Selene, associated with the crossroads, magic and witchcraft; she is regarded as a goddess of witches.

hive-off, hiving this term is used to describe the process by which Second or Third degree Wiccans (see p.36) leave the coven into which they were initiated to form their own coven.

Lilith in Jewish mythology, Lilith was Adam's first wife who stormed out of the Garden of Eden after refusing to be subordinate to Adam; she is also a Jewish demon, inhabitor of the lunar sphere of Yesod in the mystical system of the kabbalah.

neophyting the name sometimes given to formal, pre-initiation training, which might include such things as meditation and visualization exercises, learning correspondences, reading mythology. In some covens, a neophyte initiation is compulsory.

sabbat the witches' sabbat, or sabbath, was traditionally regarded as the meeting to which witches flew for their rituals. Ronald Hutton explains that the origins of the term come from the identification by early demonologists of witches with Jews, both of which were characterized as the antithesis to Christianity (Hutton, 1993, p.303).

'Sabbat' in contemporary Wicca refers to the eight seasonal festivals that are marked with ritual and which together constitute the mythic/ritual cycle known as The Wheel of the Year.

References

Adler, M. (1986) *Drawing Down the Moon: Witches, Druids, Goddess-worshippers, and other Pagans in America Today*, Boston: Beacon Press.

Baum, F.L. (1900) *The Wonderful Wizard of Oz*, New York: Bobbs-Merrill.

Berger, H.A. (1999) *A Community of Witches: Contemporary Neo-Paganism and Witchcraft in the United States*, Columbia, South Carolina: University of South Carolina Press.

Bierce, A. (1987) *The Enlarged Devil's Dictionary*, London: Penguin (first published 1911).

Bradley, M.Z. (1993) *The Mists of Avalon*, London: Penguin (first published 1983).

Briggs, R. (1996) *Witches and Neighbours: The Social and Cultural Context of European Witchcraft*, London: HarperCollins.

Cabot, L. with Cowan, T. (1990) *Power of the Witch: A Witch's Guide to Her Craft*, London: Michael Joseph.

Chapman, M. (1995) 'Conversion processes in Wicca', unpublished under-graduate dissertation, Royal Holloway, University of London.

Chichester, I. (1965) *The Witch-child*, London: Harrap.

Clute, J. and Grant, J. (1997) *The Encyclopedia of Fantasy*, London: Orbit.

Cresswell, H. (1973) *Lizzie Dripping*, London: Puffin.

Crowley, V. (1996) *Wicca: The Old Religion in the New Millennium*, London: Thorsons.

Crowley, V. (1998) 'Wicca as nature religion', in J. Pearson, R.H. Roberts and G. Samuel (eds) *Nature Religion Today: Paganism in the Modern World*, Edinburgh: Edinburgh University Press, pp.170–9.

Daly, M. (1981) *Gyn/Ecology: The Metaethics of Radical Feminism*, London: The Women's Press (first published 1978).

Edmonson, M. (1983) *Anna Witch*, London: Corgi.

Edwards, D. (ed.) (1983) *Mists and Magic*, Guildford: Lutterworth.

Furlong, M. (1987) *Wise Child*, London: Victor Gollancz.

Gage, M.J. (1972) *Women, Church and State*, New York: Arno Press (first published 1893).

Harman, C. (1989) *Sylvia Townsend Warner: A Biography*, London: Chatto & Windus.

Harrington, M. (2000) 'Conversion to Wicca?', in M. Bowman and G. Harvey (eds) *Pagan Identities*, special issue of electronic journal *DISKUS* (www.uni-marburg.de/fb03/religionswissenschaft/journal/diskus/harrington.html).

Harvey, G. (1997) *Listening People, Speaking Earth: Contemporary Paganism*, London: Hurst.

Hope-Simpson, J. (ed.) (1977) *Covens and Cauldrons: A Book of Witches*, London: Hamlyn (first published 1966).

Hume, L. (1997) *Witchcraft and Paganism in Australia*, Melbourne: Melbourne University Press.

Hutton, R. (1993) *The Pagan Religions of the Ancient British Isles: Their Nature and Legacy*, Oxford: Blackwell (first published 1991).

Hutton, R. (1999) *The Triumph of the Moon: A History of Modern Pagan Witchcraft*, Oxford: Blackwell.

Jeremy and Arihanto (n.d.) *A Pagan Child's ABC*, London: The Pagan Federation.

Kennelly, B. (1991) *Euripides' Medea: A New Version*, Newcastle: Bloodaxe Books (first published 1988).

Kirkpatrick, R.G., Rainey, R. and Rubi, K. (1986) 'An empirical study of Wiccan religion in postindustrial society', *Free Inquiry in Creative Sociology*, vol.14, no.1, pp.33–8.

Lawrence, L. (1989) *The Earth Witch*, London: Lions (first published 1982).

Lewis, C.S. (1950) *The Lion, the Witch, and the Wardrobe: A Story for Children*, London: G. Bles.

Lewis, J.R. (ed.) (1996) *Magical Religion and Modern Witchcraft*, New York: SUNY.

Lofland, J. and Skonovd, N. (1983) 'Patterns of conversion', in E. Barker (ed.) *Of Gods and Men: New Religious Movements in the West*, Proceedings of the 1981 Annual Conference of the British Sociological Association Sociology of Religion Study Group, Macon GA: Mercer University Press, pp.1–24.

Luhrmann, T.M. (1994) *Persuasions of the Witches' Craft: Ritual Magic in Contemporary England*, Basingstoke: Picador (first published 1989).

Malory, Sir T. (1917) *The Romance of King Arthur and his Knights of the Round Table*, abridged from *Morte d'Arthur* by Alfred Pollard, London: Macmillan.

Masefield, J. (1927) *The Midnight Folk*, London: William Heinemann.

Meštrović, S.G. (1997) *Postemotional Society*, London: Sage.

Murphy, J. (1974) *The Worst Witch*, London: Allison & Busby.

Murray, M.A. (1921) *The Witch Cult in Western Europe: A Study in Anthropology*, Oxford: Clarendon Press.

Neitz, M. (1994) 'Quasi-religions and cultural movements: contemporary witchcraft as a churchless religion', in A.L. Greil and T. Robbins (eds) *Between Sacred and Secular: Research and Theory on Quasi-Religion, Religion and the Social Order*, vol.4, pp.127–49.

Newlands, C.E. (1997) 'The metamorphosis of Ovid's Medea', in J.J. Clauss and S.I. Johnston (eds) *Medea: Essays on Medea in Myth, Literature, Philosophy and Art*, Princeton, NJ: Princeton University Press, pp.178–208.

Orion, L.L. (1995) *Never Again the Burning Times: Paganism Revived*, Prospect Heights, Illinois: Waveland Press.

Ovid (1955) *Metamorphoses*, trans. Mary M. Innes, London: Penguin.

Pearson, J. (2000) 'Religion and the return of magic: Wicca as esoteric spirituality', unpublished PhD thesis, Lancaster University.

Peel, E. and Southern, P. (1969) *The Trials of the Lancashire Witches: A Study of 17th Century Witchcraft*, Newton Abbot: David & Charles.

Pitcairn, R. (1833) *Criminal Trials in Scotland: from AD 1488 to AD 1624, Embracing the Entire Reigns of James IV and V, Mary Queen of Scots, and James VI*, Edinburgh: William Tait.

Pratchett, T. (1987) *Equal Rites*, London: Corgi.

Pratchett, T. (1988) *Wyrd Sisters*, London: Corgi.

Pratchett, T. (1991) *Witches Abroad*, London: Corgi.

Purkiss, D. (1996) *The Witch in History: Early Modern and Twentieth Century Representations*, London & New York: Routledge.

Puttick, E. (1997) *Women in New Religions: In Search of Community, Sexuality and Spiritual Power*, London: Macmillan.

Russell, J.B. (1991) *A History of Witchcraft: Sorcerers, Heretics and Pagans*, London: Thames & Hudson (first published 1980).

Salomonsen, J. (1996) '"I am a witch – a healer and a bender": An expression of women's religiosity in the contemporary USA', unpublished PhD thesis, University of Oslo.

Shakespeare, W. (1982) 'Macbeth', in *The Illustrated Stratford Shakespeare*, London: Chancellor Press.

Sleigh, B. (ed.) (1981) *Broomsticks and Beasticles*, London: Hodder & Stoughton.

Stark, R. and Bainbridge, W.S. (1985) *The Future of Religion: Secularization, Revival and Cult Formation*, London: University of California Press.

Tennyson, A.L. (1989) 'Idylls of the King', in C. Ricks (ed.) *Tennyson: A Selected Edition*, Berkeley: University of California Press, pp.667–975 (first published 1859).

Valiente, D. (1989) *The Rebirth of Witchcraft*, Washington: Phoenix.

Valiente, D. (1993) *Witchcraft for Tomorrow*, London: Robert Hale (first published 1978).

Warner, S.T. (2000) *Lolly Willowes, or The Loving Huntsman*, London: Virago Press (first published 1926).

Weardale, D. (1994) *The Pagan Child*, Macclesfield: New Wiccan Publications.

Wilson, B. and Cresswell, J. (1999) *New Religious Movements: Challenge and Response*, London & New York: Routledge.

Wolf, C. (1998) *Medea: A Novel*, trans. by John Cullen, New York: Virago (first published in German in 1996).

Yeats, W.B. (1992) *W.B. Yeats: The Poems*, ed. Daniel Albright, London: David Campbell (first published 1990).

Filmography

Black Sunday (1960), Mario Bava, Galatra/Jolly.

Blood on Satan's Claw (1970), Piers Haggard, written by Robert Wynne-Simmons, Tigon-Chilton.

Häxan (Witchcraft through the Ages) (1922), Benjamin Christensen, Svensk Filmindustri.

Macbeth (1972), Roman Polanski, written by Roman Polanski and Kenneth Tynan, Playboy/Caliban.

Practical Magic (1998), Griffin Dunne, written by Robin Swicord, Akiva Goldsman, and Adam Brookes, Warner Bros.

She Beast (1965), Mike Reeves, written by Michael Byron, Leith Films.

The Craft (1996), Andrew Fleming, written by Peter Filardi and Andrew Fleming, Columbia.

The Curse of the Crimson Altar (1968), Vernon Sewell, written by Mervyn Haisman and Henry Lincoln, Tigon/AIP (Tony Tenser).

The Long Hair of Death (1964), Anthony Dawson, written by Robert Bohr, Cinegai.

The Witches (1966), Cyril Frankel, written by Nigel Kneale, Warner/Hammer.

The Witches of Eastwick (1987), George Miller, written by Michael Crustofer, Warner.

The Wizard of Oz (1939), Victor Fleming, written by Noel Langley, Florence Ryerson, Edgar Allan Woolf, MGM.

CHAPTER 5

Religion, science and the New Age

RODERICK MAIN

Introduction

This chapter discusses the emergence and nature of New Age spirituality against the background of historical and contemporary interactions between religion and science. It first provides a concise historical sketch of the impact of the rise of science on religion, followed by some critical observations. It then examines some salient features of New Age spirituality which can arguably be illuminated by a consideration of the interactions between religion and science. This is followed by a case study that will help to establish these connections more vividly and in detail. The case study focuses on the psychological theories of **Carl Gustav Jung** (1875–1961), and in particular on his psychology of religion and theory of **synchronicity** (meaningful coincidence). As we shall see, these ideas are both deeply engaged with tensions between religion and science and intricately related to many forms of New Age spirituality.

Religion and science

Of all the influences on religion today, few are as pervasive as modern science. However, precisely because this influence has been so profound and far-reaching, it is difficult to specify its nature. We can note the prominent role that science, especially in the form of technology, has played in promoting some of the broad processes identified by sociologists as shaping the world within which contemporary religion exists – for example, **modernization**, **secularization** and **globalization**. Indeed, for some commentators, 'Modernity is co-extensive with science' (Segal, 1999, p.548). We can also note that science has provided explanations for the world and for human nature that are different from and, for many people, more satisfactory than the explanations traditionally provided by religion. Conspicuous examples concern the nature of the physical universe, the development of organic life on earth, the history of cultures and communities, and the functioning of the human mind. In numerous practical and ethical areas, too, developments in science have prompted a rethinking of traditional religious attitudes. For example, where the technology and resources to mitigate major sufferings such as poverty and sickness exist, it is understandable that, for some, the appeal of religious consolations should diminish. However, while at a general level we can readily acknowledge the rise of science, the challenges it has presented and the impact it has had, when we turn to the level of particular interactions between religion and science, the picture quickly becomes complicated. Religion, after all, is a global phenomenon with thousands of variants, and science, itself not a unified phenomenon, has had different kinds of impact on different cultures and individuals at different times. Cautious historical investigations generally reveal that the interactions between religion and science vary enormously, are often not what one expects and can be minutely sensitive to context (for example, Brooke, 1991; Brooke and Cantor, 1998).

A historical sketch

A widespread popular account of the interaction between religion and science pictures religion as having supplied more or less undisputedly the dominant worldview up until the seventeenth century. After that time, it is argued, developments in natural science presented a series of increasingly compelling challenges to the claims of religion. Eventually, in the late nineteenth and early twentieth centuries, science supplanted religion altogether as the intellectually most satisfying and credible explanation of the world and our being in it. According to this view, the contemporary persistence of religion indicates an inability or refusal on the part of many people to take on board the implications of science and rationality. The prevalence of this account of the interaction between religion and science makes it particularly important to appreciate the actual complexity of the situation, both historically and now.

The fields of both religion and science are extraordinarily vast and by no means static, so any attempt to discuss them in general terms is bound to be selective and questionable. In the following subsection, I shall highlight some of these difficulties. Before that, however, I offer a very brief historical sketch of some of the major episodes in the interaction between religion and science in the West from the beginning of the seventeenth to the end of the twentieth century – the period during which the supplanting of religion by science supposedly occurred. (My principal source for the following account is Barbour, 1998.)

Before the seventeenth century, the dominant worldview in Europe was the one endorsed by the Roman Catholic Church: a synthesis, largely worked out by **Thomas Aquinas** (*c.*1225–74), of Christian doctrine with the philosophical and scientific views of **Aristotle** (c.384–322 BCE) and the cosmology of **Ptolemy** (85–160). This worldview pictured a created hierarchy with the earth and human beings at the centre of a cosmic drama of redemption. Events in the physical world were explained in terms of their purposes. God was known through revelation and reason as the creator of the cosmos, the guarantor of purpose and the redeemer of fallen humanity.

During the seventeenth century, this traditional cosmology underwent a series of profound shocks, epitomized by the works of **Galileo Galilei** (1564–1642) and **Isaac Newton** (1642–1727). Rather than simply accept the authority of Aristotelian science and Ptolemaic cosmology, Galileo made his own observations of how phenomena behave. Combining these observations with mathematical calculations, he made significant discoveries, especially in the field of mechanics. Most controversially, however, his refined telescopes enabled him to make observations of celestial phenomena – mountains on the moon, spots on the sun, moons around Jupiter – that called into question the Ptolemaic cosmology in which the Church had embedded many of its doctrines. Instead, they seemed to lend support to the rival **Copernican** cosmology according to which the earth revolved around the sun. This raised serious questions for the Church, both about the authority of those scriptures that implied that the sun revolved around the earth (for example, Joshua 10:13) and about the status of a humanity no longer at the centre of the cosmos. When in 1687 Newton published his *Mathematical Principles of Natural Philosophy* formulating the laws of motion, many of Galileo's mechanical and astronomical theories, and especially his method of testing his theories against observation, received cogent endorsement. So, in addition, did the principle of explaining events not in terms of their purposes but in terms of their causes. Indeed, such was the explanatory efficiency of Newton's laws that they inspired the image of the physical universe as a perfectly law-abiding machine, a cosmic clock. This image was used to support the **design argument** for God's existence, for such an efficiently functioning clock seems to imply an intelligent clockmaker. This, and variants, forms one of the staple arguments of **natural theology** (the

Figure 5.1 Isaac Newton. Mary Evans Picture Library. 'Newton himself remarked that it was part of the business of natural philosophy to discuss such questions as the attributes of God and His relationship to the physical world' (Brooke, 1991, p.7).

understanding of God held to be obtainable through rational reflection on the world rather than through revelation).

In the eighteenth century, **Pierre Laplace** and others extended Newton's mechanical model. Where Newton had believed that certain unexplained features of planetary motion left room for occasional, necessary divine intervention, Laplace later provided the data and theories that rendered this 'God of the gaps' redundant. A worldview was becoming prominent whose main features were **determinism** (the view that all things are determined by causes) and **reductionism** (the view that complex data can be explained in terms of something simpler). Newton's own determinism had been applied to the natural world but not to the human mind. Other eighteenth-century thinkers saw no reason to draw this distinction and conceived of human mental life as equally determined. Again, Newton and many others had considered the extraordinary mechanical orderliness of the world as evidence for an intelligent Creator. However, when Napoleon observed that Laplace's book on astronomy contained no mention of the Creator, Laplace famously replied, 'I had no need of that hypothesis' (Barbour, 1998, p.35). Thus, the eighteenth century saw the rise of materialistic atheism in the West.

The tendencies of determinism, reductionism and materialism provoked reactions from various quarters. One reaction was **Romanticism**, which considered that not only reason but also the irrational faculties of imagination and intuition were essential modes of understanding the world. The Romantics rejected determinism and celebrated human freedom and creativity; they rejected the view of nature as a machine and embraced the view of nature as a living companion; they rejected materialism and acknowledged a spiritual reality. Another reaction was the revitalization of personal religion in such forms as **Pietism** in Germany and **Methodism** in Britain. The achievements of Newton had led to the view of a mechanical nature. Newton himself, and many others, continued to believe in God, but it was a God very different from the one worshipped in medieval times. Rather than being the source of revelation, miracles and providence and the guarantor of human redemption and immortality, God was increasingly conceived as a being who had created the world in the beginning but did not afterwards intervene in the course of natural and human affairs. This **Deist** understanding, of which there were many variants, failed to satisfy the need, to which Christianity had traditionally catered, for a more personal relationship with a redeeming God. It was to this neglected need that Pietism, Methodism and related movements responded.

The eighteenth century also saw the emergence of two contrasting philosophical viewpoints on the relationship between religion and science that were to have a profound impact on subsequent debates. The Scottish philosopher **David Hume** (1711–76), holding that all knowledge is derived from sensory experience, argued that there were no cogent grounds for believing anything about either the existence or nature of God, or any of the other metaphysical claims of religion. His arguments have had a profound and continuing influence on **secular humanism**. More particularly, Hume formulated some telling objections to natural theology. For example, he pointed out that even if one could, on the analogy of clocks and clockmakers, infer a maker of the world mechanism, there is nothing to guarantee that there would be only one such maker rather than a plurality of makers – a view that would not sit comfortably with monotheistic Christianity. The German philosopher **Immanuel Kant** (1724–1804), responding to Hume, agreed that the claims of knowledge must be restricted to what can be empirically observed. However, he argued that sense experience alone is not sufficient for knowledge but that the human mind supplies conceptual categories in the interpretation of sense data. In the realm of morality, he suggested that God is a necessary postulate – that is, for our assertions of moral law to make any sense they have to presuppose a lawgiver who is the source and guarantor of that law. Kant agreed with Hume that *theoretical reason* cannot prove the existence of God, but he maintained that *practical reason* requires us to presuppose His existence. Kant's manoeuvre here of assigning separate realms and functions to science (empirical knowledge) and religion (morality) is a common feature of many contemporary discussions of the relationship between religion and science.

The major event of relevance to our theme that occurred in the nineteenth century was the publication in 1859 by **Charles Darwin** (1809–82) of his *Origin of Species* and the subsequent debates about evolution. Darwin's theory proposed that biological species did not spring into being in their present forms through an act of divine creation but were the products of a long process of evolution governed by the principles of random variation and natural selection. Evolutionary ideas had existed before Darwin but only his work provided a cogent theory and adequate supporting data.

The theory of evolution had a profound impact on perceptions of the natural world and the role of humans within it. The theory gave new importance to the concepts of change and development; it highlighted the interdependence of organic forms; it greatly extended the scope of scientific law; and, above all, it placed human beings within the animal kingdom rather than as a species altogether apart. The theory presented some particularly strong challenges to religion.

First, it challenged scripture. If Darwin's theory was correct, then many passages in the Bible, especially concerning creation, could not be taken literally. This was far from being a new problem and there was already a long tradition, fully sanctioned by the Catholic Church, of interpreting biblical passages non-literally. However, non-literal interpretation of the Bible was never endorsed lightly and Darwin's theories made particularly heavy demands on this approach.

Responses to the problem ranged from outright rejection of evolution to various forms of accommodation between evolution and scripture to outright rejection of scripture.

Second, evolutionary theory challenged the design argument for God's existence, which, in spite of the philosophical criticisms of Hume and others, still held considerable sway. **William Paley**, for example, in his book *Natural Theology* (1802), argued that the complex structure of the eye is co-ordinated to the one aim of vision and that such co-ordinated structure naturally leads us to infer the existence of an intelligent designer. However, evolutionary theory could now provide an account of how the complex structure of the eye came about that appealed only to natural causes: random variation, the struggle for survival, and the survival of the fittest. Proponents of natural theology, if they accepted evolutionary theory, now had to detect God's intelligent design in the laws by which evolution proceeds or in a supposed providential guiding of the variations.

Third, evolutionary theory challenged the status of humanity. Many people felt that seeing human beings as continuous with animals compromises human dignity. Particularly objectionable was seeing the human moral sense and other higher human faculties as having evolved by natural selection, for these were traditionally the marks of our affinity with the divine. **Alfred Russel Wallace** (1823–1913), who independently discovered the principle of natural selection, was among those who claimed that it could not account for the higher human faculties.

The twentieth century saw scientific developments that were at least as significant as anything that had gone before. In physics, the theories of **relativity** and **quantum mechanics** revolutionized ways of thinking about matter and energy as well as about such

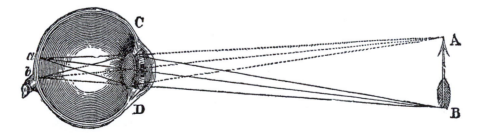

Figure 5.2 An image from William Paley's *Natural Theology: or Evidence of the Existence and Attributes of the Deity, Collected from the Appearances of Nature,* R. Faulder, London, 1802. Paley argued that the complex structure of the human eye naturally leads us to infer the existence of an intelligent designer.

fundamental categories as space, time and causality. No longer, as in classical Newtonian physics, can we describe the world 'realistically' as though it is unaffected by our observations. For experiments have shown that if we observe certain subatomic phenomena such as **photons** in one way, they behave as particles, while if we observe them in another way, they behave as waves. Our method of observation crucially influences what we observe. Nor, as in classical physics, can we describe the world deterministically. For there are events, such as the disintegration of a particular atom in a radioactive substance, that we can only predict with probability, never with certainty. Nature, it seems, is in some respects inherently indeterministic. Nor again, as in classical physics, can we explain all physical processes reductively; that is, we cannot explain all higher level processes and entities in terms of increasingly more fundamental principles and particles. For at the subatomic level there are particles, such as **quarks**, which seemingly cannot exist except as parts of a larger whole. At least some phenomena appear irreducibly **holistic**. These challenges to realism, determinism and reductionism have opened new possibilities for engagement between religion and science, for the contrary principles of participation, indeterminacy and **holism** have seemed to some to be more compatible with traditional theological notions.

In astronomy, there have been equally significant discoveries. Most conspicuous is **Big Bang cosmology** – a plausible reconstruction of cosmic history based on a series of theoretical and observational developments in physics and astronomy over the course of the twentieth century. According to this widely accepted theory, the origin of the universe can be calculated back to a hypothetical 'Big Bang' (that is, a moment when the infinitely contracted mass of the universe exploded and began to expand) approximately fifteen billion years ago. The inability of scientists even in principle to offer any picture of the situation before the initial moment of the Big Bang has encouraged some to appeal to an act of divine creation at this point. Further, calculations about the rate of expansion of the universe following the Big Bang have shown that if this rate had been smaller by one part in a hundred thousand million million or greater by one part in a million, the universe would either have re-collapsed before reaching its present size or expanded too rapidly for stars and planets to form. This has led some to suggest that the universe has been designed as though specially to enable the development of beings such as we are – the so-called '**Anthropic Principle**'. The physicist Stephen Hawkins writes: 'The odds against a universe like ours emerging out of something like the Big Bang are enormous. I think there are clearly religious implications' (Barbour, 1998, p.205) (see Colour Plate 11).

In biology, the outstanding events of the twentieth century must include the discovery of **DNA** and the subsequent gradual deciphering of the **genetic code**. This has resulted in a sharpening of the evolutionary debates of the nineteenth century. All that exists in nature, no matter how marvellous, is even more fully explicable in materialistic terms than the early proponents of evolutionary theory conceived. In this spirit, the neo-Darwinian Richard Dawkins entitled one of his books *The Blind Watchmaker: Why the Evidence of Evolution Reveals a Universe without Design* (1987). Theologians have again responded by suggesting that God either controls events that seem to be random or designed the system of law and chance by which evolution proceeds. The pattern of these debates is broadly the same as in the nineteenth century, though conducted at a greater level of sophistication. Additionally, some theologians have suggested that God takes a continuous active role in evolution not through controlling events with coercive power but through influencing them with persuasive love.

Issues arising

The preceding sketch, fragmentary as it is, demonstrates that developments in modern science, in terms of both methodology and particular theories, brought into prominence ideas that traditional religions had to engage with in one way or another. All of this provides the deeper context for appreciating the influence of interactions between religion and science on New Age spirituality. Immediately, however, we need to qualify our account in some important ways.

First, we need to note that the above account is, given the magnitude of the topic, necessarily very selective. Writers other than those on whom I have drawn would have highlighted different events in the history of science or would have handled the same ones differently. Moreover, simply by zooming in on any one of the areas covered, we will find that the issues become increasingly ambiguous. For example, we have noted that Galileo championed the Copernican cosmological view according to which the earth revolves around the sun. In 1616, the Catholic Church issued an injunction forbidding him to hold or promote this view and when, in 1632, Galileo published a work that seemed to disregard the injunction, he was tried, found guilty, forced to recant, and condemned to house arrest for the remainder of his life. This episode continues to be used as a paradigmatic example of the inveterate hostility between religion and science, with religious authority impeding the development of scientific truth (see, for example, Wilber, 1998, pp.vii-viii). However, closer historical examinations of the case have revealed that the conflict was at least as much between different scientific models and methods or between different interest groups within religion as it was between religion and science. Many of the clerics involved in Galileo's trial were sympathetic to scientific investigations and even to much of Galileo's own work. Meanwhile, Galileo was, and was acknowledged to be, a devout Catholic who argued that his cosmological views actually provided stronger support for Catholic doctrine than the traditional Ptolemaic views. Moreover, though Galileo may have been correct about the earth revolving around the sun, his telescopic observations did not decisively prove this and the main supporting argument he adduced, that the earth's motion can be inferred from the tides, is now known to be incorrect. Again, historians have shown that in important respects the trial of Galileo was not about religion and science at all. The instigator of the trial was Pope Urban VIII, formerly a friend and sympathetic patron of Galileo. At a moment of acute political vulnerability, Urban was led to believe that he had been personally insulted by Galileo's writing and consequently he wished to make an example of him (see Colour Plate 10).

Second, the above account, for all its ambitious scope and skipping over of particulars, focuses narrowly on the Christian religion and on understandings of science that originated and developed in modern Europe. This neglects all the other religious traditions of the world, as well as such alternative and arguably no less sophisticated approaches to scientific understanding as existed in ancient China, ancient Greece or medieval Islam.

Third, even within the temporal, geographical and cultural limits I have set myself, the way people have understood the terms 'religion' and 'science' has shifted continuously. Regarding religion, in medieval Europe this concept tended to be used exclusively to signify Christianity, with emphasis on the notions of faith and an organized community or church. During the Reformation in the sixteenth century, when Protestantism arose as a revolt against the perceived abuses of the Catholic Church, there emerged a greater emphasis on personal, inner, transcendental experience rather than on community organization. Later, with the increasing emphasis on reason from the Enlightenment of the seventeenth and eighteenth centuries through to the modern period, it was neither the organizational nor the experiential dimensions that were emphasized, but the philosophical and doctrinal aspects. Religion came to be conceived primarily as a system of ideas and beliefs. This coincided with an increased awareness of other systems of ideas and beliefs, in India and China for instance, which could therefore also be designated religions. Hence arose the comparative study of religions. The objectivist emphasis further developed through an increasing application of historical methods in the study of religious texts and institutions.

Regarding science, it is important to remember that as a discipline this was not clearly differentiated until the nineteenth century. Galileo, for instance, referred to himself as a mathematician or philosopher, and concerning Isaac Newton John Brooke notes the following:

> His most famous book, in which planetary orbits were explained by his gravitational theory, was entitled *Mathematical Principles of Natural Philosophy* (1687). It was not entitled *Mathematical Principles of Natural Science*. When seventeenth-century students of nature called themselves philosophers, they were identifying themselves with intellectual traditions in which broader issues than immediate scientific technicalities were discussed. Newton himself remarked that it was part of the business of natural philosophy to discuss such questions as the attributes of God and His relationship to the physical world.
>
> (Brooke, 1991, p.7)

Further, even after the scholar William Whewell coined the term 'scientist' in the 1830s, there were continual open and covert struggles over who should be entitled to apply the term to themselves, struggles bound up with the whole issue of the professionalization of science. Throughout the twentieth century, psychologists, sociologists, anthropologists and others frequently had to defend the scientific status of their disciplines. Ambiguities of language further complicated the situation. The German scholar Friedrich Max Müller (1823–1900) introduced the term '*Religionswissenschaft*' for the academic study of religions, and he translated it into English as 'science of religion'. However, *Wissenschaft* means not just science but also learning and knowledge more broadly, and so can refer to the humanities as well as the sciences. Therefore, other scholars have preferred to translate *Religionswissenschaft* as 'comparative religion' or 'history of religion'. Even at the end of the twentieth century, the boundaries of science were being vigorously contested, with debates as to whether the term could legitimately be applied to, for instance, **psychoanalysis**, **parapsychology** or the knowledge systems of the indigenous peoples of Africa, New Zealand or the Americas.

A fourth difficulty is that, even allowing for problems of definition and demarcation, the interactions between religion and science have been immensely complex. In the late nineteenth and early twentieth centuries, much of the most vocal discussion of the relationship between religion and science presented them as irreconcilable and engaged in an epic battle for intellectual and spiritual hegemony. For example, in 1875, John W. Draper published a book entitled *History of the Conflict between Religion and Science*. Twenty years later, in 1896, Andrew D. White's volume *A History of the Warfare of Science with Theology in Christendom* appeared. Recent contextual history has ensured that such simplified accounts, though still frequently promulgated, are no longer sustainable. Accordingly, responsible present-day discussions have had to find ways to acknowledge a wider range of actual and possible positions. In this chapter, I shall make use of the contemporary writer Ian Barbour's recognition of four main categories of interaction between religion and science (Barbour, 1998, pp.77–105). First is *conflict*, in which religion and science provide competing and mutually exclusive explanations for the same phenomena (for example, fundamentalist creationist accounts versus neo-Darwinian evolutionary accounts of the origin of human life). Second is *independence*, in which religion and science either account for different phenomena (for example, religion accounts for spiritual phenomena and science for material phenomena) or provide different kinds of account for the same phenomena (for example, science explains the mechanisms, religion explains the purpose); because there is no direct competition between them, these accounts are, at least in principle, compatible. Third is *dialogue*, in which religion and science, for all their differences, have sufficient areas of overlapping interest to allow for a fruitful exchange of insights and ideas (for example, Fritjof Capra (1977) highlights a shared concern with interconnectedness in some eastern religions and some theories of modern physics). Fourth and last is *integration*, in which religion and science are capable, at least at certain points, of unification into a single discourse (for example, Pierre Teilhard de Chardin (1959) weaves together biological and spiritual evolution). I will draw on Barbour's four categories especially when we come to discuss the work of Jung.

Religion, science and the New Age

The complex interactions between religion and science provide one of the major contexts within which we can understand late twentieth- and early twenty-first-century manifestations of religion. Most of the implications that we have mentioned in the preceding historical sketch have concerned the more public, institutionalized forms of religion. In the present section our focus will shift to the more private, often non-affiliated forms of contemporary spirituality, which for convenience (and with due awareness of the definitional problems noted in the introduction to this book) I am calling 'New Age spirituality'. I use this phrase as an umbrella term that includes neo-Paganism, Wicca, and other differentiated categories within contemporary alternative spirituality (cf. Heelas, 1996). In what follows, we will look at a number of salient features of New Age spirituality and consider how they may relate to interactions between traditional religion and modern science. The list of features is not meant to be either definitive or exhaustive but simply useful for the purposes of this study.

Ambivalence towards science

Overall, the New Age is ambivalent towards modern science. On the one hand, there is sharp criticism of the rationalizing and reductive tendencies of modern science and a corresponding celebration of whatever promotes a more intuitive and spiritually uplifting outlook. As Paul Heelas observes, 'the New Age is largely opposed to the rational outlook of the philosopher and the verificationist approach of the scientist, rejecting "the head" in favour of "the heart" and relying on "intuition" or "inner wisdom"' (Heelas, 1996, p.5). On the other hand, there are scientists who have been specially adopted by the New Age because the emphasis of their work seems to support some of the underlying holistic assumptions of New Age spirituality: Fritjof Capra (1977), David Bohm (1980) and Rupert Sheldrake (1981) are prominent examples.

We could formulate this ambivalence by saying that, in general, New Agers react against the reductive tendencies of modern science while at the same time selectively appropriating ideas from modern science. Sometimes, as in the cases of Bohm and Sheldrake, the New Age-friendly features of their work reflect or build on areas of genuine uncertainty and ambivalence within science itself. Other times, however, images of the development and present state of religion, science and their relationship are elaborated with little

Figure 5.3 The physicist David Bohm in dialogue with the mystic Jiddu Krishnamurti. Mark Edwards/Still Pictures.

regard for the realities and complexities of history. The historians of science John Brooke and Geoffrey Cantor have taken Capra to task on this point in their essay 'Against the self-images of the New Age' (Brooke and Cantor, 1998, pp.75–105). Even more commonly, New Agers speak and write about science, whether drawing on or denigrating it, with very little understanding of actual scientific theories or methodologies.

Psycho-spiritual transformation

Another salient feature of the New Age is its *interest in psycho-spiritual transformation*. Michael York goes so far as to suggest that 'What unites all New Agers ... is the vision of radical mystical transformation on both the personal and collective levels' (York, 1995, p.39). This interest in transformation may relate to interactions between religion and science in several ways. For instance, the transformation is often promoted by application of spiritual techniques that, as Robert Wuthnow notes, 'bear the distinctive imprint of the prevailing technological worldview' (Wuthnow, 1985, p.46). As well as providing the means of psycho-spiritual transformation (or at least the rhetoric for enhancing the attractiveness of these means), science ironically has also been largely responsible for the mind-set from which New Agers seek transformative liberation. Heelas characterizes the transformation that New Agers seek as an attempt to liberate the self through letting go of 'ego-attachments' (Heelas, 1996, p.20). These ego-attachments include the ways in which a person internalizes and conforms to social standards, but they may also more specifically refer to the kind of rational modes of thought involved in science (Heelas, 1996, p.36). Again, New Age interest in psycho-spiritual transformation may, in some cases, be an attempt to claim for personal spirituality a potential for the kind of 'progress' and 'evolution' vaunted by science (Wilber, 1998). Heelas observes: 'Modernity, in many respects, has to do with evolutionary notions of perfectibility'; 'The New Age,' he continues, 'belongs to modernity in that it is progressivistic', 'one can go on *events*, to change for the *better*' (Heelas, 1996, p.169).

Modernization, secularization and globalization

At a general level, we can see New Age spirituality, like other twentieth-century manifestations of religion, as *a response (or set of responses) to modernization, secularization and globalization*. It is problematic to claim that modern science has straightforwardly caused these processes. For instance, as Brooke notes with reference to secularization:

> The replacement of spiritual by material values would seem to owe more to the security of modern medicine, to the seduction of urban comforts and economic prosperity than to any scientific imperative. And insofar as the social functions once performed by religion have been taken over by secular groups and institutions, it is to their social and political origins one must look for insights into the redistribution of power.
>
> (Brooke, 1991, p.340)

Nevertheless, as we shall see, modernization, secularization and globalization would be extremely unlikely to have occurred without modern science.

Primarily, the New Age has responded to – indeed, has defined itself in relation to – these tendencies by resisting them. As Heelas notes, 'The New Age … runs counter to many of the great canons and assumptions of modernity', including 'the faith that has been placed in obtaining progress by way of scientific expertise' (Heelas, 1996, pp.135–6). Rather than secularization, Heelas argues, the New Age promotes the reverse process of **sacralization** ('making sacred') (Heelas, 1996, p.106). Michael York concurs that the New Age provides a counterbalance to the rationalism and scientific method-ology of modernity (York, 1995, p.14). However, in another instance of the complexity to which we are becoming accustomed in this study, Heelas's analysis explores ways in which the New Age not only breaks with but also continues many of the cultural trajectories of modernity (Heelas, 1996, pp.153–77). He refers to 'those processes – the "fall of public man", the construction of the expressivist self, the internalization of religion, and so on – which have been completed by the [New Age] Movement' (Heelas, 1996, p.154). In other words, we need to recognize Romantic as well as rationalist currents as constitutive of modernity. While opposing the rationalist currents, the New Age in many ways furthers the Romantic currents. Wouter Hanegraaff highlights the complex relationship of the New Age to secularization in the subtitle to his book: *New Age Religion and Western Culture: Esotericism in the Mirror of Secular Thought* (1996).

Again, consider globalization – the increasing worldwide link-up of political, economic and cultural systems. This has accelerated under the impact of scientific and technological developments particularly in the areas of transport and communications. Globalization has had various frequently noted effects on traditional religions. In some cases, it has arguably strengthened fundamentalist attitudes as religious groups entrench themselves in an attempt to preserve their beleaguered identities. In other cases, increasing exposure to alternative worldviews has resulted in a liberalization of attitudes and the growth of tolerance, interfaith dialogue and, for some, a more **perennialist** outlook (for example, Wilber, 1998). However, globalization also provides the context for understanding some specific features of the New Age Movement. David Spangler, co-director in the 1970s of the New Age community at Findhorn, Scotland, remarked that 'The New Age deals with issues of planetization and the emergence of an awareness that we are all one people living on one world that shares a common destiny' (Spangler, 1988). Other representatives of the New Age express the same sentiment: Marilyn Ferguson speaks of the 'global consciousness' to which the New Age aspires (York, 1995, p.35; see Ferguson, 1982) and William Bloom notes that one of the major fields comprising the New Age is ecology, which, as York puts it, 'through interdependence and interpenetration, accepts responsibility for the planetary state' (in York, 1995, p.89; see Bloom, 1991).

Non-western, pre-modern and esoteric traditions

Another significant feature of the New Age is *eclectic engagement with non-western, pre-modern and esoteric traditions*. According to York, 'New Age is a blend of Pagan religions, Eastern philosophies, and occult-psychic phenomena' (York, 1995, p.34). According to Heelas, 'From the detraditionalized stance of the New Age what matters is the "arcane", the "esoteric", the "hidden wisdom", the "inner or secret tradition", the "ageless wisdom"' (Heelas, 1996, p.27). These traditions – including **Yoga**, **Taoism**, **Gnosticism**, **divination**, **magic**, **alchemy**, and much else – may appeal partly because in them the problematic relationship between religion and science is assumed not to exist as it does in the modern western mainstream. The traditions operate before (pre-modern), distant from (non-western), or in secrecy from (esoteric) the rise of modern science. Accordingly, so it can be argued, they have been able to

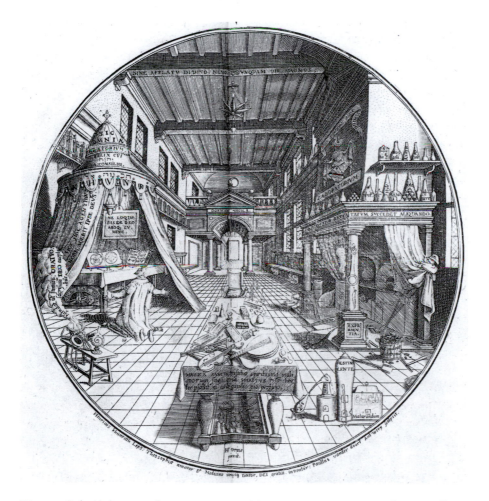

Figure 5.4 Alchemy, for many practitioners, was a spiritual as well as material pursuit. Circular plate, from *Amphitheatrum Sapientiae Solius* by Heinrich Khunrath, 1609. Bodleian Library, University of Oxford. Reference (shelfmark) R.I.9. Med.

avoid the catastrophic splitting off of the emotional and intuitive functions that took place in modern western consciousness. We can therefore turn to these traditions in order to reconnect with a more holistic outlook. Here, then, modern science and traditional religion have influenced the New Age by presenting a picture of problematic relations in contrast to which other traditions seem, often unrealistically, more attractive.

Myth

A further, closely related feature is that *New Agers often frame contemporary experience in terms of myth*. Of course, there is a mythical dimension to most if not all religions, traditional and modern (see Smart, 1997, pp.10, 130–64). I refer here to the particular salience of myth in New Age spirituality. This is especially the case with neo-Paganism, as Chapter 1 of this book showed. Beliefs and stories about Egyptian, Graeco-Roman, and northern European gods and goddesses, among many others, play a major role in neo-Pagan rituals and worldviews. Above all, the myth of the Great Goddess is invoked both to interpret and to encourage further the rise of feminine consciousness and spirituality, as in Starhawk (Miriam Simos), *The Spiral Dance: A Rebirth of the Ancient Religion of the Great Goddess* (1979). New Age uses of myth presuppose that it is not a primitive form of explanation of the physical world now superseded by science. Rather, it is a valid alternative form of cognition, with a different subject matter (the psycho-spiritual rather than the physical world) and a different function (to disclose spiritual meaning rather than to explain physical processes). This revived appeal of myth can be partly accounted for if we consider that myth, because it does not make the same claims to explanatory adequacy as religious doctrines traditionally have, is less vulnerable to direct criticism from science and so can survive better as a container of spiritual meaning.

Personal experience

Even more salient is that *New Agers generally prioritize personal experience over institutionalized beliefs*. As York observes, 'New Age is a decentralized movement – one built around not doctrines or particular belief systems but an experiential vision' (York, 1995, p.39). New Agers would mostly agree with Carl Rogers when he says, 'Experience for me is the highest authority' (Rogers, 1967, p.24). New Age appeals to experience may partly be an attempt to appropriate some of the charisma of science, for it is possible to see a loose analogy between experiencing and experimenting, inasmuch as both involve testing things for oneself rather than accepting traditionally sanctioned pronouncements. In any case, the tendency among New Agers is to move beyond socialized beliefs to the authenticity of the inner realm. Indeed, New Agers actively work to achieve liberation from social conditioning. Largely, this shift from the external and social to the inner and individual can be accounted for in terms of various institutional failures:

> The institutional fabric, whose basic function has always been to provide meaning and stability for the individual, has become incohesive, fragmented and thus progressively deprived of plausibility. Institutions then confront the individual as fluid and unreliable, in the extreme case as unreal. Inevitably, the individual is thrown back upon himself, on his own subjectivity, from which he must dredge up the meaning that he requires to exist.
>
> (Berger *et al.*, 1974, p.85)

More specifically, many women have felt that the authoritarian and patriarchal structure of the Church is irredeemably obstructive to them (see Mumm, 2002); people seeking healing have felt that conventional medicine fails to respect the wholeness of their personality; and political activists, disillusioned about significantly changing the outer structures of society, have retreated to working at inner change. This suspicion of and disillusionment with institutions may also stem from an increased awareness of the actual workings of institutions fostered by historical and social scientific analyses.

Authority of the self

Finally, and perhaps most important of all, *New Agers tend to locate spiritual and ethical authority within the individual self.* The prominent New Age teacher Sir George Trevelyan advises his listeners: 'Only accept what rings true to your Inner Self' (Heelas, 1996, p.21). Starhawk likewise places emphasis on 'self-responsibility and the individual as final arbiter for the meaning and direction of life' (York, 1995, p.113). Indeed, Heelas identifies 'Self-spirituality' as *the* defining and unifying feature of the New Age. 'Self-spirituality' involves 'the monistic assumption that the Self itself is sacred' (Heelas, 1996, p.2) and an outlook where 'The "individual" serves as his or her own source of guidance' (p.23). According to Heelas, this notion is responsible for a 'remarkable consistency' beneath 'much of the heterogeneity' of the New Age (p.2). He even proposes that 'The New Age shows what "religion" looks like when it is organized in terms of what is taken to be the authority of the Self' (p.221). This is not to deny that New Agers sometimes recognize other sources of authority besides the inner spiritual self – for example, more traditional teachers and external systems of thought – or that there is a strong social current within the New Age – for example, in its association with the Green Movement. However, as Heelas again summarizes, 'Overall, the New Age has become more detraditionalized; the shift in emphasis has been from cosmologies to experiences; from beliefs to spiritual technologies; from heeding Mahatmas to heeding the Self' (p.67). The influence on this of interactions between religion and science can probably be detected among several of the considerations that have already been mentioned. For emphasis on the self is likely to be encouraged by institutional failure, by the loose equation of experience with experiment, by concern with spiritual meaning rather than physical explanation, by retreat to a domain not so dominated by science (a domain where human subjectivity can better flourish), and by the goal of psycho-spiritual transformation.

The New Age and C.G. Jung

In the second part of this chapter, our aim is to use a more focused case study in order to gain further insight into how interactions between religion and science may have influenced New Age spirituality. This should both support and enrich our preceding observations.

A biographical sketch of C.G. Jung

Carl Gustav Jung was born in Kesswil, Switzerland, in 1875. His father, like many of his other ancestors on both sides, was a Protestant clergyman. His mother, again like other relatives and like Jung himself, was prone to paranormal experiences. Jung went to school and later to university in Basel. He trained as a medical doctor, specializing in psychiatry, and secured an appointment in the Burghölzli mental hospital in Zürich, where he worked from 1900 to 1909. At the Burghölzli, Jung worked primarily with patients suffering from schizophrenia (a severe personality disorder characterized by introversion, dissociation and an inability to distinguish reality from unreality). However, as the Burghölzli was the research hospital for the University of Zürich, Jung was also able to carry out pioneering research in experimental psychiatry (specifically, on **word association tests**) for which he gained an early international reputation. Jung's work was concerned with investigating not just conscious mental functioning but also and more especially unconscious mental processes, that is, processes of which the conscious mind is not normally aware. In this, he was part of the tradition of dynamic psychiatry or depth psychology that emerged in the latter half of the nineteenth century. During his time at the Burghölzli, Jung became aware of the work of the Austrian psychoanalyst **Sigmund Freud** (1856–1939) and his theory of psychoanalysis, which was also concerned with investigating the unconscious. The two men met and collaborated intensively between the years 1907 and 1913. For various reasons – theoretical, political and personal – the relationship ended acrimoniously in 1913. After a period of reorientation, Jung developed by 1921 his own distinctive psychological theories, which re-established his international repu-tation on a new basis and which he continued to elaborate and refine until his death in 1961. These mature psychological theories were partly a return to traditions of psychological work that had influenced Jung before his collaboration with Freud. His development of them

Figure 5.5 Jung in old age. Hulton Getty.

Figure 5.6 The Sinologist Richard Wilhelm who stimulated Jung's interests in Chinese alchemy and divination. Ullstein Bilderdienst.

was influenced by extensive studies of mythology, Gnosticism, alchemy and eastern religions; by travels in India, Africa and America; and by personal contacts with scientists (such as the physicist Wolfgang Pauli), theologians (such as the Dominican Father Victor White), and scholars of religion (such as the specialist in Chinese culture Richard Wilhelm, the specialist in Indian culture Heinrich Zimmer, and the theorist of myth Mircea Eliade). (Biographical details of Jung can be found in, for example, Hayman, 1999.)

Jung's affinity with the New Age

It may seem strange to attempt to illuminate New Age spirituality by examining the work of a thinker who died before the New Age Movement emerged as a distinctive socio-cultural force and who, in any case, arguably would have repudiated much of what goes under the New Age banner. However, there are several good reasons for focusing on the work of Jung.

If we scan the shelves of a New Age or Mind/Body/Spirit section in any major bookshop, we are likely to find not only many books by and on Jung himself, but also books on a wide range of subject matter that closely reflects the scope of Jung's interests. We will probably find books on western esotericism including magic and alchemy; divination including astrology and the **I Ching**; eastern religions from India and China; indigenous religions of Africa and North America; myths from all over the world; and reinterpretations of Christianity from a mythic or perennialist point of view. There will be books on holistic science and on healing by **creative visualization**, by connecting with one's higher self, and by various other kinds of spiritually oriented therapy. Other books will be about paranormal phenomena including hauntings, communications supposedly channelled from discarnate spirits, and UFOs. Jung, more perhaps than any other twentieth-century thinker, engaged seriously with all these subjects. Such close parallels suggest either influence or common origins.

In fact, there can be little doubt that in many cases the parallels do represent actual influences. In a survey conducted in the late 1970s, Marilyn Ferguson asked her New Age-inclined subjects to name those who had most influenced them. Among the 185 responses, Jung's name was the second most frequently cited (Ferguson, 1982). In a more recent 1994 survey of subscribers to *Kindred Spirit*, the largest-selling New Age magazine in the UK, Stuart Rose asked the same question. Among over 900 responses, Jung's name was again the second most frequently cited (Rose, 1997). Indeed, Jung's name was the only one to appear among the top ten in both surveys (Heelas, 1996, p.126). This finding is supported by indications from many other sources. To name a few: the parallels between Jung and the New Age have been considered worthy of special comment by Jungians themselves such as David Tacey, who worries that the similarities between Jung and the New Age may obscure their important differences (Tacey, 1999); by biographers such as Frank McLynn, who entitled the penultimate chapter of his life of Jung 'New Age Guru' (McLynn, 1996); by scholars of religion such as Paul Heelas, who considers Jung one of 'three key figures' (along with the Russian theosophist Helena Blavatsky (1831–91) and the Caucasian mystic George Gurdjieff (?1877–1949)) for understanding the development of the New Age Movement (Heelas, 1996, pp.46–7); and by practitioners such as the Wiccan Vivianne Crowley, who, herself a Jungian-oriented psychotherapist, observes that traditional pagan notions of gods, goddesses and magic can be and frequently are recast as Jungian notions of **archetypes** and synchronicity (Crowley, 1989).

Again, although Jung did not to my knowledge use the phrase 'New Age', he did draw attention to the inauguration of a new era with the imminent **precession of the spring equinox** from Pisces into Aquarius. The phrase 'Age of Aquarius' represented in the 1960s and early 1970s much of what later came to be represented by the phrase 'New Age' (see Ferguson, 1982). Writing in the late 1950s about the numerous reported sightings of flying saucers, Jung interprets them as signs of 'coming events which are in accord with the end of an era' (Jung, 1981b, par. 589). He explains:

> As we know from ancient Egyptian history, they [that is, these coming events] are manifestations of psychic changes which always appear at the end of one Platonic month [that is, an astronomically determined period of approximately 2,000 years] and at the beginning of another. Apparently they are changes in the constellation of psychic dominants, of the archetypes, or 'gods' as they used to be called, which bring about, or accompany, long-lasting transformations of the collective psyche. This transformation started in the historical era and left its traces first in the passing of the aeon of Taurus into that of Aries, and then of Aries into Pisces, whose beginning coincides with the rise of Christianity. We are now nearing that great change which may be expected when the spring point enters Aquarius.
>
> (Jung, 1981b, par. 589)

Finally, we may add to these outer affinities between Jung and the New Age, several deeper affinities of underlying orientation and principle. Specifically, each of the characteristic features of New Age spirituality that we identified in the previous section is also a major emphasis within Jung's psychology. Like New Agers, Jung (as we shall see) reacts against the reductive tendencies of modern science while at the same time selectively appropriating ideas from modern science; places considerable importance on notions of psycho-spiritual transformation; has an ambivalent but largely oppositional relationship to secular modernity; engages eclectically with non-western, pre-modern and esoteric traditions; frames contemporary experience in terms of myth; prioritizes personal experience over institutionalized beliefs; and locates authority in the individual self.

Differences between Jung and the New Age

In spite of these evident affinities and influences, some writers, as I have already hinted, have preferred to place the accent on the differences between Jung and the New Age. Tacey, in an article entitled 'Why Jung would doubt the New Age', has singled out two major points on which he considers Jung and the New Age to differ (Tacey, 1999, pp.36–42). One is their attitudes towards the feminine. While he acknowledges that both Jung and the New Age attach greater importance to the feminine than has traditional patriarchal European culture, he argues that their attitudes to the feminine also contrast in an important respect. The New Age, according to Tacey, tends to identify with the emergence of feminine values and swings over to a celebration of these values that is no less one-sided than was the previous commitment to patriarchal values. Jung, by contrast, recognized and described the phenomena associated with the ascendancy of the feminine but did not naively celebrate this collectively occurring process. Rather, he recommended integrating the new collective values with the old, identifying with neither but maintaining a stance of critical individuality. (It should be noted that this characterization of Jung's theoretical position regarding the feminine, though accurate, sidesteps issues such as Jung's personal attitudes towards women and his **gender essentialism** that many contemporary commentators have found problematic. See, for example, Wehr, 1987, and Young-Eisendrath, 1997.)

A second point of difference for Tacey concerns attitudes towards suffering. He considers that the New Age naively elevates bliss over suffering, whereas Jung is closer to traditional Christianity in his emphasis on the redemptive significance of suffering. New Agers, according to Tacey, aim to experience the spirit as a further form of gratification for the ego. Jung, by contrast, recognizes that spiritual development (which he termed '**individuation**') is 'an heroic and

Figure 5.7 Venus and Mercury creating the hermaphrodite Rebis. Feminine and masculine qualities combine in the alchemical symbol of the hermaphrodite. Fortean Picture Library.

often tragic task, the most difficult of all, it involves a suffering, a passion of the ego' (Jung, 1986c, par. 233, quoted in Tacey, 1999, p.40).

In regard both to the feminine and to suffering, Tacey is undoubtedly putting his finger on differences that do exist in many instances. However, the New Age is an expansive movement in which people participate in varying ways and at varying levels of sophistication. For many, the feminine is valued in much the way Tacey attributes to Jung: as a compensatory force to be brought into balanced relationship with the masculine. For example, York notes the following difference between the thinking of two prominent Wiccans, one representing the attitude Tacey criticizes, the other the attitude he favours:

> Unlike Starhawk's almost exclusively feminist brand of Wicca – one in which the male god is seen as a subordinate emanation of the

> Goddess – [Vivianne] Crowley's Alexandrian persuasion clearly
> emphasizes the male and female balance necessary within its image
> of the divine. To focus on either the Goddess or God alone, Crowley
> contends, produces both social and individual spiritual imbalance.
>
> (York, 1995, p.121)

Suffering, too, is not always treated as lightly within the New Age as Tacey implies. Heelas, for example, on the one hand can describe the New Age as 'a highly optimistic, celebratory, utopian and spiritual form of humanism' (Heelas, 1996, p.28), while on the other hand he registers the Caucasian mystic Gurdjieff as one of the 'three key figures' to have influenced the development of the New Age (Heelas, 1996, p.47). Gurdjieff's system presents a very grim picture of the human condition; transformation is possible but only through 'conscious effort and intentional suffering' (Hinnells, 1997, p.198). Furthermore, even if Tacey is largely right in identifying one-sided attitudes towards the feminine and suffering within the New Age, this need not constitute a definitive indictment. There is in principle no reason why the New Age, while retaining its basic character, should not become more balanced precisely in the ways indicated by Tacey.

In spite of some debatable differences, therefore, I would argue that the relationship between Jung's psychology and New Age thought is sufficiently close for us to gain some insight into the origin and nature of the New Age through a closer examination of Jung's work. In particular, we may gain a deeper appreciation of how interactions between religion and science have influenced New Age spirituality by examining how these same interactions have influenced Jung's psychology.

Religion and science in the psychology of C.G. Jung

Jung's lifelong preoccupation with religion and science

Jung was preoccupied with the relationship between religion and science throughout his life. In his memoirs, *Memories, Dreams, Reflections*, he recalls his youthful interest in both areas and his difficulty deciding in which direction to pursue a career: 'What appealed to me in science,' he writes, 'were the concrete facts and their historical background, and in comparative religion the spiritual problems, into which philosophy also entered. In science I missed the factor of meaning; and in religion, that of empiricism' (Jung,

1963b, p.79). However, this was not just a theoretical problem for Jung. The relationship between religion and science had become personally problematic for him when he witnessed his father, a Protestant pastor, undergoing a crisis of faith largely precipitated by the ascendancy of materialistic science. Jung writes:

> My father was obviously under the impression that psychiatrists had discovered something in the brain which proved that in the place where mind should have been there was only matter, and nothing 'spiritual'. This was borne out by his admonitions that if I studied medicine I should in Heaven's name not become a materialist.
>
> (Jung, 1963b, p.98)

A survey of Jung's work at any stage in his long career shows that this problem never left him. It is a dominant theme in the five lectures he delivered as a medical student to his fraternity the Zofingia Society (Jung, 1983, first published 1896–9). In these lectures, he acknowledges the usefulness of science but vigorously protests against the materialism and inertia of current science. He favours a more **vitalistic** understanding, asserts the inseparability of morality from science, and even argues that religion is the natural endpoint of science. The same problem is implicit in Jung's decision to base his doctoral dissertation on a case study of a spirit medium. Much of the nineteenth-century interest in spiritualism had been motivated by the aim of providing 'empirical' evidence in support of the traditional claims of religion about the existence and survival of the soul, and Jung was in part heir to these concerns. Again, the relationship between religion and science was one of the main issues that led to Jung's parting of ways with Freud and psychoanalysis. Freud was a staunch atheist and relentlessly reduced all religious phenomena to natural causes. Jung, by contrast, wished to find an honourable place for religious phenomena within psychoanalytic thinking. Later, in developing and articulating his mature psychological theory, Jung always insisted that he was working as a scientist and empiricist, but he increasingly applied his 'empiricism' to the investigation of religious phenomena. His dual interest is conspicuous in the three 'Terry Lectures' on 'Psychology and Religion' that he delivered at Yale University in 1937. These were part of a series of 'Lectures on Religion in the light of Science and Philosophy' (Jung, 1986b, p.3). They focused on a set of dreams of a scientist, showing, Jung argued, the spontaneous operation of a religious function in the psyche of someone sceptical about religion. The scientist we now know to have been the Nobel Prize-winning physicist Wolfgang Pauli, with whom Jung was later to collaborate in developing his ideas on synchronicity (Jung and Pauli, 1955).

Figure 5.8 Wolfgang Pauli, a sceptical scientist who had religious and alchemical dreams. He collaborated with Jung on the theory of synchronicity. Hulton Getty.

Pauli's dreams and visions also provided material for one of Jung's major works on alchemy (Jung, 1989). This subject, which occupied Jung in the last 30 years of his life, again unites religion and science: for alchemy, Jung shows, was not just a precursor of modern chemistry concerned with material transformations, but also, in many cases, an esoteric religious discipline concerned with the spiritual transformation of the personality. Many of Jung's other late works also evince this preoccupation with religion, science and the relationship between them – especially, as we shall see, his works on synchronicity (Jung, 1991b, 1991c).

Jung's guiding motive throughout all of this was to preserve religion in the face of science. In a 1933 letter to Pastor Josef Shattauer, Jung confided that 'it is exceedingly difficult nowadays to inculcate into people any conception of genuine religiosity. I have found that religious terminology only scares them off still more, for which reason I always have to tread the path of science and experience, quite irrespective of any tradition, in order to get my patients to acknowledge spiritual truths' (Jung, 1973, p.118). Apparently, this was his motive not just with patients but also with professional colleagues. In 1945, writing to Father Victor White, Jung claimed that a book he published in 1911–12, which precipitated his break with Freud, 'was written by a psychiatrist for the purpose of submitting the necessary material to his psychiatric colleagues, material which would demonstrate to them the importance of religious symbolism' (Jung, 1973, pp.383–4).

At early stages in his career, Jung toyed with the *conflict* model of the relationship between religion and science. In doing so, his hope was that religion might win out. For example, in the last of his Zofingia Lectures he longs for the return of a mystical approach to religion, even if this entails 'the possibility of social and scientific indifference and call[ing] into question the further progress of civilization' (Jung, 1983, par. 290). However, Jung quickly recognized that on most points of direct confrontation and conflict between religion and science, science was likely to prove the victor. 'The imposing arguments of science,' he acknowledges, 'represent the highest degree of intellectual certainty yet achieved by the mind of man. So at least it seems to the man of today' (Jung, 1981a, par. 543). Consequently, 'the guardians and custodians of symbolical truth, namely the religions, have been robbed of their efficacy by science' (Jung, 1995, par. 336).

Jung therefore increasingly appealed to the *independence* position. 'My subjective attitude,' he wrote in 1933, 'is that I hold every religious position in high esteem but draw an inexorable dividing line between the content of belief and the requirements of science' (Jung, 1973, p.125). At a talk he gave in London in 1939, a questioner put it to him that 'There is obviously, and always has been, a conflict between religion and science ... How do you bring about a reconciliation, which obviously is the sort of thing that is needed?' Jung replied: 'There is no conflict between religion and science. That is a very old-fashioned idea. Science has to consider what there is. There is religion ... Science cannot establish [or, Jung also implies, refute] a religious truth ... Our science is phenomenology' (Jung, 1993, pars. 691–2). Again, no less explicitly, he wrote in 1946: 'Science is human knowledge, theology divine knowledge. Therefore the two are incommensurable' (Jung, 1973, p.411).

From the safety of this basic position of independence, Jung explored bolder possibilities for *dialogue* and *integration* between religion and science. 'A rapprochement between empirical science and religious experience,' he writes, 'would in my opinion be fruitful for both. Harm can result only if one side or the other remains unconscious of the limitations of its claim to validity' (Jung, 1963a, par. 457). He notes that 'inside the religious movement there [have been] any number of attempts to combine science with religious belief and practice, as for instance Christian Science, theosophy, and anthroposophy' (Jung, 1986a, par. 863). However, he held these particular attempts in low esteem, and this may account for his occasional repudiation of any integrative intent on his own part. For example, to one of the same correspondents to whom he had declared his belief in the independence of religion and science, he wrote: 'I am wholly incorrigible and utterly incapable of coming up with a mixture of theology and science' (Jung, 1973, p.125). Nevertheless, he did aim to promote dialogue:

> I start from a positive Christianity which is as much Catholic as Protestant, and I endeavour in a scientifically responsible manner to point out those empirically graspable facts which make the justification of Christian and, in particular, Catholic dogma at least plausible, and besides that are best suited to give the scientific mind an access to understanding.

(Jung, 1973, pp.349–50)

Certain statements even point directly towards integration – at least if we bear in mind Jung's insistence that his psychology was scientific: 'I would surely be among the first to welcome an explicit attempt to integrate the findings of psychology into the ecclesiastical doctrine', he wrote to Father White in 1945 (Jung, 1973, p.385).

Figure 5.9 The English Dominican Father Victor White who hoped to integrate Jungian psychology with Catholic doctrine. Dominican Archives.

The influence of religion and science on Jung's psychological theories

From the above account, Jung's preoccupation with the interactions between religion and science is clear. We can see, too, that there is no simple answer to the question of how he conceived of their relationship; for his conception was different at different times. We now need to look more closely at the impact of this on some aspects of Jung's particular psychological theories. It is beyond the scope of this chapter to explain these theories fully, so we will restrict ourselves to considering only some of their most distinctive features. We will briefly look at Jung's notion of **psychic reality**, and his core concepts of the **collective unconscious**, archetypes, individuation, and the **self**. In the following section, we will take a more detailed look at his theory of synchronicity.

The relationship between religion and science influenced a notion that is fundamental to Jung's psychological model: his belief that the only reality of which we can be immediately aware is psychic reality. Based on his understanding of Kant's theory of knowledge, Jung argued that things in themselves, whether physical things or spiritual things, cannot be known other than as mediated to consciousness in the form of psychic, that is, mental, images. It is our psychic image of the table that we immediately experience, not the table itself; similarly, it is our psychic images of gods and spirits that we immediately experience, not the gods and spirits themselves. This notion of the primacy of psychic reality allowed Jung to attach equal importance to both religious imagery (stemming from the realm of spirit) and scientific imagery (stemming from the realm of matter), for both kinds of imagery, whatever their putative origin, are experienced as psychic. Thus, the notion provides an experienceable middle ground in which these two kinds of imagery (and by implication the two realms from which the imagery stems) can interact and possibly achieve some measure of dialogue and integration. Jung's arrival at such a middle position arguably was influenced by his dual commitment to religion and science, for one of his requirements of any satisfactory psychological theory would have been its compatibility with both of these commitments.

The relationship between religion and science also clearly influenced Jung's core psychological concepts of the collective unconscious and archetypes. For Jung, as for others, the unconscious 'covers all psychic contents or processes that are not conscious, that is, not related to the ego in any perceptible way' (Jung, 1991a, par. 837); it is that part of a person's inner world that is unknown.

However, Jung further differentiates between the **personal uncon-scious** and the collective unconscious. The personal unconscious comprises those contents of a person's inner world that have their origin in the person's individual life, are currently unknown, but could just as well be known: 'all the acquisitions of personal life, everything forgotten, repressed, subliminally perceived, thought, felt' (Jung, 1991a, par. 842). The collective unconscious, by contrast, is transpersonal in the sense that it comprises those contents of a person's inner world that 'do not originate in personal acquisitions but in the inherited possibility of psychic functioning in general, that is, in the inherited structure of the brain' (Jung, 1991a, par. 842). More specifically, Jung refers to the manifested contents of the collective unconscious as **archetypal images**. They are the spontaneously occurring, observable expression of 'irrepresentable, unconscious, pre-existent' forms that he calls archetypes (Jung, 1981c, par. 847). For Jung, archetypes are 'typical modes of apprehension', that is, ways of conceiving the world, and there are as many of them as there are typical human situations. Every archetype can express itself through an indefinite number of possible archetypal images. The ways we relate to parents, siblings, children, friends, lovers, enemies and authority figures; the particular interests we pursue in life; how we respond to such major transitions of life as birth, maturity, marriage, sickness and death all may be governed by archetypes and expressed in terms of archetypal imagery, which may include personifications, symbols and mythic narratives. The archetypal character of these behaviours and images is indicated by a certain spontaneity, autonomy and emotional intensity that attaches to them (Jung, 1981c, par. 847).

Jung claimed that his theory of archetypes was derived empirically, which for him meant scientifically, from 'the repeated observation that, for instance, the myths and fairy tales of world literature contain definite motifs which crop up everywhere. We meet these same motifs,' he added, 'in the fantasies, dreams, deliria, and delusions of individuals living today' (Jung, 1981c, par. 847). Nevertheless, this is not reductive science. One of the primary attractions of the theory of archetypes for Jung was precisely that it provided a means of countering the reductive tendencies of alternative psychological theories such as Freud's theory of psychoanalysis. The tenor of Freud's theory was to explain all unconscious psychological mani-festations, including ostensibly religious ones, in terms of the experiencers' personal histories and ultimately their biology. By asserting the existence of psychic contents that could not be explained simply in terms of personal history and biology, Jung hoped to escape the materialistic implications of Freud's position and so preserve the validity of the sphere of religion.

Jung's struggles with religion and science also influenced his conception of the core process of the psyche: individuation. Individuation is the process of psychic development itself. As Jung defines it, 'Individuation means becoming an "in-dividual," and in so far as "individuality" embraces our innermost, last, and incomparable uniqueness, it also implies becoming one's own self. We could therefore translate individuation as "coming to selfhood" or "self-realization"' (Jung, 1990, par. 266). Individuation proceeds through a continual, arduous integration of unconscious contents into consciousness, first the contents of the personal unconscious and then those of the collective unconscious. The involvement of the collective unconscious ensures that individuation is a transpersonal or spiritual process. However, the influence of Jung's struggle with religion and science is most conspicuous in the characterization of individuation as an inherently goal-oriented or **teleological** process. In this, it stands opposed to the assumption of most modern science that nature is fundamentally aimless and mechanistic.

All the above features of Jung's psychological model come together in his concept of the self. For Jung, the self is at once the symbol of psychic totality, the central archetype of the collective unconscious and the goal of individuation. 'The self,' he writes, 'is our life's goal, for it is the completest expression of that fateful combination we call individuality' (Jung, 1990, par. 404). The self, as Jung understands it, needs to be differentiated from the ego. While the ego is the centre of consciousness, the self is the hypothetical centre of the whole psyche, consciousness and the unconscious together. It is pre-eminently a spiritual concept. Indeed, Jung finds images of the self functionally indistinguishable from images of God, so that the self 'might equally well be called the "God within us"' (Jung, 1990, par. 399).

Jung's core psychological concepts of psychic reality, the collective unconscious, archetypes, individuation and the self provide resources for continuing to accord a central importance to the sphere of religion even in the midst of rampant secularization. In this, Jung's work has been an inspiration to the similar project of much New Age thought. Indeed, parallels between Jungian and New Age notions are easy to find. The notion of the primacy of psychic reality naturally leads to the kind of emphasis on inner experience found in New Age thinking. The concept of the collective or transpersonal unconscious finds reflection in the New Age belief that 'the person is, in essence, spiritual' (Heelas, 1996, p.19). The archetypes, as we have already noted, are sometimes equated with neo-Pagan gods and goddesses.

Individuation finds its parallels in New Age notions of psycho-spiritual transformation, which also have a teleological emphasis. Above all, close parallels exist between Jung's concept of the self and the spiritual self singled out by Heelas as the defining characteristic of the New Age. For New Agers,

> To experience the 'Self' itself is to experience 'God', the 'Goddess', the 'Source', 'Christ Consciousness', the 'inner child', the 'way of the heart', or, most simply and, I think, most frequently, 'inner spirituality'. And experiences of the 'Higher Self', to use another favoured term, stand in stark contrast to those afforded by the ego.
>
> (Heelas, 1996, p.19)

Late in life Jung gave his psychological model an important final twist with his theory of synchronicity. This theory represents the culmination of Jung's lifelong struggle with the relationship between religion and science and has profound implications for his understanding of both fields.

Jung's theory of synchronicity

Jung was in his mid seventies before he formally set down his thoughts about synchronicity, which he defined in a variety of ways. Most succinctly, he defined it as 'meaningful coincidence' (Jung, 1991c, par. 827), as 'acausal [not involving the relation of cause and effect] parallelism' (Jung, 1963b, p.342), or as 'an acausal connecting principle' (Jung, 1991c). More fully, he defined it as 'the simultaneous occurrence of a certain psychic state with one or more external events which appear as meaningful parallels to the momentary subjective state' (Jung, 1991c, par. 850). Familiar examples of the kind of occurrences that could be deemed synchronistic include dreaming of some unlikely event that afterwards actually happens, or thinking about a person one has not heard from in years only to have one's thoughts interrupted by a phone call from that person. Jung's own best-known account of a synchronistic experience concerns a young woman patient whose excellent but excessive intellectuality made her 'psychologically inaccessible', closed off from a 'more human understanding'. Unable to make headway in the analysis, Jung reports that he had to confine himself to 'the hope that something unexpected would turn up, something that would burst the intellectual retort into which she had sealed herself'. He continues:

> Well, I was sitting opposite her one day, with my back to the window, listening to her flow of rhetoric. She had had an impressive dream the night before, in which someone had given her a golden scarab – a

costly piece of jewellery. While she was still telling me this dream, I heard something behind me gently tapping on the window. I turned round and saw that it was a fairly large flying insect that was knocking against the window-pane in the obvious effort to get into the dark room. This seemed to me very strange. I opened the window immediately and caught the insect in the air as it flew in. It was a scarabaeid beetle, or common rose-chafer (*Cetonia aurata*), whose gold-green colour most nearly resembles that of a golden scarab. I handed the beetle to my patient with the words, 'Here is your scarab.' This experience punctured the desired hole in her rationalism and broke the ice of her intellectual resistance. The treatment could now be continued with satisfactory results.

(Jung, 1991b, par. 982)

Referring back to the definitions, we can see that the psychic state is indicated here by the patient's decision to tell Jung her dream of being given a scarab. The parallel external event is the appearance and behaviour of the real scarab.[1] Neither of these events discernibly or plausibly caused the other by any normal means, so their relationship is acausal. Nevertheless, the events parallel each other in such unlikely detail that one cannot escape the impression that they are indeed connected, albeit acausally. Moreover, this acausal connection of events is both symbolically informative (as we shall see) and has a deeply emotive and transforming impact on the patient and in these senses is clearly meaningful. (Jung's requirement that the parallel events be simultaneous is more problematic. For present purposes, it is sufficient to know that Jung does also allow for paralleling between events that are not simultaneous. Thus, the patient's dream, rather than her decision to tell the dream, preceded the actual appearance of the scarab by several hours. Yet, Jung would certainly have considered the coincidence between the dream and the actual appearance synchronistic even if the patient had not decided to tell the dream at just that moment.)

Jung attempts to account for synchronistic events primarily in terms of his concept of archetypes. For this purpose, he highlights the nature of archetypes as 'formal factors responsible for the organization of unconscious psychic processes: they are "patterns of behaviour"'. At the same time,' he continues, 'they have a "specific charge" and develop **numinous** effects which express themselves as *affects*' (Jung, 1991c, par. 841). They 'constitute the structure' not of the personal but 'of the collective unconscious ... a psyche that is identical in all individuals' (Jung, 1991c, par. 840). Also relevant is that they typically express themselves in the form of **symbolic** images.

[1] The scarab beetle was an ancient Egyptian symbol of rebirth. See Colour Plate 12.

Jung considered that synchronistic events tend to occur in situations in which an archetype is active. Such activation of archetypes in the life of a person is governed by the process of individuation – the inherent drive of the psyche towards increased wholeness and self-realization. Individuation in turn proceeds through the dynamic of **compensation**, whereby any one-sidedness in a person's conscious attitude is balanced by contents emerging from the unconscious which, if successfully integrated, contribute to a state of greater psychic wholeness. Relating these psychological dynamics to the example, Jung suggests that it has 'an archetypal foundation' (Jung, 1991c, par. 845) and, more specifically, that it was the archetype of rebirth that was activated. He writes that 'Any essential change of attitude signifies a psychic renewal which is usually accompanied by symbols of rebirth in the patient's dreams and fantasies. The scarab is a classic example of a rebirth symbol' (Jung, 1991c, par. 845). The emotional charge or numinosity of the archetype is evident from its having 'broke[n] the ice of [the patient's] intellectual resistance'. The compensatory nature of the experience is also clear: her one-sided rationalism and psychological stasis were balanced by an event that both in its symbolism and in its action expressed the power of the irrational and the possibility of renewal. Finally, that all of this promoted the patient's individuation is implied by Jung's statement that 'The treatment could now be continued with satisfactory results'.

The influence of science and religion on Jung's theory of synchronicity

The theory of synchronicity drew on both religious and scientific influences. The scientific influences are the more obvious, as Jung pushed these to the fore when presenting his theory. In the first place, there was Jung's usual 'empiricism', that is to say, his accumulation of observational data. He refers to 'the innumerable cases of meaningful coincidence that have been observed not only by me but by many others, and recorded in large collections' (Jung, 1991b, par. 983). In the second place, there was Jung's familiarity with recent discoveries in physics. Einstein was Jung's dinner guest on several occasions between 1909 and 1912 and, says Jung,

> It was Einstein who set me off thinking about a possible relativity of time as well as space, and their psychic conditionality. More than thirty years later this stimulus led to my relation with the physicist Professor W. Pauli and to my thesis of psychic synchronicity.
>
> (Jung, 1976, p.109)

Through discussions with Pauli, Jung deepened his understanding of such features of quantum physics as **complementarity** and acausality, both of which were to figure in Jung's presentation of synchronicity. In the third place, there was Jung's interest in the newly developed field of experimental parapsychology. He was particularly inspired by Joseph B. Rhine's experiments at Duke University in the USA in the 1930s, which seemed to provide robust statistical evidence for the existence of **extra-sensory perception** and **psychokinesis**: in other words, for connections between events that did not depend on any known form of psychic or physical causation and even seemed to transgress the barriers of time and space.

The religious influences on Jung's theory of synchronicity are less explicit – interestingly so. In his efforts to highlight the scientific evidence for his theory, Jung introduces the religious influences on it covertly in scientific, philosophical or historical disguise. For example, one major influence is the Chinese divinatory system of the I Ching. This is deeply embedded in Chinese religious thought but Jung emphasizes its 'experimental foundation', its 'experiment-

Figure 5.10 A contemporary I Ching diviner, dividing a bundle of stalks as part of the procedure for accessing the oracular texts (here in Chinese). Fortean Picture Library.

with-the-whole' (Jung, 1991c, par. 865); in an earlier discussion he had referred to the I Ching as the standard textbook of Chinese science.

Again, instead of referring to the traditional religious concern with the existence of the soul after death, Jung refers to out-of-body and near-death experiences as studied empirically by psychical researchers (Jung, 1991c, pars. 949–55). Where he might have discussed religious notions of providence, he refers to philosophical notions of pre-established harmony (Jung, 1991c, pars. 937–39). And he mentions Christian religious thought as having influenced him not in terms of its doctrines and theology but primarily through providing historical instances of synchronicity encountered in the course of his research into symbols (Jung, 1963b, p.210).

This foregrounding of the scientific credibility of his theory and downplaying its, nevertheless easily detectable, religious influences illustrate Jung's awareness that the route to intellectual respectability lay through science. Nevertheless, it is interesting that, in covertly introducing the religious influences, Jung sometimes implicitly demonstrated the extent to which he felt the religious and scientific categories could interact – and no longer simply on the basis of their shared grounding in the psyche. For example, he implies that the concept of science should be broad enough to accommodate the kinds of 'experimental' observation involved in divination, and that the concerns of religion, such as the survival of the soul, should not be kept insulated from the investigative procedures and insights of the sciences. Further, if we recall Jung's complaint that 'In science I missed the factor of meaning; and in religion, that of empiricism' (Jung, 1963b, p.79), we can sense the measure of integration he has achieved for himself with his theory of synchronicity. For in this theory Jung has championed precisely the factor of meaning; and he has done so on as solid a base of empiricism as he could manage.

Synchronicity and the New Age

The notion of synchronicity directly figures in the New Age in a number of ways. For instance, some neo-Pagans explain the alleged efficacy of their magical practices in terms of synchronicity rather than, as formerly, in terms of 'correspondences' between the spiritual and material worlds ('as above, so below') (York, 1995, p.120). Synchronicity also features as part of the general New Age concern with the paranormal and psychic ('psi') experiences. Of the over 900 respondents to Stuart Rose's survey of subscribers to the New Age magazine *Kindred Spirit*, 40 per cent reported having experienced synchronicity (Rose, 1997). Again, New Agers for whom external religious forms have lost their authority, and who therefore look to their inner self for guidance, sometimes also appeal to chance outer events as signs or omens. These chance events may be deliberately generated by means of a method of divination such as the I Ching or they may occur purely spontaneously. In either case, they are treated as synchronistic events: chance but meaningful. This use of synchronicity as a form of spiritual guidance is epitomized in James Redfield's *The Celestine Prophecy* (1994). This popular New Age adventure story involves the sequential discovery by its protagonist of a series of nine key insights, the first of which is that 'coincidences are real, synchronistic events, and once you become sensitive to them they will lead to your individual spiritual truth' (Beaumont, 1994/5, p.18). Synchronicity therefore accords with New Age sensibilities in being a form of direct personal experience and in looking towards the inner individual rather than towards external institutionalized authorities.

There are also many less direct parallels between synchronicity and the New Age. For instance, we have seen that synchronicity can promote psycho-spiritual transformation in its Jungian form of individuation. Again, not only does synchronicity engage with non-western, pre-modern and esoteric traditions, but it derives directly from them and, by Jung's own account, is largely a translation of them into modern idiom. Further, as Jung's example of the scarab beetle indicated, the content of synchronistic events is often mythic. This is not surprising if we bear in mind that, for Jung, synchronistic events are based on the activation of archetypes and myths are the narrative elaboration of archetypal motifs.

Most significantly, however, synchronicity shares with the New Age a profoundly ambivalent attitude towards science. Like the New Age, the theory of synchronicity represents both a reaction against the reductive tendencies of modern science and a selective appropriation of ideas from modern science. Synchronicity expresses the same valuation of holism as does the New Age and similarly aspires towards an integration of the material and spiritual realms. Indeed, the theory of synchronicity attempts what may also be a deeper aspiration of the New Age: to bring about a major revision of our understanding of both religion and science as well as of their relationship.

The influence of synchronicity on science and religion

In a 1955 letter to R.F.C. Hull, his English translator, Jung reported: 'The latest comment about "Synchronicity" is that it cannot be accepted because it shakes the security of our scientific foundations, as if this were not exactly the goal I am aiming at' (Jung, 1976, p.217). Specifically, Jung thought that his work on synchronicity demonstrated the need to expand the current conception of science in order to include, in addition to the classical concepts of time, space and causality, a principle of acausal connection through meaning. This, he concluded, would introduce the psychic factor of meaning into our scientific picture of the world, help get rid of 'the incommensurability between the observed and the observer', and make possible a 'whole judgement' (Jung, 1991c, par. 961) – that is, a judgement that takes into consideration psychological as well as physical factors. Because for Jung the psychological mediates between the physical and the spiritual, to link the physical and psychological in this way entails setting up a potential bridge between the physical and the spiritual, hence between science and religion. These bold conclusions and implications from Jung's work on synchronicity resonate with many subsequent attempts to develop more holistic models of science.

Jung applied his theory of synchronicity to religious phenomena less systematically. He invokes it on several occasions when discussing the possibility of life after death, arguing that the apparent ability of synchronistic experiences to connect present and future events suggests the possibility of a kind of 'existence outside time', which may therefore also be 'outside change' and possess a kind of eternity (Jung, 1976, p.561). He also invokes synchronicity both as a descriptive equivalent of religious miracles and as a theory for trying to understand them. However, it remained for later writers, notably Robert Aziz (1990), to draw out the most important implication of the theory of synchronicity for Jung's understanding of religion. Jung's psychology of religion was often criticized by theologians for being a form of psychological reductionism. Jung may have been well-disposed towards religion, and he may have provided a strategy for taking religious phenomena seriously in the face of the reductive claims of materialistic science, but because his model denied that anything non-psychic could be directly experienced, it seemed to many that he was in effect reducing religion to psychology. God as an objective external reality seemed to have been replaced by the image of God in a person's mind (Aziz, 1990, pp.46–9). In defence of Jung,

Aziz directs attention to synchronistic events. Such events indicate that meanings experienced psychically can also, without causal connection, be experienced outwardly. In the example given earlier, the appearance and behaviour of the real scarab beetle demonstrated that the meaning expressing itself in the patient's dream of a scarab was not only internal and subjective but could also involve the external, natural world. Neither, then, is there any reason to suppose that the meaning expressed in a person's image of God is only internal and subjective. That meaning too could express itself outwardly, without having been caused by an individual psyche (Aziz, 1990, pp.179–80).

In all of the above instances of the influence of synchronicity on Jung's understanding of religion and science, the underlying motive of promoting dialogue and integration is easily discernible. In uniting or bringing into closer relationship the inner psychic and outer material realms, Jung is establishing the basis for a corresponding rapprochement of at least some parts of the discourses of religion and science. However, in doing this, he is also advocating some major revisions to his own earlier understanding of both religion and science.

Conclusion

In this chapter, we have tried to elucidate the probable influence of interactions between religion and science on New Age spirituality. We spent some time considering various complicating factors in such a study: the selective nature of any historical narrative, the need to consider historical contexts in detail, the shifting boundaries and meanings of the terms 'religion' and 'science', and the variety of kinds of possible interaction. This complexity should make us cautious about generalizing too broadly from the particular insights we have gained. Nevertheless, we were able to trace a number of ways in which interactions between religion and science very likely did influence the emergence and nature of New Age spirituality. We then tried to amplify these insights with a case study. We noted that Jung's psychological theories demonstrably both directly influenced and are closely parallel to many aspects of New Age thought. We further noted that interactions between religion and science demonstrably influenced Jung's psychological theories. From this, we inferred that interactions between religion and science are likely to have influenced many aspects of New Age thought. Among Jung's theories, we devoted most time to synchronicity. This theory both is the culmination of Jung's lifelong struggle with the tensions between religion and science and has attracted particular interest among some New Agers. Moreover, for Jung, not only did religion and science influence the theory of synchronicity but also the theory of synchronicity, once formulated, had a reciprocal influence on his understanding of religion and science, calling for their revision. This ability of a theory to turn back on its origins and transform them only adds to the picture of complexity with which this chapter began. This may be no bad thing. As Brooke observes: 'Serious scholarship in the history of science has revealed so extraordinarily rich and complex a relationship between science and religion in the past that general theses are difficult to sustain. The real lesson turns out to be the complexity' (Brooke, 1991, p.5).

References

Aziz, R. (1990) *C.G. Jung's Psychology of Religion and Synchronicity*, Albany: State University of New York Press.

Barbour, I. (1998) *Religion and Science: Historical and Contemporary Issues*, London: SCM Press.

Beaumont, R. (1994/5) 'What value a vision?', interview with James Redfield, *Kindred Spirit*, vol.3, no.5, pp.16–20.

Berger, P., Berger, B. and Kellner, H. (1974) *The Homeless Mind*, Harmondsworth: Penguin.

Bloom, W. (ed.) (1991) *The New Age: An Anthology of Essential Writings*, London: Rider.

Bohm, D. (1980) *Wholeness and the Implicate Order*, London: Routledge & Kegan Paul.

Brooke, J. H. (1991) *Science and Religion: Some Historical Perspectives*, Cambridge: Cambridge University Press.

Brooke, J. H. and Cantor, G. (1998) *Reconstructing Nature: The Engagement of Science and Religion*, Edinburgh: T & T Clark.

Capra, F. (1977) *The Tao of Physics*, London: Fontana.

Compton's (1998) *The Complete Reference Collection*, on CD-ROM, Bath: Future Publishing.

Crowley, V. (1989) *Wicca: The Old Religion in the New Age*, Wellingborough: Aquarian Press.

Dawkins, R. (1987) *The Blind Watchmaker: Why the Evidence of Evolution Reveals a Universe without Design*, New York: W.W. Norton.

Draper, J.W. (1875) *History of the Conflict between Religion and Science*, London: Henry S. King.

Ferguson, M. (1982) *The Aquarian Conspiracy: Personal and Social Transformation in the 1980s*, London: Granada.

Hanegraaff, W. (1996) *New Age Religion and Western Culture: Esotericism in the Mirror of Secular Thought*, Lieden: Brill.

Hayman, R. (1999) *A Life of Jung*, London: Bloomsbury.

Heelas, P. (1996) *The New Age Movement: The Celebration of the Self and the Sacralization of Modernity*, Oxford: Blackwell.

Hinnells, J. (ed.) (1997) *The Penguin Dictionary of Religions*, London: Penguin.

Jung, C.G. (1983) *The Zofingia Lectures: The Collected Works of C.G. Jung* [hereafter *CW*], 21 vols., ed. Sir Herbert Read, Michael Fordham and Gerhard Adler, executive editor William McGuire, trans. R.F.C. Hull, Princeton, NJ: Princeton University Press (first published 1896–9).

Jung, C.G. (1963a) *Mysterium Coniunctionis: An Inquiry into the Separation and Synthesis of Psychic Opposites in Alchemy*, *CW* 14, London: Routledge & Kegan Paul (first published 1954–5).

Jung, C.G. (1963b) *Memories, Dreams, Reflections*, recorded and edited by Aniela Jaffé, trans. Richard and Clara Winston, London: Collins and Routledge & Kegan Paul.

Jung, C.G. (1973) *Letters 1: 1906–50*, selected and edited by Gerhard Adler in collaboration with Aniela Jaffé, trans. R.F.C. Hull, London: Routledge & Kegan Paul.

Jung, C.G. (1976) *Letters 2: 1951–61*, selected and edited by Gerhard Adler in collaboration with Aniela Jaffé, trans. R.F.C. Hull, London: Routledge & Kegan Paul.

Jung, C.G. (1981a) 'The undiscovered self (present and future)', *CW* 10, London: Routledge & Kegan Paul (first published 1957), pp.245–305.

Jung, C.G. (1981b) 'Flying saucers: a modern myth of things seen in the skies', *CW* 10, London: Routledge & Kegan Paul (first published 1958), pp.307–433.

Jung, C.G. (1981c) 'A psychological view of conscience', *CW* 10, London: Routledge & Kegan Paul (first published 1958), pp.437–55.

Jung, C.G. (1986a) 'Yoga and the West', *CW* 11, London: Routledge & Kegan Paul (first published 1936), pp.529–37.

Jung, C.G. (1986b) 'Psychology and religion', *CW* 11, London: Routledge & Kegan Paul (first published 1938/40), pp.3–105.

Jung, C.G. (1986c) 'A psychological approach to the dogma of the Trinity', *CW* 11, London: Routledge & Kegan Paul (first published 1942/8), pp.107–200.

Jung, C.G. (1989) *Psychology and Alchemy*, *CW* 12, London: Routledge (first published 1944).

Jung, C.G. (1990) 'The relations between the ego and the unconscious', *CW* 7, London: Routledge (first published 1928), pp.121–241.

Jung, C.G. (1991a) *Psychological Types*, *CW* 6, London: Routledge (first published 1921).

Jung, C.G. (1991b) 'On synchronicity', *CW* 8, London: Routledge (first published 1951), pp.520–31.

Jung, C.G. (1991c) 'Synchronicity: an acausal connecting principle', *CW* 8, London: Routledge (first published 1952), pp.417–519.

Jung, C.G. (1993) 'The symbolic life', *CW* 18, London: Routledge (first published 1939), pp.265–90.

Jung, C.G. (1995) *Symbols of Transformation*, *CW* 5, London: Routledge (first published 1911–12).

Jung, C.G. and Pauli, W. (1955) *The Interpretation of Nature and the Psyche*, London: Routledge & Kegan Paul.

Macdonald, A. (ed.) (1978) *Chambers Twentieth Century Dictionary, with Supplement*, Edinburgh: Chambers.

McLynn, F. (1996) *Carl Gustav Jung*, New York: Bantam Press.

Main, R. (ed.) (1997) *Jung on Synchronicity and the Paranormal*, London: Routledge/Princeton, NJ: Princeton University Press.

Mumm, S. (2002) 'What it meant and what it means: feminism, religion and interpretation', in D. Herbert (ed.) *Religion and Social Transformations*, Aldershot: Ashgate/Milton Keynes: The Open University, pp.115–53 (Book 2 in the *Religion Today* series).

Redfield, J. (1994) *The Celestine Prophecy*, London: Bantam.

Rogers, C. (1967) *On Becoming a Person: A Therapist's View of Psychotherapy*, London: Constable.

Rose, S. (1997) 'Transforming the world: an examination of the roles played by spirituality and healing in the New Age Movement', unpublished PhD thesis, Lancaster University.

Segal, R. (1999) 'Rationalist and Romantic approaches to religion and modernity', *Journal of Analytical Psychology*, vol.44, pp.547–60.

Sheldrake, R. (1981) *A New Science of Life: The Hypothesis of Formative Causation*, London: Blond & Briggs.

Smart, R.N. (1997) *Dimensions of the Sacred*, London: Fontana.

Spangler, D. (1988) 'Defining the New Age', in *The New Age Catalogue*, New York: Doubleday.

Starhawk [Miriam Simos] (1979) *The Spiral Dance: A Rebirth of the Ancient Religion of the Great Goddess*, New York: HarperCollins.

Tacey, D. (1999) 'Why Jung would doubt the New Age', in S. Greenberg (ed.) *Therapy on the Couch: A Shrinking Future*, London: Camden Press, pp.36–42.

Teilhard de Chardin, P. (1959) *The Phenomenon of Man*, New York: Harper & Row.

Wehr, D. (1987) *Jung and Feminism: Liberating Archetypes*, Boston: Beacon.

White, A.D. (1896) *A History of the Warfare of Science with Theology in Christendom*, New York: D. Appleton.

Wilber, K. (1998) *The Marriage of Sense and Soul: Integrating Science and Religion*, New York: Random House.

Wuthnow, R. (1985) 'The cultural context of contemporary religious movements', in T. Robbins, W.C. Shepherd, and J. McBride (eds) *Cults, Culture, and the Law: Perspectives on New Religious Movements*, Chico, CA: Scholars Press.

York, M. (1995) *The Emerging Network: A Sociology of the New Age and Neo-pagan Movements*, Lanham, MD: Rowman & Littlefield.

Young-Eisendrath, P. (1997) 'Gender and contrasexuality: Jung's contribution and beyond,' in P. Young-Eisendrath and T. Dawson (eds) *The Cambridge Companion to Jung*, Cambridge: Cambridge University Press, pp.223–39.

Glossary

(Several works have contributed to the definitions below, including the following: Barbour, 1998; Compton's, 1998; Hinnells, 1997; Macdonald, 1978.)

alchemy an early form of chemistry, with spiritual and magical associations, principally studied in the Middle Ages. It aimed at the transformation of base metals into gold and the discovery of the elixir of perpetual youth.

Anthropic Principle the assertion that the physical constants of the early universe were delicately balanced such that, if they had had even slightly different values, carbon-based life, including eventually human life, would not have been possible.

Aquinas, Thomas (*c*.1225–74) Italian Dominican theologian, who used the recently rediscovered works of **Aristotle** to produce a systematic presentation of Christian theology which until recently dominated Roman Catholic theological instruction.

archetypal images in Jung's psychology, the images by means of which archetypes express themselves.

archetypes in Jung's psychology, innate structures of the psyche that provide the form of the typical ways in which we imagine, perceive and think about the world.

Aristotle (*c*.384–322 BCE) Greek philosopher, pupil of Plato (*c*.429–347). Though more of a humanistic than a religious thinker, Aristotle's ideas were immensely influential in the late Middle Ages (twelfth century) on Judaism, Christianity and Islam.

Big Bang cosmology a plausible reconstruction of cosmic history, based on a series of theoretical and observational developments in physics and astronomy over the course of the twentieth century, which suggests that the universe is expanding from a common origin about fifteen billion years ago.

collective unconscious in Jung's psychology, a stratum of the mind, inherited rather than personally acquired, which all people possess but of which we are not normally aware.

compensation in Jung's psychology, the self-regulating process of the psyche, whereby any one-sidedness in a person's conscious attitude is balanced by contents emerging from the unconscious. The successful integration of these contents contributes to a state of greater psychic wholeness.

complementarity the relationship between contrasting models and concepts, such as 'wave' and 'particle', used to describe the same entity in quantum theory and by extension in other disciplines.

Copernican adjective drawing from Nicolaus **Copernicus** (1473–1543), Polish astronomer, considered the founder of modern astronomy.

creative visualization a psychotherapeutic and occult technique that involves attending to imaginative mental representations and allowing them to develop autonomously but in dialogue with the conscious mind.

Darwin, Charles (1809–82) English naturalist. His many observations and explanations of the mechanisms of natural selection for the first time provided this theory with a widely accepted basis.

Deist from **Deism,** the belief that God created the world in the beginning but did not afterwards intervene in the course of natural and human affairs. Deists seek to hold only those religious beliefs that they consider to be rationally warranted and tend to eschew formal religions, revelation and belief in miracles.

design argument the argument for the existence of God from evidence of design in creation.

determinism the view that everything, including one's choice of action, is the necessary result of a sequence of causes.

divination the act or practice of seeking to know the future or hidden things by magical means. Divination exists in all societies, sometimes under the auspices of religion (for example, in ancient China, Greece and Tibet), but sometimes outside or in opposition to it (for example, under Christianity).

DNA (deoxyribonucleic acid) discovered in 1953 by James Watson and Francis Crick, DNA is a complex molecule present in the chromosomes of all plant and animal cells. It carries in coded form instructions for passing on hereditary characteristics.

extra-sensory perception (ESP) a term popularized by the American parapsychologist J.B. Rhine in the 1930s that refers to the perception of information by telepathy (mind to mind), clairvoyance (object to mind), or precognition (future to present) without the use of the ordinary senses and reasoning.

Freud, Sigmund (1856–1939) Austrian neurologist and physician who developed psychoanalysis, which is both a theory of unconscious mental processes and a method of investigating them, usually with the aim of treating neuroses and some other disorders of the mind.

Galileo Galilei (1564–1642) Italian mathematician, physicist and astronomer. Many regard him as the founder of the experimental method and hence of modern science.

gender essentialism the view that masculine and feminine personality traits are the natural outcome of male and female biology rather than of socio-cultural conditioning.

genetic code the system by which genes pass on instructions that ensure transmission of hereditary characteristics.

globalization the increasing worldwide link-up of political, economic and cultural systems.

Gnosticism the eclectic doctrines of various individuals and groups, whose philosophy, especially in early Christian times, taught the redemption of the spirit from matter by spiritual knowledge, and believed creation to be a process of emanation from the original essence or Godhead.

holistic from **holism,** the view that an organic or integrated whole has an independent reality which cannot be understood simply through an understanding of its parts.

Hume, David (1711–76) Scottish philosopher. Hume developed a sceptical philosophy that restricted knowledge to actual experience and rejected most theology as an unprovable matter of belief.

I Ching ('Book of Changes') an ancient Chinese book of divination, consisting of 64 symbolic hexagrams taken to indicate wise courses of action.

individuation Jung's notion of psychic development, which involves integrating unconscious contents into consciousness in order to become a more complete and integrated individual and to realize one's self.

Jung, Carl Gustav (1875–1961) Swiss psychiatrist and pioneering psychologist of the unconscious, who for several years collaborated with the Austrian psychoanalyst **Sigmund Freud** (1856–1939) but developed markedly different theories and techniques.

Kant, Immanuel (1724–1804) German philosopher who revolutionized western philosophy by focusing on what the human mind could subjectively know rather than on what reality might be like objectively, independent of the human mind.

Laplace, Pierre (1749–1827) French astronomer and mathematician who made important discoveries about the motions of comets, planets and the moon.

magic ritual activity intended to produce results without using the recognized causal processes of the physical world.

Methodism a section of the Evangelical Revival led by John Wesley (1703–91), who taught justification by faith, Christian perfection, and the importance of personal and social responsibility.

modernization the process of increased structural differentiation in the modern period initiated by changes in technology and values.

natural theology the understanding of God held to be obtainable through rational reflection on the world rather than through revelation.

Newton, Isaac (1642–1727) English mathematician and physicist who discovered laws of motion and universal gravitation, the calculus and the variations of the light spectrum.

numinous a term coined by the German theologian Rudolf Otto (1869–1937) to refer to the inexpressible, mysterious, terrifying and fascinating nature of the divine as immediately experienced. More loosely, it can mean having an emotional and spiritual effect.

Paley, William (1743–1805) English theologian and philosopher.

parapsychology the branch of psychology that investigates such psychic phenomena as **extra-sensory perception** and **psychokinesis**.

perennialist relating to the view that all religions, in spite of their outer differences, express the same inner reality.

personal unconscious in Jung's psychology, the part of a person's mind comprising contents that have their origin in the person's personal life but are currently not available to consciousness.

photons quanta of electromagnetic energy having both particle and wave properties.

Pietism a movement in Lutheran Protestantism that stressed practical and inward religion rather than dogmatic theology.

precession of the spring equinox a slow westward motion of the point of the spring equinox along the apparent path of the sun's annual motion among the fixed stars, caused by the conical motion of the earth's axis. A complete revolution takes about 25,800 years, called the 'Platonic Year'. Consequently, the spring equinox moves clockwise through the twelve zodiacal signs, the precession through each taking an average of about 2,150 years, a 'Platonic Month'.

psychic reality for Jung, the view that mental states and contents have a reality that should be respected on its own terms and not reduced to either material or spiritual processes. Indeed, for Jung, psychic reality is the only reality of which we can be immediately aware, since material and spiritual realities are necessarily mediated to consciousness in the form of psychic images.

psychoanalysis a method, developed by the Austrian psychoanalyst **Sigmund Freud** (1856–1939) and others, of investigating mental processes and of treating neuroses and some other disorders of the mind. It is based on the assumption that such disorders are the result of the rejection by the conscious mind of factors that then persist in the unconscious as repressed instinctual forces, causing conflicts which may be resolved or diminished by discovering and analysing the repressions and bringing them into consciousness through the use of such techniques as dream analysis, free association (where a patient says whatever comes into his or her mind, however trivial, embarrassing or irrelevant it seems), and so on.

psychokinesis (PK) the apparent ability to influence physical objects and events by thought processes alone.

Ptolemy (85–160) Alexandrian astronomer, mathematician and geographer, whose geocentric (earth-centred) cosmological model, combined with ideas from **Aristotle**, provided the basis for the early and medieval Christian picture of the universe.

quantum mechanics in physics, the theory that energy consists of emissions of discrete particles, or quanta, and that this explains the behaviour of particles on the atomic and subatomic levels. It is an essential theory of modern physics.

quarks in modern physics, types of hypothetical subatomic particles, plus their antiparticles.

reductionism the view that complex data can be explained in terms of something simpler.

relativity a theory in physics advanced by Albert Einstein (1879–1955), which holds that all motion is relative and that space and time are not separate and absolute entities.

Romanticism a movement in art, literature, philosophy, science, and so on, that was prevalent in Europe in the late eighteenth and early nineteenth centuries and in subsequent revivals. Romanticism opposed the rational, intellectual approach of neo-classicism in favour of the emotional, mystical and sublime.

sacralization making sacred or holy.

secularization the process whereby, especially in modern industrial societies, religious beliefs, practices and institutions lose social significance.

secular humanism an outlook that puts human interests and the human mind paramount, rejecting the supernatural.

self for Jung, the self is the symbol of psychic totality, the central archetype of the collective unconscious, and the goal of individuation. While the ego forms the centre of consciousness, the self forms the centre of the psyche as a whole, consciousness and the unconscious together.

symbolic for Jung, a symbol is the best possible formulation of something that is part known, part unknown. Unlike conventional signs, symbols cannot be exhaustively translated into other terms.

synchronicity a term coined by Jung to refer to his theory of meaningful coincidence, according to which psychic and physical events that do not stand in any discernible causal relationship may nevertheless be connected through sharing the same meaning.

Taoism a Chinese tradition, with both philosophical and religious strands, largely based on the writings attributed to Lao Tzu (traditionally sixth to fifth centuries BCE) and Chuang Tzu (traditionally late fourth century BCE).

teleological adjective derived from teleology, the view that natural phenomena are determined not only by mechanical causes but by an overall design or purpose in nature.

vitalistic from **vitalism**, the view that the life in living organisms is caused and sustained by a vital force that is distinct from all physical and chemical forces and that life is, in part, self-determining and self-evolving.

Wallace, Alfred Russel (1823–1913) English naturalist, whose studies contributing to the theory of natural selection paralleled, but were independent of, those of **Darwin**.

word association tests psychological tests in which the person being tested responds to a stimulus word with the first word that comes to mind.

Yoga a Hindu discipline by which one seeks to achieve liberation of the self and union with the supreme spirit through intense concentration, deep meditation and practices involving prescribed postures, controlled breathing, and so on.

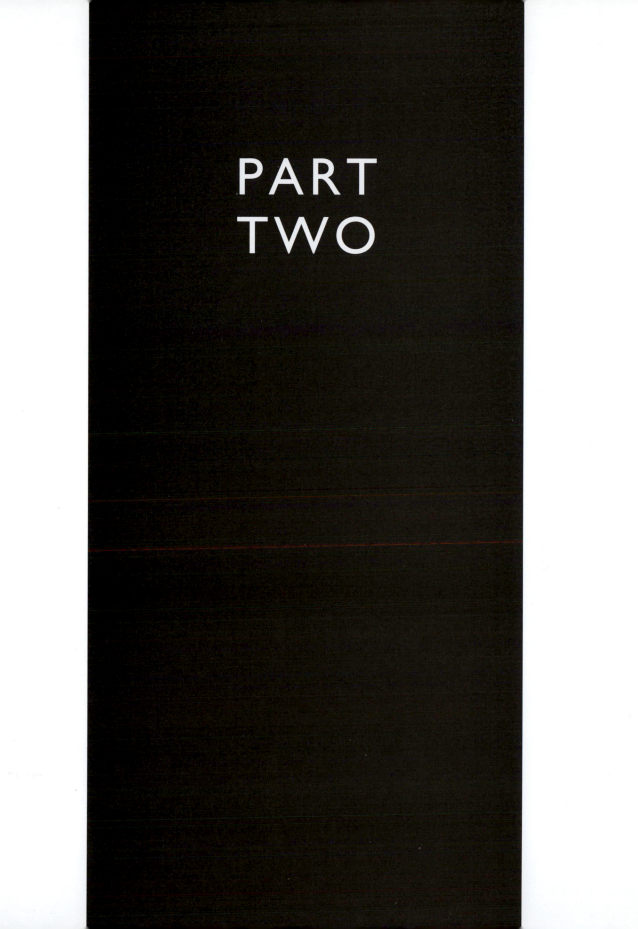

PART
TWO

The roots of modern Paganism*†

RONALD HUTTON

To speak of 'Modern Paganism' is of course to invite debate in itself, for the expression covers a multitude of faiths and practices, with only a limited (though important) amount in common. To an historian, the divisions and distinctions are of considerable moment, only some of the traditions having a long enough continuous existence in Britain to warrant investigation. Those which concentrate upon Scandinavian or Germanic deities, for example, use ancient images and ways of working but are clearly a recent revival of them based upon surviving texts. Likewise, groups working under the umbrella term of Shamanism are self-consciously a creation of the past two decades, drawing upon tribal models, often from native America, fused with ancient European imagery. Druidry, by contrast, has a well-documented history which is continuous from the late-eighteenth century. There was, however, nothing specifically pagan about any of it until the 1980s, when some overtly pagan orders were founded. Nineteenth and early-twentieth century Druidry was perfectly compatible with Christianity and indeed overlapped considerably with it, focusing upon a single creator god, identified with the sun and working through wise men.

All this puts Wicca, or Modern Pagan Witchcraft, very much in a category of its own, being from the start of its public existence (over forty years ago) both an unequivocally pagan religion and one which claimed very long roots. Where the latter actually run is now the subject of considerable debate. Until the 1970s, the matter was not seriously problematic, as the Wiccan claim fitted into an academic semi-orthodoxy; that the people persecuted as witches in Europe's Great Witch Hunt were members of a surviving pagan religion. Wicca

---

* This chapter first appeared in *Paganism Today*, edited by Charlotte Hardman and Graham Harvey, London: Thorsons, 1995, pp.3–15.

† As this essay is an interim report upon research in progress, many of the references are given in general terms, to illustrate the fields being covered, and will be provided in detail when the project is completed.

could quite plausibly be stated to be that religion, having survived in secret into the twentieth century. In the 1970s, however, this idea about the Witch Hunt collapsed inside academe, helping to instigate a search for the genuine origins of Wicca.

Much of that search has to date concentrated upon the lineages of particular Wiccan groups or traditions, and has tried to trace them back, initiation by initiation. The results so far have been interesting, but not at all conclusive, for all the documents or reliable memories seem to run out in the years around 1940, leaving a welter of modern claims about old, family-based or coven-based practices.[1] Historians are in no position to deny these but neither, in default of evidence, can they accept them. I prefer, instead of working backwards, to research forwards; to try to reconstruct the context of nineteenth- and twentieth-century culture out of which Modern Paganism either arose or resurfaced. What follows is an interim report upon that work, which is still very much in progress. In the course of my study of ancient paganism in Britain, I identified four direct lines of connection between that complex of beliefs and the present: high ritual magic, 'hedge' witchcraft, the general love affair of the Christian centuries with the art and literature of the ancient world, and folk rites. It is time to look again at all four, bearing in mind the new question of the origins of Modern Paganism.

High ritual magic consists of the summoning and control of supernatural forces by the use of invocations and sacred equipment. Some of the latter is solid, such as consecrated knives, wands, swords or flails, and some of it spatial, such as the sacred geometry of circles, quarters, cardinal points, pentagrams and triangles. This sort of magic can first be certainly identified in Hellenistic Egypt, from which it was taken and developed in Arab Spain, often by Jewish practitioners, and passed on to the late-medieval Christian world, where it was developed further in the early modern period. The main alteration thereafter was that whereas until the seventeenth century it was largely the preserve of the solitary practitioner, the 'magus', after then it was increasingly associated with magical societies, such as the Rosicrucians, the Freemasons, the New Knights Templar, the Order of the Golden Dawn, the Fraternity of the Inner Light, and the Ordo Templi Orientis.

Until the mid-nineteenth century, ceremonial magicians worked with the names of spirits or demons, often in Hebrew. After that, ancient pagan deities, especially those of Egypt or Mesopotamia,

---

[1] Compare, for example, Aidan Kelly, *Crafting the Art of Magic* (1991); Doreen Valiente, *The Rebirth of Witchcraft* (1989), and W.E. Liddell and Michael Howard, *The Pickingill Papers* (1994).

were increasingly added to invocations. In part this was simply a return to the source of the tradition which had, after all, actually come from Egypt, and could be refreshed by the study of Hellenistic texts by Victorian magicians. It was also, however, the result of archaeology, as the scholars of the century translated hieroglyphic and cuneiform script and increasing quantities of paintings, inscriptions, statues and papyri were recovered by excavation. The result is that by the early-twentieth century, it is very hard to distinguish some magical groups from pagan witchcraft; the only key difference that is immediately apparent is the lack of the name 'witch'.[2] It could, however, also be argued that the pagan element in ritual magic had remained incidental. The careers of the two best-known, best-documented and ostensibly most pagan practitioners, may illustrate this. One is Dion Fortune, whose magic became more or less Christian according to the phases of her life and seems to have ended up as a hybrid of religions.[3] The other is Aleister Crowley, who amalgamated pagan deities, Hebrew demons and redeveloped Christian ritual to produce a personal set of rites and beliefs linked by what may be termed therapeutic blasphemy.[4] In these cases, as in all documented ceremonial magic of this period, the central impulse was not essentially religious; it was not to worship or honour supernatural beings so much as to gain personal power from them.

What needs to be emphasised now is how deeply ritual magical practices had penetrated ordinary British society in the nineteenth century. Freemasonry (though now generally lacking a genuine occult content) was found even in small country towns, and had quite a high public profile; at Melrose in the Scottish Lowlands, for example, the local lodge paraded through the streets carrying torches every Midsummer's Eve. All its branches preserved rituals of initiation and celebration which had a quasi-magical character, and Masons

---

[2] For overviews, see Francis X. King, *Ritual Magic in England* (1970); Kenneth Grant, *The Magical Revival* (1972); James Webb, *The Occult Establishment* (1982), and *The Occult Underground* (1988); Francis X. King and Isabel Sutherland, *The Rebirth of Magic* (1982). For rituals, see Israel Regardie, *The Golden Dawn* (4 vols., 1937–40), and *The Secret Rituals of the O.T.O.,* ed. Francis King (1973).

[3] The best guide to Fortune's thought is in her own writings, the best known probably being *The Sea Priestess* and *Moon Magic*. The biography is by Alan Richardson, *Priestess* (1987).

[4] Again, his many publications are the best guide to his thought. A good starting-point could be *Magick* or *Magick Without Tears*. For commentaries of varying quality, see John Symonds, *The Great Beast* (1954) and *The Magic of Aleister Crowley* (1958); C.R. Cammell, *Aleister Crowley* (1969); Kenneth Grant, *Aleister Crowley and the Hidden God* (1973); Francis X. King, *The Magical World of Aleister Crowley* (1977).

referred to their traditions collectively as 'the Craft'. Then there were Friendly Societies or Benefit Clubs, rudimentary insurance societies to provide members with sick pay, unemployment benefits and a decent funeral. These sprang up in both town and country in the early-nineteenth century, flourished until its end, and incorporated ceremonies loosely modelled upon those of Freemasons. They could be very dramatic; one initiation rite of the Oddfellows, for example, involved leading the newcomer blindfolded into a circle of members and tearing off the blindfold to reveal that a sword was pointed at his chest. He then had to take the oath of secrecy and fidelity to the society. It is worth bearing in mind through all this that what he was actually supposed to be doing was buying an insurance policy! Membership of these groups was often linked to a particular trade or 'craft', and meanwhile the old-style trade guilds or 'crafts' still survived in many towns. Some adopted the trappings of the quasi-ceremonial societies; in Shrewsbury in 1840, a trade guild bought up a job-lot of Masonic regalia for its meetings in order to add dignity and excitement to them.[5]

Such groups continued to proliferate into the early twentieth century. Some were drinking clubs in which the rites were largely humorous, such as the Royal Antediluvian Order of Buffaloes.[6] Others were much more serious. One of the most important was the Order of Woodcraft Chivalry, a socialist and pacifist alternative to the Boy Scouts and Girl Guides, inspired largely by the writings of the American, Ernest Thompson Seton. It met in woodlands, especially the New Forest, and conducted ceremonies within a sacred circle, consecrated by people standing at the quarters in the order east then south then west then north. Its leaders were called the Witan, Anglo-Saxon for 'wise'; and so its practices were 'the craft of the wise'. In 1938, the Order went into schism, and split into a number of different groups, meeting at different places in the New Forest in subsequent

---

[5] Among what is, again, a very large literature, basic reading could be William Preston, *Illustrations of Free Masonry* (1788); George Oliver, *Signs and Symbols of Freemasonry* (1856); A.E. Mason, *The Accepted Ceremonies of Craft Freemasonry* (1874); P.H.J.H. Gosden, *The Friendly Societies in England 1815–1875* (1961), and *Self-Help: Voluntary Associations in Nineteenth-century Britain* (1973); Margaret Fuller, *West Country Friendly Societies* (1964); Mark C. Carnes, *Secret Ritual and Manhood in Victorian America* (1989); and H. Polling, A *History of British Trade Unionism* (1956) (the Shrewsbury reference is on p40). The 'folkloric' rituals are in *British Calendar Customs: Scotland* (Folk-Lore Society, 1937–41).

[6] Into which Robert Graves was initiated in 1914: Graves, *Goodbye to All That* (1929), pp105–6.

years and developing their own rituals of which more later.[7] It seems to be clear, therefore, that Victorian and Edwardian society was filled with groups which practised secret rites and demanded initiation, most of them linked to the word 'craft'. The terms 'Hereditary Craft' or 'Traditional Craft' consequently represent such a wide category as to be almost meaningless to an historian.

The second important link between old and modern Paganism is what can conveniently be called 'hedge witchcraft', the popular magic of the local wise woman and cunning man. It is clear that these people were not merely respected because they had a knowledge of herbs, cures and spells, for virtually everybody in traditional British society knew some of these. They were regarded, rather, as possessing some personal magical powers in addition. A huge amount of information upon these people was gathered in the late-nineteenth century by middle- and upper-class folklorists, to whom they represented the very essence of a romantic, rural world which the collectors were trying to rediscover. The data is so rich that a large book could probably be written upon that from Somerset and Essex alone.

Two things are plain from even a cursory investigation of it. The first is that these local practitioners formed part of a spectrum with 'high' ritual magic, rather than representing a self-contained world. Most cunning men were known to have owned books, and when these are itemized in the occasional court case, they turn out to be manuals, or grimoires, of old-fashioned ceremonial magic. The second rapid discovery is that these individuals were not very important in the development of modern Paganism. For one thing, they were almost always solitary workers; they are increasingly significant as role models now that the individual practice of witchcraft is coming into ever greater vogue, but they have little relation to the essentially communal character of mid-twentieth century paganism. For another thing, there is no evidence that they worshipped pagan deities. The closest approach that I have found to such worship is in the tale of a Herefordshire witch who, when asked to swear by God, carefully swore only by 'her' god. Unfortunately for its use as an example, the story makes plain that the god concerned is the Devil, whom the woman is thus forced to acknowledge as her

---

[7] The Order's history can be traced through its periodical, *Pine Cone*. I am grateful to Messrs Glynn Faithfull and Bran Labworth for clarifying additional points.

master, and the whole anecdote is a cautionary one, rather than an account of an actual incident reported by a witness.[8]

Nevertheless, the low-level folk magic is significant for our purposes because of its overlap with occult societies. The most widespread and remarkable of the latter was the Horse Whisperers, also known as Toadmen or the Horseman's Word. They practised folk magic concerned with the management of horses, but were organised in a society and had an initiation ceremony. In north-east Scotland, at least, this was rumoured to involve the confrontation of the novice by a personification of the Devil. The all-important 'word' itself turns out to be a Latin term of conjuration familiar in traditional grimoires.[9] Such meetings could look, to outsiders at the time and later, very like witches' covens.

The third strand of connection, the love affair with the pagan ancient world, has remained strong throughout the Christian centuries. The latest study of early medieval monastic literature, by Ludo Millis, concludes that the monks were so overawed by the Greek and Roman classics that this stifled their creativity.[10] When the most original twelfth-century scholar, Pierre Abelard, dedicated himself to a life of learning (by definition, within the Church), he described himself as 'kneeling at the feet of Minerva'. This addiction to classical imagery and quotation was, of course, massively reinforced by the Renaissance. In nineteenth-century England there were three distinct attitudes (in this case the fashionable term 'discourse' is absolutely appropriate) to the pagan past. The first characterised pagans as enemies of Christianity and civilisation, who bowed down to idols, made blood sacrifices, tortured saints to death or threw them to lions, and enjoyed sexual orgies. Such a discourse could be readily absorbed from the most widely read of all books, the Bible, and hitched to one of progress by equating paganism with barbarism. It was widely employed to describe and condemn the

---

[8] There are hundreds of such studies, compiled between 1800 and 1980 and usually arranged by county when in book form, or else published in *The Folk-Lore Journal* and then in *Folk-Lore*. The best way of conducting a detailed local study seems to be to begin with these and then to work systematically through newspapers and Quarter Sessions records, using parish registers and Poor Law entries to trace especially interesting individuals. The anecdote is from Ella Mary Leather, *The Folk-Lore of Herefordshire* (1912).

[9] Compare, for example, George Ewart Evans, *The Horse in the Furrow* (1960), pp239–71; Ronald Blythe, *Akenfield* (1969), p54; J.M. McPherson, *Primitive Beliefs in the North-East of Scotland* (1929), pp290–1; Ian Carter, *Farmlife in Northeast Scotland 1890–1914* (1979), pp154–6. There is a large correspondence on the subject in national and local newspapers.

[10] Ludo J. Millis, *Angelic Monks and Earthly Men* (1993), pp92–100.

religions of tribal peoples and of old Asiatic cultures with which Europeans were colliding in the expansion of trade and Empire.[11] It also represented the view of ancient civilisation taken by the popular novels of Bulwer Lytton and Marie Corelli, and later became the dominant one in Hollywood historical epic.

It co-existed, however, with a tremendous admiration for the achievements of ancient Greece and Rome, and a tendency to identify with them, inculcated further in the educated by the predominance of Greek and Latin classics in the school and university curricula. The quintessential Victorian muscular Christian, Charles Kingsley, could tell his juvenile readers approvingly that they would find the Greeks all round them in the language of 'well-written books', the buildings of 'great towns' and the decorations of 'well-furnished rooms'. On that most characteristic monument of the age, the Albert Memorial, Homer sits enthroned, with Shakespeare at his feet. The Tory, William Huskisson, could be said to have been the first politician to die in a truly modern way, run down by a railway train in 1830; yet his memorial statue in Pimlico portrayed him wearing a Roman toga. As the British were Protestants, and traditionally allergic to religious statuary, there were far more pagan deities than Christian saints decorating their parks and public buildings.

If the Greeks stood for thought and exploration, the Romans represented imperial destiny. Both were patterns not only of beauty and wisdom, but of moral force; as Richard Jenkyns has put it, 'if something was Hellenic, then it was almost bound to be pure'. In this second discourse, the ancient world was only deficient in its religion, not because the latter was barbarous, but because it was immature, better fitted for entertainment and secular edification than as a vehicle of divine revelation. This discourse also drew upon the Bible, but not on the Old Testament (upon which the first had relied) so much as upon the New; in this the Jews could be discerned to be the villains, while the pagan Roman Pontius Pilate featured as a bemused and well-meaning gentleman.[12]

There was, however, a third set of attitudes, which glorified ancient paganism itself. To John Keats, the latter was a culture of innocent joy and close identification with the beauties of nature. In the second half of the century, the intimate association with the natural world was retained, but the joy was no longer so innocent; to poets such as Rossetti, Swinburne and Wilde, paganism had been a carefree

---

[11] There is a rich harvest of such works easily found by following up the footnotes to J.G. Frazer, *The Golden Bough* (1890).

[12] For an assortment of images like these, see Richard Jenkyns, *The Victorians and the Greeks* (1981), and *Dignity and Decadence* (1991).

celebration of sexuality as part of its uninhibited 'naturalness'. This discourse was fast developing into a counter-cultural attack upon Christianity and conventional morality. Muted but persistent echoes of it are found in the novels of Thomas Hardy, in which the word 'pagan' is used repeatedly for many different purposes and in different contexts, but always with the same shiver of the alluring, the abandoned, and the amoral.

Underlying the last two discourses, moreover, was a tremendous qualitative change in nineteenth-century English attitudes. Its source may be expressed in a simple statistic: in 1810, twenty per cent of the English had lived in towns while, by 1910, the proportion had risen to eighty per cent. England had become the first urbanised and industrialised nation, the balance between town and country tipping (neatly) in the 1850s. After then it seemed a real possibility that the whole land would turn into one vast, smoking conurbation. From the 1870s, therefore, an almost hysterical celebration of rural England began, gaining strength into the early-twentieth century; a phenomenon well studied recently by Alice Chandler, Alun Howkins and Jan Marsh.[13]

What concerns us most here is the way in which (like all Victorian civilisation) it drew upon ancient images. One of the most important was the figure of the Greek god of nature, Pan. It must be emphasised that Pan was actually a minor Greek deity; Ken Dowden, author of the best recent introduction to Greek mythology, has termed him 'the Citroen 2CV of Greek gods'.[14] To the classical ancient world, as to the succeeding centuries until the nineteenth, the favourite deities had been those of civilisation. Now, however, the wild, horned and goat-footed god came into his own, featuring as the patron of Kenneth Grahame's *The Wind in the Willows*, being hailed by Oscar Wilde, and appearing in the works of a host of lesser writers. Others preferred to adopt another ancient Greek image, that of Gaia, the presiding female spirit of the globe itself, so that references to Mother Earth and Mother Nature began to multiply, reverently, in the literature of the age. By 1900, the poetic vision of the English, when

[13] Alice Chandler, *A Dream of Order: The Medieval Ideal in Nineteenth-Century English Literature* (1971); Jan Marsh, *Back to the Land: The Pastoral Impulse in England, from 1880 to 1914* (1982); Alun Howkins, 'The Discovery of Rural England', in Robert Collis and Philip Dodd (eds.), *Englishness: Politics and Culture 1880–1920* (1986), pp62–88.

[14] Ken Dowden, *The Uses of Greek Mythology* (1992), p126.

contemplating the rural world, was dominated as never before by the great goddess and the horned god.[15]

The same development had a marked impact upon attitudes to the fourth direct link between pagan past and pagan present: folk custom and rituals. Scholars had believed ever since the Renaissance that many of these derived from the old religions, and current research can establish that in a few cases at least this is perfectly correct. In the sixteenth and seventeenth centuries, antiquaries tended to assume that they came down from Roman festivals, while in the eighteenth and early nineteenth it became more fashionable to attribute them to the Druids. In the late-nineteenth century this long-established assumption was given a new importance by the work of (above all) Sir Edward Tylor, Sir Lawrence Gomme, and Sir James Frazer. These writers were inspired by the new theory of biological evolution and the discovery of the fossil record of the past, which suggested to them the possibility that surviving folk customs could be fossils of old religions, embedded in later society. If this were so, they reasoned, then a close comparative study of these survivals might enable specialists to reconstruct these religions.[16]

It should be stressed that Tylor and Frazer were both motivated by a distaste, rather than an admiration, for all religious beliefs and practices. They especially despised those like paganism and Roman Catholicism which relied heavily upon ritual. Their ultimate aim was to discredit all religion, including Christianity, as part of a progress towards a wiser and more rational society. Nor was their theory of survivals ever fully accepted by the scholarly community. At the opening of the twentieth century, the Folk-Lore Society held a full-scale debate upon it by devoting most of an issue of its periodical, *Folk-Lore,* to reviews of Frazer's key work, *The Golden Bough.* One historian and expert in comparative religion after another examined Frazer's methodology and pointed out serious faults in it. The notable exception was Sir Lawrence Gomme's wife, Alice, a pioneer of the collection of children's lore, who said that she was not an expert in the material of *The Golden Bough,* and knew little about it, but that Frazer's arguments just sounded right to her.

This established the pattern of the future: historians lost interest in the Folk-Lore Society and it became almost wholly the preserve of people like Lady Gomme, enthusiastic collectors of folk customs who

---

[15] There are surveys in Helen H. Law, *Bibliography of Greek Myth in English Poetry* (1955), and Patricia Merivale, *Pan the Goat-God: His Myth in Modern Times* (1969).

[16] J.W. Burrow, *Evolution and Society* (1966); Robert Ackerman, *J.G. Frazer: His Life and Work* (1987); Gillian Bennett, 'Geologists and Folklorists', *Folklore* 105 (1994), pp25–37.

uncritically accepted Frazer's view of them as pagan survivals. They simply fitted the data which they observed into his interpretative framework. This pattern also harmonised perfectly with the new nostalgia for the English countryside and the idealisation of the natural world. If the theory of survivals was correct, then apparently old rural customs literally were solemn and sacred rites; by linking them to an old fertility religion of greenery and nature spirits, Frazer had told the public exactly what it most wanted to hear. His work helped to perfect a vision of a timeless, sealed off, rural world, full of ancient secrets.[17]

But how did all this get linked to witchcraft? The answer lies in a political debate over the origins of the Great Witch Hunt, the roots of which, in turn, run far back into the eighteenth century. During that century it became generally accepted by the educated elites of Europe that magic did not exist. If this was so, then logically the Witch Hunt had been a terrible mistake, and could be used by the liberals of the Enlightenment to castigate and mock the traditional order in Church and state. This situation invited a reaction, and one appeared during the period of intensely conservative government often characterised as the Age of Metternich. Two scholars serving authoritarian German rulers, Karl Jarcke and Franz Josef Mone, suggested that the witches persecuted during the early modern period had in fact been practitioners of a surviving pagan religion; a view which, if it were true, made the persecution rational and even justifiable.[18]A reply to it was demanded in turn from the liberal camp and was provided resoundingly by one of the nineteenth century's great radical historians, the Frenchman Jules Michelet. Michelet was a bitter enemy of the Catholic Church and the feudal aristocracy, an unqualified admirer of the French Revolution, and an author of vivid and immensely popular books. He knew literally nothing of the Middle Ages except romances and fairy tales, and virtually all his information upon the Witch Hunt was taken from anti-clerical pamphlets. This did not inhibit him at all. In 1862, he published *La Sorciere,* a bestseller which portrayed the pagan witch religion postulated by Jarcke and Mone as having been the repository of

[17] Georgina Boyes, 'Cultural Survivals Theory and Traditional Customs', *Folk Life* 26 (1987–8) pp5–10; Gillian Bennett, 'Folklore Studies and the English Rural Myth', *Rural History* 4 (1993), pp77–91; Theresa Buckland and Juliette Wood (eds.), *Aspects of British Calendar Customs* (1993).

[18] Karl Ernst Jarcke, 'Ein Hexenprozess', in *Annalen der Deutchen und Auslandischen Criminal-Rechts-Pflege* 1 (1828), p450; Franz Josef Mone, 'Uber das Hexenwesen', in *Anzeiger fur Kunde der Teutschen Vorzeit* 8 (1839), pp271–5, pp444–5.

liberty all through the tyranny and obscurantism of the Middle Ages. In his dream of it, it was feminist, led by a priestess. It was nature-loving and also joyous, democratic, and peaceful. Michelet, indeed, went far further than even the most uninhibited modern pagan writer, to claim that the Renaissance had been caused by the natural wisdom of the witch religion working its way upward to artists and writers. After the commercial success of *La Sorciere*, it is easy to believe that Wicca was a religion waiting to be re-enacted.

Perhaps it was, indeed, re-enacted soon afterwards. There is, however, no firm evidence of this, and it is not difficult to see why not. French culture of the time did not include the same reverence of the countryside and respect for rural people that the English were acquiring. Nor does France seem to have had the same tradition of popular quasi-magical societies. Although the British cultural elite certainly read *La Sorciere*, and admired it, they could do so only because they spoke French; it was not available in English until 1904. By then an English readership also had Charles Godfrey Leland's *Aradia*, published in 1899. Inspired directly by Michelet, it purported to provide the gospel of the Italian branch of his witch religion. Leland likewise made his political purpose clear; to argue against a newly-fashionable nostalgia for the Middle Ages which offended his own radical ideas. His text was yet more feminist than Michelet's, for it made the main deity of the religion a goddess. The theory was finally given academic respectability in 1921 by the English archaeologist Margaret Murray, who was acquainted with the work of both Michelet and Leland and was, moreover, a member of the Folk-Lore Society and an admirer of Sir James Frazer. Her work on witch trial records (proved much later to have been selective, inaccurate and misleading) united Frazer's old rural fertility religion with modern folk customs and Michelet's witch cult, upon an apparently sound basis of evidence. Murray's own attitude was strictly rationalist, based upon a dislike of all religion and superstition. Nevertheless, as time wore on her antipathy towards Christianity became more overt and her sympathy for ancient paganism correspondingly more pronounced. If her first book on the subject, in 1921, had won the respect of academe, her second, *The God of the Witches*, published in 1933, made a much greater impact upon the public. It portrayed the witch religion as having been the universal one of ancient northern Europe, carefree and natural.

It is hardly surprising, therefore, that it is in England towards the end of the 1930s that the first apparently reliable evidence can be traced of groups who embodied this religion. They range from a set of Cambridge students, to a gathering of middle-class intellectuals, including individuals with a colonial background, to a convention of ordinary, if very literate, lower-middle-class people.[19] This chapter can end, however, with a quick glance at the man who was to be the first publicist, and perhaps the co-founder, of Wicca, Gerald Gardner. Even a relatively swift examination of his social world between his arrival in England in 1936 and his first 'Wiccan' publication in 1949, reveals that he was a Freemason, a Rosicrucian, a spiritualist, a friend and probable member of the Ordo Templi Orientis, a member of the governing council of a Druid order, a very active member of the Folk-Lore Society and fervent admirer of Margaret Murray, and a member of one of the divisions of the Order of Woodcraft Chivalry. Representatives of all or most of these were active in the New Forest area in the time around 1940, when Gardner later claimed to have been initiated into Wicca.[20] It is no wonder that when one reads his books or (more to the point) reads his papers in Toronto and his surviving manuscripts of Wiccan rituals, one likewise finds elements from all or most of them as well as direct borrowings from authors such as Crowley and Leland and grimoires such as the Key of Solomon.

The story suggested here is no more than an outline, and still leaves mysterious the matter of how exactly particular modern Pagan groups and traditions came into existence. There is room for a very large quantity of further research, and much of it will, undoubtedly, be carried out by academics as part of the burgeoning scholarly interest in new and revived religions, of which Newcastle University's conference, 'Paganism in Contemporary Britain' was in itself a striking manifestation. Modern pagans themselves have, however, a clear opportunity to preempt an academic investigation which may prove to be insufficiently sensitive or sympathetic for the liking of some, by conducting research into their own traditions.[21] If the data which they provide is susceptible to proof by scholarly analysis, then they will earn the respect and gratitude of professionals and possess much of the initiative in the study of their own history. What this

---

[19] This would include Gardner's original circle, the 'Pentacle Club' at Cambridge, and the Chanctonbury group, all based upon the testimony, written or spoken, of former members.

[20] Some of this information is in his biography by Jack Bracelin. The manuscript diary of Aleister Crowley confirms Gardner's membership of the O.T.O., and the minutes of the Ancient Druid Order place him upon its council. His activity in the Folk-Lore Society can be traced through its periodical *Folk-Lore* (after 1960, *Folklore)* between 1938 and 1963, and Bran Labworth testifies to his connection with the Woodcraft Chivalry.

[21] This is the subject of work in progress by Aidan Kelly, Ceisiwr Serith, and Gareth Medway.

chapter has suggested is that the task is likely to be long, complex and fascinating. It proposes that modern Paganism was neither the descendant of a continuous sectarian witch cult, nor born fully-fledged from the imagination of one man in the 1940s. It is, on the contrary, a particular, and extreme, incarnation of some of the broadest and deepest cultural impulses of the nineteenth and twentieth century British world.

Madame Blavatsky's children: Theosophy and its heirs*

KEVIN TINGAY

Introduction

The Theosophical Society (hereafter 'TS') has for most of its history been the object of opprobrium from mainstream Christianity, and either ridiculed or ignored as a movement of marginal interest by students of religion until recent years. Yet the writings of Theosophists appear as a constant backdrop to many of the alternative spiritual traditions of the twentieth century. The society can be seen as the major institutional culmination of the growth of interest in occultism in the nineteenth century and its influence continues to be felt in our own times. The history and significance of the movement await a major study but work is beginning to be published which has moved on from the propaganda and polemic which has often characterised comment on Theosophy and its ramifications over the past one hundred and twenty years.[1]

*This chapter first appeared in *Beyond New Age: Exploring Alternative Spirituality*, edited by Steven Sutcliffe and Marion Bowman, Edinburgh: Edinburgh University Press, 2000, pp.37–40, 43–5, 46–50.

[1] Several biographies of the chief founder H.P. Blavatsky have been produced since her death in 1891. Most adopt a partisan attitude for or against the proposition that she was a major spiritual teacher of the nineteenth-century. Amongst more recent works are Meade (1980) (*against*), Fuller (1988), and Cranston (1993) (*for*). The co-founder of the Society, H.S. Olcott, has been memorialised from within the movement by Murphet (1972), and his place in the revival of Buddhism in Asia has been analysed by Prothero (1996). Studies of the history of the Theosophical movement as a whole have been written from within the parent society by Ransom (1938), from the Pasadena position by Ryan (1975), and from the traditionally anonymous standpoint of the independent United Lodge of Theosophists in *The Theosophical Movement* (1951). A general academic survey of the subject is to be

The key themes of modern Theosophy are to be found in the writings of H.P. Blavatsky and her followers. They are not original to her and she did not claim that they were. She gathered together ideas which she thought represented the tradition of an 'Ancient Wisdom', and which she believed had been expressed through the ages in widely dispersed circumstances. We summarise them as follows for brevity's sake:

- The existence of a perennial wisdom tradition
- Its esoteric or gnostic character
- Its manifestation through exoteric religious traditions
- The existence of adepts or 'Masters of the Wisdom'
- Reincarnation and the law of karma
- A view of the human constitution as functioning in a series of interpenetrating 'bodies' from physical, etheric, emotional, mental, to 'higher self'
- An evolution of the spirit undergirding physical evolution
- A vision of universal brotherhood
- Western acceptance of Asian spiritual traditions
- Techniques of clairvoyance, divination and healing

The prime founder of the Theosophical movement was born Helena Petrovna Hahn in Ekaterinoslav in the Ukraine in 1831. She was by all accounts an unconventional child of her class, and did not fit at all into the pattern set for a young Russian woman of the minor aristocracy. She took a great interest in the folklore and popular religious practices of the local peasant community, especially psychic phenomena, magic and shamanism. Three weeks before her seventeenth birthday she was married to Nikifor Blavatsky, often described as an elderly military officer, but in fact a middle-aged provincial governor in Armenia. After a few weeks, however, Helena abandoned her husband and in 1848, the 'Year of Revolutions', began a series of travels and adventures which resulted in the foundation of the Theosophical movement twenty-seven years later.

found in Campbell (1980), and particular studies have been made of Theosophy in Australia (Roe, 1986), New Zealand (Ellwood, 1993), and Russia (Carlson, 1993). A popular work which accepts uncritically the accusations that Blavatsky was a 'fraud', but nevertheless goes on to chart some of the links between Theosophy and other twentieth-century movements, has been written by Washington (1993). Detailed academic studies of the movements and personalities which predated the foundation of the TS but whose influences are significant are to be found in Godwin (1994) and Faivre (1994).

No child was born to this union. Indeed Blavatsky later wrote that the marriage was never consummated and that a combination of her distaste for sex and gynaecological problems precluded any consideration of child-bearing. Some biographers have asserted that she did in fact give birth to a son, Yuri, in 1861, and that the child died in infancy. This has always been denied by Blavatsky and by Theosophical biographers. The name of Blavatsky was not to be lost to posterity by lack of issue, however, as Madame Blavatsky, or 'HPB' as she is referred to in Theosophical occultist circles, lives on through a far-reaching series of activities. This essay outlines how the life and activities of this curious Russian woman, of no formal education, have been perpetuated in writings that have remained in print over the century since her death on 8 May 1891, and in a host of organisations expressing what we now call 'alternative spiritualities' from then until the present day. It will dwell no more on the details of her earlier life, fascinating though it was, but will describe something of what followed from it. Blavatsky travelled in Europe, the Middle East and Central Asia in search of spiritual wisdom. Contacts with the early Spiritualist movement led her to the United States where, in 1874, she met Colonel Henry Olcott (1832–1907) who was also investigating Spiritualism. These two drew together a small group to discuss how they might facilitate the study of occultism and related matters.

The birth of the Theosophical Society

The Theosophical Society was founded in 1875 in New York. Blavatsky contributed a charismatic enthusiasm for the occult and claimed to have access to teachings on the subject which had hitherto been concealed. Olcott, who had a background in law and administration, provided an organisational impetus for the movement. He became its first president and remained in that office until his death. The founders travelled to India in 1879 and in 1882 established the headquarters of the now flourishing society at Adyar near Madras. The society had been established as a response to the growing interest in occultism, Spiritualism and comparative religion which had developed in the latter half of the nineteenth century. The reasons for the move to India are not obviously apparent, but it proved fruitful in terms of the growth of the movement, enabling links to be established with both Hindus and Buddhists, and bringing it closer to those 'Masters of the Wisdom' whom the founders believed to reside in the Himalayas. From that time onwards the spirituality of Theosophists was clearly rooted in eastern rather than western esoteric traditions.

The original single object of the society at the time of its foundation was 'to collect and diffuse a knowledge of the laws which govern the universe.' After some modification its objects were established in 1896 as:

1 to form a nucleus of the Universal Brotherhood of Humanity, without distinction of race, creed, sex, caste or colour

2 to encourage the study of comparative religion, philosophy and science

3 to investigate unexplained laws of nature and the powers latent in man[2]

But the society was not an assembly in the tradition of nineteenth-century literary or scientific societies. Blavatsky claimed that she had been instructed in an Ancient Wisdom that underlay the teachings and practices of all the world's faiths, and that that instruction had come from hidden adepts – the Masters of the Wisdom. These adepts were alleged to be human beings who had reached the peak of human evolution through many reincarnations and were the custodians of this wisdom. Two such beings – Koot Hoomi and Morya – had chosen her to proclaim the teachings to a world that was deemed ready for their reception. The Theosophical Society was the mechanism by which this plan was to be achieved.[3]

From its earliest days the movement had to cope with the inbuilt tension between the wide-ranging scope of its three objects and the apparently definitive teachings of Blavatsky and her hidden teachers. Despite its claims not to be a religious body it has in fact provided for many of its members doctrinal and ethical teachings traditionally associated with religion. In common with many movements of the period, the society's predominant public activity was to arrange lectures and publish literature, both being directed to the propagation of the teachings and the recruitment of members. Meetings for members generally took the form of lectures or the group study of Theosophical texts. Though the TS itself did not for the most part provide devotional or liturgical activities, these did in fact emerge in a number of associated movements.

[...]

---

[2] Ransom (1938: 545ff).

[3] Letters alleged to be from these Masters were published by Barker in 1923. Details of physical and clairvoyant contacts with various Masters appear through much of Theosophical literature up to the 1950s. Johnson (1994) attempts to correlate Blavatsky's descriptions with identifiable historical figures.

Esoteric elaborations

The aforementioned three objects of the Theosophical Society did not mention Masters of the Wisdom or concealed teachings directly and there have always been members who did not concern themselves too much with these matters. For those who did, however, provision was made from the start of the movement for detailed teachings of an occult nature and the possibility of being put in closer contact with the Masters. The 'ES' (at various times these initials stood for the 'Esoteric Section', the 'Eastern School' or 'Esoteric School' of Theosophy) had its origins in the personal pupils of Blavatsky. They had to follow an ascetic spiritual regime and to declare confidence in the legitimacy of Blavatsky and her successors as the approved agents of the Masters, and to commit themselves to work for the society to the best of their abilities. Membership of this inner group has provided the leadership of the TS in most parts of the world until the present day. Other controlled groups – that is, those which restricted themselves to TS members – included at various times The Temple of the Rosy Cross (1912), The Krotona Drama (1921), The Egyptian Rite of the Ancient Mysteries (1930), The Temple of the Motherhood of God (c.1924), and the Ritual of the Mystic Star (1935), all of which offered ceremonial expression to Theosophy. Some of these were short-lived, while others endured for longer periods. In the social field the Theosophical Order of Service (1908) co-ordinated work of a philanthropic nature. The Theosophical Fraternity in Education (1916) was the focus for progressive developments in schools and evolved into the wider New Education Fellowship. Less successful was the Theosophical World University project (1925) which envisaged a chain of progressive centres of higher learning around the world. It never developed further than a series of public lectures and some vague and grandiose planning. A number of activities for children enjoyed greater popularity in the period up to 1930. Lotus Circles (1892), the Order of the Golden Chain (1899) and the International Order of the Round Table provided opportunities for children of different ages to be exposed to the ethical and spiritual teachings of Theosophy. Since the 1930s the first two of these groups have been subsumed into the Order of the Round Table, which still functions in several countries and uses ceremonies based on the Arthurian legends. The bulk of its membership comes from the children of Theosophical families.

Those movements I have designated 'controlled' had links with the TS built into their individual constitutions, but there were two larger movements which sought, amongst other things, to explore Theosophy through ceremonial expression. They had no formal links with

Theosophy and did recruit some of their membership from outside Theosophy, but its influence remained as a vital component and hence they can fairly be described as 'influenced' movements. These two groups were The Liberal Catholic Church (hereafter 'LCC') and The Order of International Co-Freemasonry (generally referred to as 'Co-Masonry'). The LCC derived from an attempt to establish a branch of the Dutch Old Catholic Church in England in 1908. This attracted a number of Theosophists who enthusiastically adopted a rich catholic liturgical practice and interpreted it from an esoteric viewpoint. This appealed to those who had reluctantly left established churches as a result of their Theosophical interests, but also antagonised members who saw Theosophy as a rejection of Christianity. The LCC developed a hierarchy of bishops (who have generally been Theosophists) in many parts of the world, has endured a number of schisms, and has reflected the general decline in Theosophical membership in its own decline in numbers. C.W. Leadbeater, an Anglican clergyman prior to becoming a disciple of Blavatsky, became a bishop in this church in 1916 and subsequently wrote prolifically on ecclesiastical topics. His *Science of the Sacraments* offered the student of Christian liturgy his clairvoyant Theosophical insights into what was going on in the inner worlds during the celebration of Mass and the administration of the sacraments.

The Co-Masonic Order had its origins in France and is still governed from Paris. In 1882 a French masonic lodge decided to initiate a woman. This resulted in their being expelled by their governing authority and they established a masonic order of their own which admitted men and women on equal terms. Annie Besant was initiated in 1902 and the movement expanded through her enthusiasm, particularly in the English-speaking Theosophical world. Since World War II this order has recruited less from the Theosophical movement and, like the LCC, has declined in recent years. In France, however, where the Theosophical influence was only peripheral, it has continued to grow. Several of the later generation of Theosophical leaders were active in this movement and have written on masonic symbolism, and in some cases the masonic ritual was elaborated along Theosophical lines. Some freemasons from lodges of the United Grand Lodge of England and the Grand Lodge of Scotland associated themselves with the new order, but the ruling authorities of those bodies did not take kindly to this feminine development and forbade their members from having any contact with it. Some men did in fact throw in their lot with the new body and assisted in its growth. After a few years of activity, in which several new lodges were founded in Great Britain, a faction of initiates who did not find themselves in sympathy with the Theosophical influence separated themselves. Their endeavours evolved into two separate orders of Freemasonry for women only which continue to the present day and have no connection with their co-masonic forebears.

[...]

Theosophists at work in the world

Such was the organisational fruit of Blavatsky's endeavours, manifested in movements that attempted in some way or another to express the inner or spiritual aspect of her teachings. How far she saw her movement as having a wider social function is a matter of debate, but the influence of Annie Besant propelled many of the members into social action. Amongst the 'progressive' causes which they espoused were alternative medicine, vegetarianism, animal welfare, progressive education, female suffrage, the Garden City movement and the struggle for Indian independence. We should also note some influence on artistic and literary trends in the period from 1880 to 1914.[4]

The excitements of the 1920s were followed by a period of retrenchment after the departure of Krishnamurti and the death of Annie Besant, and through the difficult years of World War II. A resolution, originally passed by the general council of the society in 1924 and regularly reproduced in *The Theosophist*, its international journal since the 1930s, illustrates the movement away from dogmatic pronouncements by authoritarian leaders towards a more dispersed pattern of authority:

> As the Theosophical Society has spread far and wide over the world, and as members of all religions have become members of it without surrendering the special dogmas, teachings and beliefs of their respective faiths, it is thought desirable to emphasise the fact that there is no doctrine, no opinion, by whomsoever taught or held, that is any way binding on any member of the Society, none which any member is not free to accept or reject. Approval of its three Objects is the sole condition of membership. No teacher, or writer, from H.P. Blavatsky downwards, has any authority to impose his teachings or opinions on members. Every member has an equal right to attach himself to any school of thought which he may choose, but has no right to force his choice on any other. Neither a candidate for any office nor any voter can be rendered ineligible to stand or to vote because of any opinion he may hold, or because of membership of any school of thought to which he may belong. Opinions or beliefs neither bestow privileges nor inflict penalties. The Members of the General Council earnestly

---

[4] Nethercot (1961, 1963) provides the most accessible source of reference for these activities.

request every member of The Theosophical Society to maintain, defend and act upon these fundamental principles of the Society, and also fearlessly to exercise his own right of liberty of thought, and of expression thereof, within the limits of courtesy and consideration for others.

In common with other movements with a mission in a pre-electronic age, Theosophy used the printed word to embody its teachings. A great volume of books, pamphlets, and periodical literature poured from the presses. Their sales went beyond the membership of the specifically Theosophical, which might lead us to suppose that there were many more who took an interest in esoteric ideas than actually joined organisations, a situation which I suspect applies as much today as it did a century ago. The writings of Blavatsky remain in print, as do many by Annie Besant and C.W. Leadbeater. The TS, which still runs publishing houses in India, the USA and elsewhere, has produced a wide range of books over the past one hundred years. We summarise the genres, with examples, as follows:

- Foundational texts of H.P. Blavatsky – *Isis Unveiled* (1877), *The Secret Doctrine* (1888) and *The Key to Theosophy* (1889).

- Channelled/'received' texts – *The Mahatma Letters* (written in the 1880s, published 1923).[5]

- Descriptions of supersensible experiences or observations – *Man, Visible and Invisible* (1902) and other titles by C.W. Leadbeater.

- Translations and commentaries on classical oriental texts – *The Bhagavad Gita* translated by Annie Besant.

- Cosmological and anthropological schemas and accounts of past lives – *Man, Whence, How and Whither* (1913) by Besant and Leadbeater.

- Guides to spiritual practices, meditation, yoga, etc.

- 'Esoteric' Christianity – *Esoteric Christianity* (1905) by Besant, *The Christian Creed* (1917) by Leadbeater.[6]

[5] The Mahatma Letters were purported to have been 'precipitated' by occult means from the Masters to A.P. Sinnett, Blavatsky and others. Other Theosophists have from time to time made claims to the reception of what is now referred to as 'channelled' communications from the same source.

[6] Esoteric Christianity, so-called, generally turns out to be old gnosticism in new clothing. Theosophists from Blavatsky onwards subscribe to the theory that the Church throughout the ages has conspired to keep the true message of Jesus Christ a closely guarded secret.

The other movements already noted engendered a corresponding volume of printed material. Perhaps the greatest number of Blavatsky's 'children' are these now largely neglected texts which expressed the hopes and fears of their earnest authors.[7]

Our opening summary of Theosophical interests and our outline of the movements and activities over the past one hundred and twenty years points to the place where Blavatsky's children mostly seem to dwell in our own times – the New Age. Blavatsky is not the only mother of that age but surely one of the most significant. The movements and activities which she and her successors instigated provided a comprehensive range of opportunities for seekers of esoteric spirituality. The parent society might be likened to a Clapham Junction for occult travellers, who entered from various directions and travelled on to several destinations beyond. Some were quite famous names, and there has always been a faithful core of members who saw it as the centre of their spiritual world, but today the Theosophical Society is a rather faded shadow of its grand former self. For the seeker after ancient wisdom, there is now a bewildering variety of alternative transport. A century ago Theosophy had the major share of the market; now it is almost submerged by the brightly packaged products of the New Age. In 1889 H.P. Blavatsky wrote some words towards the end of her book *The Key to Theosophy* which now have a prophetic ring:

> Every such attempt as the Theosophical Society has hitherto ended in failure, because, sooner or later, it has degenerated into a sect, set up hard-and-fast dogmas of its own, and so lost by imperceptible degrees that vitality which living truth alone can impart. You must remember that all our members have been bred and born in some creed or religion, that all are more or less of their generation both physically and mentally, and consequently that their judgement is but too likely to be warped and unconsciously biased by some or all of these influences. If, then, they cannot be freed from such inherent bias, or at least taught to recognise it instantly and so avoid being led away by it, the result can only be that the Society will drift off on to some sandbank of thought or another, and there remain a stranded carcass to moulder and die.
>
> (Blavatsky, 1893: 193)

---

[7] No comprehensive bibliography covers the whole of the period of Theosophical history, but Gomes (1994) covers the period up to 1900.

Bibliography

Barker, A. Trevor (1923) *The Mahatma Letters to A.P. Sinnett* (London: T. Fisher Unwin).

Blau, Evelyne (1995) *Krishnamurti – 100 years* (New York: Stewart, Chabori and Chang).

Blavatsky, Helena P. (1893) *The Key to Theosophy*, 3rd edn (London: Theosophical Publishing Society).

Campbell, Bruce J. (1980) *Ancient Wisdom Revived – A History of the Theosophical Movement* (Berkeley: University of California Press).

Carlson, Maria (1993) *'No Religion Higher Than Truth' – A History of the Theosophical Movement in Russia 1875–1922* (Princeton: Princeton University Press).

Cranston, Sylvia (1993) *H.P.B. – The Extraordinary Life and Influence of Helena Blavatsky* (New York: Putnam).

Ellwood, Robert S. (1993) *Islands of the Dawn – The Story of Alternative Spirituality in New Zealand* (Honolulu: University of Hawaii).

Faivre, Antoine (1994) *Access to Modern Esotericism* (New York: State University of New York Press).

Fuller, Jean Overton (1988) *Blavatsky and her Teachers* (London: East-West Publications).

Godwin, Joscelyn (1994) *The Theosophical Enlightenment* (New York: State University of New York Press).

Gomes, Michael (1994) *Theosophy in the Nineteenth Century: an Annotated Bibliography* (New York: Garland).

Johnson, K. Paul (1994) *The Masters Revealed* (New York: State University of New York Press).

Leviton, Richard (1994) *The Imagination of Pentecost – Rudolf Steiner & Contemporary Spirituality* (Hudson, NY: Anthroposophic Press).

Lutyens, Mary (1990) *The Life and Death of Krishnamurti* (London: John Murray).

Meade, Marion (1980) *Madame Blavatsky – The Woman behind the Myth* (New York: Putnam).

Melton, J. Gordon (1989) *The Encyclopaedia of American Religions* (Detroit: Gale Research).

Murphet, Howard (1972) *Hammer on the Mountain – The Life of Henry Steel Olcott (1832–1907)* (Wheaton, IL.: Theosophical Publishing House).

Nethercot, Arthur H. (1961) *The First Four Lives of Annie Besant* (London: Rupert Hart-Davis).

Nethercot, Arthur H. (1963) *The Last Five Lives of Annie Besant* (London: Rupert Hart-Davis).

Prothero, Stephen (1996) *The White Buddhist – The Asian Odyssey of Henry Steel Olcott* (Bloomington: Indiana University Press).

Ransom, Josephine (1938) *A Short History of the Theosophical Society* (Adyar: Theosophical Publishing House).

Roe, Jill (1986) *Beyond Belief – Theosophy in Australia 1879–1939* (Kensington, NSW: University of New South Wales Press).

Ryan, Charles J. (1975) *H.P. Blavatsky and the Theosophical Movement* (San Diego: Point Loma Publications).

Schuller, Govert (1997) *Krishnamurti and the World Teacher Project: Some Theosophical Perceptions*, Theosophical History Occasional Papers, Vol. V (Fullerton, CA.: Theosophical History).

The Theosophical Movement 1875–1950–1952 (Los Angeles: The Cunningham Press).

Washington, Peter (1993) *Madame Blavatsky's Baboon – Theosophy and the Emergence of the Western Guru* (London: Bloomsbury).

The faith of the fringe: perspectives and issues in 'Celtic Christianity'*

DONALD E. MEEK

Although 'Celtic Christianity' appears to be thoroughly contemporary in its profile as an 'alternative' form of Christianity, and is strongly influenced by postcolonial perceptions of primal religions elsewhere in the world, it is nevertheless grounded in a particular view of culture and history which, at first sight, appears to conflict with the progressive mindset of modernity, though it is not necessarily in conflict with the tenets of postmodernity. 'Celtic Christianity' is highly retrospective in its view of 'Celtic' tradition. Comparatively few of its promoters are themselves participants in the affairs of the contemporary 'Celtic' world, and know little of how that world functions.

In their broadly retrospective and romantic 'vision', the exponents of 'Celtic Christianity' follow an approach which can be traced through Arnold and Renan and as far back as Macpherson's Ossianic translations of the early 1760s. [...] They also pursue outdated lines of scholarship. Alongside collections like *Carmina Gadelica* [...], several key writers such as Ian Bradley, Esther de Waal and David Adam are rediscovering influential scholarly studies and translations which derive from the turn of the twentieth century. As most of the modern writers are not themselves Celtic scholars, and (with some more honourable exceptions) generally not speakers of a Celtic language, they are often unaware of the extent to which earlier perspectives have been superseded by much more recent scholarly inspection. They are therefore primarily observers of a culture which is, on the one hand, remote from them, but, on the other, accessible, recoverable and even transferable, through the labours of earlier scholars who have furnished translations of key texts. Without the impediments of the distinctive Celtic languages of the British Isles, the

---

* This text first appeared in *The Quest for Celtic Christianity*, Donald E. Meek, Edinburgh: Handsel Press, 2000, pp.79–102.

appropriation of the 'Celtic' material is greatly facilitated, and an alternative 'Celtic' culture is created largely for the consumption of 'outsiders' and non-speakers of Celtic languages who continue to colonise the 'Celtic Fringe', either physically or spiritually.

The debt of modern writers to late nineteenth-century and early twentieth-century scholarly translators and interpreters is writ large on one of the standard themes of contemporary 'Celtic Christianity', namely the 'peripherality' of the Celtic areas of the British Isles. As appropriation of the 'periphery' takes place, a primitivist vision of the 'Celtic Fringe' also reasserts itself. This primitivist vision is, however, frequently counterbalanced by a (post)modernist vision which derives from the imagination and creativity – literary, philosophical, and theological – of the English-language world with which the writers are, of course, much more familiar. The beguilingly contemporary profile of 'Celtic Christianity' is further enhanced by its apparent relevance to, and ability to resolve, a raft of issues of common contemporary concern which were of no relevance whatsoever to the real Celts of these islands before 1100. Paradoxes of this kind are the stuff of 'Celtic Christianity'. This chapter will examine the main concerns of contemporary 'Celtic Christianity', and assess their validity in the light of contextual, historical and literary evidence earlier than the twelfth century.

Postmodern primitivism

The primitivist, peripheralist vision at the heart of 'Celtic Christianity' is articulated by its modern advocates at every possible opportunity. Thus, Ian Bradley is able to write eloquently (*The Celtic Way*, p.30):

> Celtic Christianity is a faith hammered out at the margins. The Celts lived on the margins of Britain, on the margins of Europe and on the margins of Christendom. They lived close to nature, close to the elements, close to God and close to homelessness, poverty and starvation ...

> The great upsurge of interest in Celtic Christianity in recent years can be compared to the re-evaluation of the religious beliefs of other peoples who have lived on the margins like the Australian Aborigines and the native Indians of North America. It reflects a realisation that what is primitive and simple can also be profound and highly original. It expresses also a deeply Christian view that it is among the voices of the most marginalised and oppressed that we may find the greatest wisdom.

Bradley's perspectives are those of a post-imperial and postcolonial society with a conscience about the exploitation of the 'natives' by earlier imperialism [...]. They are also those of a technologically advanced society, no longer 'primitive and simple', but aware of the pains and aches of its own progress, and prepared to recognize, in a somewhat patronising way, the achievements of a 'primitive and simple' society. They also encapsulate a reaction against the squalor of contemporary urban life; a vision of 'cardboard city' appears to underlie such words as 'close to homelessness, poverty and starvation', and implies that the 'Celts' have something to say to those who endure such problems nowadays.

Such perspectives, however, are not necessarily relevant to the early Christian 'Celts'. It is unlikely that 'Celts' would have regarded themselves as being in any way 'marginalised and oppressed' when their culture was at its strongest. Such a view of the past is constructed from an eastern and southern British point of reference which sees the contemporary 'Celts' as inhabitants of a remote fringe. It is, in fact, historically inaccurate to claim that 'the Celts lived on the margins of Britain, on the margins of Europe and on the margins of Christendom.' Celtic cultures were extensive in the British Isles in the so-called Dark Ages, and the regions which archaeologists and others have identified as the homelands of the continental Celts were hardly on the 'margins' of Europe.

Misleading concepts of marginality have become pervasive in the twentieth century as the majority mass culture of the British Isles has developed an increasing interest in the 'Celtic Fringe'. They reflect an external and essentially Anglocentric standpoint. Even today, the crofting communities of the Western Isles do not necessarily see themselves as marginal. They may be perceived as such by others, and the failures of economic macro-forces to acknowledge their needs may compel them to believe that they are indeed regarded in that way by those who control the 'energy centres' of modern society; but they are central to their own existence, and Glasgow and Edinburgh, to say nothing of York or Canterbury or Rome, are (from the West Highland perspective) the periphery.

Contrary to the view of many of the proponents of 'Celtic Christianity', Christians in the so-called 'Dark Ages' were not out of touch with Rome. In fact, Christians in Ireland were regularly in contact with Rome in the seventh and eighth centuries, and at no time considered themselves to be beyond its grasp. Issues pertaining to the dating of Easter [...] were discussed with Rome, and important letters were exchanged. Again, the evidence of religious manuscripts and works from early Ireland shows few signs of intellectual isolation on the periphery of Christendom; the commentaries on religious texts make it quite clear that Irish monks were au fait with many of the latest European writings. They were, for example, among the very earliest users and admirers of the etymological works of Isidore of Seville (c.550–636). Furthermore, the use of the terms 'primitive' and 'simple' underestimates the skills that were regularly employed by the Insular Celts. In terms of the value-system of the areas thus described, the terms 'advanced' and 'sophisticated' might be better. Where, today, is the person who can reproduce the brilliance of the Book of Kells, or the artistry of the Class Two Pictish stones? Yet all of that was normal to those 'primitive' and 'simple' folk who lived on the 'periphery'.

The natural world

Modern 'Celtic Christianity' places a strong emphasis on the harmonious relationship which is perceived to have existed between early 'Celtic Christians' and their environment. The early Christian Celts, according to Ian Bradley and numerous other commentators, lived 'close to nature'. In this too the paradigm is running along primitivist lines, and following the arguments elaborated by Douglas Hyde and Kuno Meyer, but it is also supplemented by some of the perceptions of more recent scholars of primal religion. It is, however, now stimulated primarily by modern ecological issues.

It needs to be made clear that living 'close to nature' was not an option for the Celts of the British Isles. Of course, their natural environment was less spoilt by human hands, and they were not faced with modern ecological issues – environmental degradation caused by cities, industries, fossil fuels, CFC gases and other alleged sources of ozone depletion. That, however, is not to say that they may not have played their own part in disfiguring the landscape. Some scholars would argue that large centres of population were unknown in Ireland before the Viking period, but others have claimed that the creation of monasteries, some developing into mini-cities, was the first step towards urbanisation. If this is the case, Celtic Christians, far from protecting the environment, laid the foundation of the urban lifestyles which are rejected by contemporary 'Celtic Christianity'. The attempt to make the Celts role-models for environmental conser-vation may thus be somewhat misguided. Like several of the themes discussed in this chapter, it presupposes a dichotomy which was not of any relevance in the early Middle Ages.

Literary sources, in Early Gaelic and Early Welsh, in both poetry and prose, demonstrate that the Celts did have an appreciation of the world around them, in all the variety of its forms. However, exponents of 'Celtic Christianity' argue that there is a special affinity between 'Celtic' monks and the natural world, an affinity which is said to stand in contrast to the lack of concern for nature which is typical of modern Western Christianity. Douglas Hyde, in his *Story of Early Gaelic Literature* (published in 1895), linked Columba very closely with poetry and with nature (p.148). 'Columkille', he wrote,

> like Ossian and the Pagan Irish, was enthusiastically alive to the beauty of Nature. If – apart from form – there is one distinguishing note more than another, peculiar to the literature of the ancient – and to some extent the modern – Gael, it is his fondness for Nature in its various aspects. He seems at times to have been perfectly intoxicated with the mere pleasure of sensations derived from scenery.

Less than a decade later, Kuno Meyer [...], in the introduction to his anthology of translations, *Selections from Ancient Irish Poetry*, reinforced Hyde's sentiments and created what has become a virtually indissoluble connection between 'Celtic Christianity' and nature:

> Many of [these quatrains] give us a fascinating insight into the peculiar character of the early Irish Church, which differed in so many ways from the rest of the Christian world. We see the hermit in his lonely cell, the monk at his devotions or at his work copying in the scriptorium or under the open sky; or we hear the ascetic who, alone or with twelve chosen companions, has left one of the great monasteries in order to live in greater solitude among the woods or mountains, or on a lonely island. The fact that so many of these poems are fathered upon well-known saints emphasizes the friendly attitude of the native clergy towards vernacular poetry.

> In Nature poetry the Gaelic muse may vie with that of any other nation. Indeed, these poems occupy a unique position in the literature of the world. To seek out and watch and love Nature, in its tiniest phenomena as in its grandest, was given to no people so early and so fully as to the Celt.

In this way, Meyer sets up the unique 'Gaelic' response to nature, based on his reading of early Irish poetry, and transmits it to 'the Celt'. Underlying Meyer's deductions is the notion that such poems record real experiences and are directly attributable to hermits or monks who are living the ascetic life in close communion with nature. This perception was developed even more fully by Meyer's former student, Eleanor Hull, who contrasted the world-affirming vision of the Irish hermit with the world-rejecting perspectives of the great Cistercian abbot, Bernard of Clairvaux (1090–1153), noted for his strictures on luxury and excessive embellishments (*Poem-Book of the Gael*, p.xx):

St Bernard, walking round the Lake of Geneva, unconscious of its presence and blind to its loveliness, is a fit symbol of the tendency of the religious mind in the Middle Ages. Sin and repentance, the fall and redemption, hell and heaven, occupied the religious man's every thought; beside such weighty themes the outward life became almost negligible. If he dared to turn his mind towards it at all, it was in order to extract from it some warning of peril, or some allegory of things divine.

But the Irish monk showed no such inclination, suffered no such terrors. His joy in nature grew with his loving association with her moods. He refused to mingle the idea of evil with what God had made so good. If he sought for symbols, he found only symbols of purity and holiness. The pool beside his hut, the rill that flowed across his green, became to his watchful eye the manifestation of a divine spirit washing away sin; if the birds sang sweetly above his door, they were the choristers of God; if the wild beasts gathered to their nightly tryst, were they not the congregation of intelligent beings whom God Himself would most desire?

Thus Eleanor Hull – conveniently overlooking the very evident fact that sin and repentance and other 'weighty themes' are extremely prominent in early Irish monastic literature (see below) – shaped the idea of the nature-adoring 'Irish monk' and the 'Celtic hermit' in a manner which is repeated *ad infinitum* in present-day writings. Modern Celtic scholars, however, are uneasy with the notion that such poems, extolling the great outdoors, were produced by hermits *in situ*. They stress that there is little or nothing in the literary context of these poems to link them directly with eremitic authorship. They are aware that poets, then as now, could assume poses and pretend that they were experiencing a particular set of circumstances. In the case of so-called 'hermit poetry', the pose need not require any active participation in the 'hermit experience'. All that was needed was a scribe who, when wearied of copying a dull manuscript in a scriptorium, glimpsed the sunshine and the trees outside the monastery, and scribbled a few wistful verses in his margins. He would not have considered for a moment that his humble doodles would later assume so much significance for twentieth-century romantics panting for the hermit life.

Broader themes of exile and separation, closely associated with Columba, for instance [...] could be fashioned in a similar way, and ascribed to the appropriate saintly 'voice'. Such poems would express an ideal along the lines of 'this is how we feel it must have been, or how we would like it to be'. The main aim of some at least would be 'idealisation of the ideal'.

In certain poems, nature may be no more than a pretext for the expression of less exalted sentiments which are quietly tucked into the lines. In one of the best known of these early nature poems, the 'hermit' leads us to believe that he is writing in arboreal bliss. His lines are translated by Kuno Meyer as follows (*Ancient Irish Poetry,* p.99):

The scribe

A hedge of trees surrounds me,
A blackbird's lay sings to me;
Above my lined booklet
The trilling birds chant to me.
In a grey mantle from the top of bushes
The cuckoo sings:
Verily – may the Lord shield me! –
Well do I write under the greenwood.

Professor Patrick Ford has recently suggested (in 'Blackbirds, Cuckoos and Infixed Pronouns') that this poem may be a wry, scholarly, off-the-cuff attempt to demonstrate the working of forms of the infixed pronoun found in Early Irish. Several uses of the first person singular pronoun are evident, even in the translation, and the poet may have been trying to show the richness of early Irish grammar in respect to such pronouns. The poem, in fact, occurs in the context of a copy of Priscian's Latin grammar preserved at the continental monastery of St Gall, but probably written in ninth-century Ireland. Although it is ostensibly a poem 'about nature', its immediate context may be indicative of an interest in the *minutiae* of language rather than the 'tiniest phenomena' of the natural world.

While it cannot be doubted that Celtic literature across the centuries does show a lively response to nature, it is highly unlikely that any significant link between 'happy hermits' and early Irish nature poetry can be sustained. The validity of the larger claims that 'to seek out and watch and love Nature ... was given to no people so early and so fully as to the Celt' has likewise been challenged by modern scholars, who point out that there is nothing uniquely Celtic in such a response to nature. Hebrews (in the Old Testament), Greeks, Romans and Romanised Africans (like Augustine of Hippo) also responded positively and appreciatively to the natural world. The supposedly 'Celtic' response to nature has also been shaped across the centuries by external influences, as diverse as the Bible and James Thomson's eighteenth-century verse on *The Seasons* [...]. In the minds of the modern advocates of 'Celtic Christianity', however, the perceived uniqueness of Celtic nature poetry, developing in isolation from the rest of the world, becomes the basis for its distinctiveness.

Essentially the 'happy hermit' of 'early Celtic nature poetry' is a version of the myth of the Noble Savage, which has been reshaped and given a spiritual profile. It contains an element of sharp contrast with other ecclesiastical or environmental approaches. Further overlays give it a present-day resonance. Modern writers commonly weave the body of 'hermit nature verse' into an interpretative pastiche which, while acknowledging the objectivity of such poetry, covers it with a subjective, highly romantic, eco-friendly, and frequently pagan-friendly, glow. Some spiritualise the 'Celtic' view of nature into a belief-system reminiscent of modern descriptions of African primal religion, and they also draw attention to similar themes in Native American spirituality [...]. The great virtue of the Irish poetry – its unadorned detail – thus stands in sharp contrast to the elaborate manner of its modern presentation. The overall aim of this presentation appears to be to produce a distinctively 'Celtic' brand of 'creation spirituality', but the allusions to other 'creation spiritualities' suggest that wider agendas are at work and that the final product is by no means uniquely Celtic.

Simplicity

Given the supposedly close-to-nature lifestyle of the Celts, it is not surprising to find that, in writings on 'Celtic Christianity' generally, there is a presupposition that the Celts did not have complex structures of any kind. These writings express unease with what may be termed broadly 'metropolitan structures'; that is to say, organisations and value systems which are held at the centre by an influential body or group of bodies and exercise control of people's lives. Such metropolitan structures can be political, social or religious; they are often large-scale, as in the case of the Church of England, or the Church of Scotland, or the Roman Catholic Church, or the concept of the United Kingdom itself. Reaction against the metropolitan structures can take a variety of forms, including a flight to the 'periphery'. For those who are weary of the metropolitan lifestyle or value-system, the primitive periphery holds out the hope that a less demanding, less pressurised, less angst-ridden and ultimately more caring form of life may be preserved somewhere in the world.

Reaction against metropolitan control reveals itself in a rejection of central authority and authority figures, and also in the displacement of structured forms of worship in favour of the unstructured, the spontaneous and the individualistic. The trend is consistent with the ethos of post-Impressionist, culturally modernist Britain (and doubtless also Ireland). 'Modernism as a cultural phenomenon', writes

Professor David Bebbington, 'was ... the result of a shift of sensibility as major as the transition from the Enlightenment to Romanticism a century before' (*Evangelicalism*, 233). The movement was carried over into postmodernism.

Modernism began to affect religious life in the British Isles after 1970. British churches then became familiar with the charismatic movement, which emphasized spontaneity, unstructured worship and individual participation, with such other manifestations as glossolalia (speaking in tongues) and prophecy. Some would contend that certain features of this movement bordered on the anarchic, while others, in more positive vein, would stress its contribution to personal spiritual development, by allowing people to come out of the shadow of the 'one-man ministry'. The ideals of the charismatic movement, however, while modern and even postmodern in ethos, reflect a form of primitivism (and thus of romanticism): its practitioners, in abandoning hierarchical structures, believe that they are returning to the form of the early churches in the New Testament.

The Celts, perceived to have been simple and uncomplicated souls, have become role-models or at least validators for this new anti-hierarchical movement. Thus David Dewey, who reviewed Ian Bradley's book in the *Baptist Times* (21 January 1993), rams home the point:

> Celtic Christians had little time for a hierarchical ecclesiastical order. Their worship was centred in independent monastic communities led by an abbot (or abbottess [*sic*]) rather than a parish structure replete with diocesan bishop and ornate cathedral.

This statement minimises the amount of structure that most definitely existed within individual monasteries and in the wider *familiae*. Abbots like Columba had a general jurisdiction over a set of monasteries which they themselves had founded. This must have required planning and meetings and conflicts with local big-wigs and politicians. The clergy of the Gaelic west also attended synods and councils; Columba is said to have been excommunicated by one such synod. Clergy from the Gaelic world were also much involved in ecclesiastical legislation. Adomnán's *Lex innocentium* ('Law of the innocents'), promulgated at Birr in 697, was one such measure. The fact that it was supported by no less than ninety-one guarantors, consisting of forty ecclesiastics and fifty-one kings, suggests that churchmen were active political and social lobbyists, as well as formidable organisers within their own structures (see also David Dumville, *Councils and Synods of the Gaelic Early and Central Middle Ages*). A committee-free Arcadia may be very appealing to burnt-out clerics in present-day national churches, but it is unlikely to have existed in the Celtic west.

In an earlier article in the *Baptist Times* (20 February 1992), Dewey pointed up the alleged contrast between Celtic Christians and those sent to Britain as missionaries from Rome:

> When the British Isles were first evangelised, the missionaries came from two directions. From across the Channel those sent from Rome, speaking Latin and representing the culture of the – by then – Christianised Roman Empire. There was a formal Christianity with its hierarchical structures of church authority.
>
> Then there were those who came from Ireland into Scotland and Northern England. Their Christian faith was less formal. Following a monastic way of life with a key centre on Holy Island, they were unencumbered by wealth and less bothered by status and power. They demonstrated a simplicity and lightness of touch that their Latin counterparts often lacked; in many ways they were the charismatics of their day.

Again, this passage demonstrates the dangers of over-simplification, and repeats the groundless stereotyping typical of nineteenth-century writings on the 'Celtic Church' [...]. Celtic monks would have been more than familiar with Latin, and, to put it mildly, Irish monasteries had a tremendous interest in power, and in the advance of their own cause. It is certainly true that Irish monks in their cells could have great visions (as Columba is represented as having in the island of *Hinba*), but similar visions are ascribed to monks within the Anglo-Saxon world. Whether such visions are sufficient to make them 'charismatics' in the modern sense is open to doubt.

Ecumenism

As Dewey's enthusiastic support of 'Celtic Christianity' shows, the new movement is able to span the denominational divisions of Christianity. Members of relatively old denominations and religious bodies such as Baptists, historically hostile to monasticism, wary of liturgies, and suspicious of symbols such as crosses, are prepared to accommodate these elements into their 'Celtic' experiments. The establishment of pilgrimages to holy places, retreats into meditative communities and liturgies such as the Northumbrian Office, are now acceptable to many who, twenty years ago, would have been uneasy at any of these prospects. Here one can perceive the decay of doctrinal and theological distinctivism, in the face of a new, syncretic 'pick and mix' approach to religious belief. In addition, one notices the growing trans-denominational allure of what Professor

Bebbington, in the context of his penetrating discussion of the charismatic movement, has called 'an extraordinarily unEvangelical delight in symbol – "a love of oil, candles, crosses etc."' (*Evangelicalism,* 244). The knots and crosses of the Celts are easily assimilated into this medley of charismatic catholicity, and become the keys by which the 'Celtic mind' is supposedly unlocked. All denominations are united as they admire their own reflections, intermingling with those of others, in the hall of mirrors which is revealed by opening the mysterious 'Celtic mind'.

The supposed ecumenicity of 'Celtic Christianity' derives from a number of modern perceptions which are projected into the past. First, there is the general idea that, as an expression of faith, 'Celtic Christianity' predates Roman Catholicism. It is thus perceived to be earlier than the major schisms and fractures of Christianity, although some would claim that its real roots lie in Eastern (Greek) Orthodoxy, rather than Roman (Latin) Catholicism [...]. There is certainly evidence of Coptic influence on the early Christian tradition of Ireland, but Christianity in the Celtic lands was in touch with Rome, not Constantinople. To subscribe to 'Celtic Christianity', whatever its roots, is allegedly to enter a purer world, devoid of denomination-alism, and to entertain the hope that 'we can get back to where we used to be before things went wrong'. Second, many believe that 'Celtic Christianity' was free from doctrinal distinctiveness of the kind that has (in their view) bedevilled the later expression of the faith, and has separated believers from one another (see the discussion of theology below). In contrast to modern denominationalism, 'Celtic Christianity' is broad enough to accommodate every shade of faith and practice.

Unfortunately, the historical evidence presents difficulties which militate against the easy acceptance of these views. The Christian faith in the Celtic lands did indeed take root at a time when there were no major denominational differences (as we would define them) within Christendom, but this surely suggests that 'Celtic Christianity' is irrelevant as a supposedly unifying force or model of practical ecumenism. The growing separation between what became Eastern and Western (Roman) Christendom reached its final breaking-point only in the eleventh century. There was thus no need for a unifying body on any significant scale before 1000.

Furthermore, the expression of the faith before that date, even in the Celtic areas, was not without its doctrinal disagreements and squabbles, caused by issues such as Pelagianism, and the dating of Easter. On the latter bone of contention, there were some 'Celts' who had no desire to compromise, and events at Whitby in 664 [...] may be closer to late twentieth-century ecclesiastical controversies regarding points of order and practice than we might care to admit. Some 'Celts', on the arrival of Augustine in 597, showed no great willingness to accommodate the 'Roman' mission [...]. Ecumenism was not part of the spirit of their age. It seems, rather, that there might be innate conservatism and a spirit of competitive expansionism among some Christian communities. Expansionist strategy appears to have been embraced readily by some early Irish monasteries, and is scarcely a good model for ecumenism even in the local context.

It also needs to be recognized that contemporary 'Celtic Christianity' is a curiously double-edged weapon to use in the ecumenical cause. It is frequently employed by its supporters in all bodies to berate what they perceive to be the top-heavy bureaucracy of their own churches, and they appear to be less than kindly disposed to Canterbury, to say nothing of Rome. Rome is commonly portrayed as the oppressor, the papal-driven steamroller that crushed the gentle 'Celts'. By claiming an ecumenical agenda for itself, the vision of the 'aboriginal' Christian faith in these islands is self-contradictory; on the one hand it is seen to hold out hope for unity, but, on the other, it seems to be a tool for the creation of distinctiveness, discord and (ultimately) disunity. This is one of the most perplexing paradoxes of the new movement, particularly since, in its eyes, Rome often appears to be more of an enemy than a friend. The unity to which the movement aspires thus seems to be one which embraces the disillusioned in all camps, rather than one which reconciles these camps.

In this particular context, as in others, the historical facts are disregarded, and the 'Celts' become the ultimate primitivist symbols, capable of being refashioned according to the needs of the seeker, regardless of his or her denomination – but with the capacity (if needed) to validate or challenge trends within that denomination. Charismatic power, artistic brilliance, quiet meditation, uncontentious Christianity – all of these are symbolised in the Celts, who become all things to all men (and women, too), as the occasion demands. Now unable to answer for themselves, these pliable people represent still another modern virtue which lovingly beckons the world-weary, spiritual pilgrim who is tired of clash and clamour – tolerance.

Tolerance

Tolerance, leading to the acceptance of a variety of religious groupings, both Christian and non-Christian, is one of the keynotes of the late twentieth century. This may mean overlooking significant differences while making contact with similarly minded individuals who are likewise chafing under their own metropolitan yoke. Thus, the charismatic movement helped to foster ecumenism by bringing 'charismatics' within the Roman Catholic Church to the attention of those beyond it. In Britain today, with its multi-faith society, there is a strong emphasis on tolerance at various levels, especially in the religious context, where major distinctions may be apparent between Christianity and other world religions.

This irenic approach to beliefs has brought the Celts into favour, since they are perceived to have been tolerant of pagan customs and beliefs which predated the arrival of Christianity. The tolerance of the 'Celts' is stressed time and again by writers within the new movement. Esther de Waal, in *A World Made Whole* (p.68), writes:

> The perception of the holiness of the earth and the sacredness of matter belonged to the world familiar to them, the world in which the natural and the divine still met. Elsewhere in Europe the Christian Church was fulminating against the natural world, imposing its strictures on the landscape, cutting down sacred trees, despoiling sacred wells, and denying the natural rhythm that depended on the slow turning of the sun and moon and planets. The anti-pagan violence and admonitions of the councils in sixth-century Gaul and Spain, which were nothing less than a conflict between man and nature, had no place in the Celtic approach to God.

This passage, beautifully and movingly written, as are many of the books on 'Celtic Christianity', simplifies greatly the range of attitudes to paganism displayed by the church in early medieval Europe. To ascribe a single monolithic anti-pagan position to 'the Christian Church' while exonerating pagans from environmental degradation is broadly misleading, as Professor Ronald Hutton – not a supporter of Christianity of any kind! – makes clear in his book on *The Pagan Religions of the Ancient British Isles* (pp.252–3). He asks – and answers – the critical question:

> Did the early Christian Church encourage a more destructive attitude to the natural environment? Again, the evidence at first sight seems to support the proposition. Pagans all over Europe venerated certain groves of trees as sacred. The Romans believed that all natural things were associated with spirits which had to be respected, while the Irish Celts believed that every district was under the protection of a goddess, whose custody of the land had to be honoured. Christians, on the other hand, taught that the whole natural world had been given into the dominion of humans, and cut down the old sacred groves. But such a contrast will not stand up to further analysis. The followers of Christ may have felled the groves, but they sanctified many springs in the name of their own faith and they stopped the ritual slaughter of

huge numbers of animals in the course of rituals. More important, the peoples of Europe and the Mediterranean lands have shown the same disposition to destroy or manipulate the natural world since the Stone Age. Comments upon the damage done in the British Mesolithic, Neolithic and Bronze Age have been made ... the Iron Age Celts in what became England may have had their holy stands of trees, but this did not stop them from clearing virtually all the large areas of forest spared by their predecessors, especially in the midlands. Under the pagan Roman Empire, the remaining woods were stripped from much of the North African coast, producing an ecological catastrophe when most of the ploughed-up soil was washed into the Mediterranean. It seems to have been in the same period that the lion was exterminated in Europe, the elephant and the hippopotamus in North Africa and the bear in England. Christianity was absolutely irrelevant to this process.

In early Ireland, the law tracts show that it was necessary to legislate for the protection of trees and woodland, a point which hardly suggests that the natural world in a Celtic Christian society was somehow secure from human rapacity. Fines and penalties for tree-damage were extensive and detailed. Different levels of fine existed for different types of trees. Professor Fergus Kelly (*Early Irish Farming*, pp.387–8) notes that:

> In legal material a distinction is regularly made between trees which are classed as *nemed* 'sacred, privileged', and those which are not. The penalty for damage to a sacred tree (*fidnemed*) is much higher than for an ordinary tree (*fid comaithchesa*). For example, the penalty-fine (*díre*) for an apple-tree classed as *nemed* is given as twenty *séts*, four times greater than for an ordinary apple-tree ... A tree's status may make it a target for enemy attack: the *Annals of Ulster* record how the Ulstermen chopped down sacred trees (*biledha*) at the royal inauguration site of the Cenél nEóghain at Telach Óc in AD 1111.

The evidence thus indicates that sacred trees individually were highly esteemed, but this did not render them inviolate. As Kelly further points out, 'early Irish tradition lays much more stress on single trees than on trees as a group'. It is therefore difficult to claim that Christianity in the Celtic areas somehow gave the natural world greater protection than was the case elsewhere. It is unlikely that environmental protection (in our terms) was of any real significance as a general principle in early Irish society, or indeed in any of the early Celtic societies of the British Isles. Woodland was to be found in abundance, and only the particularly special specimens – special because of their religious function, and not because they were trees as such – were of great value.

The desire to turn 'Celtic Christianity' into a tolerant, nature-protecting, and ultimately pagan-affirming, faith also leads its supporters to underestimate the extent of confrontation between pagans and Christians, as exemplified in the Lives of Patrick and Columba, for example. Tolerance was not always a feature of the Celtic saints, whose capacity to curse to death any recalcitrants or opponents is well attested in the writings of their biographers [...]. Selectivity with the evidence does, nevertheless, present a picture of accommodation and co-operation broadly in tune with the feelings of our own day.

Such accommodation results in a moderation of the traditional evangelical emphasis on 'aggressive' evangelism. This intention was especially evident during the 1990s, which had been designated the Decade of Evangelism by evangelistic Christian bodies. The reviewer of Ian Bradley's book in the *Baptist Times* wrote appreciatively:

> Celtic missionaries lacked nothing in their zeal to win people for Christ, but their evangelism knew little of the aggressive, confrontational stance adopted in some quarters today. Instead they sought to get alongside people and to build on whatever positive good they could find in the culture in which they bore witness.

What is surely most significant here is that the Celts, viewed through the prism of modern society, become the model for action, rather than the New Testament itself. 'Celtic Christianity' has become an anodine substitute for New Testament Christianity.

The theology of 'Celtic Christianity'

Although 'Celtic Christianity' in its alleged social, cultural and ecclesiastical contexts is perceived within an essentially primitivist frame by its advocates, its theology appears to be remarkably up-to-date. When it came to theology, the Celts were apparently very much in advance of their time, since they appear to have anticipated many of the thoughts and theories of the most significant modern theologians of Europe. Their theology somehow leapt centuries ahead of itself, thus defying the stasis which dominated their social setting.

Because of the restricted source-base used by most popular writers, the theological positions which are often said to be representative of popular 'Celtic Christianity' are seldom deduced from detailed analysis of sources in early Irish or Welsh. They are usually derived, in the first instance, from *Carmina Gadelica,* supplemented by observations based on a few well-known Early Irish hymns and other readily accessible material. [...] The *Carmina* act as a form of lens, through which the available bits and pieces of genuine evidence are viewed.

Contemporary theology too is used to unlock the 'Celtic' past. The first of the recent flow of modern Protestant writers were generally theologically liberal, and read their version of 'Celtic Christianity' not only through the lens of the *Carmina,* but also through the lenses supplied by liberal theologians. Thus they endowed the 'Celts' with the views of much more recent (and often modern) theologians and philosophers. [...] [T]he more academic exponents of 'Celtic Christianity' are fond of citing the controversial Roman Catholic philosopher Pierre Teilhard de Chardin (1881–1955) on 'the sacredness of matter', and occasionally they refer to the existentialist theologian Karl Rahner (1904–84), 'probably the most important and influential Roman Catholic theologian of the twentieth century', who argued that it was possible for salvation to be realized 'without knowledge of the historical Christian revelation and, without explicit faith in Christ, by "anonymous Christians"' (*New Dictionary of Theology,* pp.556–7). The insights of Jürgen Moltmann (1926–), a highly respected German Reformed theologian, are quoted with approval in a number of books. Another modern authority of very considerable influence is Thomas Merton (1915–68), a Trappist monk, mystic and devotional writer resident in Kentucky, whose reflections have appealed to Anglicans such as Esther de Waal. Merton's later interests included Zen Buddhism and Eastern spirituality. Quotations from these writers are often a fairly conspicuous part of volumes on 'Celtic Christianity', whereas quotations from authentically Celtic sources (especially those from the period before 1100) are sometimes remarkably few.

The logic of such quotations would suggest that whatever is being offered in such books is unlikely to be distinctively 'Celtic' since it is so readily paralleled among modern theologians who have no connection whatsoever with the Celtic lands. The frames of reference which are used to define 'Celtic Christianity' are largely external to the proper Celtic community of faith; we have already noted similar perspectives in the use of African insights and comparisons [...]. This process no doubt helps to validate 'Celtic Christianity' in a global perspective, but it also raises the suspicion that the 'Celts' are being used to further particular agendas, and even to inject subtle doses of (generally) liberal theology into the popular spiritual mainstream. The silence of the Celts as primitivist icons – more spoken about than speaking – permits writers to ascribe modern theology of this kind to their account. In this way, 'Celtic Christianity', braced by 'evidence' from the world of twentieth-century theology, has a deceptively authoritative validating power similar to that of the 'old Celtic Church' [...].

Unfortunately, there is (so far) no comprehensive scholarly account of the theological understanding of early 'Celtic' Christians, though an expanding range of texts is gradually being made available by scholars. Exponents of 'Celtic Christianity' therefore tend to rely on one another's works, for this as for much else. The evangelical writers have usually arrived at 'Celtic Christianity' by reading the books of more liberal commentators. The latter frequently expound the 'Celtic' approach to conversion, for example, as 'process' rather than 'crisis'; 'Celtic Christians' are thus invoked in order to put a dampener on 'aggressive evangelism'. This is echoed in the writings of evangelicals too, who are currently putting a great deal of emphasis on 'lifestyle evangelism'.

Liberal writers are also more sympathetic to the accommodation of Celtic culture within a Christian perspective, and this lesson is applied to the modern church, which is believed to be much less open to secular culture. Evangelical writers (who belong, on the whole, to the charismatic wing of church life) are similarly anxious to claim 'Celtic Christianity' as a model for conservative Protestant practice. Some, like Ray Simpson, are prepared to challenge the New Age and the creation spirituality of Matthew Fox, but succeed only in producing a more benign form of 'the mixture as before', with some additional spurious ingredients such as the perspectives of Jungian psychology. Others make light of, or completely avoid, those aspects of early medieval Catholic doctrine and practice which are characteristic of real Celtic Christianity. Protestant writers who wish to claim 'Celtic Christianity' as their model make little or no mention of the mass, the practice of penance or the widespread belief in the efficacy of relics. Thus it can be said fairly that, while the exponents of 'Celtic Christianity' often assert its distinctiveness, they also use it as a means of eroding the distinctiveness of existing doctrines within Protestantism and Roman Catholicism. The 'Celtic Fringe' ultimately becomes the theologically misty Middle Ground.

Sin and penance

The modern doctrinal reformulations of 'Celtic Christianity' are well illustrated by the ways in which contemporary authors present key doctrines of the faith, particularly those relating to God and human nature. Selective use of the original material and a failure to read the sources relevant to the period result in major generalisations and ultimately in overall misrepresentation. Thus Philip Newell (*Listening for the Heartbeat of God,* p.59) can speak of 'Celtic spirituality's emphasis on our essential goodness'. In this Newell, basing his views mainly on *Carmina Gadelica*, is at variance with at least one major Irish monk from the late sixth and early seventh century, namely Columbanus, who (as Kathleen Hughes observed in *The Modern Traveller to the Early Irish Church*, p.2) was 'deeply aware of human sin'. In fact, Columbanus went so far as to justify severe asceticism on the grounds that 'it requires great violence to seek by toil and to maintain by exertion what a corrupted nature has not kept.' The fact that the flesh was perceived to be, in the words of Columbanus, 'unclean by nature' was the greatest single reason for the practice of penance by the real Celtic Christians; the urge to clean the flesh led Columbanus to compile what Hughes has described as 'the most brutal of all the Irish penitentials'.

The better-informed writers on 'Celtic Christianity' are usually aware that the curing of sinners by means of penance was of central importance in all the 'Celtic' churches of the early Middle Ages, but, on the whole, the theme is generally seriously underplayed in popular books, and direct quotations from the penitentials are either carefully filtered or conspicuous by their absence. However, the particularly heavy emphasis on penance characteristic of real Christian Celts is one of the few basic practices which unequivocally unite the churches of the Scots, the Irish and the Welsh, and its influence is evident in the contribution which they made to the development of the sacrament of penance throughout Europe. Due partly to the influence of British (Welsh) and Gaelic (including Irish) practices of private penance, involving individual confession before a confessor, known in Irish as *anamchara* ('soul friend'), the earlier practice of public penance, which was a once-in-a-lifetime event and often delayed until shortly before death, was discontinued, and private penance was adopted as the norm throughout Western Christendom by the twelfth century.

The privatisation of penance led to extensive codification, by which lists of sins were compiled and penances prescribed for each. These compilations, which acted as handbooks for the confessors, are known as 'penitentials', the most significant of which, like that of Columbanus, are ascribed to several of the founding fathers of the monastic movement, including Gildas and Finnian. The compilers strove to provide a remedy for every conceivable form of sin. The penitentials define the minutiae of sins, and prescribe penalties accordingly, to an extent that seems unhealthy and even prurient to modern readers. Charles Plummer, an outstanding scholar of medieval Irish Christian literature, and editor of many saints' Lives and other key texts, decried the genre: 'The penitential literature,' he wrote, 'is in truth a deplorable feature of the medieval Church. Evil deeds, the imagination of which may perhaps have dimly floated through our minds in our darkest moments, are here tabulated and reduced to system. It is hard to see how anyone could busy himself with such literature and not be the worse for it' (cited by O Cróinín, *Early Medieval Ireland,* p.198). More recent writers have drawn attention to the concern with sexual deviance which seems to be such a prominent feature of these texts. Professor Dáibhí Ó Cróinín (*ibid.,* p.199) has noted that:

> ... there was apparently no crime that could not be thought of: heterosexual and homosexual relations (male and female), the regulation of 'proper' methods of intercourse, aphrodisiacs and potions, physical relations, bestiality (Columbanus has two canons on the subject, one for clerics or monks, the other for laymen), wet dreams, stimulation, abortion, contraception, abstinence from sexual relations, and an endless litany of reprobate behaviour that ranged from drinking in the same house with a pregnant servant woman to keening or wailing for the dead.

Sexual sin is, however, only a part of the concern of the penitentials. True to biblical teaching, they cover the sins of the heart as well as those of the body. For example, the *Old Irish Penitential* tackles such vices as avarice and envy. With regard to the latter, it states bluntly (Bieler, p.269): 'Anyone in whom is the nature of envy and malice, there is no dwelling for God in his heart, and so there will be no dwelling for him with the God of heaven.' It goes on:

> Anyone who makes mischief against his brother through (love of) talk or drunkenness, let him spend a day in a silent fast. If it be through gossiping that he finds fault, he recites twelve psalms, or receives a hundred blows on his hands.

Whether we like it or not, the basic premise of penance and of penitentials is that humanity is, as Columbanus claimed, 'unclean by nature'. Although the *anamchara* is commonly reduced in popular writing to little more than a spiritual chum, in historical reality the confessor was regarded as the stringent physician of the soul, with a deep concern to cleanse the flesh, and to prepare it for readmission to the spiritual community here on earth, or ultimately to lessen the severity of processes of purification in the afterlife. As we have seen in the case of malicious talk, the specific sin had to be counteracted by means of its opposite; thus gluttony was cured by an appropriate period of fasting, and sexual indulgence by abstinence and bread-and-water diets. Dietary restrictions were supplemented by pilgrimages, floggings, and recitations of the penitential psalms in uncomfortable physical positions. Commutation was possible, whereby the original penalty could be commuted for a less time-consuming mode of atonement.

The compilers of the penitentials were by no means cloistered in their perspectives; their writings are filled with a wider concern for the well-being of society. 'Therefore', says the *Old Irish Penitential*, 'is envy to be shunned beyond everything, because it creates enmity between son and father, and between daughter and mother, and between king and queen, and between kinsmen so that each of them slays the other.' Malefactors guilty of serious crimes such as homicide and kin-slaying required an extensive period of rehabiliation away from normal society, and were sometimes sent to serve their sentences in isolated penitentiaries. Within the monastic *familia* (or family of monasteries) of Columba, for example, certain communities were apparently set aside for rehabilitation of this kind, notably in Tiree and *Hinba* (perhaps to be identified with Oronsay, close to Colonsay). By sending serious offenders to such institutions, monastic leaders in the early British Isles provided what were in effect spiritual, reformative prisons which complemented the punitive regimes of secular society [...].

Nevertheless, indigenous 'Celtic' theology, allegedly exemplified chiefly in the works of Pelagius (*floruit* c. 410) and John Scotus Eriugena (c.810–c.877), is presented by exponents of 'Celtic Christianity' as supposedly sympathetic to the foibles of human nature and the natural world. Such perspectives are commonly contrasted with the views of Augustine of Hippo (354–430). The latter is considered to be hostile to the natural world, stressing the fallenness of humanity, and is held responsible for introducing the concept of original sin, together with the split between spirit and matter allegedly characteristic of Western Christianity. Pelagius, of course, is held in high regard by enthusiasts of 'Celtic Christianity' because he does not adhere to the doctrine of original sin. The penitentials, however, are based firmly on the view that sin is indeed a part of human nature.

Given the drift of modern society, it is readily understandable that some critics will regard the penitentials as a form of voyeurism by monks who, because of monastic rules, were unable to express their natural desires except covertly and in manuscript. Again, one can understand why the prescriptive nature of the penitentials, laying down stiff penalties for 'sin' which is not regarded as such today, should be unpalatable to those who are trying to formulate a type of 'Celtic Christianity' which is compatible with the aspirations of postmodernity. The 'grubby' side of human life conflicts with the desired romantic image of a comfortable 'Celtic' spirituality, designed for people who have lost the concept of sin.

God and judgement

Just as the natural world is generally perceived within modern 'Celtic Christianity' as essentially good, and in harmony with humanity (and vice versa), God is also seen to be close to his creation. Thus it is common to find that exponents of 'Celtic Christianity' emphasise God's 'nearness', rather than his 'apartness'. He is perceived to be all around, a pervasive Presence, involved in people's daily chores, and not aloof, as he supposedly is in modern Western Christianity. The 'Celtic vision' presents a God who is immanent rather than transcendent. Here too, most writers take their cue from the standard interpretation of the prayers found in Carmichael's *Carmina Gadelica*. The evidence of hymns and nature poetry composed before 1100, on the other hand, shows that early Irish Christians invoked *Rí secht nime*, 'the King of seven heavens', and *Airdrí nime*, 'the High-king of heaven' (as in 'Be Thou my Vision', originally composed in Early Middle Irish, and popularised in Eleanor Hull's translation). They assumed no automatic availability of his grace or protection. Their experience of his creation caused them to wonder at his power and his goodness to them.

Again, 'Celtic Christianity' draws attention to God's love rather than his judgement, and downplays the latter. Early Irish believers, in contrast to modern romantic liberals, had a very strong awareness of judgement, damnation and hell, and acknowledge their need of Christ's protection and deliverance (see Murphy, *Early Irish Lyrics*, pp.23–7). These themes, along with the transcendence and power of the Creator, are frequently portrayed in early hymns, including the celebrated seventh-century *Altus Prosator*, attributed to Columba (Clancy and Márkus, *Iona*, p.49). To judge by this hymn, the faith ascribed to Columba was something very different from that of his latter-day 'Celtic' admirers. It gives a particularly graphic description of hell:

> It seems doubtful to no one that there is a hell down below
> where there are held to be darkness, worms and dreadful animals;
> where there is sulphurous fire burning with voracious flames;
> where there is the screaming of men, weeping and gnashing of teeth ...

Such sentiments were not the peculiar property of the poets. They form the essence of some of the 'vision literature' which has come down to us in Latin and early Irish. The description of hell offered in *Fís Adomnáin* ('The Vision of Adomnán') is probably unsurpassed (even in Protestant evangelical preaching and writing) for the wealth of lurid detail with which it describes the fiery fate which befalls different categories of sinners. The text survives in a twelfth-century source, and is retrospectively attributed to the biographer of Columba.

One sample alone will be sufficient to give its flavour (Carey, *King of Mysteries,* p.271):

> There are others with streams of fire in the orifices of their faces, others again with nails driven through their tongues, still others with nails driven into their heads. Those who endure that torment are the folk given to grasping and refusal, lacking charity and the love of God; thieves and perjurors and traitors and slanderers and ravagers and raiders, unjust judges and troublemakers, witches and satirists, relapsed brigands and scholars who teach heresy.

This awesome portrayal of the fate of the damned – a mere prelude to the even more excruciating torments which they will endure after the Day of Judgement – occupies the second half of the 'Vision'. The first half describes heaven, the eternal home of the saints, as 'a fruitful, radiant country'. Entry into heaven and progression through the 'seven heavens' involve testing and cleansing by fire even for the saints themselves, because the soul has previously been 'the companion and neighbour of the flesh with its slumber and luxury and comfort'.

Such, in reality, were the exacting standards of the real Christians of early Ireland, and they go far towards explaining why they were determined to 'mortify' their flesh, as Columbanus sought to do, through penance and the tough prescriptions of penitentials. The self-indulgent 'soft theology' expounded by many advocates of 'Celtic Christianity' bears little relationship to that found in the original Irish or Welsh texts, and it would be unrecognizable, except as a poor caricature, to the Celtic saints. They might well conclude that it had been manufactured by those 'scholars who teach heresy', mentioned by the composer of *Fís Adomnáin.*

Dreams and visions

The bulk of this chapter has been devoted to modern writers' perceptions of the relationship between 'Celtic Christians' and the world around them, both the natural world and that of the church. Writers on 'Celtic Christianity' do not regard the 'Celts' as deep or profound thinkers in theological matters; rather, they are seen to be 'simple' folk, possessed of mystical, dreamy characteristics which modern authors consider to be distinctive of the psyche of the 'Celts'. Racial stereotyping of this kind, deriving from nineteenth-century perspectives [...], is particularly evident in Ian Bradley's *Celtic Way*. 'As we begin to discard some of the excessive rationalism of Western

Christianity,' he writes (p.92), 'we can perhaps begin to appreciate too that other great feature of the Celtic Christian imagination, its tendency to dream dreams and see visions, experience premonitions and feel hidden presences.' Bradley (p.93) believes that in explaining the Celts' alleged propensity towards 'sightings of angels and visions and of the world to come ... perhaps the most important factor was the Celtic temperament, dreamy and other-worldly, given to possessing second sight and experiencing premonitions and omens. This marked feature of the pagan Celtic outlook was, like so much else, baptised and incorporated into Celtic Christianity. Where pagan Celts had seen fairies and felt premonitions of impending doom, their Christian descendants saw angels and had visions of the Last Judgement.'

Within contemporary 'Celtic Christianity', the supposedly visionary dimension of the Celts has a particular allure for modern charismatic Christians, who lay emphasis on dreams, visions, and 'signs and wonders'. As Andy and Jane Fitz-Gibbon amply demonstrate by their book, *Prophetic Lifestyle and the Celtic Way,* some charismatic enthusiasts believe innocently that, in giving a place to dreams, they are following the distinctive example of 'Celtic Christians'.

Even if we were to allow that the Celts had a propensity to visionary experiences, this would not make them distinctive within the early medieval world. Visions of various kinds were fairly common within a wide range of cultures; the most far-reaching vision of all was that of the Roman Emperor, Constantine, who saw a vision of the cross in the sky prior to the battle of the Milvian Bridge in 312. His subsequent victory was an important turning-point towards the eventual supremacy of the Christian faith in Europe in the following centuries. The Christian faith in Anglo-Saxon England also ascribed importance to dreams and visions, as Bede's *Historia Ecclesiastica* amply indicates.

Critical issues

Modern 'Celtic Christianity' thrives on reinventing the romantic, 'Renanesque' constructs of the 'Celts' that were produced in the nineteenth century. In the present day these are presented in contrast to the tenets of 'conventional' Christianity, usually by reducing the latter to simple negative propositions, and ascribing correspondingly positive – and simplistic – positions to 'Celtic Christianity'. Generalisations and assumptions abound, and wishful thinking reaches its zenith. Despite the denials of several writers, a second Celtic Twilight glows attractively in many of the concepts at the heart of the movement, glossing over the less appealing features of the real faith of Christians in these islands in the early Middle Ages. As a result of further make-overs and manipulations, 'Celtic Christianity' functions largely as an up-to-date 'designer spirituality' which has been constructed to meet a range of contemporary needs. Because the Celts are perceived to be so 'far out', so utterly dead in historical terms, they can be treated with impunity as a *tabula rasa* on which to inscribe consoling responses to contemporary concerns. Somewhat paradoxically, the creators of 'Celtic Christianity' have thus disguised any possible distinctiveness in the 'Celtic' expression of the Christian faith under a cover of contemporary theory and creativity. The 'primitive' context is intended merely to carry and to affirm the modernist message, which, for the most part, has nothing whatsoever to do with the historical Christianity of the Celtic areas.

The distinctiveness of 'Celtic Christianity' is a key question worthy of further study. Was 'Celtic Christianity' really different from other forms of Christianity in the period before 1100? Is it correct to draw a firm line between 'Roman Christianity' and 'Celtic Christianity'? We have already noted that Christians in the Celtic areas of the British Isles were not out of step with Rome on major doctrines. The main differences were over the timing of the celebration of Easter and the form of the tonsure. Christianity in the British Isles was contextualised in terms of Celtic societies, but that does not mean that its fundamental beliefs and doctrines were different from those of the rest of Europe.

A further critical question relates to the alleged continuity of 'Celtic Christianity' into the present century, if not down to the present day. Does 'Celtic Christianity' still exist? [...] At the heart of the 'historical' perspective, as popularly construed, however, there lies the 'Celtic Church'. This acts as a powerful symbol of 'Celtic' spiritual cohesion and supposed continuity across the centuries, offering a bridge from the historical to the contemporary [...].

Select bibliography

Bebbington, David, *Evangelicalism in Modern Britain: A History from the 1730s to the 1980s* (Unwyn Hyman, London 1989).

Bieler, Ludwig, *The Patrician Texts in the Book of Armagh* (Dublin 1979).

Bradley, Ian, *The Celtic Way* (DLT, London 1993).

Carey, John (ed.) *King of Mysteries: Early Irish Religious Writings* (Four Courts, Dublin 1998).

Carmichael, Alexander, *et al.* (eds), *Carmina Gadelica*, 6 vols (Oliver and Boyd *et al.*, Edinburgh 1900–71).

Clancy, Thomas Owen, and Márkus, Gilbert (eds), *Iona: The Earliest Poetry of a Celtic Monastery* (Edinburgh University Press, Edinburgh 1995).

de Waal, Esther, *A World Made Whole: Rediscovering the Celtic Tradition* (Fount, London 1991).

Dumville, David N., *Councils and Synods of the Gaelic Early and Middle Ages* (Department of Anglo-Saxon, Norse and Celtic, Cambridge 1997).

Ferguson, Sinclair B., and Wright, David F. (eds), *New Dictionary of Theology* (Inter-varsity Press, Leicester 1988).

Fitz-Gibbon, Andy and Jane, *Prophetic Lifestyle and the Celtic Way* (Monarch, London 1997).

Ford, Patrick K., 'Blackbirds, Cuckoos and Infixed Pronouns: Another Context for Early Irish Nature Poetry', in Ronald Black, William Gillies, and Roibeard Ó Maolalaigh (eds), *Celtic Connections: Proceedings of the Tenth International Congress of Celtic Studies*, Vol. 1 (Tuckwell Press, East Linton 1999), pp.162–70.

Hughes, Kathleen, and Hamlin, Ann, *The Modern Traveller to the Early Irish Church* (SPCK, London 1977; Four Courts, Dublin 1997).

Hull, Eleanor (ed.), *The Poem-Book of the Gael* (Chatto and Windus, London 1912).

Hutton, Ronald, *The Pagan Religions of the Ancient British Isles: Their Nature and Legacy* (Blackwell, Oxford 1991).

Hyde, Douglas, *The Story of Early Gaelic Literature* (Fisher Unwin, London 1895).

Kelly, Fergus, *Early Irish Farming* (Dublin Institute for Advanced Studies, Dublin 1998).

Meyer, Kuno, *Selections from Ancient Irish Poetry* (Constable, London 1911).

Newell, Philip, *Listening for the Heartbeat of God* (SPCK, London 1997).

Ó Cróinín, Dáibhí, *Early Medieval Ireland 400–1200* (Longman, London 1995).

Renan, Ernest, *Poetry of the Celtic Races and other Essays*, transl. William G. Hutchison (Walter Scott Publishing Co., London [1896]).

Wanting to be Indian: when spiritual searching turns into cultural theft*

MYKE JOHNSONT†

Note

Many people are searching for a deeper spiritual engagement with the world, and feel a hunger unmet by the teachings and services of traditional religious institutions. Some have begun to take an interest in Native American spiritual practices, and one can easily find workshops and lectures offering Indian rituals and ceremonies to non-Indian people. However, many Native people, including highly respected religious elders, have condemned such 'borrowing'. They identify it as a form of cultural exploitation, gravely detrimental to the survival and well-being of Indigenous people.

In this paper, I will be discussing the ethical questions raised by White peoples' exploration of the religious ceremonies and beliefs of American Indians. What is at work here which makes sincere spiritual searching an act of cultural theft? Why are Native peoples endangered by this interest in their beliefs and rituals? How can we respect the cultural integrity of Indian people, and yet also honor deep-felt spiritual desires?

[...]

---

* This essay was published by Respect Inc., Brewster MA., 1995, web site http://www.dickshovel.com/respect.html

† I dedicate this paper to my German-American paternal grandmother, born Mary Lucille Heisler, who died March 9, 1995, at the age of 98.

My own background

First, I want to introduce myself in relation to this issue. I am a White woman related by matrilineal ancestry to the Innu people, called by the French 'Montagnais', who are indigenous to the land which is now called Quebec and Labrador. I grew up in White U.S. Christian culture, with fair skin and red hair, and only a reminder that we were 'part-Indian' to link me to any other culture. To be White is to fit into the norm in ways that give one certain advantages denied to those who are not White. And yet the influence of my Innu great great great grandmother also shaped my consciousness in a certain way. It was a window in the wall of my white identity which drew me to explore and eventually make a commitment to Native struggles.

This consciousness made it more complex and confusing to speak about this issue, even as it formed the heart of my commitment and responsibility to it. Even grammatically, I questioned how to use 'we' and 'they' when I might be included in both, but not quite contained in either category. I had heard many Indian people speak out about these issues. I decided that it was most useful for me to speak as a White woman, to raise the issues in the context of the feminist spirituality movement of which I am a part, that we might be true to our commitment to the survival and liberation of all people. Furthermore, while for me there is an element of seeking my own Native heritage, the current phenomenon of outside interest in Native spirituality is a phenomenon of White culture, and this White phenomenon affects all of us who find ourselves interested in Native Americans. It has been important for my search to get inside this White thing about Indians, to explore and understand how it works in White people, of which I am a part, so that I can also understand how it affects those of us with some Native ancestry.

Since childhood, I have been a spiritual person. As I was becoming an adult, the values of the gospel led me into political activism on behalf of justice and liberation. This path of justice activism led me to understanding the oppression of women, and of myself as a woman. One of the places where women experience oppression is in the area of spirituality and religion. So feminism instigated for me a spiritual search and a transformation, and with many other women I began to seek and create what we called women's spirituality. This is when I also began to be interested in Native American spirituality.

The stereotype Indian and Native American spirituality

There is a phenomenon in White culture which affects any interaction between White people and Native Americans. White culture has created an image and called it 'Indian'. But this image is a stereotype, and not really informative or accurate about real Native Americans, who are of many diverse cultures. All of us could give details about this stereotype 'Indian'. An important aspect of this stereotype 'Indian' is that it has two sides, like the two sides of a coin.

One side of the stereotype Indian is the Hostile Savage – the dangerous, primitive warrior who attacked the settlers of the West, or the irresponsible reservation drunk who couldn't be trusted, the Indian of which it was said, 'the only good Indian is a dead Indian'. The other side of the stereotype Indian is the Noble Savage – the innocent primitive who was naturally spiritual and lived in idyllic harmony close to the earth, the Indian of the Thanksgiving stories who helped the Pilgrims survive. These images are embedded deeply in our culture, and are a subliminal backdrop to any of our interactions with Native people or concepts.

When we hear about Indians sharing spiritual wisdom with White people, they call to mind this second stereotype, the friendly noble Indian. When we hear the anger of Indians, it is easy for the first stereotype Indian to re-emerge, the hostile savage. We might feel angry or defensive or fearful.

It is important to realize that these images are really fantasies – projections of fears and dreams of White people onto those perceived as 'other'. While the second image, the noble spiritual wise Indian, might seem to be an improvement on the first, it is actually also harmful to Native people. So for any of us with some desire to learn more about Native people, the first layer we encounter is this layer of distortion, like a mask which obscures the voices and experiences of actual Native peoples.

What is called 'Native American spirituality' in various New Age movement settings is actually a part of this distorted image. So-called 'Native American spirituality' draws on the 'Noble Savage' stereotype, mixed with elements of symbol and ritual from various actual Native religious practices. What interests us about these Indians might be the way they are portrayed as having a spiritual world view, while mainstream culture seems increasingly secular. We might be looking for an emphasis on female deities and positive roles for women, or a focus on the earth, grounded in the interconnectedness of all beings. Men have seen the Indian as an image of manhood to be reclaimed.

These can all be important visions, and contain elements of truth. But the mask is still a mask. Andrea Smith, Cherokee activist and member of Women of All Red Nations, points out, 'The "Indian ways" that these white, new-age "feminists" are practicing have very little basis in reality ... these new agers do not understand Indian people or our struggles for survival and thus can have no genuine understanding of Indian spiritual practices'. (Andrea Smith, 'The New Age Movement and Native Spirituality,' in *Indigenous Woman*, Vol.I, No.1, Spring 1991, p.18.)

Resistance, colonialism and structural racism

Of course, I didn't know any of this right away. I mentioned that spirituality had led me into political activism. As part of my journey, I was also drawn into political activity with Native people. It was in this context that I began to learn about the lives and issues faced by actual Native Americans. I learned about the continued theft of the land and displacement of its inhabitants. I learned about forced acculturation through forbidding people to practice their religions, sending their children to boarding schools, and forbidding them to speak their languages. I learned about the mining of coal and uranium on reservations with disregard for the consequences on the lives of the communities there. And on and on.

I also learned about the reclamation of Indian pride and identity and the history of resistance to genocide. I learned about current resistance: A.I.M. and Alcatraz and the Wounded Knee occupation. I learned about people like Anna Mae Pictou Aquash and Leonard Peltier. Eventually, I met the Innu people of my own heritage, who have been currently engaged in a battle against the destruction of their land and way of life as they try to stop the building of a huge hydroelectric project, the Saint Marguerite 3 dam. These real people and real struggles began to cut through the stereotypes fostered by our culture, and help me to understand about Native American realities today.

In this way I began to see the vast differences between what was being promoted as 'Native American spirituality' and what was actually true for Native peoples' lives. These differences are not something that can be corrected with more accurate recordings of ceremonies or better teachers. Rather, they are about context and underlying values. They are about power and a history of colonialism.

It is important to look at the bigger context for these questions. We get used to thinking of ethics as an individual matter, where good intentions are uppermost, and right or wrong is something we each of us choose. These are important, but there is another way of thinking about ethics which I find helpful here. That is social ethics – looking at the structures of society and their impact on people. The context here is structural racism.

Structural racism is a system of oppression in which the structures of society are operated and controlled by White people. Racism combines prejudice against people of color with political, economic, and social power over their lives. Racism is in the air we breathe. It is not so much about individual guilt or innocence, as it is an atmosphere of injustice with which we all have to reckon in some way.

We live in a colonialist society. It was built upon the European theft of land. It was built by conquering and destroying the nations of people already here, and it continues its assault on Native lands and culture. This isn't something we chose, but something we inherited, and thus have to reckon with.

It is in this context that Native Americans identify the use of Native symbols and ceremonies as cultural appropriation. Cultural appropriation is a form of racism. Cultural appropriation is a weapon in the process of colonization. Cultural appropriation is when a dominating or colonizing people take over the cultural and religious ceremonies and articles of a people experiencing domination or colonization. When Euro-Americans take Native American symbols and ceremonies and use them for our own purposes, we are participating in the process of colonization and the destruction of Native culture.

Janet McCloud, Tulalip elder and fishing rights activist, tells us, 'First they came to take our land and water, then our fish and game ... Now they want our religions as well. All of a sudden, we have a lot of unscrupulous idiots running around saying they're medicine people. And they'll sell you a sweat lodge ceremony for fifty bucks. It's not only wrong, its obscene. Indians don't sell their spirituality to anybody, for any price. This is just another in a very long series of thefts from Indian people and, in some ways, this is the worst one yet.' (From 'Spiritual Hucksterism: The Rise of the Plastic Medicine Men', in Ward Churchill, *Fantasies of the Master Race: Literature, Cinema and the Colonization of American Indians*, (Monroe, ME: Common Courage Press, 1992) p.217. Originally published in *Z Magazine*, Dec. 1990.) Cultural appropriation is a theft from a people, and also a distortion, a lie spread about a people. It is an assault on the cultural integrity of Native people, and ultimately threatens even the survival of Native people.

Three traps that non-Indians fall into

When we live in the history of this theft and domination, how do we get to a place of positive connection or cultural sharing? Unfortunately, sincerity is not enough. There are three different traps we can fall into as we attempt to reckon with Native American people.

Denial

The first trap is denial. European settlers on this continent had a view of a divinely ordained progress: it was their destiny to take over Native lands. This view is currently maintained through the premise that Native Americans benefit by being assimilated into White culture. For people who are enjoying the privileges of White society, there can be a strong tendency toward this belief. But for Native people, the view is different. They can see the wounds and scars of oppression every day.

Denial also creates the myth that Native people don't exist anymore. They are often referred to as the dying race. If Indians are seen as only part of the past, White people can justify moving on, living only in the now. We can justify taking or using artefacts from Native culture as a way of preserving them. When Native people break the silence about injustices, or even assert their existence, they cut through the cultural denial. And the response of the officials has often been increasingly destructive silencing.

Cultural denial has similarities to the process of denial in individuals. When someone is an abuser, and hurts a victim, there is a psychological propensity to scapegoat the victim, and to deny one's own culpability. There is a belief that if the victim can be destroyed, the guilt can be destroyed.

Even if justice-minded people don't get caught in this trap of blatant denial, there are two other traps which are more subtle. These traps can obscure situations of cultural exploitation and make them appear honorable.

Wanting to be Indian

One of these traps I refer to as 'wanting to be Indian'. In fact, American Indians have a name for people in this trap, the Wannabe Indians. This trap is an identification with the Indians, most likely out of our own distress or oppression, our disenfranchised desire. Indians become the 'utopic other' holding the dreams we wish were true, whatever they may be. And here the romantic stereotypes take over. So for example, we might say, 'In tribal cultures ... women were held in respect'. 'In tribal cultures ... everything was shared communally.' 'In tribal cultures ... people lived in harmony with the earth.' And so on, filling in the blanks. We desire that utopia, want to be those romanticized Indians.

Guilt seeking redemption

The other similar trap I call 'guilt seeking redemption'. In this trap, we are aware of and acknowledge what White culture has done and reject that, but get stuck in the feeling of guilt. We desire release from the guilt of association with White culture. And so we seek out Indians to say we're okay, to offer forgiveness, and welcome us, adopt [us] into their own better ways.

We can see an example of this trap in current movies about Indians. Movies went from those portraying Indians as the bad guys who threatened the survival of the White heroes, to a movie like 'Dances with Wolves', where the White hero is the exception to the destructiveness of White culture, and is adopted by the Indians. This trap explains the appeal of an Indian like Sun Bear who taught spirituality to White people, and started a non-Indian entity called the Bear Tribe. He was considered a sell-out by many traditional Native people. However, many White people felt welcomed and assumed a new identity as 'tribal' members of a so-called Rainbow Tribe.

So what's the problem

What are the problems with these three traps?

First of all, this redemption we find is really a cheap grace. It makes us feel better but doesn't transform the situation of Native peoples. The injustices keep happening.

Secondly, by denying the spiritual and political autonomy of Indian people, the New Age 'rainbow' people subvert whatever good intentions they may have about multi-cultural community. What gets created is multi-cultural white middle class dominance in yet another form.

Thirdly, these options perpetuate the fantasy image of the Indian, and distort the real picture. They prevent us from seeing the real lives of Native people. They obscure and drown out their voices and expression of self.

Pam Colorado, Oneida activist, says, 'The process is ultimately intended to supplant Indians, even in areas of their own customs and spirituality. In the end, non-Indians will have complete power to define what is and is not Indian, even for Indians. We are talking here about an absolute ideological/conceptual subordination of Indian people in addition to the total physical subordination they already experience. When this happens, the last vestiges of real Indian society and Indian rights will disappear. Non-Indians will then "own" our heritage and ideas as thoroughly as they now claim to own our land and resources'. (Pam Colorado, quoted in Wendy Rose, 'The Great Pretenders: Further Reflections on Whiteshamanism', in M. Annette Jaimes, *The State of Native America: Genocide, Colonization, and Resistance*, (Boston: South End Press, 1992), p.405. Original quote in Ward Churchill, 'A Little Matter of Genocide: Native American Spirituality and New Age Hucksterism,' *Bloomsbury Review*, Vol. 8 No.5, Sept/Oct 1988, pp.23–4. Her tribal affiliation was mentioned in *Indigenous Woman* magazine.)

Examples of cultural appropriation

The mother goddess of Europe

Let me present another example to help distinguish cultural appropriation from appropriate cultural sharing. This example is from European history and may speak to White women interested in feminist criticism of male-dominated spiritualities. Cultural appropriation is one of the ancient tools of domination and colonization. It has been going on throughout history, whenever one culture has attempted to conquer another. Battles are not fought only by the force of arms, but also by images and ideas. Any context of domination will include such cultural imperialism.

Many feminist scholars have pointed to evidence suggesting that there were early female images of divinity throughout 'pre-historic' Europe. According to some scholars, the Catholic church took the image of the great mother goddess, and incorporated it as the virgin Mary, Mother of God. It used her early sacred sites for building its shrines to Mary. The church absorbed many such pagan symbols, yet distorted and transformed their meaning and their impact on the lives of the people.

The shift of context, control, and usage created important shifts of meaning and power. The conquerors took what had been an image of empowerment and valuing of women and turned it into an image promoting female acquiescence to male pre-eminence. They were able then to redefine female goodness as obedience, humility, and renunciation of sexual energy. To capture and transform the image of goddess in this way served to further solidify the subjugation of women and undermine ideas fostering resistance.

The vision quest of the Lakota

How is this similar to the cultural appropriation of Native images and practices by the New Age movement? I will use the example of one practice, the 'vision quest,' a ritual found in Lakota culture (with variations in many other Native nations), which is now offered for a price in many New Age contexts. In traditional Lakota culture, the vision quest was a time of fasting and prayer in the mountains, and fit into the unfolding of a person's role within their community. The elders of the community sent the individual forth with prayers, and received them back offering interpretation of their visions and guidance for living out their implications. The context was a belief that the person's individual life and calling was a gift for the whole group, and their connection to the spirit world would bring them into deeper connection with the community, bringing life to the community. Each existed in balance with the other. (One account of the vision quest is given in Black Elk, *The Sacred Pipe*, (New York: Penguin Books, 1971), pp.44–66.)

When this ritual is brought into a New Age context, its meaning and power are altered. The focus shifts to White people's needs and visions, which in most New Age venues are about individual growth and prosperity. There is no accountability to a community, particularly any Native community. Rather, White people get to experience their own distorted idea of being spiritual and 'Indian,' without any sense of the responsibility which is fundamental to Native religion.

The form and structure of the ritual itself have been changed. For example, the giving and receiving of the Native way are transformed into buying and selling, a sacrilege in Native contexts. The use of images of wild animals and plants by urban White vision-questers trivializes the wholeness of the intimate relationship of a community to a specific region of land, and the inhabitants therein who provide food, clothing, inspiration and survival.

There is no harm in White people's retreating into solitary places for spiritual insight and growth. This has been a part of most religious traditions. So the popularity of calling such a retreat a 'vision quest' comes from the commodification [...] of Native Americans as the latest consumer fad. By turning Indians into commodities, they are incorporated into capitalism's way of perceiving and valuing reality. Their own perceptions and values are thus undermined. What is called 'Indian spirituality' has actually become a distortion. These words then cannot be relied on, they have been warped to fit another agenda. By this, the attempt to hold onto authentic Indian spiritualities has been rendered more difficult.

What are some of the effects of this warped agenda on Native people? The actual realities of Native communities are erased. Native communities have been under assault for 500 years, and are facing issues of dislocation, continued theft of land, poverty, unemployment, addiction, suicide, and despair. In Native communities, the recovery of traditional practices such as the vision quest helps build identity and community pride, helps empower Native communities for life struggles against a racist mainstream. If these ceremonies are diluted by misuse in White America, the communities are weakened in their struggles for survival.

What can white people do?

So to summarize, White people finding themselves interested in Native Americans first have to deal with the stereotype image Indian, a projection of White fears and hopes which is an undercurrent to any understanding we seek. We have to reckon with an inheritance of White colonialism and a context of structural racism. In such a context sincere spiritual searchers face three traps which can short circuit ethical right relations between White people and Native people: denial, wanting to be Indian, and guilt seeking redemption. But what can we do? I believe there is a response which offers an ethic we can stand on. It has two parts: become an ally and do our own spiritual work.

Become an ally

The first part is to become an ally. If you are familiar with the twelve step programs you may have heard of 'making amends'. This means that it is important to take stock of one's past and take responsibility for righting the wrongs that one can. I believe this can also function on a cultural level. To take responsibility on a cultural level would be to identify one's cultural location and the realities of colonialism and structural racism. To take responsibility includes acknowledging the problem as bigger than individual guilt or innocence. In other words, we didn't individually cause this injustice, so we don't need to get stuck in individual guilt or shame. Rather, our responsibility is to work against racism, to be an ally to those who are oppressed.

It is important to point out that Indian people are not saying, 'Don't learn about Indian culture or religion'. Rather the appeal is that White people learn more deeply and accurately about Indian cultures and in a context which does not foster their destruction. Oren Lyons, a traditional chief of the Onondaga Nation says, 'We've got real problems today, tremendous problems which threaten the survival of the planet. Indians and non-Indians must confront these problems together, and this means we must have honest dialogue, but this dialogue is impossible so long as non-Indians remain deluded about things as basic as Indian spirituality'. (Churchill, *Fantasies of the Master Race*, pp.216–7.)

Since there are so many distortions, information is important. We can educate ourselves and our children and friends about the issues and struggles facing Native peoples today. Help can be given beginning in forms as simple and concrete as money, or appealing to our congressional leaders to support Native religious freedom issues and land claims.

There are many community-rooted Indian writers, artists, scholars, and cultural workers we can support, for example, by buying their books instead of the New Age impostor books. (For those who would like to learn more about the experience of Indian people and support Native women writers, I would recommend the books of the following Native writers, as a start: Paula Gunn Allen, Betty Louise Bell, Beth Brant, Maria Campbell, Chrystos, Louise Erdrich, Janice Gould, Janet Campbell Hale, Joy Harjo, Linda Hogan, M. Annette Jaimes, Lee Maracle, Leslie Marmon Silko, Anna Lee Walters.)

> '... for those of you who want to know what Aboriginal people are like, let us tell you. Participate in our writings, feel our visual art, move with our music, hear in your heart our stories.'
> (Joy Asham Fedorick, 'Fencepost Sitting and How I Fell Off to One Side', in *Give Back: First Nations Perspectives on Cultural Practice*, (North Vancouver, BC, Canada), Gallerie: Women Artists' Monographs, Issue 11, 1992, p.42.)

Native people need allies. White people have a choice. We can pretend there is no problem. We can get stuck in grief or guilt about what has happened. Or we can use our privilege as White people as a resource for Native peoples' needs and concerns. Audre Lorde, an African American poet and justice worker said, 'Use what power you have to work for what you believe in'. (Paraphrase from a lecture.) The process of learning and responding will in itself be a life-long spiritual journey.

Cultural sharing involves interaction with the whole of a person and community, reciprocal giving and receiving, sharing of struggle as well as joy, receiving what the community wants to give, not what we want to take. Cultural sharing begins in respect, with patience not to make assumptions but to risk stepping outside of our own frame of reference. On a fundamental level, cultural sharing will not be possible until we end racism. In the meantime, only when we wholeheartedly join the struggle to end racism, and all oppression, can we begin to experience cultural sharing.

Do your own spiritual work

The second part of what we can do is to do our own spiritual work. When we put Indians into the stereotype of spiritual gurus, or 'utopic other', we use them like spiritual surrogates. When we use someone as a surrogate, we occupy them in a way which prevents them from bearing their own children. Native spiritualities have a purpose in the communities in which they originate. They are fundamental for the Native cultural struggle against genocide. They are not empty symbols into which we can put our struggles, use them, for example, for the empowerment of women, or an affirmation of male bonding. (Joanna Kadi describes how cultural appropriation treats objects as 'ahistorical and culturally empty'. See 'Whose Culture Is It Anyway?', *Sojourner*, Vol.18, No.2, October 1992, pp.5–6.)

Since we have projected an image onto the Indian, one part of doing our own spiritual work is to bring back that image into ourselves. We can use the 'Indian' stereotype which we have created to learn about our selves. What do we see there? Can it teach us what we are hungry for? What do we long for? If we recognize it as a projection, we can use the stereotype 'Indian' to help us do our own spiritual work.

The image 'Indian' holds for us the idea of mysticism and spirituality. We live in a society which seems to give us a choice between secularism or a rigidly-defined male God. Part of what feeds cultural appropriation is a deep spiritual hunger in White people. This sense of starvation is very real, but we must realize: Native people are not keeping us from spirit. White culture has broken and disrupted its own spiritual heritage. If we believe there is such a thing as spirit, we can recreate a path to it, we can hope that it will help us in that process. I believe our desire itself, our desire for spirit, is a powerful magic which can open the doorway for us.

In popular consciousness, the 'Indian' is seen as linked to the earth and other species. We are hungry for this connection. But, in reality, we all live here on this earth, our lives equally enmeshed with the fate of countless other beings around us. These beings can teach us if we are quiet with them. Connect directly with the source. We can pay attention as we walk in the woods, or on a city block. We need to trust that we can begin where we are, who we are, in our own lives. What are the animals and plants we rely on? What feeds us? How can we honor that gift? How can we give back?

When we fantasize Indian religion, we might imagine a community of greater belonging and interconnection. We need to explore the links of spirit to community, ask ourselves, Who is my community? How do we negotiate the world together? Where do we find our power? What breaks us apart? What gives us meaning? What is our relationship to the world around us?

We also see in so-called Indian spirituality a link to ancestors, to tradition. We are hungry for this link to ancestors. Native people have encouraged us to explore the earth-centered traditions of our own ancestors. Some might object that those traditions are too hard to find, too far away. Yet often there are remnants so close we don't notice them. For example, the celebration of Christmas contains countless elements from the ancient ceremonies of the Yule, the Winter Solstice: lights in the night, evergreen trees, gift-giving, reindeers pulling sleighs through the sky, a grandfather of generosity who comes from the north, who comes into the house through the hearth chimney, carols, elves, the four candled circle of the advent wreath, the special ham dinner ... all of these were once imbued with sacred meanings and powers – perhaps to be reclaimed.

I think it is also important for White women to acknowledge the fears and risks involved in exploring a woman-valuing Euro-descent spirituality. European Christian history includes the destruction of the earth-centered religions and the women who held roles of wisdom and spiritual power. Perhaps millions of women accused of being witches were burned and tortured. We carry in our collective European psyche the memory of this gynocide (sic). While the fantasy image of the 'Indian' has been romanticized and spiritualized, the fantasy image of the 'witch' is as sinister and belittling as ever, despite the occasional 'good witch of the North'.

When I face my spiritual ancestry as a European descent woman, I face this loss, this tremendous assault on female power and value, perpetrated upon us by my own people. To embrace woman-valuing spirituality that is Euro-based implies a rebellion against the dominant 'spirit-world' of Euro-Christianity. For White women, we must ask ourselves how the word 'witch' is used against us, and whether we might reclaim the word, to bring this rebellious aspect of our search into the open. There is a risk in this and tremendous power.

If we jump into a quick fix 'Indian spirituality' we end up neglecting the real and serious spiritual questions in our own lives, in our own communities. By turning away from using others as surrogates, we are able to do our own spiritual and communal work, bear our own spiritual 'children'. For some that may mean going back to the distress which sent us searching in the first place, to see what's going on in a deeper way. We need to acknowledge our own oppression, so that we are able to fight our own political and spiritual battles. We need to find or create our own ceremonies for our struggles. This too can be a life-long journey. And why not? To take our own spiritual path seriously is to honor our place in the universe and the importance of our lives.

Are there any times when non-Indians may take part in native rituals?

At this point, some might still ask the question, are there any times when it might be appropriate for non-Indians to take part in Native rituals and ceremonies? The answer is complex, since it involves cutting through the stereotypes and understanding certain dimensions of Native religions, differences which are often overlooked.

'Indian religions are community based, not proselytizing religions.' (Andrea Smith, 'For All Those Who Were Indian in a Former Life', *Sojourner*, Vol.16, No.3, Nov. 1990, p.8.) They tie together the heart and life of a specific group of people. In contrast, many of us are more familiar with religions like Christianity or Islam, which have an evangelizing impulse which encourages the conversion of others to their way of belief. (Jewish White women are an exception here since Judaism, like Indian religions, is a community based religion.)

Indian religions are not something one can convert to, as one might to Christianity, by adopting a set of beliefs or principles. Indian religions are built upon systems of relationships.

So, if one is entering into relationship with Indian people, participating in an Indian community's life and struggles, often one will be included in various elements of ritual or spiritual life. For example, when White people have joined in activities protesting the building of the hydrodam on Innu land, they participated with Innu people in ceremonies and prayers which were part of the struggle. White people have also become a part of Indian community through marriage or friendship.

This is not the same as White people adopting Indian spiritual practices; rather it reflects the power of the community to adopt, to make relationship with a person. Paula Gunn Allen, Laguna Pueblo author and teacher, sums it up by saying, 'You cannot do Indian spirituality without an Indian community ... it's physical and social and spiritual and they're fused together'. (Jane Caputi, 'Interview with Paula Gunn Allen,' *Trivia* 16/17, Fall 1990, p.50.) It is our link with Native people as allies and friends which creates a spiritual relationship, rather than a spiritual rip-off.

Summary and further questions

If there are two things I could impress upon your hearts, I hope you will take these with you: the choice to become allies and the choice to do our own spiritual work. I hope that you might honor the desire in your hearts, the interest in things Indian, and use it to really learn about Native lives and struggles. Use it to cut through the stereotypes, find out the deeper realities, and then to use the power you have to act in solidarity with Native people. I also hope that you might trust in our ability to do our own spiritual work, trust that we can find a way to do it with each other. I ask you to believe with me that the spirit is here in our midst.

For those who have begun this journey, I would also like to offer some further questions and reflections which have emerged on this path of creating anti-racist woman-valuing earth-centered spiritu-alities. For this paper, I can merely give voice to some of the issues which are raised, in the hope of sparking further discussion.

The earth

What does it mean for an earth-centered spirituality, that the particular land on which we live is stolen land? What about the grief of the land for her original people? Are there ways to be welcomed here? This is the land of our birth, perhaps for many generations. I believe we do belong on the earth, she is the mother of us all. But how do we live here with honor? Is it the responsibility of all of us who love this land to restore her original people?

It seems to me that the land in all her specificity – this stream, that mountain, that group of trees – not only has been stolen. She has also been kidnapped from a people who regarded land as unownable and possessed of consciousness which demanded respect, and enslaved into the hands of a people who has reduced her from 'person' to 'property.' How can the earth be our goddess when we have made her our property? The very idea of ownership of land goes against the ethic of an earth-based spirituality. It seems to me that there are parallels here with White society's capacity to sustain the ownership of people as slaves. When we live in a culture which takes for granted the ownership of land, what is our power as individuals to alter that? In this country even having access to land can be a privilege of comparative wealth. Do we have any power to free land from ownership?

What does it mean that we live in a culture which is polluting and destroying the land? Concrete, buildings, chemicals, pesticides, monocrop agriculture and many other aspects of our culture upset the balance of nature. Our food comes from far away, and through an industrialized process [that] makes use of other animals and plants. What is our responsibility to the earth's environment?

Spirits and implications

There may be non-Indian persons who feel they have been visited by Native spirits. What if the power is really there? One of the reasons the traditional elders withhold access is because of the dangers of certain powers if they are not in a proper balance. So if we really believe the powers exist, it seems that one step is to acknowledge the depth of it, not play games with it. What are the consequences and responsibilities we have if we have become implicated in these powers? What do you do if the spirits have claimed you?

What about those who have participated in some way in Native rituals? What are the implications of that? One of the principles of many Native traditions is the belief that knowledge equals responsibility. So some of the dangers of these rituals are the ways in which we are implicated by them. How have we taken on commitments and responsibilities which we might not even be aware of? I think of the old movies where the explorer takes a bowl of soup from the pretty Native maiden and discovers in the ensuing hours that he has married her without knowing it. What have we committed ourselves to unawares, and what should we do about it now? Also, what about those who have participated in distorted or muddled ceremonies? Are there purifications that should be done?

Multicultural community

What do we do in the context of multicultural settings of women, when we seek to create ritual among us? There has been a mingling of peoples and cultures, with beneficent as well as oppressive links. What ceremonies can hold us all, honor us all, respect the pain between us? I believe that finding and sharing our own ancestral resources might be one step, but then what? If White women turn to our own ancestral traditions only, how are we being different from racist segregationists? How do we recognize our interrelatedness with all peoples, as well as the brokenness between us? Is it possible to create a way to pray together to bring us power for the struggles we face together? As we create real instances of multicultural linking do the 'rules' change?

Can a Puerto Rican-American, a Jewish-American, a Scandinavian-American, an African-American, and a Native American do ritual together as women? What about a group which is 80% White women, with 20% women of color from various cultures? If Native women want to keep ceremony only in a Native context, given the appropriation which is rampant, is there a way for White, Black, Asian, and Latina women to honor the situation? If some Native women want to share ritual or teach, and others don't, how do we approach that? Are we attaching a higher standard of authority for Native women, while we let White or Black women be 'spiritual teachers' with no authority but their own?

Ancestry

What about those of us who are of partial Native ancestry, but were raised in White culture with White privilege? What is our heritage and our responsibility? How is this different or the same for Black people of partial Native ancestry? Is there a legitimate calling from the ancestors which draws us into connection with Native spirituality? How do we sort through the culture's racist and distorted images to find access to something we can rely on? Does biological heritage make a difference here, or is our adoption into White or Black culture the primary kinship in which we must make community?

And for those of any descent, how does ancestry influence spirituality? How does it shape our spiritual and ethical responsibilities? What about those women who were adopted or in some way cut off from their biological roots? What is the interplay between biology and community and spirituality? What about for those who have been abused by their kin? How do gay and lesbian people reconstitute family and kin in the face of rejection for sexual orientation? Are there certain responsibilities for those who go between various cultures and classes of people?

Despite the complexity of these issues which are raised, I believe the journey we embark on is not so difficult or unwieldy. It is rooted in a commitment to the life of the people, and a trust that we are not alone. In closing, I would like to remember the advice offered by the Menominee two-spirit poet, Chrystos:

> Take nothing you cannot return
> Give to others
> give more
> Walk quietly
> Do what needs to be done
> Give thanks for your life
> Respect all beings
> simple and it doesn't cost a penny

… from the poem, 'Shame On!' in *Dream On*, (Vancouver: Press Gang, 1991), pp.100–101.

From the Devil's gateway to the Goddess within: the image of the witch in neopaganism*

WOUTER J. HANEGRAAFF

Sticks and stones may break my bones,
but names can never hurt me

Introduction[1]

Other than what the well-known children's rhyme suggests, history teaches us that names *can* hurt people. During the sixteenth and seventeenth centuries the name 'witch' was a deadly weapon: far more deadly, in act, than the 'sticks and stones' that had occasionally been turned against women accused of maleficent magic during earlier periods. The classic western stereotype of the witch, as it took shape since the fourteenth century as an outgrowth of older traditions, has occupied the European imagination ever since. Originally, it pictured witches quite unambiguously as supreme embodiments of antihuman evil. After the great witch hunts had subsided, the witch survived in fairy tales, children's stories, novels

* This text first appeared in *Female Stereotypes in Religious Traditions*, edited by Ria Kloppenborg and Wouter J. Hanegraaff, Leiden, New York, Cologne: Brill, 1995, pp.213–19, 234–42.

[1] This research was supported by the Foundation for Research in the Field of Philosophy and Theology in the Netherlands which is subsidized by the Netherlands Organisation for the Advancement of Research (NWO).

and films as a figure inspiring either mild horror or, at best, amused laughter and ridicule.

Against this background, it is easy to see why the presence in contemporary western society of people who call themselves witches has been highlighted, by one author, as 'one of those supreme ironies that historians of religion find so fascinating'.[2] The irony results from an apparent incompatibility between the traditional witch stereotypes, on the one hand, and the self-image of modern witches, on the other. It seems puzzling, given the almost completely negative nature of the stereotype, that intelligent people with high ethical ideals would choose to characterize themselves as witches.[3] On the following pages I will attempt to shed some light on this problem. Why do modern people come to call themselves witches? How do they manage, for themselves, to reinterpret the traditional stereotype into a positive image inspiring pride? And how do they deal with the inevitable negative reactions from outsiders? Special attention will be given to the significance, in this process of revaluation, of the traditional linkage between witchcraft and femininity.

The making of a stereotype

To contemporary Europeans and Americans, the word 'witch' immediately evokes a complicated cluster of associations. On closer analysis, the different components of this cluster appear to be derived from a wide variety of popular and 'official' traditions in western religion and culture. Within the extremely complicated history of these ideas[4] a very general distinction can be made between two historical strands.[5] One consists of traditional folk beliefs concerned with maleficent sorcery (*maleficium*), flying night-witches, or 'ladies of the night'. The other consists of the belief in a secret sect that worships Satan and engages in evil and unnatural activities, including

[2] Howard Eilberg-Schwartz, 'Witches of the West: Neopaganism and Goddess Worship as Enlightenment Religions', *Journal of Feminist Studies in Religion* 5:1 (1989), 77.

[3] Cf. T.M. Luhrmann, 'Witchcraft, Morality and Magic in Contemporary London', *International Journal of Moral and Social Studies* 1:1 (1986), 82–85.

[4] See in particular: Norman Cohn, *Europe's Inner Demons*, Sussex Univ. Press 1975 (Paladin repr. 1976); Carlo Ginzburg, *Ecstasies: Deciphering the Witches' Sabbath*, Random House 1991 (Penguin repr. 1992).

[5] I follow Norman Cohn, *Demons*; and id., 'The Myth of Satan and his Human Servants', in: Mary Douglas (ed.), *Witchcraft Confession & Accusation*, London 1970.

child cannibalism and incestuous orgies.[6] In the mind of Europeans this second strand was not originally associated with witchcraft at all but with heresy. The theological reinterpretation of folkloric witchcraft beliefs in terms of satanism is a comparatively modern phenomenon starting in the late fourteenth century. In the specific historical and social context of the period, and particularly from the late fifteenth century on, this particular combination of folk beliefs and theology proved extremely combustible. The novel perception of 'witches' as heretics and members of a subversive satanic cult served as the theoretical legitimation for the great witchhunts of the sixteenth and seventeenth centuries. As observed by Norman Cohn, 'it gave the traditional witchcraft beliefs of Europe a twist which turned them into something new and strange – something quite different from, and vastly more lethal than, the witchcraft beliefs that anthropologists find and study in primitive societies today'.[7]

It is this specifically western, hybrid stereotype that concerns us here. Its main elements, in the period of the witchhunts, were the following. 1. Witches are members of a sinister *underground cult* hostile to the norms and values of Christianity.[8] 2. They gather secretly at nightly meetings known as *sabbaths*.[9] 3. They travel to these sabbaths by *flying* through the air by magical means, often in

---

[6] Ironically, the first victims of these accusations were the Christians of the second century (Minucius Felix, *Octavius*, quoted in Cohn, *Demons*, 1).

[7] Cohn, 'Myth of Satan', 3; cf. Keith Thomas, *Religion and the Decline of Magic: Studies in Popular Beliefs in Sixteenth- and Seventeenth-Century England*, 1971, London repr. 1988, 521.

[8] Cohn, *Demons*, ch. 6.; id, 'Myth of Satan'.

[9] The witches' sabbath was modelled partly on the earlier concept of the heretical sabbath (*Ketzersabbat*) allegedly practiced already by the Cathars. The original term 'Synagoga Satanae' was adopted from Revelations 2,9, but the term 'synagogue' later gave way to 'sabbath'. Both terms obviously reflect the strong antisemitic sentiments of the time (Dagmar Unverhau, 'Frauenbewegung und historische Hexenverfolgung', in: Andreas Blauert (ed.), *Ketzer, Zauberer, Hexen: Die Anfänge der europäischen Hexenverfolgungen*, Frankfurt a.M. 1990). A second source of the concept, explored at great length by Carlo Ginzburg, can be found in folk beliefs about nocturnal gatherings centering around the pagan goddess Diana. These beliefs inspired Margaret Murray's now discredited thesis that witchcraft was not a collective delusion but an actually existing fertility religion of pre-christian origins (M.A. Murray, *The Witch-Cult in Western Europe*, 1921, Oxford repr. 1962; Cohn, *Demons*, 210–224; Ginzburg, *The Night Battles: Witchcraft and Agrarian Cults in the Sixteenth and Seventeenth Centuries*, Baltimore 1983; id., *Ecstasies*, see especially the discussion of Murray and Ginzburg's reply to Cohn, 8–11).

the shape of animals.[10] 4. The sabbaths are presided over by *Satan* (often in animal shape), with whom witches have sealed a pact and whom they serve as their master.[11] 5. *Sex* is central to the rituals: witches copulate with Satan and the sabbath usually culminates in an incestuous orgy.[12] 6. *Ritual child murder and cannibalism* takes an equally central place: fetuses and babies are slaughtered and eaten,

[10] This element seems to be rooted in folk beliefs, reported already from Roman antiquity, about night-witches (*striges*): cannibalistic women who can magically change themselves into birds and fly through the air to attack babies in their cradles (Cohn, *Demons*, 206–210; Waltraud Jilg, '"Hexe" and "Hexerei" als kultur- und religionsgeschichtliches Phänomen', in: Georg Schwaiger, *Teufelsglaube und Hexenprozesse*, München 1987 46–50). A second source may be found in the belief that the followers of the 'religion of Diana' (cf. note 9) used to fly to their gatherings through the air, often riding animals. These 'ladies of the night' included the souls of the dead. They were not regarded as destructive and demonic spirits, but as benevolent and protective ones (Cohn, *Demons*, 216; Ginzburg, *Night Battles*). Cohn suggests that the element of flight was essential in order to give intellectual credence to the Sabbath: '... before the great witch-hunt could begin ... intellectuals had to persuade themselves that witches could fly. So long as witches were supposed to proceed to their meetings on foot, those meetings could not plausibly be represented as either very frequent or very large' (*Demons*, 205).

[11] The original accusations against Christians (cf. note 6) included worship of a donkey's head. In later accusations against the Paulicians (early eighth century), its place had been taken by the devil (Cohn, *Demons*, 18), and this became the standard pattern in accusations of heresy. Satan frequently appeared in animal shape and demanded to be honoured by obscene kisses, 'whether as a cat, abominably, under the tail; or as a toad, horribly, on the mouth' (Gulielmus Alvernus, early thirteenth century, quoted in Cohn, *Demons*, 22). This also became a standard motif. The 'pact' in which the witch pledged herself to the service of Satan was sealed by a visible mark on the body. In witchcraft trials, the presence of a small irregularity of the skin (such as a wart or scar) was used as legal evidence sufficient to condemn the accused. The concept of the demonic pact goes back to antiquity (Roland Götz, 'Der Dämonenpakt bei Augustinus', in: Schwaiger (ed.), *Teufelsglaube*, 57–84).

[12] The incestuous orgy figures already in the early accusations against Christians (cf. note 6). It also figures prominently in Christian polemics against gnostics (the so-called 'libertinistic gnosis', cf. for instance Kurt Rudolph, *Gnosis: The Nature and History of Gnosticism*, San Francisco 1983, 247ff) and became a standard ingredient of heresy accusations. Copulation between demons and human beings (*incubi* and *succubi*) is already mentioned by Augustine in *De Civitate Dei*. Its reality came to be widely accepted by laymen and theologians (for relevant quotations, cf. Montague Summers, *The History of Witchcraft and Demonology*, 1926, London repr. 1969, 89–109).

and their blood drunk in a purposeful perversion of the eucharist.[13] 7. *Blasphemous utterances and acts* are directed against God, Christ and the symbols of Christianity.[14] 8. Witches practice *maleficium*,[15] i.e., they harm neighbours by occult means. 9. Finally, witches are predominantly or even exclusively *women*.[16]

The widespread belief that this stereotype describes an actual reality is usually assumed to have died out, completely or almost completely, under the impact of Enlightenment rationality and the triumph of a scientific worldview. Modern people supposedly no longer believe in witches and their immoral activities. We will see later that this view is misleading. The secularization of western society is by no means as pervasive as we are often led to believe, and the idea that 'irrational beliefs' are of marginal importance in our culture is largely a product of wishful thinking.[17] Of course this does not detract from the momentous impact which the rise of secular thought did indeed have on the social function of the witch stereotype. From being a real menace to society she became a powerful figure in literature and the visual arts. The collections of

[13] This motif, again, can be traced back to accusations against Christians and gnostics during the first centuries and became a standard ingredient of heresy accusations (Cohn, *Demons*, 1 and *passim*; Rudolph, *Gnosis*, 249). Cannibalistic infanticide was equally characteristic, as we saw (note 10), for the folk belief in *striges*.

[14] According to Cohn (*Demons*, 97), the theme of 'apostasy, deliberate renunciation of Christ and of Christianity' is a relatively late element that clearly emerges for the first time in the accusations against the Templars (early fourteenth century).

[15] The suspicion of *maleficium* could be aroused by any kind of misfortune: illness, mental disorder, death, sterility or impotence, miscarriages, cattle diseases, hailstorms that destroy crops, etc. (cf. Cohn, *Demons*, esp. chapter 8; Thomas, *Decline*, esp. chapter 14; Jilg, "'Hexe'", 44–46). Suspicions of *maleficium* were common throughout the Middle Ages. Occasionally they led to lynchings of suspected witches, but seldom to official trials. Cohn (*Demons*, 160–163) explains the dramatic increase of official accusations since the sixteenth century from changes in the legal system. The so-called 'accusatory' procedure that obtained throughout the Middle Ages favoured the accused rather than the accuser, because the latter risked a grave penalty known as the *talion* if he failed to convince the judge. The new 'inquisitorial' procedure, in contrast, shifted the burden of (dis)proof from the accuser to the accused. Under the accusatory procedure, *maleficium* was almost impossible to prove (Cohn, *Demons*, 162); under the inquisitorial procedure it became almost impossible for the accused to prove his/her innocence.

[16] For discussion, see below.

[17] Cf. the opening paragraphs of Robert Galbreath, 'Explaining Modern Occultism', in: Howard Kerr & Charles L. Crow (eds.), *The Occult in America: New Historical Perspectives*, Urbana & Chicago 1986.

German *Märchen* published by the Grimm brothers contain a wealth of folk material about witches[18] which heavily influenced the Romantic movement and continues to be transmitted in children's stories. Shakespeare's *Macbeth* and Goethe's *Faust* are only two among the better known examples from 'high literature'. Witches have been a common motif in the visual arts ever since the very beginning of the witchhunts,[19] and the tradition has been continued on the film screen during this century.[20] The essential thing to note is that each single element of the classical witch stereotype has been preserved (although with varying emphasis and not necessarily always all at the same time) in these secular derivations. At most, it might perhaps be argued that the elements which are at least partly derived from folklore (the nightly gatherings, flying and animal transformation, child cannibalism, *maleficium*, femininity) are somewhat more prominent than the elements that are exclusively connected with the heretical/satanic cult (subversive organization, satan, sex, blasphemy).[21] This is, however, at most a very relative distinction. The traditional association of 'witchcraft' with 'sin, sex and satan' remains, as before, a very natural one.[22] The main difference lies in the degree of seriousness: literary adaptations of the witch motive usually employ the demonic association as a means to create suspense and drama, whereas its original religious function was to inspire moral indignation.

[18] Cf. Walter Scherf, 'Die Hexe im Zaubermärchen', in: Richard van Dülmen (ed.), *Hexenwelten: Magie und Imagination vom 16.–20. Jahrhundert*, Frankfurt a.M. 1987.

[19] Sigrid Schade, 'Kunsthexen – Hexenkünste: Hexen in der bildenden Kunst vom 16. bis 20. Jahrhundert', in: van Dülmen (ed.), *Hexenwelten* (richly illustrated).

[20] Rolf Giesen, '"Queens of Horror", böse Märchenhexen, zauberhafte Frauen: Hexenfiguren in Film, Trickfilm und Filmkomödie', in: van Dülmen (ed.), *Hexenwelten*.

[21] Cf. Jilg, "Hexe", 40.

[22] Cf. Ted Peters, 'Sin, Sex, and Satan at the Bookstore', *Dialog* 29 (1990). Many examples of these associations could be given. Take, for instance, the popular 1987 movie *The Witches of Eastwick* (dir. George Miller), starring Jack Nicholson as the devil who lures three young women into his power by seducing them. The three 'witches' finally manage to beat the devil by using *maleficium*, after first having turned the same weapon of seduction on him.

There is general agreement that 80 to 90 percent of the victims of the witch persecutions were women.[23] The witch stereotype, although not 'sex-specific', is therefore certainly 'sex-related.[24] Explanations of this phenomenon are a hotly-debated issue, not in the least because of the obvious emotional and political sensitivity of the subject for scholars working with a feminist agenda.[25] In order to reach some clarity about this problem, it is necessary to make a clear demarcation between traditional witchcraft beliefs as a cross-cultural phenomenon, on the one hand, and the very specific historical phenomenon of the European witchhunts, on the other. The strong predominance of women in traditional witchcraft beliefs, both in Europe and abroad, undoubtedly presents a formidable theoretical problem.[26] Sociological, anthropological, psychoanalytic and feminist explanations, and their various combinations, compete for prominence. I will not attempt an even cursory evaluation here, remarking only that the cross-cultural character of the belief that witches are women is sufficient in itself to reject the traditional misogynist tendencies of Catholic theology (see below) as a sufficient explanation of the European witchhunt.[27] If, for the purposes of this article, we have to accept the *general* prominence of women in witchcraft beliefs as given, the massive victimization of women during the European witchhunts can be explained as resulting from the convergence of these longstanding folk traditions with a very specific Christian demonology. Traditional folk beliefs about female witches would never by themselves have created the witchhunts,[28]

[23] Clarke Garrett, 'Women and Witches: Patterns of Analysis', *Signs* 3:2 (1977), 462; Nelly Moia, 'Comment on Garrett's "Women and Witches"', *Signs* 4:4 (1979), 799; Daniela Müller, 'Procès de sorcellerie et répression féminine', *Heresis* 12 (1989), 33; Nel Noddings, *Women and Evil*, Berkeley, Los Angeles & London 1989, 44.

[24] The distinction derives from Christina Larner, referred to in Andreas Blauert, 'Die Erforschung der Anfänge der europäischen Hexenverfolgungen', in: Blauert (ed.) *Ketzer*, 12.

[25] See literature quoted in Blauert, 'Erforschung', 34 note 4. Publications that take issue with feminist approaches include Unverhau, 'Frauenbewegung'; Müller, 'Procès'; and Cohn, *Demons*, x–xi, 248ff).

[26] Blauert, 'Erforschung', 12; Garrett, 'Women', 461; Geoffrey Parrinder, *Witchcraft: European and African*, London 1963, 60; cf. the old study of Nikolaus Paulus, *Hexenwahn und Hexenprozess, vornehmlich im 16. Jahrhundert*, Freiburg i.Br. 1910, chapter XI: 'Die Rolle der Frau in der Geschichte des Hexenwahns', esp. 198–203.

[27] This argument is found for instance in Nelly Moia, 'Comment', but had been refuted already by Paulus, *Hexanwahn*, 203.

[28] Cohn, *Demons*, 252.

but they did provide a fertile substratum. As Norman Cohn remarks, 'When the authors of the *Malleus Maleficarum* produced quasi-theological reasons to explain why witches were generally female, they were simply trying to rationalize something which peasants already took for granted'.[29] Equally important, the reinterpretation of witchcraft in terms of Satanism could fall back on a longstanding tradition of misogynist theology, exemplified by Tertullian's description of women as 'the devil's gateway'.[30] The witchhunter's manual *Malleus Maleficarum*, published in 1486/87 by the Dominican inquisitors Jacob Sprenger and Heinrich Kramer, represents perhaps the ultimate example of this tradition.[31] The argument that women, being created from Adam's bent rib, must be regarded as *animal imperfectum*,[32] an imperfect animal, was to inspire serious theological debates on the question of whether women were at all human. Among the many vices attributed to women, her carnal nature which tempts men into sin is highlighted as the characteristic of witchcraft *par excellence*: 'All witchcraft comes from carnal lust, which is in women insatiable'.[33]

The combination of theological views of women as demonic temptresses, with the picture of the satanic cult engaging in satanic

[29] Cohn, *Demons*, 251.

[30] Noddings, *Women and Evil*, 35; Nancy van Vuuren, *The Subversion of Women as practiced by Churches, Witch-hunters, and other Sexists*, Philadelphia 1973, 29. About Christian misogyny in general cf. van Vuuren, *Subversion*; Moia, 'Comment'; Müller, 'Procès', 44–45; E-berhard Berent, *Die Auffassung der Liebe bei Opitz und Weckherlin und ihre geschichtlichen Vorstufen*, The Hague/Paris 1970, 13–23 (chapter 'Frauenhass').

[31] For a good discussion, see Sydney Anglo, 'Evident Authority and Authoritative Evidence: The Malleus Maleficarum', in: Anglo (ed.), *The Damned Art: Essays in the Literature of Witchcraft*, London, Henley & Boston 1977. The title of the manual was inspired by Pierre Mamor's *Flagellum maleficorum* (1462), but Sprenger and Kramer characteristically changed the grammatical gender to *maleficarum* (Emile Brouette, 'De zestiende-eeuwse christelijke beschaving en het probleem van de duivel', in: *Satan*, Voorhout 1949 [Dutch transl. from a French volume edited by 'Les Études Carmélitaines' in 1948, no editors mentioned], 360).

[32] Montague Summers (ed.), *Malleus Maleficarum* [English translation with introduction], 1928, London repr. 1969, 46.

[33] Summers (ed.), *Malleus*, 47. This sentence has been quoted over and over from Summers' translation. In fact, although Summers' rendering certainly reflects correctly what Sprenger and Kramer meant to say, the crucial words 'witchcraft' and 'women' do not appear in the original: 'Concludamus. Omnia per carnalem cocupiscentiam [sic], quae quia in eis est insatiabilis'. 'Omnia' refers to the witchcraft practices just discussed, 'eis' to women. This adaptation of the original into a quotable formula is certainly not unrelated to Summers' own admiration for the *Malleus* (cf. Parrinder, *Witchcraft*, 62).

sex and child-cannibalism, resulted in an explosive amplification of traditional beliefs about female *maleficium*. Once intellectuals had successfully 'unmasked' practitioners of *maleficium* as satanic heretics, the stage was set[34] for a potentially unlimited chain-reaction of accusations. It is true that, at its height, the dynamics of suspicion came to endanger both women and men.[35] But this hardly need surprise us. Of course, both sexes were considered susceptible to sin, but few theologians doubted that it had been woman who brought it into the world. By the time the holocaust came to its end, the image of the witch as a fear-inspiring woman had taken root in the popular imagination more strongly than ever, and associations with the devil would continue to haunt her twentieth-century admirers.

Neopagan witchcraft

[...]

If the neopagan view of witchcraft is an outgrowth of Romantic (semi)scholarship, then it is here that we should look in order to find an explanation for the neopagan inversion of the witch stereotype. There are several reasons why religious anthropology of a Romantic type would tend to look at witchcraft in a positive light. Romanticism as such is both a reaction to and an outgrowth of the eighteenth-century Enlightenment. It has been pointed out that, with hindsight, eighteenth-century Deism shares many concerns with modern neopaganism: a critical attitude towards the Judaeo-Christian tradition, interest in ancient paganism as a source of inspiration, a concern to rehabilitate a 'religion of nature' as antidote to human alienation, anticlericalism, individualism, rejection of the doctrine of original sin, location of the source of truth within the human being, and denial of 'the difference between various antitypes and ourselves'.[36] Traditional examples of such antitypes included the 'Jew', the 'Mohammedan' and the 'Savage'. The criticism of religious 'antityping' was to play an important role in the growing interest in other cultures and religions which in time was to inform religious anthropology. Combined with the general relativist potential of the

[34] Given, of course, the crucial changes in the legal system mentioned in note 15.

[35] Cohn, *Demons*, 248.

[36] Eilberg-Schwartz, 'Witches'. Quotation on page 85. The only weakness in Eilberg-Schwartz' brilliant article is, in my view, the surprisingly small attention given to Romanticism.

so-called 'counter-enlightenment' tradition,[37] of which Romanticism is a manifestation, the foundations were laid for a systematic deconstruction of the traditional perception of western culture and religion as the universal norm for humanity and the epitome of human progress. As demonstrated paradigmatically by Rousseau's view of the 'noble savage', it was no longer unthinkable to regard modern Christian civilization as actually inferior to the culture of 'primitive' paganism. To these factors may be added some general Romantic concerns: the search for a religion of nature; a new interest in 'magic' (including the 'occult' phenomena associated with the *Nachtseite der Natur*); and the emphasis on personal experience, intuition and mystery over against Enlightenment rationality. A detailed description of these developments would obviously take us far beyond the scope of this article. It is not difficult to see, however, that from a romantic/counter-enlightenment perspective the 'witch' was bound to appear in a new light. She seemed a perfect example of a traditional antitype: cruelly persecuted by religious fanatics, and obviously related to the pagan 'antiquities' and folklore traditions which were yet another preoccupation of the times.[38]

In terms of such a context, authors like Murray, Leland, Michelet and others, and of course Gerald Gardner, could reconstrue the witch as a *positive antitype* which derives much of its symbolic force from its implicit criticism of dominant Judaeo-Christian and Enlightenment values. That the witch is an antitype with regard to dominant western traditions is obvious, but it should now be clear that this does not automatically have to entail a negative evaluation of what she stands for. It is only from the perspective of those who maintain the values of the dominant culture that her essence must necessarily be 'evil'. For those who criticize or reject those very values, the antitype can become a symbol for positive but as yet not sufficiently explored alternatives. This is the simple reason why Romantic authors could reinterpret, and neopagans adopt, a stereotype which is unambiguously negative from the perspective of dominant cultural suppositions. Having convinced themselves that the undisputedly evil aspects of the stereotype (infanticide and cannibalism) had been imputed on innocent victims by the inquisition and that some other elements (satanism, sexual orgies, etc.) had resulted from misunderstandings and misrepresentations of unfamiliar practices, both neopagans and their Romantic predecessors could end up with a picture of witchcraft which is ethically acceptable and theoretically

---

[37] See Isaiah Berlin, 'The Counter-Enlightenment', in his *Against the Current: Essays in the History of Ideas*, Oxford 1981.

[38] Richard M. Dorson, *The British Folklorists: A History*, London 1968.

defendable, while still retaining its full culture-critical potential. Actually, the 'witch' is an appropriate symbol precisely *because* she is controversial and threatens the status quo: arguably, there is hardly a better way to express one's rejection of the values informing mainstream society than claiming the name of its traditional enemies. Given the fact that these perceived 'enemies' were, in fact, victimized brutally and on a massive scale, it was easy to sympathize with them. To openly call oneself 'witch' became a potent means of reminding the mainstream culture of its crimes, while simultaneously expressing solidarity with its innocent victims. In this sense, the blood of the martyrs once again became the seed of a new religion.

The dialectics of a stereotype

I have emphasized the culture-critical belief structure of neopagan witchcraft as the principal reason for its conscious adoption of a 'negative' stereotype. It should be added that it does not follow that neopagans engage in subversive activities to 'overthrow' society. As typical heirs of the 'interiorization' of the counterculture of the 1960s, *Wiccans* agree with most New Age adherents that positive change can only be implemented by changing oneself first. Modern witches do not proselytize, and they mostly practice their rituals in private. New members should come to the movement as the result of an inner need. Typically, attempts to 'change the world' take the shape of magical ritual workings designed to have a positive impact on events. Although many rituals have rather unpretentious goals – such as helping a sick friend or relative to get well again, or locate a lost pet – magic can also be used with intentions such as to help victims of the Bosnian war, to prevent an oil spillage from getting out of hand, and so on. Tanya Luhrmann, who knows the subculture in question as few other scholars do, confirms that 'the goals are lofty, commendable and ideal. Witchcraft goals ... centre primarily on maintaining 'harmony' with the earth'.[39] In the context of American Goddess-

---

[39] Luhrmann, 'Magic', 84. Although the boundaries are rather fluent, neopagan witchcraft as such must be distinguished from the 'western mysteries' groups which practice 'high' ceremonial magic in the traditions of western occultism rather than neopaganism. These 'magicians', as distinguished from 'witches', tend to be more ambitious. As remarked by Luhrmann, 'Magicians' groups use arresting metaphors: they are the watchdogs, the silent shepherds, the spiritual commandos, of a naïve humanity'. This reflects the conviction that, behind the scenes of world events, a metaphysical war is going on between the forces of light and evil, in which magic – white against black – plays a crucial role. The pronounced ethical dualism of these magicians, envisioning themselves in heroic roles, sets them in a category apart from the holistic orientation of neopagans.

spirituality, strongly influenced by the political traditions of militant feminism, the picture is somewhat different. The Goddess spirituality of Starhawk, arguably the most influential American witch, strongly emphasizes the need for political action. Starhawk describes public rituals performed during street demonstrations and blockages of nuclear power plants. In this type of witchcraft, the culture-critical content of neopaganism is expressed far more explicitly than in the low-profile Gardnerian or Alexandrian covens. For those who know her work there can be little doubt that Starhawk's motivations are basically ethical: very seriously concerned about the situation of the modern world, she believes that only the recovery of an essentially pagan, 'creation-centered' ethic – an ethic, to be sure, which is regarded as not alien even to the core of the Judaeo-Christian tradition[40] – can save us from self-destruction. It is only in the radical feminist witchcraft represented by Zsuzsanna Budapest that the culture-critical background of neopaganism leads to a complete and uncompromising rejection of Christianity and of 'patriarchy' in general. Budapest sees Christianity as the sworn enemy of her own religion, and rejects all attempts at reconciliation. With regard to the representants of 'patriarchy' in general, Budapest diverges from the main trend of neopaganism in actually recommending black magic. The traditional neopagan belief that each action returns threefold to the actor does not seem to worry her, because *maleficium* against villains is simply not unethical.[41]

Budapest is an extreme case. Neopagans in general repeat over and over again that their aims are fully positive, that they do not worship the Christian devil, and that they are not out to harm anyone or anything. Quite the reverse: their professed aim is to be a positive force against the powers of destruction which threaten the world. In other words, we have a situation in which ideological opponents of modern western society seek to convince members of that same society of their fully positive intentions. In such a context, the role played by the traditional witch stereotype must inevitably be ambiguous. Neopagan advocates of witchcraft reject its traditional associations as a malicious caricature reflecting a misguided

---

[40] For this reason, Starhawk has been working at the 'Institute for Creation-Centered Spirituality' founded by the controversial Dominican priest Matthew Fox. Fox believes that Christianity should move away from a morbid theology based on the doctrine of original sin, to its forgotten panentheistic traditions of 'creation spirituality', which focus on creation as 'original blessing' (cf. Matthew Fox, *Original Blessing: A Primer in Creation Spirituality*, Santa Fe 1983; *The Coming of the Cosmic Christ: The Healing of Mother Earth and the Birth of a Global Renaissance*, San Francisco 1988).

[41] Budapest, *Holy Book*, 30–31, 43, 133.

worldview. But a caricature is, by definition, only a *partial* distortion, in which essential features of the original remain visible. It would not be correct, therefore, to say that neopagans reject the traditional stereotype and replace it with something else (by removing all controversial aspects and replacing them with socially acceptable alternatives). Instead, by calling themselves 'witch', neopagans use the very ambiguity of the stereotype in a profoundly dialectical fashion. Some elements are simply rejected; others are proudly accepted; and yet others are given a new meaning. This can be illustrated most easily by looking at the way neopagans react to the different elements of the classical and modern antisatanist stereotypes.

	Classic (A)	*Modern Anti-satanist (B)*	*Neopaganism (C)*
1	Underground sect	Underground sect	Successors to underground sect; now more accessible
2	Sabbath	Secret meetings	Private meetings (incl. 'sabbaths')
3	Magical flight	Psychedelic 'flights'	Guided imagination
4	Satan	Satan	Goddess/horned god
5	Sex	Sex	Ritual nudity/Great rite
6	Infanticide/cannibalism	Infanticide/cannibalism	–
7	Blasphemy	Blasphemy	–
8	Maleficium	Maleficium	Positive magic
9	Predominantly women	Both sexes	Both sexes, but majority women

1. Neopagan witches confirm that witchcraft has indeed been an *underground religion* (A). This was not for sinister reasons, however: witchcraft was driven underground by the persecutions of mainstream Christianity. The antisatanist idea of an underground sect of satanists (B) is usually rejected as reflecting the same dangerous paranoia and religious fanaticism which produced the 'burning times' (a preferred neopagan term for the period of the great witchhunts). Still, given their belief in the efficacy of white magic, few neopagan witches will deny that black magic exists as well, and many of them may suspect self-avowed satanists of practicing it. The idea of 'dark forces' working for destruction is not prominent in neopaganism *per se*, but fits well within its wider occultist context.[42] Somewhat ironically, therefore, neopagan witches may well believe that there is at least a core of truth in the satanism scare, and in principle they may

[42] Cf. Luhrmann, *Persuasions*, 19 note 1, and 81: 'magicians seem very concerned about morality. They talk about black magic; they usually tell you that there are black magicians elsewhere and stress that they, by contrast, are very white'.

be as concerned about it as any fundamentalist Christian. As for their own character as a 'secret cult' (C), neopagans emphasize that theirs is a mystery religion based on successive initiations. It would be unwise and dangerous to expose unprepared, i.e., uninitiated persons to forces they would not be able to handle. 2. The classic picture of the witches' *sabbath* (A) is mostly rejected either as a fabrication or, more often, as a distortion of a genuine pagan cult. As for the secret meetings of supposed satanists (B), witches will simply say that they know as little about it as everyone else. However, *Wicca* does know 'sabbaths' (C). Following Margaret Murray, the classic witches' sabbath is interpreted as a caricature of the yearly cycle of eight pagan festivals.[43] These yearly festivals are the religious high points of the Wiccan year. 3. Neopagans are apt to recognize in the traditional tales about *magical flight* (A) a remnant of experiences of astral travel during so-called 'altered states of consciousness'. Although they deny using drugs (B), they do use non-drug techniques for inducing altered states (C). Ritual as such already has this effect, and guided imagery techniques (particularly so-called 'pathworkings') are a prominent part of neopagan practice. Magical work may include travels on the 'inner planes'. 4. *Satan* (A–B) is regarded as a Christian invention without any connection to the pagan worldview. It is a common neopagan assumption that the Christian devil supposedly worshipped during classical witches' sabbaths is actually a perversion of the vegetation deity known as the 'horned god' in *Wicca*. This god is not evil or demonic at all, but simply represents the male counterpart of the Goddess (C). 5. Traditional tales of *sexual orgies* (A, repeated in B) are again rejected as Christian misrepresentations. However, we already saw that neopagans reject the association of sex with sin, and that their fertility religion reserves a central place for the mysteries of sexuality. Wiccan rituals seldom involve sexual promiscuity,[44] but may involve symbolic or actual practice of the 'great rite' (C; see above). 6. *Infanticide and cannibalism* (A–B) is, of course, rejected as completely alien to what *Wicca* stands for. 7. As for anti-christian *blasphemy* (A–B), most neopagan witches would answer that they

---

[43] The cycle of eight festivals was introduced by Gerald Gardner, who combined the principal Celtic festivals (based on the lunar calendar) with the solstices and equinoxes (based on the solar calendar). The sabbaths take place appr. February 2 (Imbolc) – March 21 (Spring Equinox) – April 30 (Beltane) – June 22 (Midsummer Solstice) – July 31 (Lammas) – September 21 (Autumn Equinox) – October 31 (Samhain) – December 22 (Winter Solstice or Yule). Note that Murray denies that the word 'Sabbath' is derived from Judaism at all, suggesting a connection to the french *s'esbattre*, 'to frolic' instead (Murry, *Witch-Cult*, 97).

[44] Z. Budapest, again, is an exception: *Holy Book*, 98–100.

have better things to do than offending the gods of an other religion. In any case, such practices would not accord with the fundamental tolerance of a religion which defends both polytheism and religious diversity as according best with an ecological worldview. 8. *Maleficium* (A–B), as we saw, is regarded as possible in principle but unethical and self-defeating: every action will rebound threefold on the actor. Contrary to the stereotype, modern witches work *positive* magic (C), in the traditions of the healers and 'wise women' whose successors they feel themselves to be. 9. Finally, neopagans confirm the traditional predominance of *women* in witchcraft (A). However, traditional Gardnerian/Alexandrian Wicca, and most of their 'liberal' derivations, accept men and women as equal members. Indeed, at least one man is necessary in order to ritually represent the God. In the less traditional Goddess-movement, feminist separatist groups have emerged. This development, exemplified most typically by Z. Budapest, regards witchcraft as 'wimmin's religion'[45] concerned with women's mysteries, and does not admit men.

Concluding remarks

But even though modern witches may do what they can to introduce a new stereotype, outsiders still often judge them according to the old ones. Neopagan reactions to public suspicions and attacks conform to what might be expected. They have reacted against countersubversionist attacks by denying, again and again, any connection with satanism, and by ever-renewed attempts to explain the difference. The vehemence of the debate has led to the founding of organizations specifically devoted to fighting prejudice.[46] As we saw above, attempts to educate the public into distinguishing between neopagan witchcraft and satanism seem to have met with moderate success. We also discussed the reasons why probably no amount of such education will succeed to convince the hard core of Christian fundamentalist antisatanists. However, it would be a mistake to conclude that the modern persistence of the classic witch stereotype can be explained exclusively from biblical literalism and continued belief in the metaphysical reality of the demonic. One further dimension of the problem should be mentioned, which focuses attention on the contribution of modern secular thought to the creation and preservation of the classic witch stereotype. For

[45] In an attempt to avoid all reference to men, Z. Budapest for a long time spoke of 'women' (sing.) and 'wimmin' (plur.) She later dropped this.

[46] York, 'Néo-paganisme'. See for instance the British 'Sorcerer's Apprentice Legal Fighting Fund' (SAFF).

academic scholars – products and representatives of secular modernity – it is tempting to assume that, once the evil of persecution has
comfortably been located in 'others' (such as 'Christian fundamentalist fanatics'), the dynamics of stereotyping are sufficiently
accounted for. Actually, however, it may be argued that these
dynamics touch upon the very foundations of modernity itself.

There can be no doubt that witchcraft, like such ill-defined but
obviously related phenomena as 'magic' or 'the occult', is commonly
associated with the 'dark side of things'. While doing research in the
field, one quickly becomes familiar with the fact that mere mention of
these domains tends to evoke remarkably strong and emotional
reactions from outsiders. Prior to rational reflection, and usually
without being able to give even a remotely relevant definition,
people tend to dismiss 'the occult' out of hand and express various
kinds of objections to 'it'. Whether or not they are right to do so is
irrelevant to our concerns.[47] However, the similarity of such reactions
to an automatic defensive reflex *is* highly relevant. Somehow,
modern westerners seem to have internalized a strong belief that
certain domains are 'danger zones': potential threats to sanity and
order, both on the level of society and of the individual psyche. These
domains are felt by many to be representative of everything
responsible people should avoid and fight against, lest chaos invade
our world and wash away all certainties. A well-known anecdote
about Sigmund Freud seems paradigmatic in this regard. Freud once
tried to convince C.G. Jung to never, ever give up the sexual theory of
psychoanalysis. He implored him, in tones of obvious concern, that it
should be made into a 'dogma', an 'unshakeable bulwark'. To Jung's
question against what danger this bulwark should be set up, the
answer was: 'against the black tide of mud … of occultism'.[48]

Freud is known as one of the 'masters of suspicion' who have laid
the foundations of modern secularism, and it is this very
representativeness which makes for the delicacy and the significance
of Jung's anecdote. Modern society, too, seems to be highly nervous
and irritable whenever it is confronted with the 'shadow' cast by the

[47] Empirical research into esotericism, as in religion generally, cannot afford to
express opinions about the truth or falsity (either in a religious or in a philosophical
sense) of belief systems. Scholarship has access only to the empirical level, i.e., to
religious phenomena as they appear in space and time; it is bound to a stance of
methodical agnosticism with regard to their 'meta-empirical' reference. This
precludes the expression of personal value judgments. Cf. W.J. Hanegraaff,
'Empirical Method in the Study of Esotericism', *Method and Theory in the Study of
Religion* 7:2 (1995).

[48] Carl Gustav Jung, *Memories, Dreams, Reflections*, Collins/Fontana edition 1971,
173.

Enlightenment.[49] A final explanation for the continued force of the negative witch stereotype *and* for its neopagan reversion into a positive antitype may be found in this circumstance. The attitude of modern representatives of Enlightenment values towards 'the occult' seems to imply that the 'darkness' of the occult and the irrational must be fought in the name of the 'light' of reason. The urgency with which this message is repeated again and again may be rooted in fears on which modern psychology could perhaps throw some light. In any case, it certainly reflects a deeply-felt concern.[50]

Neopagan witchcraft, as opposed to modern secularism, is historically connected to 'occultist' traditions *and* deeply influenced by the psychology of Jung.[51] It is well known that Jung did not heed Freud's advice, but continued to emphasize the need to confront and integrate the 'shadow' rather than alienate it as 'the other'. The neopagan reaction to modern persecution is deeply informed by this Jungian approach. While they publicly fight against prejudice, neopagans privately interpret it as a sign of psychological immaturity. The battle of the Enlightenment and its contemporary heirs against 'the occult' is interpreted by them as the reflex mechanism of a culture which fears to confront its own shadow. The result, according to the neopagan perspective, is evident: in lieu of being properly integrated, the shadow of the western collective psyche now confronts humanity in the outside world, threatening real destruction. The rejection and alienation of the purportedly 'irrational' in the name of reason stimulates ways of behaviour that are objectively irrational, because they destroy the very world on which humans depend for their survival. In the perception of neopagans, the witch is a figure *par excellence* who knows of these 'dark and fearsome', but all-important secrets of personal and global healing, transmutation, and potential destruction. They feel that by ignoring and forgetting those secrets and by persecuting their keepers, her enemies have put all creation at risk.

[49] Cf. Herbert Leventhal, *In the Shadow of the Enlightenment: Occultism and Renaissance Science in Eighteenth-Century America*, New York 1976.

[50] Very good examples are to be found in the modern 'skeptical' movement. See George P. Hansen, 'CSICOP and the Skeptics: An Overview', *The Journal of the American Society for Psychical Research* 86 (1992), 19–63.

[51] See for instance Crowley, *Wicca*. That the affinities between occultism and Jungian thought are not accidental is demonstrated in Richard Noll, *The Jung Cult: Origins of a Charismatic Movement*, Princeton 1994. Cf. also the observations in chapter two of Dan Merkur, *Gnosis: An Esoteric Tradition of Mystical Visions and Unions*, Albany 1993.

It is perhaps not inappropriate to end our discussion of the witch stereotype on this dark note. Obviously, whether the 'fear of the occult' is convincingly accounted for by a neo-jungian explanation is a problem which neither can nor should be addressed here. That this fear *exists*, however, and that it deeply informs any discussion of the subject, seems evident. Serious reflection on the reasons for this fear, and on the rational validity of those reasons, will be highly important to the future academic study of occultism. The methodological debate in this domain (as in the study of religion generally) should not be limited exclusively to the rational validity of research strategies and methods. It should also consider the non-rational factors (rooted in personal biography) which lie behind the preference of individual scholars for this or that methodological school or approach, and their frequent aversion to others.[52] Unless this methodological meta-issue is seriously addressed, the academic study of occultism will remain haunted by implicit stereotypes.

[52] Cf. my discussion of the 'ideological mechanism' in philosophy and science, with reference to the methodology of A.O. Lovejoy (Hanegraaff, 'Empirical Method').

The witch in history*

DIANE PURKISS

A Holocaust of one's own: the myth of the Burning Times

> Popular history, and also the history taught in schools, is influenced by this Manichaean tendency, which shuns half-tints and complexities; it is prone to reduce the river of human occurrences to conflicts, and the conflicts to duels – we and they, the good guys and the bad guys respectively, because the good must prevail, else the world would be subverted.
>
> Primo Levi, *The Drowned and the Saved*

Here is a story. Once upon a time, there was a woman who lived on the edge of a village. She lived alone, in her own house surrounded by her garden, in which she grew all manner of herbs and other healing plants. Though she was alone, she was never lonely; she had her garden and her animals for company, she took lovers when she wished, and she was always busy. The woman was a healer and midwife; she had practical knowledge taught her by her mother, and mystical knowledge derived from her closeness to nature, or from a half-submerged pagan religion. She helped women give birth, and she had healing hands; she used her knowledge of herbs and her common sense to help the sick. However, her peaceful existence was disrupted. Even though this woman was harmless, she posed a threat to the fearful. Her medical knowledge threatened the doctor. Her simple, true spiritual values threatened the superstitious nonsense of the Catholic church, as did her affirmation of the sensuous body. Her independence and freedom threatened men. So the Inquisition descended on her, and cruelly tortured her into confessing to lies about the devil. She was burned alive by men who hated women, along with millions of others just like her.

* This text first appeared in *The Witch in History: Early Modern and Twentieth-Century Representations*, by Diane Purkiss, London and New York: Routledge, 1996, pp.7–10, 13, 15–16, 17–20, 22–4, 276, 282–3.

Do you believe this story? Thousands of women do. It is still being retold, in full or in part, by women who are academics, but also by poets, novelists, popular historians, theologians, dramatists.[1] It is compelling, even horrifying. However, in all essentials it is not true, or only partly true, as a history of what happened to the women called witches in the early modern period. Thousands of women were executed as witches, and in some parts of Europe torture was used to extract a confession from them; certainly, their gender often had a great deal to do with it; certainly, their accusers and judges were sometimes misogynists; certainly, by our standards they were innocent, in that to a post-Enlightenment society their 'crime' does not exist. However, the women who died were not quite like the woman of the story, and they were not killed for quite the same reasons.

[...]

Around 1968, the 'action wing' of New York Radical Women formed, and they chose a striking new name: WITCH. The name exploited the negative associations of the witch as woman of dark power, but the group's members also played with the signification of the term in their presentation of it as an acronym for Women's International Terrorist Conspiracy from Hell. The meaning discovered in the term 'witch' by that acronymic rendering is interesting because it goes beyond any simple reclamation of the witch as a foresister in order to assign explicit meaning to the figure. 'Woman' names the witch as gendered, while 'international' asserts the ubiquity of witches, and 'terrorist' marks witches as violent. 'Conspiracy' deliberately flirts with fears of a secret organisation of subversive women, while 'from Hell' draws attention to the origin of witches' otherness while pointing to women's oppression. This adds up to an image of the witch as violent and empowered woman. WITCH's members hexed the Chase Manhattan bank, and invaded the Bride Fair at Madison Square Gardens dressed as witches. Despite the disjunction between self and role implied by such flagrant theatricality, WITCH also inaugurated many of the myths of witch-craft which have become central to many radical feminists and most modern witches. Describing witches, the collective wrote:

---

[1] Recent historical restatements include Marianne Hester, *Lewd Women and Wicked Witches,* London: Routledge, 1992; Anne Llewellyn Barstow, *Witchcraze: A New History of the European Witch Hunts,* New York: HarperCollins, 1994; and Uta Ranke-Heinemann, *Eunuchs of the Kingdom of Heaven: The Catholic Church and Sexuality,* trans. Peter Heinegg, Harmondsworth: Penguin, 1990. Recent polemical usages include Joan Smith, 'Patum Peperium' in *Misogynies,* London: Faber, 1989, pp. 55ff. I discuss literary uses below.

They bowed to no man, being the living remnant of the oldest culture
of all – one in which men and women were equal sharers in a truly
cooperative society before the death-dealing sexual, economic, and
spiritual oppression of the Imperialist Phallic Society took over and
began to destroy nature and human society.[2]

[...]

Th[is] example ... stand[s] for the extraordinary flexibility of the
term 'witch' as a signifier within all feminist discourse. Constantly cast
and recast as the late twentieth century's idea of a protofeminist, a
sister from the past, the witch has undergone transformations as
dramatic as those in any pantomime. The figure of the witch has been
central to the revival of women's history over the past two decades.
That revival has been carried out by academic historians, but not only
by them; the original impetus behind the attempt to uncover
women's past came from activists in the women's liberation movement, and partly from the fact that witches were among the few
women given any space whatever in pre-feminist history. The witch
has consequently been caught up in virtually all of feminist history's
debates about itself and its own project. The enormous changes in
the standard feminist narrative of the witch and her place in history
reflect feminism's attempt to ask and answer questions about what
history is, what feminist history is, what might count as authority and
authenticity, and where the intersections are between history and
textuality, history and politics. The figure of the witch mirrors – albeit
sometimes in distorted form – the many images and self-images of
feminism itself. Originally, women's history was inspired by the wish
to uncover the truth about women, and this led to a yearning to find
oneself in the past, to locate real women who share our natures and
problems. The witch offers opportunities for both identification and
elaborate fantasy, standing in a supportive or antagonistic relation to
the contemporary feminist-activist-historian inscribing her.

[...]

Gesturing away from its own immediate past and towards the
stories it narrates, the radical feminist history of witches often appears
to offer a static, finished vision of the witch. However, feminist
histories of witchcraft are not finished artefacts, but stages in a
complicated, conflictual series of processes within the public sphere,
processes which involve both the writing of women's past and the
rewriting of their present and future. Since all feminist histories offer
to ask – and sometimes answer – the question 'What is a woman?', all

---

[2] WITCH, 'Spooking the patriarchy', in *The Politics of Women's Spirituality: Essays
on the Rise of Spiritual Power within the Feminist Movement*, ed. Charlene
Spretnak, New York: Doubleday, 1982, p.76.

feminist histories of witchcraft are caught up in contemporary questions of authority, authenticity and public politics.

[...]

[For example, in Mary Daly's *Gyn/Ecology*,] Witchcraft persecution is enlisted alongside Chinese footbinding, Indian suttee, genital mutilation in the Arab world, American gynaecology and Mengele's medical experiments to illustrate Daly's thesis that patriarchy means the relentless persecution of women by physical torture. This agenda involves a great deal of conflation of cultures, but the figure of the witch is central to the narrative, owing to Daly's rewriting of the term hagiography as Hag-ography. Daly explicitly invokes the hag as a role model: 'our foresisters were the Great Hags whom the institutionally powerful but privately impotent patriarchs found too threatening for coexistence ... For women who are on the journey of radical be-ing, the lives of the witches, of the Great Hags of hidden history are deeply intertwined with our own process. As we write/live in our own story, we are uncovering their history'. But our story *is* their story, it seems: 'crones are the survivors of the perpetual witchcraze of patriarchy, the survivors of the Burning Times'. The Burning Times 'is a crone-logical term which refers not only to the period of the European witchcraze but to the perpetual witchcraze which is the entire period of patriarchal rule'. A woman becomes a crone, Daly explains, 'as a result of ... having dis-covered depths of courage, strength and wisdom in her self.'[3] At this point, it becomes clear that Daly's narrative account of the Burning Times is less a presentation of external events than the story of an internal voyage, a metaphorical journey into the heart of patriarchal darkness.

[...]

Dworkin uses both the image of the demonised witch-stepmother of fairy tales and the figure of the persecuted witch-victim of the Burning Times as figures for the suffering woman-victim of pornography and rape.[4] Similarly, Daly's witch-narrative conflates the persecution of witches with these notions of patriarchy so that the witch can become a synecdoche of female victims of sexualised violence.

Ironically, the seductiveness of the witch's place as ultimate victim is that the learned world had always sided with her against her oppressors. From Reginald Scot's alignment of witch-beliefs with ignorant peasants, to Arthur Miller's representation of the victims of House Committee for Un-American Activities via the Salem witch-

---

[3] Daly, *Gyn/Ecology*, pp. 14–15, 16.

[4] Andrea Dworkin, *Woman-Hating*, New York: Dutton, 1974, pp. 34–46, 118–50.

trials, the witch-craze has been a synonym for pointless persecution. Far from revealing a narrative long lost by patriarchal history, radical feminists were plodding along in the footsteps of every liberal from the Romantics onwards who deplored witch-hunting as a sign of barbarity. The witch's status as victim of prejudice and superstition could be enlisted to portray feminism as enlightened. As well, the witch became crucial to the effort to make men and especially women *believe* in women's oppression, always a daunting task. 'It would be unthinkable' remarks Daly, 'for scholars to refer to Jewish pogroms or to lynchings of blacks as therapeutic'.[5] Pogroms, lynchings and above all the Holocaust do make it more difficult (though *not* impossible) to deny the very existence of racism and ethnocentrism. The Burning Times myth offers to play the same role in women's history, to authorise the need for struggle and authenticate the forms that struggle takes.

[...]

[However,] at times there does seem to be a race on to prove that women have suffered more than victims of racism or genocide (as though women have not been *among* the victims of racism and genocide). [...] [The] stress on *burning* itself seems to allude to the crematoria, although it may also point to Dresden and Hiroshima. Radical feminist witches *always* burn; they are never hanged.

[...]

The myth of the Burning Times is not politically helpful. It might seriously be doubted whether a myth that portrays women as nothing but the helpless victims of patriarchy, and the female body as nothing but a site of torture and death is enabling, especially if these portrayals are taken to define what woman under patriarchy is, for all time. The ahistorical character of the myth of the Burning Times is alarming: Daly wants women to be Hags, but she also wants to say that what happened to Hags once is happening to them again. Indeed, one way of recognising Hags – defining their identity – is by persecution. Another way to read the ahistoricity of the Burning Times myth, however, is to see it as an attempt to lend dignity to kinds of oppression which are usually too 'trivial' to register as problems.

[...]

What of the victim of this endless cycle of patriarchal violence? In the story with which I began this chapter, she is the impossibly innocent, exceptionally knowing midwife-healer, and she derives from Barbara Ehrenreich and Deirdre English's influential pamphlet

---

[5] Daly, *Gyn/Ecology*, p.185.

on women healers.[6] Ehrenreich and English argued that the witch-craze was caused by the attempt on the part of rising male medical professionals to take over and control the regulation of women's bodies. In order to do this, doctors removed the women healers and midwives on whom the community had previously relied. These guardians of the female body therefore found themselves accused of witchcraft by those who wished to wrest control of that body from them. Using a different model of essential femininity, not as silent victim or wild Hag but as gentle, maternal, close to the earth, Ehrenreich and English added to the fantasy of the Burning Times by creating an utterly innocent victim. She was us as we should have been; she was the perfect nurturing mother that we were not, the useful woman who cared nothing for orthodox power, but who had at her disposal awesome knowledge. Above all, she is free, free of church, state, men, and the unlawful wishes for power and money which they might wickedly inspire.

Ehrenreich and English's pamphlet is light on evidence.[7] However, unlike Daly, Ehrenreich and English do not offer their work as a challenge to the patriarchal norms of history as a practice, but only to its domination by men and male agendas. They are really challenging another body of professional expertise altogether, the expertise of the medical profession, especially in relation to gender-specific issues, and some at least of their appeal rests on women's assent to the proposition that Western medicine has damaged women. Once this proposition is agreed, imagining an alternative becomes seductive. As well, the figure of the healer-witch reflects assumptions about the Middle Ages: the midwife-herbalist-healer-witch seems a spectacular collage of everything which feminist historians and others see as the opposite of medieval patriarchy, and in this way she has come to subtend a certain notion of what patriarchy is. Barbara G. Walker, for example, writes:

[6] Barbara Ehrenreich and Deidre English, *Witches, Midwives and Nurses: A History of Women Healers*, London: Writers and Readers Publishing Cooperative, 1973.

[7] On midwives, see Clive Holmes, 'Popular culture? Witches, magistrates and divines in early modern England', in *Understanding Popular Culture: Europe from the Middle Ages to the Nineteenth Century*, ed. Steven Kaplan, Berlin: Houton, 1984, and 'Women, witnesses and witches', *Past and Present*, 140 (1993), pp.45–78; Richard Horsley, 'Who were the witches? The social roles of the accused in European witch trials', *Journal of Interdisciplinary History*, 9 (1979), pp.714–15; David Harley, 'Ignorant midwives: a persistent stereotype', *The Society for the Social History of Medicine Bulletin*, 28 (1981) pp.6–9, and 'Historians as demonologists'; *Wiesner, Women and Gender*; J. A. Sharpe, 'Witchcraft and women in seventeenth-century England: some northern evidence', *Continuity and Change*, 6 (1991), pp.179–99.

> The real reason for ecclesiastical hostility [to midwives] seems to have been the notion that midwives could help women control their own fate, learn secrets of sex and birth control, or procure abortions. The pagan women of antiquity had considerable knowledge of such matters, which were considered women's own business, and not subject to male authority.[8]

Here the midwife simply is the female sexual autonomy which the church cannot tolerate. There is no need to cite evidence showing that midwives were great purveyors of birth control or abortifacients to women; the myth thrives not on evidence but on a sense of likelihood deriving from *twentieth*-century political struggles. Reproductive rights, central to the myth of the healer-witch, came to the fore as a central organising principle of the women's movement in the mid-1970s, about the time when Ehrenreich and English's pamphlet was published.[9] Like Daly's work, this story is shaped by specific political realities.

Thus the healer-witch, too, is a fantasy grounded in present-day social reality; here is Starhawk's version:

> The old woman carries a basket of herbs and roots she has dug; it feels heavy as time on her arm. Her feet on the path are her mother's feet, her grandmother's, her grandmother's grandmothers'; for centuries, she has walked under these oaks and pines, culled the herbs and brought them back to dry under the eaves of her cottage on the common. Always, the people of the village have come to her; her hands are healing hands, they can turn a child in the womb; her murmuring voice can charm away pain, can croon the restless to sleep.[10]

Starhawk evokes an unchanging identity ('Her feet on the path ...') in an unchanging world; the ideal antidote to the fragmented postmodern self. The figure of herbs and herb lore is central to this portrayal. It stands both for agriculture and for untamed nature, both of which are familiar to the old woman. It also stands for professionalism and professional knowledge, as do the woman's midwifery skills; and for domestic labour: gardening, cooking, nursing. The herbalist-witch represents a fantasy of a profession which blends into rather than conflicting with the ideology of

---

[8] Barbara G. Walker, *The Woman's Encyclopedia of Myths and Secrets,* New York: Harper & Row, 1985, pp.654–5. The idea that women in (say) ancient Athens had more power than modern women is especially risible.

[9] See Sheila Rowbotham, *The Past is Before Us: Feminism in Action Since the 1960s,* Harmondsworth: Penguin, 1989, pp.61–85, esp. p.71.

[10] Starhawk, *Dreaming,* p.183.

femininity constructed for and in the domestic sphere; more simply, it expresses a fantasy in which domestic skills are valued in the community as if they were professional skills. There is more than a passing resemblance between the witch-herbalist and the fantasy superwoman heroine of the 1980s and 90s, professional women who have beautiful country gardens, bake their own bread, make their own quilts, and demonstrate sexuality at every turn.

[...]

Characteristically, women writers have seen in the witch a figure of all that women could be were it not for patriarchy. In Sylvia Townsend Warner's novel *Lolly Willowes,* Lolly is a shy spinster-aunt, disregarded by the women of her family. But when she buys a cottage in the Chilterns, Lolly discovers that everyone in the village regards her as a witch, and from this comes a new, and much more powerful identity. To be recognised as a witch is to be recognised as free and independent.[11] In a much more complex and anxious way, Sara Maitland's story 'The Burning Times' dramatises the witch as a figure of all that women want to be. The story is narrated by the daughter of a woman denounced as a witch and burned, and it gradually emerges that it is the narrator herself who has given evidence against her mother. The narrator is self-oppressed. Mother of sons who disregard her and wife to a bullying husband, she dwells constantly on the image of her powerful and confident mother, who ran her own lacemaking business, while engaging in a voluptuously detailed lesbian affair with another strong woman called Margaret. It is her mother's lesbian sexuality and her own unrecognised desire for Margaret that lead the narrator to denounce her mother, but plainly this daughter envies her mother at every possible level. Though the reader is encouraged to identify with the mother against the jealous daughter, the story also mobilises our fears that we may be the 'good' cowardly woman and not the confident 'witch'. Though the reader's negotiation of these categories is unstable, the categories themselves are rigidly absolute; there is nothing strong about the daughter and nothing weak about the witch-mother. The witch as martyr emerges as a signifier that resolves the conflict the story establishes by allowing the reader to absolve herself of guilt for being a wimp; we would all be strong, the story implies, were it not for the Inquisitors and fembots who dog our footsteps, making us fearful of our own sexuality.[12]

[11] Sylvia Townsend Warner, *Lolly Willowes*, London: Virago, 1995, first published 1926.

[12] Sara Maitland, 'The Burning Times', in *Women Fly When Men Aren't Watching*, London; Virago, 1993, story first published 1983.

In Anne Sexton's poem, 'Her Kind', Sexton claims kinship with the witch as desirable version of the self. This was the poem which Sexton used to define her public identity as poet, beginning her readings with it: 'I have gone out, a possessed witch / haunting the black air ... A woman like that is not a woman, quite/I have been her kind'. Sexton's witch is not fully incorporated into the social category 'woman'; she represents a kind of Kristevan negativity, a 'that's not it' and 'that's still not it'. But Sexton is also attracted by the spectacle of suffering woman; the last stanza of the poem describes the witch burning in a kind of ecstasy of death and pain: 'survivor / where your flames still bite my thigh ... A woman like that is not ashamed to die'.[13] This association of woman with erotic burning and death also figures in Sylvia Plath's work. Though Plath chose to use the Holocaust and Hiroshima as her central myths of burning, her juvenilia contains a poem which shows her experimenting with this alternative figure of female suffering.[14] Later, however, Plath followed Sexton in writing 'Witch Burning', which dwells on the sensuousness of being burned in a manner which looks forward to 'Fever 103°': 'My ankles brighten. Brightness ascends my thighs'. For both Plath and Sexton, only fire can affirm the sexuality of the female body; being burned is a metaphor for a caress that accepts the body's responsiveness, and pain a symbol of passion.[15] The title of Plath's 'Three Women' alludes to the Weird Sisters of *Macbeth* as well as the Fates and the Furies. Like others informed by psychoanalysis, Plath uses the witch as a figure of the mother, since the poem concerns three women, a mother, woman miscarrying, and a woman giving birth but abandoning her baby.[16] Ironically, it is Ted Hughes who understands the witch in ways much closer to the ideas of Mary Daly in his poem 'Witches': 'Once was every woman the witch/To ride a weed the ragwort road/Devil to do whatever she would'. Hughes, full of touchingly *passé* tough-guy talk, makes this an occasion for near-comical male fear: 'Bitches still sulk, rosebuds blow/And we are devilled. And though these weep/Over our harms, who's to know Where their feet dance while their heads sleep?'[17] Hughes's poem makes gratifying reading for any woman who wants to see the witch

[13] Anne Sexton, *The Complete Poems*, Boston: Houghton Mifflin, 1981, p.15.

[14] 'Sonnet to Satan', in Sylvia Plath, *Collected Poems*, edited by Ted Hughes, London: Faber, 1981, p.323.

[15] Plath, *Collected Poems*, p.135. See also Plath's juvenile poem 'On Looking Into the Eyes of a Demon Lover', p.325.

[16] Plath, *Collected Poems*, pp.176–87, 272.

[17] Ted Hughes, *Selected Poems 1957–1981*, London: Faber, 1982, p.56.

as the ultimate threat to patriarchy, except that Hughes fully subscribes to the fantasy. Although the poem is terrified of what women may be doing 'while their heads sleep', it also yearns to see them at their secret rites to know what they are up to when beyond male control. This is the kind of poem one might expect from Hughes, who later brought us the full-scale Robert Graves old sow myth of material femininity in *Shakespeare and the Goddess of Complete Being*.[18] Hughes's fantasy fits perfectly with Sara Maitland's, who thinks that 'women fly when men aren't watching'. It is only that Hughes would love to watch.

[...]

Bread into gingerbread and the price of the transformation

[...] In laying hold of the witch, in making her our own, we have also lost her, or perhaps lost what she once was for her original owners. Now she stands like a country house, with so many additions from diverse historical periods that the original structures are no longer visible from any angle. For despite the subtleties of radical feminists, historians and modern witches, the dominant image of the witch is still of a shrieking hag on a broomstick, the Wicked Witch of the West.

The witch's consignment to the world of childhood infects historical accounts of her. She is the bogey of Western society's infancy, a feature of our early years as a culture. She exemplifies the dark ages, the primitive, the superstitious, the unenlightened. It is right for her to wear black, because her black clothes show she is from the deep unknown past. She also represents the dark forces of unreason which may return at any moment to menace civilisation. But it is not so much she herself who represents these things. It is belief in her, belief in her power, and also a willingness to act on that belief by killing her. Because it is impossible for most of us to be who we are and also to accept the knowledges of early modern believers about the witch, those knowledges have to be understood in other terms, our terms.

[...]

This process of transformation, which is not without its contestations, involves a series of noticeable losses. For the essence of the early modern witch is fear, and we no longer find the witch

---

[18] Ted Hughes, *Shakespeare and the Goddess of Complete Being*, London: Faber, 1993.

frightening. Charles Lamb might have said that it would have taken a brave constable to arrest the Weird Sisters, but most of us would see even those flying night-hags as sad, deluded old ladies, with such conviction that they might see themselves that way too, and go quietly. Even in the nursery the witch is no longer a terror. Yet unless we can for a moment understand what it is to fear the witch, we cannot understand her early modern incarnations. Anyone who wishes to feel such real fear might try reading 'Chips', a story told to the young Charles Dickens by his nanny Mary Weller.[19] The story is about a man whose family all sell their souls to the devil. He does everything he can to avoid doing so, but at last he is forced into the pact, and the devil kills him in the most awful way imaginable, with plenty of warning to draw out his fear and ours. It terrified the young Dickens, and it should strike fear into any sane reader, because it is about the inescapability of the discovery that you may yourself be the worst thing in the world. The real terror of the witch lies in this mixture of familiarity and unbearable strangeness. She represents what we cannot bear to acknowledge as ours, the feelings, violence, dirt and filth that we cannot own without destroying our pleased sense that we are good and kind and clean.

It is easy for us to feel superior to the early modern men and women who thus expunged their worst feelings and attached them to another person. Superiority should, however, be tempered with caution. Although we no longer fear the witch, we still have not owned those dark feelings. Rather, we have sanitised the witch, so that she can become acceptable, transforming her into another one of our better selves. Now she is clean, pretty, a herbalist with a promising career in midwifery, a feminist, as good a mother as anybody if not rather better than most, sexually liberated (without anything too kinky). If a constable did pluck up enough courage to arrest the Weird Sisters, we would probably feel indignant on their behalf rather than impressed with his nerve ('Free the three!'). It is Macbeth, with his broadsword militarism, who endangers us. We are all Romantics now, all more taken with sexy and cynical Vivian than

---

[19] Originally in Charles Dickens, 'Nurse's stories', *The Uncommercial Traveller*, 1860. Mary Weller told Dickens a number of frightening tales; she used to signal their onset by clawing the air and groaning. Dickens would beg her to stop, but she was relentless. Robert Louis Stevenson was also told his most frightening witch-story by his Scottish nanny Cunnie; the story is the horrible 'Thrawn Janet'. A good third to these is 'Jinny's Gibbet', a traditional gipsy folktale about a witch who cuts a hand of glory from a hanged man, only to realise that the same hand had gently touched her breast as the owner fed from it. The hanged man is her son. This story is retold in *Folktales of England*, ed. Katherine Briggs and Ruth Tongue, London: Routledge & Kegan Paul, 1965.

with boring old Arthur and moralistic old Merlin. Vivian's transgressions are mild; to us, her sexuality is not a transgression at all, but a point in her favour. She is the mother of those near-pornographic fantasy creatures who roam freely in the films of Ken Russell, for whom the label 'witch' is simply an excuse for a lot of uninhibited nudity and nook. Any crimes grimier than this, like eating babies, can be dismissed as libels.

[...]

The dark sister of the charming herbalist with the well-scrubbed pine table and the bunches of herbs drying in the rafters is for us nothing but a mass of bygone prejudices, a marker which divides us from the benighted and bigoted past into which we have abjected so much of our worst selves. The bright, steady lights of empirical history and symptomatic ego-psychoanalysis can illuminate that darkness (in which case it ceases to be dark). For if we can no longer feel fear when contemplating the witch, we can at least feel its supposedly more rational double, curiosity. All our witches are the daughters of the Weird Sisters, because all our witches, from the Witch of Atlas to Starhawk, are displays. All our witches exist to satisfy curiosity about witches, and I too am of that happy breed, having written this book to satisfy my own curiosity and in the hope that it will allow others to do the same. Our witches, like the Weird Sisters, are displays of lost lore, displays of a past always already going out of fashion, dissolving, requiring exorcism or preservation, but always requiring action on our part. This book, inevitably, is part of the process of keeping the witch in play, playing with her, creating new meanings for her so that she remains one of the dominant figures of our mental landscape.

Acknowledgements

Grateful acknowledgement is made to the following sources for permission to reproduce textual material in this book:

Hutton, R. (1996) 'The roots of modern paganism', in Hardman, C. and Harvey, G. (eds) *Paganism Today*. Thorsons/HarperCollins Publishers Ltd.; Tingay, K. (2000) 'Madame Blavatsky's children: Theosophy and its heirs', in Sutcliffe, S. and Bowman, M. (eds) *Beyond New Age: Exploring Alternative Spirituality*, Edinburgh University Press, reproduced by permission; Meek, D.E. (2000) 'The faith of the fringe: perspectives and issues in "Celtic Christianity"', in *The Quest for Celtic Christianity*. ISBN1871828511, The Handsel Press Ltd.; Johnson, M. (1995) *Wanting to be Indian: When Spiritual Searching turns into Cultural Theft*. Respect Inc. Taken from web site http://www.dickshovel.com/respect.html; Hanegraaff, W.J. (1995) 'From the Devil's gateway to the Goddess within: the image of the witch in neopaganism', in Kloppenborg, R. and Hanegraaff, W.J. (eds) *Female Stereotypes in Religious Traditions*, Brill Academic Publishers; Purkiss, D. (1996) 'A Holocaust of one's own: the myth of the Burning Times' and 'Bread into gingerbread and the price of the transformation', in *The Witch in History: Early Modern and Twentieth-Century Representations*. Routledge/Taylor & Francis Books Ltd.

Every effort has been made to trace all the copyright owners, but if any has been inadvertently overlooked, the publishers will be pleased to make the necessary arrangements at the first opportunity.

Index

Abelard, Pierre 230
Abramelin Magic 28, 46
Adam, David, Vicar of Holy Isle (Lindisfarne) 89, 251
Adler, M. 133
Adomnán, *Lex innocentium* 259
age distribution of Wiccans 138, 142, 143
Albanese, Catherine 8
alchemy 23, 46, 189, 217
    Jung's work on 194, 200
Alexandrian Wicca 34–6, 37, 43, 44, 120, 198, 309
    initiated witches 138
    and traditional and hereditary witches 134
Allen, Paula Gunn 290
Alpha et Omega 22, 23
Anderson, Victor and Cora 38
Ansell, George 79
Anthropic Principle 180, 217
anthroposophy 201
antiquarianism
    and Celtic Christianity 87
    and Celtic spirituality 57, 58
    and the Druids 71
    and folklore 62
    Aquinas, Thomas 175, 217
archaeological remains, and Celtic spirituality 64–5
archetypes
    in Jungian psychology 195, 205, 217
        and synchronicity 207–8
Argenteum Astrum (AA) 31
Aristotle 175, 217, 221
Arthurian legends 84, 87
    images of the witch in 148, 155–6, 162, 323–4
    and the Theosophical Society 243
'aspirational Indians' 1, 114, 115, 117–20, 282–3
astrology 23, 46
'Atlantic Celts' 64
Atlantis 8, 29
Aubrey, John 70, 80
Augustine of Hippo 257, 270
Australian aborigines 4, 59, 76
Australian Wiccans
    age 142
    educational background 145
    gender 145
authenticity
    and Celtic spirituality 56–7, 90–4

and Native American spirituality 114, 121–4
    and Wicca 134
authority of the self, and New Age spirituality 191–2
Avalon 8, 29
Avebury, Wiltshire 72, 81, 83, 92–3
Aziz, Robert 212–13

Bainbridge, William Sims 136
Baptist Times 259, 260, 265
Barbour, Ian 184
Barrie, J.M., *Peter Pan* 17
Bath, eighteenth-century Druidic connections 71–2, 84
Baum, Frank L., *The Wonderful Wizard of Oz* 151
BDO (British Druid Order) 81, 82
Bebbington, David 259, 261
Bede 86
    Historia Ecclesiastica 273
Beltane 39, 46, 76
Berengaria Order of Druids 82
Berger, P. 191
Berkhofer, R.F. 104, 106, 107
Bernard of Clairvaux 255–6
Besant, Annie 21, 25, 32, 245, 246
Besant-Scott, Mrs 32
Bewitched 149, 160–1
Biblical criticism, and Christianity 21
Bieler, Ludwig 269
Big Bang cosmology 180–1, 217
biology, twentieth-century developments in 181
Black Elk Speaks 123–4
Black Sunday (film) 160
Blake, William 84
    Jerusalem 72
    prophetic books 28, 46–7
    The Serpent Temple 72
Blavatsky, Helena Petrovna 21, 22, 25, 26, 73, 195, 239, 240–1, 242, 245
    The Key to Theosophy 247
Blood on Satan's Claw (film) 160
Bloom, William 188
Boas, George 120
Bohm, David 185, 186
Book of Kells 56, 60, 254
Book of Shadows 150, 168
boundaries
    between mainstream and alternative religion 1–2
    in Wicca 41

Boy Scouts 106
Boyle, Robert 46
Bradley, Ian 86–7, 251, 254
    The Celtic Way 59, 252–3, 259, 265, 272–3
Bradley, Marion Zimmer 162
brainwashing 138
bricolage, and Native American spirituality 116, 117
British Circle of the Universal Bond 84
British Druid Order (BDO) 81, 82
British identity, and Celtic languages 68
Brooke, John 183, 186, 187, 214
Brown, Terence 73
Buckland, Raymond 36
Budapest, Zsuzsanna 38, 40, 164, 306, 309
Buddhism
    and Celtic spirituality 58, 89
    and Native American spirituality 125
    and the Theosophical Society 25, 241
Burne-Jones, Edward 154
    The Beguiling of Merlin 155–6
Burning Times *see* Great Witch Hunt

Cabot, L. 162
calendars
    eightfold Celtic calendar 92
    see also Wheel of the Year
Cantor, Geoffrey 186
Capra, Fritjof 184, 185
Cardiac Celts 63–4, 94–5, 96
Carey, John, *King of Mysteries* 272
Carmichael, Alexander, *Carmina Gadelica*
    69–70, 81, 89, 90, 251, 265, 266, 268, 271
Casaubon, Isaac 24, 48
The Cauldron: Pagan Journal of the Old Religion 42
Celtic Christianity 1, 56, 58, 59, 60, 86–90, 251–75
    and the Celtic Church 87–8, 258–60
    and the Celtic fringe 251–2, 253, 267
    critical issues in 273–4
    dreams and visions 272–3
    and ecumenism 260–2
    God and judgement 271–2
    and the natural world 254–8
    and postmodern primitivism 252–4
    revival of 86–6
    sin and penance 267–70
    theology of 265–7
    and tolerance 262–5
Celtic Connections: The Journal of Celtic and Related Subjects 57

Celtic diaspora 64
Celtic languages 67–8, 81, 91
Celtic literature 68–70, 91, 93
Celtic Orthodox Church 56
Celtic spirituality 1, 3, 10, 11, 55–101
    authenticity of 56–7, 90–4
    and Cardiac Celts 63–4, 94–5, 96
    and the Celt as walker between the
        worlds 98
    and the Celtic fringe 59–60, 95–6
    and the Celtic revival 57–8, 94–5
    and 'Celticity' 55
    contemporary perceptions of 56–7
    and CyberCelts 96–7
    festivals 72–3, 75–6, 78, 92
    as native religion 75–8
    and Paganism 56, 58, 75–8
    and popular culture 65
    and primitivism 61–2
    and ritual 3
    and shape shifting 58, 98
    sources for images of the Celts 63–75
        Celtic language and literature 67–70
        classical 66–7
        eighteenth-century Celts and Druids
            71–3
        Iron Age 64–5
        and native peoples 70
    Theosophical Celts 73–5
    witches and Celtic identity 133–4
    see also Druidry
Chaldean Oracles 28, 47
Champion, Timothy 64–5
channelling, and Celtic spirituality 93
Chapman, M. 66, 90, 95, 139
    The Celts: The Construction of a Myth 65
charismatic movement, and Celtic Christianity
    259, 261, 263, 273
Charmed 150
Charnwood Grove of Druids 83
Cher 160, 162
Chichester, Imogen, *The Witch-child* 148–9
Chief Piercing Eyes 114
children
    and the Theosophical Society 243
    of Wiccan parents 141–2, 143
children's literature and films, images of witches
    in 148–53
Chinese science, I Ching 194, 209–10, 211, 219

Christian missionaries
    and Druids 85, 86
    and Native Americans 106
Christian Science 201
Christianity
    charismatic movement 259, 261, 263, 273
    and Druidry 85–6
    esoteric 246
    and Gnosticism 23, 47–8, 189, 194, 219
    and the Hermetic Order of the Golden
      Dawn 28–9, 31
    and images of witches 162
    and Jungian psychology 196–7
    and Native American spirituality 108, 117,
      123, 289, 290
    and Paganism 18–19, 20
        festivals and Pagan children 141–2
        neo-Paganism 306, 307–9, 310
    and science 21
    and the Theosophical Society 25
    and Wicca 143, 144
    and witchcraft 297–9, 301–3
    see also Celtic Christianity; Protestantism;
      Roman Catholicism
Chrystos (Native American poet) 293
Churchill, W. 103, 117, 119–20, 281, 287
Circe 154–5
Clan Keltoi 97
classical sources
    on the Celts 66–7
    on Druids 67
    Paganism and classical literature 230–1
Co-Masons 32, 244–5
Cochrane, Robert 34
Cohn, Norman 297, 302
collective unconscious
    in Jungian psychology 203–4, 205, 218
        and synchronicity 207
colonialism, and Native American spirituality
    280–1
Colorado, Pam 283–4
Columba 255, 256, 259, 260, 265, 270, 271, 272
Columbanus 268, 269, 272
Columbus, Christopher 104
conflict between religion and science 184
    and Jungian psychology 201
Constantine, P. 55, 60
Constantine (Roman Emperor) 273
conversion motifs 137–40
Cooper, Guy 112
Copernican cosmology 175, 181, 218

Cornwall
    Gorsedd 79–80, 81
    Men-an-tol at Anguidal Down, Madron 77
Corpus Hermeticum 23–4, 46
cosmology 175, 181–2
    Big Bang 180–1, 217
Cotswold Order of Druids 82, 84
counter-culture (1960s)
    and Native American spirituality 107, 109
    and New Age spirituality 1
covens 32, 33, 34, 35, 42, 47, 135
    finding a coven 136–7, 138–9
    hiving off 136
    and initiation 140
The Craft (film) 42, 136, 153, 162
creative visualization 194, 218
Crowley, Aleister 24, 29, 30, 227, 236
    Law of Thelema 31, 41, 50
Crowley, Vivianne 6, 9, 43, 146–7, 195, 198
cultural erosion, and Native American spirituality
    115
cultural evolutionism, and Celtic spirituality 60–1,
    77
cultural primitivism
    and Celtic spirituality 61–2
    and Native American spirituality 120–1
cultural theft
    and Druidry 83
    and Native American spirituality 117, 126–7,
      129–31, 277–93
The Curse of the Crimson Altar (film) 160, 161
CyberCelts 96–7
Cynan 79

Daly, Mary 43, 318
    Gyn/Ecology 163, 316, 317, 319
Dark Ages, and Celtic Christianity 253–4
Darwin, Charles 25, 218, 222
    *On the Origin of the Species by Means of
      Natural Selection* 21, 60, 178
Davies, John 78, 94–5
Dawkins, Richard, *The Blind Watchmaker* 181
Dead Sea Scrolls 48
deep environmentalists 107, 124, 125–6
Deism 177, 218, 303
Deloria Jr, Vine 110, 111, 117, 119, 120
depth psychology 193
design argument for God's existence 175, 179,
    218
determinism 177, 180, 218
Dewey, David 259, 260

dialogue between religion and science 184
and Jungian psychology 201–2
Dianic witchcraft 38, 47
Dickens, Charles 323
divination 189, 218
DNA (deoxyribonucleic acid) 181, 218
Dowden, Ken 232
Draper, John W., *History of the Conflict between Religion and Science* 184
Droogers, André 117
Druidry 2, 56, 67, 75, 78–86
and Awen 81–2
and the Celtic tradition 82–3
and the channelling of information 93
and Christians 85–6
'cultural' and esoteric or 'believing' 79
eighteenth-century sources of 71–3, 84
festivals 79–80, 81, 84–5
as native spirituality 83
and nature religion 9–10
Orders 56, 82–4
and Paganism 225
as local religion 19–20
rituals 3, 4, 81
and Stonehenge 71, 72, 80–1
sweat lodges 83
varieties of 82
The Druids' Voice 75, 82
Drury, N. 121
Duncan, John, *St Bride* 74
Dürer, Albrecht, *The Four Witches* 157
Dworkin, Andrea 316
dynamic psychiatry 193

Earth First! 124, 125–6
ecofeminism 124, 127
ecumenism, and Celtic Christianity 260–2
educational background of Wiccans 145
Egypt
and high ritual magic 226–7
occultism and the Theosophical Society 25
Egyptian Book of the Dead 28, 47
Ehrenreich, Barbara 317–18, 319
Einstein, Albert 208, 221
Eliade, Mircea 120–1, 194
English, Deirdre 317–18, 319
English language, and Celtic literature 68–70
Enochian Magic 28, 47
environmental awareness
and activism 9–10, 17
and Celtic Christianity 254, 263–4

and Native American spirituality 107, 118, 124–6, 291–2
and New Age spirituality 188, 192
and Paganism 17
Eriugena, John Scotus 270
esoteric Christianity 246
esoteric traditions
and New Age spirituality 188–90
Western Esoteric Tradition 23–5, 26, 29, 44, 46, 50
European unity, and the Celts 64–5
evolutionary theory 21, 25, 178–9
and Celtic spirituality 60–1, 77
extra-sensory perception (ESP) 218
and Jung's theory of synchronicity 209

Faery Wicca 38, 47
Farr, Florence 22, 23
Farrar, Stewart and Janet 34
Fellowship of Crotona 32
feminism
ecofeminism 124, 127
feminist witchcraft 36, 37–9, 40, 44, 144, 161, 197–8, 314–15
images of the witch 164, 165, 166
and Native American spirituality 278, 279, 280
and the occult 21, 22
and Wicca 145
Ferguson, Marilyn 188, 194
festivals
and Celtic spirituality 72–3, 75–6, 78, 92
Druid 79–80, 81, 84–5
and Native American spirituality 289
Pagan 2, 4–6, 50
and Pagan children 141–2
Wiccan 35, 50, 169, 308
Ficino, Marsilio 22, 23–4, 48
films, images of witches in 151–2, 159–62
fin de siècle
and Celtic spirituality 58
occult community 20–3, 29, 32, 44, 135
Findhorn community 188
First World War, and the occult revival 29
Folk-Lore Society 233–4, 235
folklore, and Celtic spirituality 62, 63, 69–70
Forbes, Jack D. 111
Ford, Patrick 257
Fortune, Dion 29, 30, 227
Fox, Matthew 89, 267
Fraternity of the Inner Light 29

Fraudulent Mediums Act (1951) 32, 50
Frazer, Sir James 231, 233, 235
freemasonry 22, 47, 226, 227–8
    and the Hermetic Order of the Golden
        Dawn 26, 27, 28
    and the Theosophical Society 244–5
French Druids 82
Freud, Sigmund 193, 199, 201, 219, 310
    theory of psychoanalysis 204–5, 221
Furlong, M. 133

Galileo Galilei 175, 181–2, 183, 219
Gardnerian Wicca 33–4, 35, 36, 43, 44, 120, 309
    initiated witches 138
    and traditional and hereditary witches 134
Gardner, Gerald 31, 32–4, 35–6, 38, 148, 163, 236, 304
    Witchcraft Today 149
gender essentialism 196, 219
genetic code 181, 219
Geoffrey of Monmouth 80
Ghost Shirts 116
Glasgow Museums, and the Lakota Ghost Shirt 116
Glassie, Henry 97–8
Glastonbury
    Celtic spirituality in 76, 92–3
    Druid College of Avalon 84
globalization 173, 219
    and New Age spirituality 187, 188
Gnosticism 23, 47–8, 189, 219
    and Jungian psychology 194
God
    in Celtic Christianity 271–2
    science and arguments for the existence of 175–9, 180–1
    synchronicity and images of 212–13
Goddess Movement 36–7, 38, 39, 190, 197–8, 306, 309
gods and goddesses
    Celtic 76
    and Jungian archetypes 195, 205
    mother goddess of Europe 284
    New Age 8
    Pagan 2, 15, 16–17, 20, 232–3
    and Wicca 35, 37, 308
Golden Dawn *see* Hermetic Order of the Golden Dawn
Gomme, Alice and Lawrence 62, 233–4
Gorsedd Prayer 73
Gorseths 81

Bath Gorseth 84–5
Cornish Gorseth 79–80, 81
Welsh Gorsedd 72–3, 79, 81
Goya, Francisco 159
    The Spell 157
    Witches' Sabbath 157
Grahame, Kenneth, *The Wind in the Willows* 17, 232
The Grapevine 90
Great Witch Hunt 19, 37–8, 134, 148, 150, 159–60, 167
    and the myth of the Burning Times 313–24
    origins of the 225–6, 234–5
    and women 163–4, 301–3, 313–24
Greece, Ancient
    and the Celts 66–7
    and Paganism 231
Green movement *see* environmental awareness
Grien, Hans Baldung, *Two Witches* 157, 158
Gurdjieff, George 195, 198

Hale, Amy 76, 79
Hall, S. 94
Hanegraaff, Wouter 162
    New Age Religion and Western Culture 188
hard primitivism 61
Hardy, Thomas 232
Hassidic Druids 82
Hawkins, Stephen 180–1
Häxan (film) 159, 160
Heathenism 2, 4, 6
Hecate 154, 159, 168
hedge witchcraft 229–30
Heelas, Paul 185, 187, 188, 189, 191–2, 195, 205
    on the self 206
hell, and Celtic Christianity 271–2
hermaphrodites 197
Hermes Trismegistus 18, 23, 24, 48
Hermetic Brotherhood of Luxor 25–6
Hermetic Order of the Golden Dawn 21–2, 23, 24, 26–31, 75, 226
Hermetic Society 25
hermeticism 22, 23, 24, 48
hermit poetry 256–8
high ritual magic 226–9
Highwater, Jamake 114
Hinduism
    and Celtic spirituality 58
    and Native American spirituality 110
    and the Theosophical Society 25, 241
history, and the origins of the Celts 65–6

holism 180, 219
    and synchronicity 211, 212
Holman Hunt, William, *Converted British Family Sheltering a Christian Priest from the Druids* 86
Horniman, Annie 21, 22
Horse Whisperers 230
Hughes, Kathleen, *The Modern Traveller to the Early Irish Church* 268
Hughes, Ted, 'Witches' 321–2
Hull, Eleanor, *Poem-Book of the Gael* 255–6, 271
Hull, R.F.C. 212
Hultkrantz, Abe 112
human sacrifice, and Druidry 67
Hume, David 177–8, 219
Hume, L. 5, 138
Huskisson, William 231
Hutton, R. 15, 18–19, 20, 44, 92, 165
    The Pagan Religions of the Ancient British Isles 263–4
Hyde, Douglas 254
    Story of Early Gaelic Literature 255

I Ching 194, 209–10, 211, 219
independence of religion and science 184
    and Jungian psychology 201
indigenous peoples
    and Celtic Christianity 252–3
    and Celtic Pagan spirituality 76–7
    and the Celts 70
    knowledge systems of 183
    and nature religion 9
    see also Native American spirituality
individuation
    in Jungian psychology 196–7, 205, 219
        and New Age spirituality 206, 211
        and synchronicity 207, 211
Insular Order of Druids 82, 93
integration between religion and science 184
    and Jungian psychology 201–2
Internet
    and CyberCelts 96–7
    and Native American spirituality 112
    and Paganism 135
    and Wicca 135, 167
Iona 87, 89, 92–3
Ireland
    Celtic Christianity in 253–4
        and nature poetry 255–8
        and sacred trees 264
Iron Age, and Celtic culture 64–5

Isle of Man, Museum of Witchcraft and Magic 32, 163

James, Simon 59, 64, 65–6, 95
James VI, *Demonology* 164–5
Japanese New Religious Movements (NRMs) 117
Jarcke, Karl 234–5
Jenkyns, Richard 231
Jewish kabbalah 24, 48
Johnson, Myke 126
Judaism, as the religious background of Wiccans 143–4
Jung, Carl Gustav 1, 4, 10, 46, 173, 184, 198–213, 219
    biographical sketch of 192–4
    Memories, Dreams, Reflections 198–9
    and neo-Paganism 310, 311
    and New Age spirituality 194–8
    religion and science in the psychology of 198–206
    'Terry Lectures' on 'Psychology and Religion' 199
    theory of synchronicity 173, 200, 206–14
    and Wicca 6
    Zofingia Society lectures 199, 201

kabbalistic teachings 22, 23, 24, 48
Kabbalistic Tree of Life 28, 48
Kant, Immanuel 178, 203, 219–20
Karnak 29
Keats, John 16, 231
Kells, Book of 56, 60, 254
Kennelly, Brendan 153–4
Key of Solomon 28, 48, 236
Kiberd, Declan, *Inventing Ireland* 67
Kindred Spirit 194–5, 210–11
King, Matthew 103
Kingsford, Anna 21, 25, 26
Kingsley, Charles 231
Kipp, Woody (Blackfeet Nation) 118–29
Kramer, Heinrich 302

Lakota beliefs and customs 123–4
Lamb, Charles 323
Lame Deer (John Fire) 118
languages, Celtic 67–8, 81, 91
Laplace, Pierre 176, 177, 220
Las Casas, Bartolomé 104
Leadbeater, C.W. 246
    Science of the Sacraments 244
Leerssen, Joep 68

Leland, Charles Godfrey 236, 304
    Aradia 235
Lévi, Eliphas 24
Levi, Primo 313
Lewis, C.S., *The Lion, the Witch and the
    Wardrobe* 148
ley lines 83
Lhuyd, Edward, *Archaeologia Brittanica* 67–8
Liberal Catholic Church, and the Theosophical
    Society 243
Lilith 148, 168
Lindisfarne Gospels 60
literature
    Celtic 68–70, 91, 93
    images of witches in 148–51, 299–300
    Paganism and classical literature 230–1
'locality' meaning of Paganism 19–20
Lofland, John 137, 138
The Long Hair of Death (film) 160
Lorde, Audre 287
Lovejoy, Arthur 120
Love's Enchantment (Flemish School
    painting) 157
Low, Mary 69
Lubbock, Sir John, *The Origin of Civilization and
    the Primitive Condition of Man* 60
Luhrmann, Tanya 305
Lyons, Oren 286–7

McCloud, Janet 126, 281
McGrath, Michael, Archdruid of Tara and Ireland
    75
McLynn, Frank 195
Macpherson, James 96, 251
magic 189, 220
    high ritual 226–9
    and Paganism 3, 23
    and the Western Esoteric Tradition 24
    and Wicca 44
Mahatma Letters 246
mainstream religion
    bridges between the alternative and 1
    and Paganism 7
Maitland, Edward 25
Maitland, Sara, 'The Burning Times' 320, 322
maleficium, and witchcraft 299, 300, 303, 309
Malleus Maleficarum 302
Malory, Sir Thomas, *Morte d'Arthur* 156
Martello, Leo 165
Martinez, Dennis 127
materialism 177
    Jung's critique of science and 199

Mathers, Moina 22, 23
Mathers, S.L. MacGregor 22, 26, 27, 31
Matthews, Caitlin 77–8, 92, 93
Matthews, John 77–8
Means, Russell 103
Medea 153–4, 162, 166
Medici, Cosimo de 23
Meek, D.E. 55, 60, 69, 91
    on Celtic Christianity 87, 88, 89, 90
men
    and images of the witch 154
    and Native American spirituality 279
    and Wicca 144–5
Merlin (wizard) 148, 155–6
Merton, Thomas 266
Methodism 177
metropolitan control, reaction against 258–9
Meyer, Kuno 254
    Selections from Ancient Irish Poetry 255, 257
Michelet, Jules 304
    La Sorcière 234–5
Millis, Ludo 230
Minor Arcana 142
Mirandola, Giovanni Pico della 22, 23, 24
modernism, and Celtic Christianity 258–9
modernization 173, 220
    and New Age spirituality 187–8
Moltmann, Jürgen 266
monasteries and monks, and Celtic Christianity
    88, 253–4, 254–5, 259, 260, 262
Mone, Franz Josef 234–5
Montgomery, Elizabeth 160
montheistic religion 20, 48
Morgan le Fey 148, 155, 162
Morganwg, Iolo (Edward Williams) 72–3, 79, 81
Mount Haemus Grove 84
Müller, Friedrich Max 183
multiculturalism, and Native American spirituality
    282–3
Murphy, Jill, *The Worst Witch* 149, 150
Murray, Margaret 236, 304, 308
    The God of the Witches 235
    The Witch Cult in Western Europe 166
mystery religion 48
    Wicca as a 37, 43, 139
mysticism, and Theosophical Celts 73–5
myth
    in Jungian psychology 204
    and New Age spirituality 190
    and Paganism 2

Native American spirituality 1, 3, 10, 11, 59,
        103–31
        and aspirational Indians 1, 114, 115, 117–20,
                282–3
        and authenticity 114, 121–3
        beliefs 108–10
        and bricolage 116, 117
        and Celtic spirituality 76–7
        and the Celtic view of nature 258
        and the counterculture 107, 109
        and cultural primitivism 120–1
        and cultural theft 117, 126–7, 129–31,
                277–93
        *Declaration of War Against Exploiters of
                Lakota Spirituality* 129–31
        defining indigenous religions 110–12
        and environmental awareness 107, 118,
                124–6, 291–2
        and Ghost Shirts 116
        and 'hobbyists' 107
        Hopi religion 104
        Lakota beliefs and customs 123–4, 285
        and medicine bags 115
        medicine men 113–14
        and Native American tribes
                distribution of 105
                diversity of 107–8
        and Native ancestry 293
        and New Age spirituality 108, 112–14,
                118–20, 124–7, 129–30, 279, 285
        ownership, power and control issues in
                118–20
        and Pan-American Indians 114
        and revived religion 7
        rituals 3, 4, 110, 112, 117–18, 118–19
                isolation/vision quests 117–18
                and non-Indians 290, 292
                Sundance 112, 118–19
        and shamanism 2, 120–1, 122, 124
        and the stereotype Indian 279–80, 286, 288
        sweat lodges 112, 113
        and syncretism 116–17
        and totem poles 115–16
        and witches 134
Native Americans, and the Celts 70
native peoples *see* indigenous peoples
native religion
        Celtic spirituality as 75–8
        Druidry as native spirituality 83
natural theology 175–6, 178, 220

nature
        and Celtic Christianity 254–8, 263–4
        and Paganism 2, 6, 20, 29, 39
        and Wicca 9, 17, 35
        see also environmental awareness
nature religion 8–10
nature/culture duality 9
neo-Paganism 16, 190
        children in neo-Pagan families 141
        images of the witch in 303–12
        and Native American spirituality 125, 126
        rituals 305
        and synchronicity 210
        see also New Age spirituality; Paganism
Neo-Pythagoreanism 23
neophyting courses in Wicca 136, 168
NeoPlatonism 23, 48–9
New Age spirituality 1, 3, 10
        and the authority of the self 191–2
        and Celtic spirituality 56, 58, 60
        and Jungian psychology 194–8
                theory of synchronicity 210–11
        and modernization, secularization and
                globalization 187–8
        and myth 190
        and Native American spirituality 108,
                112–14, 118–20, 124–7, 129–30, 279, 285
        and non-western, pre-modern and esoteric
                traditions 188–90
        and Paganism 2, 6–7
        and psycho-spiritual transformation 186–7
        and revived religion 7–8
        and ritual 3
        and science 173, 181, 185–92
                ambivalence towards 185–6
                and personal experience 190–1
        and the Western Esoteric Tradition 24–5
New Religious Movements (NRMs) 7–8, 10
        Japanese 117
Newell, Philip, *Listening for the Heartbeat of God*
        267–8
Newton, Isaac 175, 176, 177, 183, 220
        *Mathematical Principles of Natural
                Philosophy* 175
Newton, Sir Isaac 46
Noble Savage concept
        and Celtic spirituality 61–2, 96
        and early Celtic nature poetry 258
        and Native American spirituality 104–6, 119,
                279
        and Paganism 304

North America
    and 'Atlantic Celts' 64
    neo-Paganism in 16, 141, 305–6
    and New Age spirituality 6
    Paganism in 16, 36–7, 137
    Wicca in 33, 36–9
        and gender 144–5
        religious background of Wiccans
            143–4
    witches 133, 161–2
        age of 142
Northumbrian Office 260
nudity, and witches 157–8
numinous effects 220
    and Jung's theory of synchronicity 207, 208

OBOD (Order of Bards, Ovates and Druids) 83–4
occultism 24, 29
    Western Esoteric Tradition 23–5, 26, 29, 44,
       46
    see also Paganism; Wicca
occupational background of Wiccans 145
O'Cróinín, Dáibhí 269
Oddfellows 228
Olcott, Colonel Henry Steel 25, 26, 241
Old Irish Penitential 269, 270
Order of the Silver Star 31
Order of Woodcraft Chivalry 106, 108, 228–9
Ordo Templi Orientis (OTO) 31, 32, 49, 226
Orientalism 68, 121
Orthodox Christianity, and the Celtic Church 261
Ossian 95–6, 251
Ovid, Metamorphoses 153, 159

Pagan Dawn (journal) 141
Pagan Druidry see Druidry
Pagan Ethic 39–41
Pagan Federation 39–41, 42, 136, 138, 139
    and Pagan children 141
    and teenagers 142
    The Wiccan (later Pagan Dawn) 34, 39, 41
Pagan shamanism see shamanism
Paganism 1, 2–3, 10, 11
    and alchemy 23, 46
    ancient 16
    and Celtic Christianity 263–5
    and Celtic spirituality 56, 58, 75–8
    and folklore 63
    Goddess spirituality 36
    and the Great Witch Hunt 18

    and the Hermetic Order of the Golden
       Dawn 21–2, 23, 24, 26–31
    history and development of 15–31
    influence of the fin de siècle on 20–3, 29
    and the Internet 135
    meanings of the word 16–20
        'civilian' 18–19
        'country dweller' 16–18
        'locality' 19–20
    and nature religion 9
    and New Age spirituality 2, 6–7
    non-aligned Pagans 2–3, 4
    in North America 16, 36–7, 137
    pagan children 141–2
    Pagan groups 3
    and revived religion 7
    rituals 2, 3–6
    roots of modern 225–37
    and the Theosophical Society 21, 22, 25–6,
       28, 29, 50, 239–49
    and the Western Esoteric Tradition 23–5, 26,
       29, 44, 46, 50
    and Wicca 36, 39–45, 236
    see also neo-Paganism
Paley, William 220
    Natural Theology 179
Pan (goat-god) 16–17, 232–3
Pan-American Indians 114
pan-Celticism 68
pantheism 49
    and Paganism 2, 17, 20
parapsychology 220
    and Jungian psychology 183, 194, 209, 210
Pauli, Wolfgang 194, 199–200, 208–9
Peel, E. 164
Pelagius 270
penance, and Celtic Christianity 267–70
Pendderwen, Gwyddion 38
Pendragon, Arthur Uther 84, 85, 155
perennialist view of religion 188, 220
personal experience, and New Age spirituality
    190–1
personal unconscious, Jung's concept of the 203
Pfieffer, Michelle 162
photons 180, 220
physics
    and Jung's theory of synchronicity 208–9
    twentieth-century developments in 179–81
Piccini, Angela 65, 70
Pietism 177, 220
Piggot, S. 61, 67, 70, 78

pilgrimages, to Celtic sacred sites 76
Plath, Sylvia 321
Platonism 23
Plummer, Charles 268–9
Plymouth Brethren 31, 49
poetry
        early Celtic nature poetry 255–8
        on witches 321–3
political activism
        and environmental awareness 9–10, 17
        and Wicca 36
polytheism 49
        and Paganism 2, 15–16, 20
Pompeii, Villa of the Mysteries 157
Porterfield, Amanda 106, 114
postmodern primitivism, and Celtic Christianity
        252–4
Powers, William K. 123–4
Practical Magic (film) 162
Pratchett, Terry 147–8, 153
precession of the spring equinox 195, 220–1
primitivism, and Celtic spirituality 61–2
progress, and Celtic spirituality 60–1
Protestantism
        and Celtic Christianity 87, 89, 267
        and the Reformation 87, 88, 182
        and science 182
        and Wicca 143, 144, 145–6
psychic reality, in Jungian psychology 203, 205,
        221
psycho-spiritual transformation 186–7
psychoanalysis 183, 204–5, 221
psychokinesis (PK) 221
        and Jung's theory of synchronicity 209
Ptolemy 175, 221
Purkiss, Diane 154
        The Witch in History 151, 161
Puttick, Elizabeth 135

quantum mechanics 179–80, 221
quantum physics, and complementarity 209
quarks 180, 221

racism
        and cultural primitivism 121
        structural, and Native American spirituality
                280–1
Rackham, Arthur 156
Rahner, Karl 266
Ransom, J. 25
reason, rejection of 21

Reclaiming witchcraft 36, 38–9, 40
Redfield, James, *The Celestine Prophecy* 211
reductionism 177, 180, 221
Reformation 182
        and the Celtic Church 87, 88
reincarnation
        and Celtic spirituality 73, 93
        and the Theosophical Society 240, 242
relativity, theory of 179–80, 221
Restall Orr, Emma 9–10, 19–20, 82, 83, 93
revived religion 7–8, 10
Rhine, Joseph B. 209
rites of passage 4
Rogers, Carl 190
Rollright Stones 81
Roman Catholicism
        and Celtic Christianity 87–8, 260, 261–2,
                267, 274
        and the charismatic movement 263
        and Japanese New Religious Movements
                117
        and Jungian psychology 202
        and science 175, 178, 181–2
        and the Virgin Mary 284
        and Wicca 143, 144, 146
Romance of Merlin 156
Romans, ancient
        and the Celts 66–7
        and Paganism 231
Romanticism 177, 221
        and Celtic Christianity 87
        and Celtic spirituality 57, 62, 75
                Druidry 78
        and Native American spirituality 104–6, 107
        and New Age spirituality 188
        and Paganism 16
        and witchcraft 300, 303–5, 316, 323–4
Rose, Stuart 194, 210–11
Rossetti, Dante Gabriel 154, 231–2
Rosicrucians 26, 49
Russell, George 74

sabbats 159, 168–9
Sabians 18
Sabrina the Teenage Witch 149, 150
sacralization 221
        and New Age spirituality 187–8
Said, Edward 68
Salomonsen, Jone 143
Sanders, Alex 34–5, 148
Sanders, Maxine 34, 35

Sandys, Frederick 154
    Morgan le Fay 155
Sarandon, Susan 162
Satanism, and witchcraft 297–9, 302–3, 307–8, 309
Saunders, Kate, *The Belfry Witches* 149, 150
science and religion 1, 10, 11, 21, 173–222
    and esotericism 24, 188–90
    four categories of interaction between 184
    history of interaction between 174–81
    and Jungian psychology 196
        theory of synchronicity 208–10,
            212–13
    nature religion 9
    and New Age spirituality 173, 181, 185–92
Scotland, Celtic fringe in 95–6
Scott, Sir Walter 96
Sebastion, Tim 63–4, 84, 85–6
secular humanism 177, 222
Secular Order of Druids (SOD) 63–4, 84, 85
secularization 173, 222
    and New Age spirituality 187–8
the self
    in Jungian psychoanalysis 203, 205, 222
    and New Age spirituality 206
self-help movements, and Native American
    spirituality 125
self-spirituality 191–2
Seton, Ernest 106–7, 108, 228
Sexton, Anne, 'Her Kind' 321
sexuality, and witchcraft in films 160
Shakespeare, William, *Macbeth* 153, 159, 300, 321
Shallcrass, Philip 81, 82, 83, 93
shamanism
    and Celtic spirituality 77–8
    and Native American spirituality 2, 120–1,
        122, 124
    and Paganism 225
    rituals 4
    and Wicca 36
Sharp, William 74–5
Sharpe, Eric 60, 62
Shattauer, Pastor Joseph 200
Shaw, George Bernard 22
She Beast (film) 160
Sheldrake, Rupert 185
Shelley, Percy Bysshe 16
Shinto 110
Simes, Amy 6
Simos, Miriam *see* Starhawk (Miriam Simos)
Simpson, Revd Ray 267
sin and penance, and Celtic Christianity 267–70

Skonovd, Norman 137, 138
Slotkin, J.S. 110
Smith, Andrea 280
Snyder, Gary 124
SOD (Secular Order of Druids) 63–4, 84, 85
soft primitivism 61–2
Southern, P. 164
Spangler, David 188
Spence, Lewis 74
Spencer, Herbert, *First Principles* 60
spiritualism 21, 26, 28, 49–50
    and Jung 199
    and the Theosophical Society 25, 241
Sprenger, Jacob 302
spring equinox, precession of the 195, 220–1
Stanton Drew stone circles 72
Starhawk (Miriam Simos) 36, 38–9, 40, 144, 191,
    197, 306, 319, 324
    The Spiral Dance 190
Steele, Barbara 160, 161
Stella Matutina 29
Stoicism 23, 50
Stonehenge 71, 72, 80–1
structural racism, and Native American spirituality
    280–1
Stukeley, William 80, 84, 85
    *Stonehenge: A Temple Restor'd to the British
        Druids* 71
suffering, Jungian and New Age views on 196–7,
    198
Sun Bear 113, 125
survivals, and folklore 62, 63
sweat lodges
    Druid 83
    and Native American spirituality 112, 113
Swinburne, Algernon Charles 231–2
symbolic images, in Jungian psychology 207, 222
synchronicity
    Jung's theory of 173, 200, 206–14
        and the New Age 210–11
syncretism, and Native American spirituality
    116–17

Tabitha 161
Tacey, David 195, 197, 198
Tantric worship 157
Taoism 189, 222
Taylor, Bron 8, 124, 126, 127
teenage Wiccans 142
Teilhard de Chardin, Pierre 184, 266

teleological processes 222
    in Jungian psychology 205
    in New Age spirituality 206
television programmes, images of witches in
    149–51
Tennyson, Alfred, Lord, *Idylls of the King* 155
Thabit ibn Qurra 15, 18
Thelema Abbey, Sicily 31
Thelema, Law of 50
Theosophical Society 21, 22, 25–6, 28, 29, 50,
    239–49
    at work in the world 245–7
    and Celtic spirituality 73–5
    esoteric elaborations 243–4
    and New Age spirituality 247
    origins 241–2
    publications 246–7
theosophy 201
theurgy 38, 50
Thomson, James, *The Seasons* 257
Thunder Chicken Group (now Pan-American
    Indians) 114
tolerance, and Celtic Christianity 262–5
totem poles 115–16
Toulson, Shirley 88–9
Traditional and Hereditary Witchcraft 33–4
trees, Celtic Christianity and sacred trees 264
Trevelyan, Sir George 191
Tuatha De Danann myth 38
Tylor, Edward 62, 233
    Primitive Culture 62

Uffington White Horse, Oxfordshire 81
unconscious
    Freud's theory of the 204–5
    Jung's concept of the 203–4, 205
United Kingdom
    British Pagans, and Christianity 18–19
    and New Age spirituality 6
    and Wicca 32–6, 37, 143, 144
Urban VIII, Pope 182
urbanization, and Paganism 16–17, 232

Valiente, Doreen 9, 34, 157
Victorian age, and Paganism 16–17, 21–2
vitalism 199, 222
Vivianne/Nimuë (the Lady of the Lake) 148,
    155–6, 323–4

Waal, Esther de 25, 266
    A World Made Whole 263

Waite, A.E. 28
Walker, Barbara G. 318–19
Wallace, Alfred Russel 179, 222
Warner, Sylvia Townsend, *Lolly Willowes, or The
    Loving Huntsman* 165–6, 320
Waterhouse, John William
    Circe Invidiosa 154
    Circe Offering the Cup to Ulysses 154–5
    The Magic Circle 155
    The Sorceress 154
Watts, George Frederick 154
Weller, Mary 323
Welsh Eisteddfod 73
Welsh Gorsedd 72–3, 79, 81
Welsh Pagans 78
West Kennett Long Barrow, Wiltshire 65
Westcott, Dr William Wynn 26–7
Western Esoteric Tradition 23–5, 26, 29, 44, 46, 50
Wheel of the Year 3, 4–6, 9, 50
    Beltane 39, 46, 76
    and Celtic spirituality 75–8
    and feminist witchcraft 37
    and Wicca 169
Whewell, William 183
White, Father Victor 194, 200–1, 202
Whole Earth Review 164
Wicca 1, 2, 10, 29, 31, 32–45, 133–72
    age distribution 138, 142, 143
    Alexandrian 34–6, 37, 43, 44, 120, 134, 138
    as an esoteric mystery religion 37, 43, 135
    books on Wicca and witchcraft 147–8
    boundaries in and distinctiveness of 41–2
    children of Wiccan parents 141–2, 143
    covens 32, 33, 34, 35, 42, 47, 135
        finding a coven 136–7, 138–9
        hiving off 136, 168
        and initiation 140
    Craft of the Wise 136–7, 139, 146
    educational and occupational background
        of Wiccans 145
    Faery Wicca 38, 47
    festivals 35, 50, 169, 308
    Gardnerian 33–4, 35, 36, 37, 43, 44, 120, 134,
        138
    gender of Wiccans 144–5
    history of 32–6
    and images of the witch 164, 166–7
    initiation 35, 37, 41, 42, 43, 137, 167
        age of 142
        conversion motifs 137–40
    and the Internet 135

and magic 44
and Native American spirituality 125
and nature 9, 17, 35
neophyting courses 136, 168
and New Age spirituality 6, 185, 305
origins of 146–7, 225–6
and Paganism 36, 39–45, 236
'popular' 42–3
priests and priestesses 41, 43
Rede 31, 39–41
religious background of Wiccans 143–4,
    145–6
and revived religion 7
rituals 3–4, 35, 157, 226
sabbats 159, 168–9
Study Group 136, 137, 139
and the Western Esoteric Tradition 24
and witchcraft 36–9
workshops 136–7, 139
see also witchcraft; witches
Wilde, Oscar 231–2
Wilhelm, Richard 193, 194
Williams, Edward see Morganwg, Iolo
Williamson, Cecil 32, 163
Witch Craze see Great Witch Hunt
WITCH (Women's International Terrorist
    Conspiracy from Hell) 314–15
witchcraft 1, 36–9
    exoteric 43–4
    feminist 36, 37–9, 40, 44, 144, 161, 197–8,
        314–15
        images of the witch 164, 165, 166
    hedge 229–30
    'slippery' status of 168
    Traditional and Hereditary 33–4
    see also Wicca
Witchcraft Act, repeal of (1951) 32, 50
Witchcraft Anti-defamation League 161
witches
    images of 133–5, 146–68, 295–312
        in Arthurian legend 148, 155–6, 162
        in children's literature and films
            148–53
        Circe 154–5
        early modern 163–5, 167
        in film 159–62
        Hecate 154, 159, 168
        herbalist witches 313, 318–20, 323–4

in late Victorian art 154–6
in literature and the arts 299–300
Medea 153–4, 162, 166
in neo-Paganism 303–12
nude paintings and engravings 157–8
and Satanism 297–9, 302–3, 307–8,
    309
in Shakespeare's Macbeth 153, 159,
    300, 321
stereotypical wicked witch 153,
    296–303, 322–3
twenty-first century 166–7
see also Great Witch Hunt
The Witches of Eastwick (film) 161–2
The Wizard of Oz (film) 151–3
Wolf, Christa, Medea: A Modern Retelling 154
women
    and Celtic spirituality 76
    and the Goddess Movement 36–7
    and the Hermetic Order of the Golden
        Dawn 27–8
    Jungian and New Age attitudes to the
        feminine 196, 197–8
    and Native American spirituality 279, 289,
        292–3
    and the revival of the occult 21–3
    and Wicca 144–5
    and witchcraft 309
        the Great Witch Hunt 163–4, 301–3,
            313–24
        images of witches 133–5, 146–67
    see also feminism
Wood, John the Elder 71–2, 84
Woodcraft Society (Order of Woodcraft Chivalry)
    106, 108, 228–9
Woodford, Revd A.F.A. 26
Woodman, Dr W.R. 26
Woolf, Virginia 166
word association tests 193, 222
Wuthnow, Robert 186

Yeats, W.B. 29, 47, 74, 133
Yoga 189, 222
York, Michael 186, 188–9, 190, 191, 197–8

Zen Druids 82
Zimmer, Heinrich 194
Zofingia Society 199, 201